First World War
and Army of Occupation
War Diary
France, Belgium and Germany

61 DIVISION
Headquarters, Branches and Services
Royal Army Medical Corps
Assistant Director Medical Services
2 May 1915 - 31 March 1919

WO95/3038/2

The Naval & Military Press Ltd
www.nmarchive.com
Published in association with The National Archives

Published by

The Naval & Military Press Ltd

Unit 10 Ridgewood Industrial Park,

Uckfield, East Sussex,

TN22 5QE England

Tel: +44 (0) 1825 749494

www.naval-military-press.com

www.nmarchive.com

This diary has been reprinted in facsimile from the original. Any imperfections are inevitably reproduced and the quality may fall short of modern type and cartographic standards.

Contents

Document type	Place/Title	Date From	Date To
Heading	WO95/3038/2		
Heading	61st Division Asst Dir. Medical Services 1915 May-1919 Mar		
Miscellaneous	Proposals Of A.D.M.S, 61st (S.M) Division For Draft for Divisional Operation Orders.	12/10/1915	12/10/1915
Operation(al) Order(s)	R.A.M.C. Operation Order No. 3 by Colonel W.H. Bull K.H.S. V.D. A.D.M.S. 61st (S.M.) Division	12/10/1915	12/10/1915
Heading	War Diary A.D.M.S 2/1st (S. Mid) Division May 1915-May1916		
War Diary		02/05/1915	22/05/1916
War Diary	War Diary August 1915	01/08/1915	01/11/1915
War Diary		01/09/1915	30/09/1915
Heading	War Diary Of The ADMS 61st (S.M.) Division From 1st December 1915 To 31st December 1915 Volume 2		
War Diary	Headquarters 61st S.M.D Boreham House, Chelmsford Essex	01/12/1915	31/12/1915
Heading	War Diary Of A.D.M.S. 61st (S.M) Division From 1st January 1916 To 31st January 1916 Volume 2		
War Diary	Headquarters 61st (S.M) Div Boreham House Chelmsford Essex	01/01/1916	31/01/1916
Heading	A.D.M.S 61st Division May 1916		
War Diary	Le Havre	23/05/1916	24/05/1916
War Diary	St. Venant	25/05/1916	31/05/1916
Heading	War Diary A.D.M.S 61st Division June 1916		
War Diary	St. Venant	01/06/1916	11/06/1916
War Diary	La. Gorgue	12/06/1916	30/06/1916
Heading	War Diary A.D.M.S 61st Division July 1916 Volume 3		
War Diary	La. Gorque	01/07/1916	31/07/1916
Miscellaneous	Appendix 1 Operations July 19th-1916	19/07/1916	19/07/1916
Heading	War Diary August 1916 A.D.M.S 61st Division Vol 4		
War Diary	La. Gorgue L.35.b.4.6	01/08/1916	31/08/1916
Heading	War Diary A.D.M.S 61st Division Period 1-30th September 1916 Volume 5		
War Diary	La. Gorgue L.35.b.4.6.	01/09/1916	30/09/1916
Heading	A.D.M.S 61st Division Oct 1916		
War Diary	La. Gorgue	01/10/1916	28/10/1916
War Diary	St. Venant	29/10/1916	31/10/1916
Heading	War Diary A.D.M.S 61st Division Period 1st-30th November 1916 Volume 7		
War Diary	St. Venant	01/11/1916	02/11/1916
War Diary	Chelers	03/11/1916	04/11/1916
War Diary	Rollecourt	05/11/1916	06/11/1916
War Diary	Frohen Le Grand	07/11/1916	17/11/1916
War Diary	Contay	18/11/1916	22/11/1916
War Diary	Bouzincourt	23/11/1916	30/11/1916
Heading	War Diary A.D.M.S 61st Division December 1916 Volume 8		
War Diary	Bouzincourt	01/12/1916	31/12/1916
Heading	War Diary Of A.D.M.S 61st Division From January 1st 1917 To January 31st 1917 Volume 9		

War Diary	Bouzincourt	01/01/1917	15/01/1917
War Diary	Marieux	16/01/1917	16/01/1917
War Diary	Bernaville	17/01/1917	18/01/1917
War Diary	Brailly	19/01/1917	31/01/1917
Miscellaneous	Appendix 1		
Miscellaneous	61 Division RAMC Order 1208	13/01/1917	13/01/1917
Miscellaneous	Appendix 2		
Miscellaneous	Instruction As To Harding Over And Moving Out And March		
Heading	War Diary Of A.D.M.S 61st Division From February 1st 1917 To February 28th 1917 Volume 10		
War Diary	Brailly	01/02/1917	04/02/1917
War Diary	Long	05/02/1917	13/02/1917
War Diary	Guillaucourt	14/02/1917	17/02/1917
War Diary	Harbonnieres	18/02/1917	28/02/1917
Miscellaneous	Appendix 1		
Operation(al) Order(s)	61st Div R.A.M.C. Order No. 9		
Miscellaneous	Appendix 2		
Miscellaneous	61st Div R.A.M.C. Warning Order	10/02/1917	10/02/1917
Miscellaneous	Appendix 3		
Operation(al) Order(s)	RAMC Order No. 10	12/02/1917	12/02/1917
Miscellaneous	Appendix 4		
Miscellaneous	Appendix 5		
Operation(al) Order(s)	61st Div R.A.M.C. Order No 11.	16/02/1917	16/02/1917
Miscellaneous	Amendment To RAMC ORDER No 11	17/02/1917	17/02/1917
Miscellaneous	Appendix 6		
Map	Map		
Operation(al) Order(s)	61st Div. RAMC Order No. 12	25/02/1917	25/02/1917
Heading	War Diary Of The A.D.M.S 61st Division From March 1st 1917 To March 31st 1917 Volume No. 11		
War Diary	Harbonnieres	01/03/1917	28/03/1917
War Diary	Guizancourt	29/03/1917	31/03/1917
Operation(al) Order(s)	61st Division R.A.M.C.Order No. 13.	17/03/1917	17/03/1917
Operation(al) Order(s)	R.A.M.C. Operation Order No. 14	18/03/1917	18/03/1917
Operation(al) Order(s)	61st Division R.A.M.C. Order No 15.	19/03/1917	19/03/1917
Operation(al) Order(s)	61st Divisional R.A.M.C. Operation Orders No. 16.	20/03/1917	20/03/1917
Operation(al) Order(s)	61st Division R.A.M.C. Order No 16.A	27/03/1917	27/03/1917
Miscellaneous	March Table Issued With RAMC Order No:16		
Operation(al) Order(s)	61st Division R.A.M.C. Order No. 17.	28/05/1917	28/05/1917
Operation(al) Order(s)	61st Division R.A.M.C. Operation Order No. 18	30/03/1917	30/03/1917
Operation(al) Order(s)	61st Division R.A.M.C. Operation Order No. 19.	31/03/1917	31/03/1917
Heading	War Diary Of The A.D.M.S 61st Division For The Month Of April 1917 Volume No. 12		
War Diary	Guizancourt	01/04/1917	11/04/1917
War Diary	Voyennes	12/04/1917	21/04/1917
War Diary	Auroir	22/04/1917	30/04/1917
Operation(al) Order(s)	61st Division R.A.M.C. Operation Order No. 20	01/04/1917	01/04/1917
Miscellaneous	Issued With R.A.M.C. Operation Order No. 20	01/05/1917	01/05/1917
Operation(al) Order(s)	Issued With R.A.M.C. Operation Order No. 21.	02/04/1917	02/04/1917
Operation(al) Order(s)	61st Division R.A.M.C. Order No 22	04/04/1917	04/04/1917
Operation(al) Order(s)	61st Division R.A.M.C. Order No 23.	08/04/1917	08/04/1917
Operation(al) Order(s)	61st Division R.A.M.C. Order No 24.	10/04/1917	10/04/1917
Operation(al) Order(s)	61st Division R.A.M.C. Order No 25.	18/04/1917	18/04/1917
Heading	War Diary Of The A.D.M.S 61st Division From May 1st To May 31st 1917 Volume 13		
War Diary	Auroir	01/05/1917	15/05/1917

War Diary	Vignacourt	16/05/1917	20/05/1917
War Diary	Doullens	21/05/1917	22/05/1917
War Diary	Le Cauroy	23/05/1917	29/05/1917
War Diary	Warlus	29/05/1917	31/05/1917
Operation(al) Order(s)	61st Division Administrative Order No. 27.	12/05/1917	12/05/1917
Operation(al) Order(s)	61st Division R.A.M.C. Order No. 28	13/05/1917	13/05/1917
Operation(al) Order(s)	61st Division R.A.M.C. Order No. 29.	14/05/1917	14/05/1917
Operation(al) Order(s)	61st Division R.A.M.C. Order No. 30.	19/05/1917	19/05/1917
Miscellaneous	Medical Arrangements for 61st Division On Relieving 37th Division	29/05/1917	29/05/1917
Operation(al) Order(s)	61st Division R.A.M.C. Order No. 31	29/05/1917	29/05/1917
Heading	War Diary Of The A.D.M.S 61st Division From June 1st-30th 1917 Volume 14		
War Diary	Warlus	01/06/1917	01/06/1917
War Diary	Arras	02/06/1917	12/06/1917
War Diary	Warlus	13/06/1917	30/06/1917
Map	Map		
Operation(al) Order(s)	61st Division R.A.M.C. Order No. 32	08/06/1917	08/06/1917
Map	Map		
Miscellaneous	Warning Order	20/06/1917	20/06/1917
Map	Map		
Operation(al) Order(s)	61st Division R.A.M.C. Order No. 33.	21/06/1917	21/06/1917
Heading	War Diary Of A.D.M.S 61st Division From July 1st 1917 To July 31st 1917 Volume 15.		
War Diary	Willeman	01/07/1917	26/07/1917
War Diary	Zeggers Cappel	26/07/1917	31/07/1917
Miscellaneous	R.A.M.C. Administrative Instructions No. 34	24/07/1917	24/07/1917
Heading	War Diary Of A.D.M.S 61st Division From August 1st To August 31st 1917 Volume 16		
War Diary	Zaggers Cappel	01/08/1917	14/08/1917
War Diary	Poperinghe	15/08/1917	18/08/1917
War Diary	Mersey Camp	18/08/1917	31/08/1917
Operation(al) Order(s)	61st Division R.A.M.C. Administrative Order No. 35	13/08/1917	13/08/1917
Operation(al) Order(s)	61st Division R.A.M.C. Order No. 36	13/08/1917	13/08/1917
Miscellaneous	61st Division RAMC Administrative Instruction		
Map	Wattou & Brandhoek Areas		
Operation(al) Order(s)	61st Division R.A.M.C. Order No. 37	16/08/1917	16/08/1917
Miscellaneous	Medical Arrangements 61st Division		
Miscellaneous	Summary of Medical War Diaries of 61st Div. 8th Corps.		
Heading	War Diaries of Medical Units 61st Division From September 1st To September 30th 1917 Volume 17		
Miscellaneous	Operations Z		
Heading	War Diary Of A.D.M.S 61st Division Volume 17 Period September 1st To September 30th 1917.		
War Diary	Mersey Camp	01/09/1917	14/09/1917
War Diary	Wat(T)ou (Sheet-27)	15/09/1917	17/09/1917
War Diary	Duisans	18/09/1917	24/09/1917
War Diary	St Nicholas Camp	25/09/1917	30/09/1917
Operation(al) Order(s)	61st Division R.A.M.C. Administrative Order No. 38	12/09/1917	12/09/1917
Miscellaneous	Appendix To 61 Division RAMC Order No: 38		
Miscellaneous	Move Table		
Map	Wattou & Brandhoek Areas		
Operation(al) Order(s)	61st Division R.A.M.C. Administrative Order No. 39	16/09/1917	16/09/1917
Operation(al) Order(s)	61st Division R.A.M.C. Order No. 40	19/09/1917	19/09/1917
Miscellaneous	Addendum To 61 Division RAMC Order No:40.		

Heading	War Diary of A.D.M.S. 61st Division From October 1st To October 31st 1917 Volume 18		
War Diary	St Nicholas Camp	01/10/1917	28/10/1917
War Diary	Arras G.27.b.8.4.	29/10/1917	31/10/1917
Heading	War Diary Of A.D.M.S 61st Division Period November 1st-30th 1917 Volume 19		
War Diary	Arras	01/11/1917	30/11/1917
Operation(al) Order(s)	R.A.M.C. Order No. 41 by Colonel C.H. Howkins D.S.O. A.M.S.	27/11/1917	27/11/1917
Heading	War Diary Of A.D.M.S 61st Division Period December 1st To December 31st 1917 Volume 20		
War Diary	Etricourt Man Ref. 57 C. V.14.a.8.8.	01/12/1917	04/12/1917
War Diary	Etricourt	05/12/1917	11/12/1917
War Diary	Etricourt	12/12/1917	22/12/1917
War Diary	Mericourt T. Map Ref. Sheet No. Amiens 17	23/12/1917	29/12/1917
War Diary	Mericourt Sur-Somme	30/12/1917	30/12/1917
War Diary	Harbonnieres Map Ref Amiens	31/12/1917	31/12/1917
Operation(al) Order(s)	R.A.M.C. Order No. 42 by Colonel C.H. Howkins D.S.O. A.M.S.	02/12/1917	02/12/1917
Miscellaneous	Administrative Order	02/12/1917	02/12/1917
Miscellaneous	Medical Arrangements		
Miscellaneous	61st Division Medical Arrangements No:1		
Miscellaneous	Medical Arrangements for The evacuation of founded 61st division	16/12/1917	16/12/1917
Operation(al) Order(s)	R.A.M.C. Order No. 43 by Colonel C.H. Howkins D.S.O. A.M.S. A.D.M.S. 61 Div	18/12/1917	18/12/1917
Operation(al) Order(s)	R.A.M.C. Order No. 44 by Colonel C.H. Howkins D.S.O. A.M.S. A.D.M.S. 61 Division	21/12/1917	21/12/1917
Miscellaneous	March Table		
Operation(al) Order(s)	R.A.M.C. Order No. 45 by Colonel C.H. Howkins D.S.O. A.M.S. A.D.M.S. 61 Div	29/12/1917	29/12/1917
Heading	War Diary of A.D.M.S 61st Division Volume No. 21 From January 1st To 31st 1918		
War Diary	Harbonnieres Map Ref: Amiens 17	01/01/1918	06/01/1918
War Diary	Nesle Map Ref. Amiens 17.	07/01/1918	11/01/1918
War Diary	Auroir Map Ref. Sheet 66d.	12/01/1918	31/01/1918
Operation(al) Order(s)	61 Division R.A.M.C. Order No. 46	06/01/1918	06/01/1918
Operation(al) Order(s)	61 Division R.A.M.C. Order No. 47	08/01/1918	08/01/1918
Heading	War Diary of A.D.M.S 61st Division From February 1st 1918 To February 28th 1918 Volume 22		
War Diary	Auroir 66.d.	01/02/1918	28/02/1918
Operation(al) Order(s)	61 Division R.A.M.C. Order No. 48	20/02/1918	20/02/1918
Heading	War Diary of A.D.M.S 61st Division From March 1st To March 31st 1918 Volume 23		
War Diary	Auroir Sheet 66D.	01/03/1918	22/03/1918
War Diary	Rethonvillers Map Sheet Amiens 17	23/03/1918	24/03/1918
War Diary	Parvillers Map Sheet Amiens 17	25/03/1918	25/03/1918
War Diary	Beaucourt Map Sheet Amiens 17	26/03/1918	27/03/1918
War Diary	Villers Bretonneux Map Sheet Amiens 17.	28/03/1918	28/03/1918
War Diary	Boves. Map Sheet Amiens 17	29/03/1918	31/03/1918
War Diary	War Diary of A.D.M.S. 61st Division From April 1st 1918 To April 30th 1918 Volume 24		
War Diary	Boves. Sheets Amiens & Dieppe 1/100000	01/04/1918	01/04/1918
War Diary	Pissy Sheet Amiens 17	02/04/1918	10/04/1918
War Diary	Aire (Ref Sheet Hazebrouck 5a)	11/04/1918	30/04/1918

War Diary	War Diary of A.D.M.S 61st Division From May 1st 1918 To May 31st 1918 Volume 25		
War Diary	Aire Map Sheet Hazebrouck 5a	01/05/1918	17/05/1918
War Diary	Lambres Sheet 36A	18/05/1918	31/05/1918
Heading	War Diary of A.D.M.S. 61st Division From June 1st 1918 To June 30th 1918 Volume 27		
War Diary	Lambres Sheet 36A	01/06/1918	30/06/1918
Miscellaneous	Medical Arrangements	23/06/1918	23/06/1918
Heading	War Diary of A.D.M.S. 61st Division From July 1st 1918 To July 31st 1918 Volume 27		
War Diary	Lambres Sheet 36A	01/07/1918	13/07/1918
War Diary	Norrent-Fontes Sheet 36.A	14/07/1918	21/07/1918
War Diary	Wardrecques Sheet 36A	22/07/1918	31/07/1918
Miscellaneous	Medical Arrangements 61 Division on Relief By 74th Division	09/07/1918	09/07/1918
Miscellaneous	Collection of Sick etc on Completion of Relief	09/07/1918	09/07/1918
Miscellaneous	Medical Arrangements 61 Division	10/07/1918	10/07/1918
Miscellaneous	Medical Arrangements In connection with 61 Divisional defence Instructions No 1.	27/07/1919	27/07/1919
Miscellaneous	Stretcher Bearers Competition	30/07/1918	30/07/1918
Miscellaneous	Provisional Arrangements for collection of Sick commencing August 1st 1918	31/07/1918	31/07/1918
Heading	War Diary of A.D.M.S. 61st Division From August 1st 1918 To August 31st 1918 Volume 28		
War Diary	I.19.d.1.9 Sheet 36 A	07/08/1918	31/08/1918
Miscellaneous	Medical Arrangements 61 Division	03/08/1918	03/08/1918
Miscellaneous	Medical Arrangements In connection with 61 Division defence Instruction No:3	03/08/1918	03/08/1918
Operation(al) Order(s)	R.A.M.C. Order No. 65 by Colonel C.H. Howkins D.S.O. A.M.S. A.D.M.S. 61 Division	04/08/1918	04/08/1918
Miscellaneous	Provisional Medical Arrangements For left Sector of XIth corps front	04/08/1918	04/08/1918
Miscellaneous	Medical Arrangements In case of an Advance 61 Division	07/08/1918	07/08/1918
Operation(al) Order(s)	Light Railway Arrangements For Evacuation of wounded Issued with 61 Division RAMC Order No:66	10/08/1918	10/08/1918
Miscellaneous	RAMC Order No:66 By Colonel C.H. Howkins D.S.O. A.M.S. A.D.M.S. 61 Division	10/08/1918	10/08/1918
Operation(al) Order(s)	R.A.M.C. Order No. 67 by Colonel C.H. Howkins D.S.O. A.M.S. A.D.M.S. 61 Division	27/08/1918	27/08/1918
Operation(al) Order(s)	61st Division R.A.M.C. Order No. 68	31/08/1918	31/08/1918
Heading	War Diary of A.D.M.S. 61st Division From September 1st 1918 To September 30th 1918 Volume 29		
War Diary	Annay Sheet 36.A.1/40000	01/09/1918	08/09/1918
War Diary	Croix-Marraise J.21.C. Sheet 36A. 1/40000	09/09/1918	30/09/1918
Miscellaneous	Medical Arrangement 61 Division	08/09/1918	08/09/1918
Operation(al) Order(s)	61 Division R.A.M.C. Order No. 68	31/08/1918	31/08/1918
Operation(al) Order(s)	R.A.M.C. Order No. 69 By Lieut-Colonel Geo Mackie DSO. RAMC. TF Acting A.D.M.S. 61 Div	28/09/1918	28/09/1918
Miscellaneous	Medical Arrangements 61 Division	28/09/1918	28/09/1918
Miscellaneous	Reference R.A.M.C. Order No. 69	29/09/1918	29/09/1918
Heading	War Diary of A.D.M.S. 61st Division From October 1st 1918 To October 31st 1918 Volume 30		
War Diary	Croix Marraisse	01/10/1918	05/10/1918
War Diary	Doullens	06/10/1918	08/10/1918
War Diary	Lagnicourt	09/10/1918	12/10/1918

War Diary	Noyelles	13/10/1918	18/10/1918
War Diary	Rieux	19/10/1918	23/10/1918
War Diary	St Aubert	24/10/1918	25/10/1918
War Diary	Vendigies	26/10/1918	31/10/1918
Operation(al) Order(s)	R.A.M.C. Order No. 70 By Lieut-Colonel Geo Mackie DSO. RAMC. Acting A.D.M.S. 61 Div	01/10/1918	01/10/1918
Operation(al) Order(s)	R.A.M.C Order No. 71 By Lieut-Colonel Geo Mackie DSO. R.A.M.C.T Acting A.D.M.S. 61 Div	04/10/1918	04/10/1918
Operation(al) Order(s)	R.A.M.C. Order No. 72 By Lieut-Colonel Geo Mackie D.S.O. RAMC. T Acting A.D.M.S. 61 Div	10/10/1918	10/10/1918
Miscellaneous	Medical Arrangements	11/10/1918	11/10/1918
Operation(al) Order(s)	R.A.M.C. Order No. 73 By Colonel C.H. Howkins D.S.O. A.M.S. A.D.M.S. 61 Division	22/10/1918	22/10/1918
Miscellaneous	Medical Locations-61 Division	28/10/1918	28/10/1918
Heading	War Diary of A.D.M.S. 61st Division From November 1st 1918 To November 30th 1918 Volume 31		
War Diary	Vendegies Sheet 51.A. Scale-1/40000	01/11/1918	01/11/1918
War Diary	St Aubert	02/11/1918	07/11/1918
War Diary	Vendegies	09/11/1918	13/11/1918
War Diary	Rieux	14/11/1918	15/11/1918
War Diary	Cambrai	16/11/1918	30/11/1918
Operation(al) Order(s)	R.A.M.C. Order No. 75 By Colonel C.H. Howkins D.S.O. A.M.S. A.D.M.S. 61 Division	01/11/1918	01/11/1918
Operation(al) Order(s)	R.A.M.C. Order No. 76 By Colonel C.H. Howkins D.S.O. A.M.S. A.D.M.S. 61st Division	03/11/1918	03/11/1918
Miscellaneous	R.A.M.C. Order No:76 By Colonel C.H. Howkins D.S.O. A.M.S. A.D.M.S. 61st Division	13/11/1918	13/11/1918
Operation(al) Order(s)	R.A.M.C. Order No. 77 By Colonel C.H. Howkins D.S.O. A.M.S. A.D.M.S. 61st Division	14/11/1918	14/11/1918
Operation(al) Order(s)	R.A.M.C. Order No. 78 By Colonel C.H. Howkins D.S.O. A.M.S. A.D.M.S. 61st Division	18/11/1918	18/11/1918
Operation(al) Order(s)	R.A.M.C. Order No. 79 By Colonel C.H. Howkins D.S.O. A.M.S. A.D.M.S. 61 Division	30/11/1918	30/11/1918
Miscellaneous	Medical Arrangements In connection with 61st Div		
Heading	War Diary of A.D.M.S. 61st Division From December 1st 1918 To December 31st 1918 Volume 32		
War Diary	Bernaville	01/12/1918	07/12/1918
War Diary	St Riquier	08/12/1918	31/12/1918
Miscellaneous	Medical Arrangement 61 Division	06/12/1918	06/12/1918
Heading	War Diary of A.D.M.S. 61st Division From January 1st 1919 To January 31st 1919 Volume 33		
War Diary	St Riquier	01/01/1919	31/01/1919
Heading	War Diary of A.D.M.S. 61st Division From February 1st 1919 To February 28th 1919 Volume 34		
War Diary	St Riquier	01/02/1919	28/02/1919
Miscellaneous	61 Division Order No. 239	12/02/1919	12/02/1919
Heading	War Diary of Medical Units 61st Division From March 1st 1919 To March 31st 1919 Volume 35.		
Heading	War Diary of A.D.M.S. 61st Division From March 1st 1919 To March 31st 1919 Volume No. 35		
War Diary	St Riquier	01/03/1919	23/03/1919
War Diary	Le Treport	24/03/1919	31/03/1919
Operation(al) Order(s)	61st Division R.A.M.C. Order No. 103	22/03/1919	22/03/1919

61ST DIVISION

ASST DIR. MEDICAL SERVICES

~~MAY 1916-DEC 1918~~

1915 MAY — 1919 MAR

NO.2.

PROPOSALS OF A.D.M.S., 61st (S.M.) DIVISION
TO G.O.C., 61st (S.M.) DIVISION FOR DRAFT
FOR DIVISIONAL OPERATION ORDERS.

Reference ½" Ordmance Map, sheet 30.

-

1st Field Ambulance will work in neighbourhood from R. Blackwater to Pt 128 Road Fork, South of Beaconhill exclusive.

3rd Field Ambulance will work in neighbourhood from Point 128, inclusive to Railway, Noth of Chipping Hill exclusive.

2nd Field Ambulance will remain in reserve at Hatfield Peverel.

A Divisional Collecting station will be formed at Mission Hall, Danbury.

[signature]
Colonel,
A.D.M.S., 61st (S.M.) Division.

12.10.15.

Issued ~~P.M.~~ 9-45 am., by Hand
~~Cyclist orderly.~~

R.A.M.C. OPERATION ORDERS NO.3., BY

COLONEL W.H. BULL, K.H.S., V.D.,

A. D. M. S., 61st (S. M.) DIVISION.

Reference ½" Ordnance Map, sheet 30.

Detail.

1. At the end of the march O.C., each Field Ambulance will furnish me with a return of all sick who fall out on the march, and are unable to rejoin their Unit, and inform me of their disposal.

2. 2nd Field Ambulance will detail one Tent subsection and open a Divisional Collecting Station at Mission Hall, Danbury.

3. One officer from each Field Ambulance will attend on me for instrctions at 4.30 p.m. to-day, 12th instant.

4. All sick will be sent direct to Divisional Collecting Station at Danbury.

5. I shall be with Divisional Headquarters, The Priory, S.W. of Hatfield Green.

W.H. Bull
Colonel,
A.D.M.S., 61st (S.M.) Division.

Issued 9.30 a.m.
by Cyclist orderly.

12.10.15. Copy No.1. Filed in War Diary.
2. Operation Order file.
3. O.C., 1st Field Ambulance,
4. O.C., 2nd Field Ambulance.
5. O.C., 3rd Field Ambulance.

WAR DIARY

A.D.M.S

2/1st (S. MID.) DIVISION

May 1915 – May 1916

1915.

MAY

"War Diary." for month of May 1915

May 2nd At midnight the Divisional Sanitary Officer was called in consultation to see a doubtful case of Cerebro-Spinal-Meningites (in billets of the 2/4th Bn. Royal Berks.) Four men were found in one room, 3 sleeping in one bed. An urgent report of same was sent in.

" 3rd Requested the Divisional Sanitary Officer to meet A.D.M.S. at Danbury Huts No 1 in consultation with the A.D.M.S. 3rd Army. afternoon visited 3rd South Midland Field Ambulance Hospital.

" 5th Instructed the Divisional Sanitary Officer to accompany the A.D.M.S 3rd Army to Ingatestone to inspect the Sanitary Condition of 2/2nd S.M. Bde R.F.A. Examined crime sheets of 2/2nd Field Ambulance, found same satisfactory. Major Holland R.A.M.C.(T). 2/2nd Field Ambulance proceeded to Birmingham to take up duty as O.C 3/2nd. Field Ambulance.

" 8th Visited Witham and inspected (a) 2/1st Field Ambulance Hospital. Ordered several cases to be sent to Oaklands and sputum of 5 doubtful Tubercular cases to be sent to Colchester for Examination (B) Riding Horses, several of which had recently been sent from Remount Depot. On the whole they were a useful set. (C) Stables

" 9 Found them fairly well kept but required more ventilation The Hay was of a grossly coarse nature, full of dust, and dirty. (D) Headquarters Found them well kept. The meat

1915
May

was good, and properly hung up, on hooks and covered with canvas covering (E) Transport – 7 General Service Waggons, all in good working order, but one required new back brake. 3 Ambulance Waggons Mark 5 *, which are only fit for very slow light work & tho little weight inside. One fourwheeled covered car used as a bread cart, fit only for light work & short journeys. 4 waggons already scrapped by Ordnance Officer as unfit & useless. (7) Army Service Corp Depot (at railway siding) found carcases lying on dirty ground piled up one on top of the other, only partly covered and exposed to a hot sun and high wind – Tins of tea & bags of salt also open and exposed to dust, (which was blowing across these stores & smothering the food.) The sun was melting the frozen parts. This "filthy" state of affairs was reported & recommended that the meat be hung on hooks on a beam, and placed under shelter with proper protection – Visited Maldon V.A.D. Hospital, found Patients most comfortable. Interviewed Civil Medical Practitioner in charge of this Hospital, Ordered 7 cases to be brought over to 2/2nd Field Ambulance Hospital. Oaklands Chelmsford for further treatment. Interviewed O.C & M.O of 2/8th Worcester, found a fair amount of German Measles prevalent in town, but due precautions were taken. Was informed

1915
May

that billeting was 'almost overdone', & no more could be taken in without overcrowding (9) Visited Danbury. 2/3rd Ambulance Hospital. Inspected drainage, found every thing satisfactory. Ordered a few cases into Oaklands (for transmission to Cambridge.) Late in afternoon received instructions from Headquarters to send 1st Field Ambulance to Colchester, One officer with advance party to proceed at once, main body to proceed on the 12th.

May 10th Received very urgent request at 8 P.M. from King Edwards Horse Regiment to take in a case of Cerebro. Spinal-Meningitis from Hoddesdon

" 11th Made thorough inspection of Oaklands Hospital with Dr Thresh Medical Officer of Health Essex who was requested to examine the premises by the local Government Board.

" 12th In accordance with orders from G.O.C 2/1 S.M.D. held board at Civil Hospital on Officer of the Cyclists Co 1/1st S.M.D. who had sustained a fracture of the thigh –

13th Under orders of Southern Command (sanctioned by War Office) detailed Capt Joyce RAMC (T) 2/4 Royal Berks for duty as Registrar War Hospital Reading + placed C.M.P. (S. Come) in Medical Charge of this Unit –

" 14th Visited Colchester, inspected 2/1st S.M. F.A. at their new Headquarters (Lexden House) and also V.A.D. Hospital (Gostwycke House) and Isolation Hospital (Cambridge Road), taken over from East Anglian Division –

" 17th Owing to report of diphtheria at Browning's House Bromfield Road, visited same with

1915 May

Divisional Sanitary Officer & found two contacts only were placed there. Interviewed ADVS. as Rooms in Mornington House were being told off for his department.

May 18th At the request of Lt Col Wilkinson Local Government Board Inspector, I detailed the Divisional Sanitary Officer (with Dr McDonald the local Medical Officer of Health) to accompany him on a Sanitary Inspection. A case of Cerebro Spinal Meningitis of the 1/1st Division which had been in Kenilworth Hospital since early last February died this day.

" 19 At the request of Dr Martin Civil Medical Practitioner I conveyed by Motor Ambulance a civil case of Cerebro-Spinal-Meningitis from Broomfield Road to Kenilworth Hospl and as 5 men of 2/5th Glos Regt were billeted in same house they were sent at once to the Isolation Tent (Oaklands) for inspection by the Bacteriologist from Colchester. Visited Danbury Hutments 1 & 2 & also 2/3rd S.M.F.A. Investigated case where 2 men of the 1/3rd Field Ambulance left their billet in Chelmsford without billet being paid. Wrote overseas to the O.C. of Unit about same. Brigadier General commanding Warwick Infantry Brigade having corresponded with O.C Colchester Military Hospital with a view of obtaining the help of RAMC (Regular) Officers for some of his Units. I wired to ask if any could be spared, but received an answer in the negative from O.C. Military Hospl. —

1915 May

May 20th ADMS 3rd Army visited Oaklands, with Chief Engineer 3rd Army C.F., respecting Oaklands House being taken over entirely for use as a Hospital — Afterwards formed a Medical Board at Danbury, ADMS 3rd Army C.F. Presiding, examined draft from 2/3rd S.M.F.A. 2/4th Gloucesters & 2/6th Gloucesters. The draft recently sent to the 2/6th Glos was considered a very poor one and only 49 out of 100 were accepted for Imperial Service & several were rejected as unfit for any service

" 21st Held Medical Board at Colchester (ADMS 3rd Army presiding) drafts from following Units 2/6th 2/7th & 2/8th Btn Royal Warwick & 2/1st SMFA General Culling also inspected (Gostwycke House) V.A.D. Hospital, and Infectious Hospl & 2/1 S.M.F. Ambulance. Interviewed Brigadier General Warwick Infantry Brigade respecting Medical Officers to fill Vacancies in his Brigade.

" 22 Interviewed G.O.C 2/1 S.M.D had exceptionally heavy office work owing to absence from same on these new Medical Boards —

" 24 At the urgent request of the G.O.C, I formed a Medical Board and examined 1st Reinforcements South Midland Infantry Brigade at Terling consisting of 426 NCO & men. Of these 395 were found perfectly fit for Imperial Service 15 were temporary unfit for Imperial Service and 16 were recommended for home service only. I found the whole Btn except 38 had twice been inoculated against typhoid These 38 men were inoculated same day by one of my Medical Officers & arrangements

1915 May

have been made to administer 2nd inoculation 10 days hence –

May 25th Held a Medical Board at Oaklands. Total No of drafts 167 (~~Result~~ See Central Force order 596 22/4/1915) Result was

Category

A.	B.	C.	D.
87	7	26	37

" 27 G.O.C. 3rd Army Central Force accompanied by his Staff Officers, & G.O.C. 2/1 S.M.D & Staff inspected 2/2nd Field Ambulance, & ~~also~~ Oaklands House Hospl. –

" 28 Held Medical Board at Colchester Total No of drafts examined 211 – result as follows

Category

A.	B.	C.	D.
84	27	65	35

" 29 Formed a Medical Board at Danbury & examined 2/6th Bn Glos ~~[illegible]~~ Regt (Draft of 15)

Result: – Category

A.	B.	C.	D
8	2	4	1

" 31 Visited Maldon held Medical Board on drafts from 2/4th & 2/8th Worcesters Total 176

Result: – Category

A	B.	C	D
70	24	56	26

Visited Rivercourt (V.A.D) Hospital – Patients all comfortable – & no serious cases

Precis

The month's work has been carried on fairly

1915 May

satisfactorily, but not so thoroughly, as I should wish owing to such causes as: – (1). Central Force order (596) that Medical Boards assemble Tuesdays Thursdays & Fridays. This ~~takes~~ takes me away from office duty "3 days" per week, consequently clerical, & other, work are in abeyance. Although much is passed on to D.A.D.M.S., a fair amount demands personal attention –

(2). Extra amount of work, calling for extra reports etc: which are hurriedly & urgently required.

The three Field Ambulances are "always late" in responding punctually to my urgent demands, especially the 3rd Field Amb, which in this respect, causes me much trouble, therefore my returns (urgently asked for at Headquarters) arrive late. I have most seriously cautioned the O.C's (especially 2nd & 3rd F. Ambles) about this "slackness"

The first few medical Boards were presided over by A.D.M.S. 3rd Army C.F. who now instructs me to "carry on", ~~reporting~~ result of each Board to him, noting ~~all~~ any cases that ~~required to~~ need be brought before him.

At the Board on 2/6th Btn Glos Regt a draft of men (recently joined), were of poor type, & out of 80, only 29 were passed for Imperial Service, 20 being unfit for any service

With regard to equipment, I have sent in a full report of requirements for all Units, but up to the present they have nothing to "carry on" with, which is of serious importance, especially to the F. Ambles as it handicaps their training

1915 May

& the O.C.s are constantly calling my attention to same.

The monthly report of inoculations shows an improvement, but I find that some Officers (of middle age) for Home Service, have not been inoculated, hence low percentages in some instances—

Again I call attention to shortage of M.O.s which is more likely to get worse, than improve, until the W.O equalizes the Service.

I am glad to report no recent fresh cases of Cerebro-Spinal-Meningitis & when the last case leaves Kenilworth House I will raise the question whether that building be retained (W.O having built excellent accomodation for such cases at Civil Infectious Hospital, which has only just been completed)

The Bacteriologist at Colchester has been of great service to me in these cases & given me (through the D.S.O.(?)) untold assistance

Again I call attention to the proper care of meat & stores, which in my report I have designated as "filthy"

Attention has seriously been called to overcrowding in a House where Cerebro-Spinal-Meningitis occured, This was caused by men, "not complying with "orders" (sleeping 3 in one Bed)

1915 May

With regard to "Oaklands House" being taken over entirely as a Hospital, This is still under consideration & so far I have ~~not~~ received ~~any~~ definate orders, but the Sanitary conditions of the ~~part~~ part of the House used ~~as~~ for the ~~present~~ Hospital is receiving the attention of D.O.R.E. with whom we are in frequent communications.

June

Month of June 1915

June 1st Held Medical Board at Oaklands Inspection Room Number examined 132 Result A 99 B 8 C 8 D 17

2nd Motored over to Boreham House & interviewed G.O.C

3rd Held Medical Board at Maldon examined 172 result A 104 B 28 C 36 D 4, Owing to this heavy board at Maldon was unable to attend G.O.C's conference at 3 P.M. but was represented by D.A.D.M.S.

4th Held Medical Board at Colchester examined draft of 9 men from 2/3rd S.M. R.F.A. result A 2 B 1 C 5 D 1. One of the men Gunner Surman was a malingerer of exceptionally bad character who appeared before a Board the previous week. The Board recommended the Medical Officer to examine him under an anaesthetic. This he declined & the case was duly reported for O.C to take necessary steps. Inspected the V.A.D. Gostwycke Hospital & Military Hospital. Found everything most satisfactory

5 Held Medical Board at Ingatestone examining draft of 17 of 2/2nd. S.M.R.F.A result A 9 B 2 C 1 D 5 Motored over to Boreham House & interviewed

1915
June

Staff. At 2.30 P.M meet G.O.C at Civil Infectious Hospital & visited new War Office Infectious Pavilion which had recently been opened.
Visited Danbury and consulted with O.C 2/3rd Field Ambulance about movement of his Unit to Camp at Epping. Arranged for him to leave ½ tent section with one Medical Officer at Danbury for the use of the Gloucester & Worcester Brigade

7th Motored over to Boreham House for consultation

8th Motored over to Boreham House at 9 a.m & interviewed G.O.C. Arranged for the removal of this office to Boreham House. Held Medical Board at Oaklands Inspection room 55 men were examined, result (a. B. C. D) 46 1 5 3. Inspected Oaklands House in company with Divisional Sanitary Officer & O.C of the 2/2nd Field Ambulance & drew up, & completed report of requirements, required to be done to the house before taking all of the building over as a Divisional Hospital, & submitted same to the D.O.R.E. At Hospital examined Pte Cockle who had been sent into Hospital from detention barracks. Finding him mentally deficient, recommended his discharge

9th Held Medical Board at East Hanningfield and also at Danbury on the 1st Reinforcement Battalion of Gloucester & Worcester Brigade Number examined 79 result (a. B. C. D) 59 12 8 - also held Board at Danbury on 80 men of the 2/4th Btn

1915
June

Gloucesters, result (a. B. C. D) 40. 22 18 -

10th Attended inspection of the Division by General Sir L. Rundle G.O.C in C. C.F. at Hylands Park 9.30 a.m. & Boreham Park 11 am. & Colchester, 3. P.M.

11th Visited Eastern General Hospital at Cambridge, and interviewed Commandant and the Bacteriologist of the Hospital about many cases sent to them.

12th Held Medical Board at Colchester of the 2/5th. 2/6th & 2/8th Royal Warwick Regt. total 77 result (a. B. C. D.) 26 23 19 9. In afternoon held Board at Witham on draft of 11 men of the R. E. result (a. B. C. D) 3 1 4 3

14th The ADMS. 3rd Army C. F. inspected the 2/2nd Field Ambulance at 10. am at Oaklands & the 2/3rd Field Ambulance at Danbury. In the afternoon inspected the huts of the R. G. A Great Baddow Road, The new, War Office Infectious Pavilion, and the Hutments of the A.S.C. Chelmsford

15th Held Medical Board at Chelmsford, 33 men were examined result (a. B. C. D) 9 4 17 3. Visited Boreham House inspected marquees & tents. Arranged for Offices of A.D.M.S. A.D.V.S. D.A.D.O.S. & tents for office staff

16th Offices of A.D.M.S. & staff complete were moved from 67 New London Road to new offices at Boreham House

17th Held Medical Board at Maldon on 2/7th & 2/8th Btn. Worcesters 53 men examined result (a. B. C. D) 19 5 25 4

1915
June

18th Held Medical Board at Colchester on draft of the 2/3rd S.M. Bdge. R.F.A & 1 man of the 2/1st S.M. Field Ambulance. Total examed 35 result A. 18. B. 7 C. 8 D. 2. The Warwick Brigade were under orders to proceed this day from Colchester to Chelmsford but owing to extensive outbreak of measles 175 cases being reported by the local M.O.H. ~~that~~ in Bromfield & Great & Little Waltham I ordered these places out of bounds & other arrangements were made

21st Interviewed War Office Land Agent about giving up Kenilworth, that house being no longer required. Also interviewed D.O.R.E. about the Drains & various repairs at Oaklands. Visited Oaklands House & found everything satisfactory.

22nd Held Board at Chelmsford on 126 men result A. 28. B. 14. C. 68. D. 16. A large number (34) were found to be under age of 18 1/2 1 under age of 16 4 under 17, 20 under 18 & 11 over the age of 40. Visited Cerebro. Spinal Meningitis (Kenilworth) Hospital & found Pte Capewell the only case now left was becoming rapidly comatosed.

23rd Drew up a large number of reports on various Boards held.

24th Paid a very hurried visit to Epping Camp in response to urgent wire from Colonel Commanding South Midland Infantry Brigade asking ADMS to hold Medical Board on drafts to be sent overseas

1915
June

at once. On arrival it was found to be unnessary, as small number of men required for transfer to the 1st Reinforcement had already been seen by Medical Board & passed only awaiting final approval of the Regimental Medical Officer.

26th Held Medical Board at Danbury on Officers & men as follows, 14 Officers A. 6 B. 4 C. 4 D. – & 50 men A. 15 B. 4 C. 25. D. 6

27th Visited Oaklands Hospital & interviewed OC of the 2/1st & 2/3rd South Midland Field Ambulance

28th Visited Burnham. Consulted with O.C 83rd Prov: Batt: & with Dr Lander M.O appointed by Admiralty & arranged for V.A.D Hospital at Burnham & for the treatment of other cases. Attended in afternoon with DADMS & O.C 2/1st & 2/2nd Field Ambulances The Instructional Class (Tactical) by Captn Davies Staff Officer 2/1st S.M.D. (No 1 Attack)

29th Held Medical Board at Chelmsford number examined 42 result A. 21 B. 6 C. 14 D. 1

Held a Practical Demonstration on 1st Aid to wounded scheme being from "The Regimental Aid Posts to Rail Head", by the 2/1st & 2/2nd Field Ambulances at Oaklands which was witnessed by the G.O.C.. In afternoon attended similar class, with my officers, as previous day (but No 2 Defensive) by Colonel Heard Staff Officer 2/1st S.M.D.

" 30th Held Practical Demonstration on 1st Aid ~~[illegible]~~ (Scheme same as held previous day at Oaklands) by 2/3rd F. Amb at Epping Camp – Held Med: Board at Epping – No exam'd 37 ~~[illegible]~~
Result A. 12. B. 2. C. 14. D. 9.

1915
June

Precis

Having completed the Medical Boards, in accordance with C.I.O's. 596 d/22 4/15 and 695 d/12 5/15 – which Boards have been regularly held 3 times a-week at Chelmsford, Danbury & Maldon & Colchester, in accordance with 3A/CR/1046 M. 2871 d/17 5/15 – I now give the following report –

No of men who appeared before the Boards from 20th May to 30th June	2366.
(A). Fit for Service at Home or abroad	1292.
(B). Temporarily unfit for Service abroad	264.
(C). Fit for Service at Home only	552.
(D) Unfit for Service at Home or abroad	258.
Total	2366

A large number of above were either "under age" – or "overage" – to which I have already called attention in previous reports – Several men have been placed in Category (C) with recommendation that they should be transferred to Government works – in which they have worked previous to mobilization –

Antityphoid inoculation still continues satisfactory & it will be observed – from reports sent in – that in some instances the % among Officers is low – This is fully explained by the following facts – (A) It is unnecessary to inoculate men over the age of 55. There are many Officers over this age – (B) – many Officers who have not submitted their names for Foreign Service – decline inoculation while on "Home Service" – but are willing to be inoculated if they join the Foreign Service Units. The % of sickness during this month is most highly satisfactory – & the Division is now free of cerebro-spinal meningitis, under which circumstances I have recommended "Kenilworth House" taken over by

1915
June

the 1/1st S.M.D. for that purpose, be now given up, as the new "Infectious Pavilion" for such purposes – erected by the W.O at Great Baddow Infectious Hospl grounds – be now utilized, having been opened for use this month = It has now been definitely arranged by the 3rd Army that "Oaklands" House is to be taken over, entirely, as a Field Ambulance Hospital for the Division – and the imperfect sanitary arrangements are to be put into proper order – Already 2 new water carriage W.C's have been erected in the yard – & my Recommendations for all necessary work to be done – (before I can take it over as a Hospital) – have been forwarded through the proper channels – with urgent request for prompt & immediate action – In accordance with instructions – the Offices & Staff of A.D.M.S were moved from 67 London Road – to Horslan House Head Quarters – Marquees & tents being pitched as Offices – & accommodation for the Staff = but on 30th inst: a sudden & severe thunderstorm flooded the tents & very seriously interrupted the work – & made the floors – in places – unfit for occupation – The move of the Office – though inconvenient in many respects – will save much time & correspondence by being in immediate touch with all the Branches of Head Quarters – The training of the F. Ambulances is making decided progress – and now that some of the Equipment (so often indented for) has arrived, they can carry on work much more satisfactorily – The new (Mark 6.*) Ambulance wagons are a great acquisition but I regret that the present limited amount of Harness is most inferior, & indeed some of it unsafe for heavy work – & the number of Horses is still most limited ——

1915. Month of July

July 1st. Visited Oaklands Hospital and interviewed the O.Cs of 2/1st & 2/2nd Field Ambulances on various subjects. At 4.30 pm attended a Weekly Conference of the G.O.C.

July 2nd. Sent D.A.D.M.S to Epping Camp to make all necessary Dental arrangements with the ~~Regular~~ Civilian Dentist for treating the troops while under canvas. Sent Divisional Sanitary Officer also to Epping Camp, to meet the Sanitary Officer from Central Force to consult with him on the Camp Sanitation. Interviewed the Secy. Red Cross Socy. Chelmsford, respecting the V.A.D. Hospital at Burnham being utilized as a Hospital for the use of the 83rd Provisional Battalion if required. Visited Oaklands Hospital and afterwards called upon the C.O.R.E. respecting the Drains & repairs in Oaklands House. Owing to the urgent orders received from Headquarters, when all Officers & Men for Home Service where to proceed to Colchester on the 5th inst so as to be separated from the 2/1st Division. I wrote the D.G.A.M.S under personal instructions received from him last year regarding my Services being retained as A.D.M.S. or transferred.

July 3rd. Under Special G.O. orders held a Medical Board on Lieut. Marklew R.A.M.C. (T) of the 1/1st ~~Ambulance~~ Ammunition Column S.M.D. who was injured early in the year, but on his return to Duty last month was temporarily attached to 2/1st S.M. Fd. Ambulance.

With the Special permission of the G.O.C. I obtained permission for a weeks leave.

July 12th. Visited Oaklands Hospital & Hutments.

July 13th. Surgeon General Culling held a Staff ride at Hatfield Peverelle at 10.0 am. which was attended by myself, the D.A.D.M.S and ~~the~~ Officers of the 2/1st & 2/2nd Field Ambulances. This Staff ride covered the grounds ~~as far as~~ from [illegible] to Maldon, & all places of importance were visited. In the afternoon I carefully inspected Oaklands Hospital, Infectious Tented Hospitals & Hutments.

Action supposed to be in the vicinity of Highwood Quarter, Blackmore, Highwoods, Ingatestone & Margaretting. The D.A.D.M.S also attended these Demonstrations.

July 15th. Motored over to Colchester with D.A.D.O.S. in order to hand over Gostwycke House. V.A.D. Hospital & the Infectious Hospital Cambridge Road taken over by the 2/1st Field Ambulance from the East Anglian Division ~~and~~ the equipment of this Infectious Hospital had been disinfected in accordance with Regulations, and as the whole of same ~~were~~ was standing in my name I interviewed the ~~D.A.D.O.S.~~ Ordnance Officer Colchester to ~~return~~ retain same for Oaklands Hospital Chelmsford. Afterwards interviewed the O.C. A.S.C. Colchester & arranged with him to send same over to Chelmsford by Motor Lorry.

July 16th. Held a Course of Instructions with the 2/1st & 2/2nd Field Ambulances at Oaklands in "General Field Work."
Interviewed the D.O.R.E. and O.C. i/c Barracks with ~~a~~ regard to requirements at Oaklands also inspected Oaklands. In the afternoon held Medical Boards at Danbury & Maldon.

July 17th. Hospital equipment was sent from Colchester Infectious Hospital to Oaklands.

July 19th. Medical Boards were held on Drafts (1) sent from the 3rd line to the Warwick Infantry Brigade at

~~2~~ Chelmsford. and (2) At Epping Camp on drafts sent from the 3rd line to the South Midland Infantry Brigade.

July 20th. Surgeon Gen. Culling A.D.M.S. 3rd Army Central Force inspected with me (1) Hutments at Writtle at 10.0 a.m. and ~~at the~~ Hutments at Baddow at 4.30 p.m. accompanied by the Divisional Sanitary Officer.
Reports of this Inspection to be duly forwarded by him to the G.O.C.
The rest of the day was occupied with a Practical Demonstration of the 2/1st & 2/2nd Field Ambulances on duties connected with Field work in action. The scheme was drawn out by the General Staff 1/S. M. D.

July 21st. ~~I~~ visited Oaklands in morning.
Received urgent telegram from O.C. ordering Lieut. Marklove to proceed overseas at once, reporting himself at Southampton. Received urgent wire from C.F. asking me to supply a Medical Officer for the 1/5th Bn R. Warwick. but could not comply as only 1 M.O. was doing duty with this Unit.

22nd. Attended a Conference of the G.O.C. at Headquarters at 4/30 p.m.

23rd. The D.A.D.M.S. was granted Seven days leave of absence sanctioned by the G.O.C. to proceed home on important.

private matters. Held a Medical Board at Maldon on drafts from the 3rd Line. Lt. Moore R.A.M.C. & 7/8th Gloster Regt being on the Board. Called at Oaklands & went over the Hospital & saw the D.O.R.E. respecting work not yet done at Oaklands. Called upon the Secy. Essex Red Cross Society, respecting V.A.D. Nurses rendering help at Oaklands.

24th. Visited Oaklands & met Mrs Magor Lady Commandant of Essex V.A.D. & her assistant Nurse, Miss Craig, together with the M.O. i/c of the Hospital & the O.Cs. of the 2/1st & 2/2nd South Midland Field Ambulances, and arranged with Mrs Magor to act as Lady Commandant of the Hospital with 2 or 3 ~~Nur~~ Lady Helpers, commencing ~~for~~ duty at the end of next week.

In the afternoon held a Medical Board on a draft of 30 men at Oaklands Hospital Chelmsford. (Of the 2/8th Battn. Royal Warwick Regt.)

26th Held Medical Boards on a Draft from 3rd Line sent up to 2/7th Worcester Regiment at Maldon, also on ~~some~~ other men in the 2/7th & 2/8th Bn Worcesters Regiment, and afterwards held Medical Board on several of the R.E's at Writtam.

27th In accordance with urgent orders from A.D.M.S. 3rd Army, I met the Div. San. Officer to meet him in consultation at Southminster & Burnham. Held Medical Boards at Oaklands (~~Reception Rooms~~) Chelmsford (~~2nd S.M. F. Amb. Hos~~) on several details sent from many units. Also Medical Board on 7 Officers of the A.S.C., held Board also on several cases in the Oaklands Hospital and visited the Hospital. Held a Board on Lieut. Probyn of the 2/5th R. War. Regt. with a view to ~~him~~ joining the Royal Flying Corps.

C.R.A. interviewed me respecting Boards on Officers & Men under his command.

28th ~~Held Medical Boards at F. Amb. Reception Room Oaklands Chelmsford on 7 Officers of the A.S.C. and examined one Officer of the R.E's for the Flying Corps. Also held Boards on several detachments from other Units & upon 9 men in the Hospital.~~ Carefully inspected Oaklands Hospital, Interviewed the M.O. & found still further improvement in the arrangements. Interviewed the G.O.C. on several matters.

July 1915

29th Visited Epping Camp, accompanied by the Divisional Sanitary Officer with a view of ascertaining details for baths for the Camp as follows:- 1. At Mr Pelly's stables ideal arrangements were made for 49 men at one time to have a Hot bath. The water being discharged direct into the main sewer.

Excellent Latrine (Urinals) accommodation was provided at these places.

The only objection to these accomodations appeared to be the high charges demanded and the distance (over a mile from the Camp).

2. Inspected Mr Hollands premises at Oakridge, about half mile further off who offered his Garage, but here the accommodation was very limited, as 24 baths, at the very most, only could be provided, and half of this number must have been outside the Garage on the Concrete Washing floor which would require enclosing with screens.

3. Accommodation on the field erected by the Engineers for each Battalion. I met the Medical Officer of Health for the Rural District Council together with his Sanitary Officer & carefully inspected the whole system with the ditch leading down from the Camp, ultimately empties itself into the River.

This appeared to be the best scheme provided, the water was most carefully passed through one or two filter traps to be erected.

This scheme met with the approval of the Medical Officer of Health, who considered a large flush of water of this kind would be beneficial in keeping this ditch clean.

Afterwards interviewed the Caretaker of the Small Pox Hospital with regard to Notifiable Infectious Cases being received, and asked him to name his charge for his duty, to be paid by the Military which he stated would be 10/- per week.

Inspected the VAD ("Suyland's") Hospital were 4 cases had been admitted from the Camp. But this Hospital Everything was in splendid order.

At the Camp I found the Latrine Buckets in most instances had little or no creosole fluid in them.

In the afternoon attended the GOCs weekly conference, I brought forward the subject of Vaccination & Inoculation.

Interviewed the GOC in the morning on several important matters.

30th Received an urgent telegram at 11-0 am from M.O. [illegible] R. War. Regt. sent from Detention Barracks at Gt Baddow on the 21st instant to Stafford Prison, and a communication had just been received from the Prison Authorities that he had developed Small Pox. Have taken the very strictest precautions in the matter.

31st Owing to a very heavy demand for medical inspection of the whole Division (i Cons with G.O.C.) I arranged for M.O's of F. Ambulances to assist M.O's of Units in carrying out this work at once — Went D.A.D.M.S. to Epping — & Danbury & Maldon to expedite (& assist if reqd.) — Also interviewed Lt Col. Rogers whom I have placed in charge of this duty being carried out at once in the [illegible] with the assistance of his Officers —

1915

June July

Precis

Sickness in the Division during the last month is—(what it ought to be during this fine and healthy weather)—extremely low for the present free from notifiable infectious diseases except three cases of Measles. The Field Amb. (Oaklands) hospital has again occupied my serious attention and there is now a marked improvement in its administration. I have in consultation with the Essex Red Cross Society arranged for a Lady Commandant + two nurses to render help in the hospital. Under the most strict vigilance it will never look clean as the 3rd Army has refused my request to put the building in a proper state of repair and the boards until planed and properly treated will always look dirty regardless of labour spent in scrubbing and cleaning. Throughout the Division there is an improvement in Sanitation in general—but still there is much more to be desired. The Units do not yet grasp the all important fact that Sanitation is Life and their attention is constantly being called to it by the Div. San. Officer who pays frequent visits to each unit. During the month the Field Ambulances have had extra and special training in Field Duties and on two occasions (During Field Practice) have had the benefit of Instruction from the A.D.M.S. 3rd Army and his Staff Officer. A number of Medical Boards have again been held during the month especially on drafts sent from 3rd Line. Some of these drafts have been far from satisfactory consisting of a large number of boys under the age of 18. For example, a draft of 56 men was examined by the M.O. i/c Unit he passed 14 perfectly sound but refered 42 to a Medical Board out of which 38 were found to vary between the ages of 15 and 18.

The question of warm bath for troops at Epping Camp has received careful attention. The present scheme is almost ideal but the charges are prohibitive. I visited the Camp with

Precis.
Divisional Sanitary Officer and interviewed local M.O.H. and Sanitary inspector regarding Bathing accomodation in the Field but so regulated as to avoid fouling the ditch (Conveying the water into the river) and drew up a report for consideration of G.O.C. Owing to the order for all Home Service men to proceed to Colchester to join the 106th Provisional Battalion. Interviewed the G.O.C with regard to M.Os. In accordance with regulations there should be (exclusive of Casualty clearing station) 55 R.A.M.C. Officers in the division but at present there are only 25. out of which 14 offer their services for overseas and 11 (i.e. 9 M.Os + 2 Non Medical Officers) are for Home Service. To remove these Officers from the Division untill their places could be filled by overseas officers would be a serious matter as it is most difficult to procure the services of C.M.P.s. The 3rd Army was consulted and ruled that these M.Os should remain with the division for the present. With regard to Inoculation only slight progress has taken place since last month. I have interviewed the M.Os on the subject and issued most urgent appeals to the various O.C.s Unit calling their serious attention again to this most vital question.

August. 1915.

1st. Nil.

2nd. Sent D.A.D.M.S. to hold Boards at Maldon & Danbury.

3rd Visited "Oaklands" inspected Hospitals Held Board (by order of G.O.C.) on Capt Rose 1/4th Battn Oxon & Bucks L.I. (wounded on 11th May) at Oaklands:- called on O/c Barracks re Lt Col Craig's Camp Claims. 6 pm attended G.O.C's conference re arrangements for Lord Kitchener's inspection of the 6th inst.

4th Sent D.A.D.M.S. with D.A.Q.M.G. to Hylands re arrangements for 6th inst. Visited Oaklands Hospital motored to Ingatestone to interview Dr Sterling-Hamilton to act as Medical Officer i/c 2/3rd Royal Field Artillery Brigade. Interviewed Dr Denning Epping re attendance on Corps.

5th. Visited Oaklands (Hospital & Marquees) sent D.A.D.M.S. with D.A.Q.M.G. to Hylands with Divisional Sanitary Officer to make Sanitary arrangements for inspection on 6th inst.

6th The Secretary of State for War (Lord Kitchener) inspected 2/1st. South Midland Division in Hylands Park at 11-0. a.m.

Aug

6th At 3.0 pm held Medical Board on Capt Cheshire 4th Provisional Battalion & Lieut Large 1/7th Royal Warwickshire Regiment.
Interviewed Major Howard RAMC T. now in charge of Provisional Units at Colchester.

7th Visited Oaklands & held consultation with O. Cs. Interviewed Dr Smith in Chelmsford re taking commission as M.O. i/c 6th Gloster Regiment.
Held consultation with G.O.C.

8th Arranged for Medical Board on Lt Austin 1/8th War Regt on 16th inst but just received wire from S. C. to send his Documents to Military Hospital Warwick.

9th 2nd Lieut Solomon (1/7th War Regt) presented himself for a Medical Board, but same had been held over him in order on 2nd inst.
Reported same to G.O.C.
Visited Oaklands Hospital re application for more Hospital Equipment & fully went into the matter with O. Cs. 2/2nd & 2/3rd F.As & Lady Commandant.
The G.O.C. came in at same time & went over the Hospital.

Aug

10th Visited Oaklands Hospital.

11th Proceeded early in the morning to Epping Camp accompanied by DADMS & held Medical Board on 129 men.

12th Held Medical Board on Capt Hayne attended the G.O.C's Conference at 4.30 pm.
Visited Oaklands Hospital Interviewed O. C. A.S.C. re:- Supply of Manure of Field Ambulance Stables to Master of Workhouse.

13th Held Medical Exercises with 2/2nd & 2/3rd Field Ambulance at Ingatestone
ADMS 3rd Army was present & inspected the various advanced Dressing Stations & Divisional Dressing Stations.
Dr Appleton RAMC from Colchester attached 1/4th Bn Bells & ASC.

14th Interviewed the Clerk to the Board of Guardians with reference to use of Baths & Disinfector for cases of Itch.

16th Under instructions from 3rd Army visited Central Force who requested me to interview the D.G. A.M.S. at War Office.

17th Surgeon General Culling ADMS 3rd Army Central Force called at Headquarters & introduced to the Divisional Staff his successor, Colonel Morgan. He himself proceeding as D.D.M.S. C.F.
They inspected Oaklands Hospital

Aug

17th The Infectious Tents, the Field Ambulance Instruments & Stables.

18th Proceeded with D.A.D.M.S. to Maldon & Danbury holding Medical Boards.

19th Held Medical Boards with Major Hopton & Lt Col ~~Stallard~~ Craig at Oaklands on 2 Officers & 2 men A.S.C. 2 men 3rd Field Ambulance, & on 6 patients in Oaklands Hospital. Held consultation with O Cs of 1st 3rd Field Ambulances Interviewed Major Warwick R A M C T. at present doing Duty at Colchester Military Hospital re: being attached to 2nd Field Ambulance of this Division.
Attended G O Cs Conference at 4 30pm

20th It being reported to me that Pte Keeley of the 5th Glosters Regiment who was recommended by Medical Board on the 7/8/15 for discharge through Mental Deficiency was showing symptoms of loss of Control over his actions. I accordingly visited their Headquarters, interviewed the O.C. & ordered him to Oaklands Hospital with a

Aug

guard to be furnished by the Battalion for strict observation. Strictest Orders were given to the M.O. to carefully watch the case & report to me his condition in the evening. At 7.30pm O.C. 3rd F. Amb informed me by telephone that the man was perfectly quiet & docile & that so far it only appeared to be a case of Mental Deficiency.

21st Held Boards at Maldon (with Lt Col Rogers & Surg Capt Fowler (visited Witham & consulted with C.R.E.
Under orders from C. F. the following Officers reported themselves for duty were posted to:-

Lt Hogg. R.A.M.C.	{ R.F.A. (How) Bde & R.G.A. Gt Baddow.	
Lt Lavertine R.A.M.C.	2/3rd R.F.A. Bde Ingatestone	
22nd Lt Hutchinson RAMC.	2nd Field Amb C'ford	
Lt Graydon RAMC	1st " " Stisted	

23rd Met the A.D.M.S. 3rd Army & proceeded with him and his Staff Officer & D.S.O. of 61st (S.M.) Division ~~at~~ to inspect the following Units etc.

Danbury	4th Bn Gloster Regt.
	2nd Field Amb. Hospital
	6th Bn Glosters Regt
Maldon	7th Bn Worcester Regt
	8th Bn "

Aug

23rd & 1/E.A.D. Hospital Riverscourt.
Southminster 1/8th Bn (Cyclist) Essex
Regt, including Medical
Inspection Room Burnham-on-
Crouch. Headquarters of the
83rd Provisional Bn & 1/E.A.D.
Hospital Burnham.
A Board was held at Oaklands
Hospital on Lieut Samuels
2/3rd R.F.A. Board consisted
of Lieut Col Gray, Lt Col Rogers &
Major Porter.

24th Held a Medical Board on
Lt Col Ash 7/8th R War R under
orders of G.O.C. Proceeded
to Southend with the D.A.D.M.S.
held Medical Board on 41 men
78th Provisional Bn & interviewed
the O.C. on several details.

25th Medical Board held
at Oaklands Chelmsford
on several small drafts from
different Units.

26th Visited Epping Camp with
the D.A.D.M.S. Held Medical
Boards on Drafts from the
5th 6th 7th & 8th Battalions
Royal Warwick Regt on
1st Field Ambulance
& 1/1st S.M. R.F.A. & R.Es
These reported here for duty & attd
to 7/8th R Warwicks Regt.

Aug

26th Attended conference of G.O.C
at 11 30 pm.

27 Held Medical Board on
2nd Lieut Large 1/7th R War Regt
Interviewed Quartermaster
Captain W.J. Kingston transferred
from 1st S.M. F. Ambulance
to Colchester.
Met A.D.M.S. 3rd Army with
his Staff Officer & the
D.W.P.O. visited & inspected
Oaklands Hospital &
Hutments & the Hutments
at Writtle (2/2nd R.F.A.)
& Baddow Road (R.F.A.)
Hutments at Gt Baddow
(2/4th (How) R.F.A. Brigade) &
Henry Street Chelmsford
(A.S.C). The Medical Officer
~~of the~~ 2/2nd R.F.A at
Writtle has engaged the
small Mission Hall as a
Medical Orderly Room & told
off part of it with 4 beds in
case of extreme emergency.
The whole arrangements are
well carried out.

28th Sent the D.A.D.M.S. to
interview the O.Cs Field Amb
Oaklands with regard to
Horses & Mules about to be supplied

Aug to the Three Field Ambulances.

29th Sunday)

30th Interviewed D.O.R.E. respecting the unsatisfactory state of the kitchen at Oaklands Hutment which has not yet received attention & which has been unfavourably reported upon for many weeks past by the A.D.M.S. 3rd Army the D.S.O. & myself.

31st. In conjunction with Lt Col. Rogers & Major Hopkin held Medical Boards at Oaklands Hospital. Notified Capt Burroughs M.O. i/c 1/8th Essex Cyclists Battalion.

August 1915 **Precis.**

During the last month the Division has been very free from sickness, no serious case occuring for many weeks.

A Transport man in 9/5th Bn Royal Warwick Regiment was killed at Epping Camp being thrown from a mule which kicked him causing fracture of the Skull.

Oaklands Hospital under new arrangements (made with the Essex Red Cross Society) has shown considerable improvement, but some of the Wards require urgent attention in the shape of distempering floors, planing etc, & until same is done & unhealthy wall paper removed it will never have the appearance of an up-to-date Hospital, this however the authorities decline to do. The Sanitation in the Division is most satisfactory & receives the constant attention of the Divisional Sanitary Officer. The Hutments are well cared for & kept clean, but the Road & approaches should receive the immediate attention of the Authorities before the approaching winter. This has several times been prominently brought before the notice of the D.O.R.E. The training of the Field Ambulances continues very satisfactory now they are receiving their full complement of Horses & proper ~~(Cart)~~ military Harness has just been ~~expected to be~~ delivered. During this month Central Force has detailed 5 R.A.M.C. Medical Officers for temporary duty, but the Shortage of M.Os is still serious and will become more so when those for Home Service only are transferred to Home Service Battalions. I fear this shortage will remain until the War Office fixes their pay at the same rate as those joining the New Army. A large number of Medical Boards have been held during the month & again a fair percentage of Recruits are found under age. Inoculations have made decided progress during the last month, but a few units are still showing a low percentage. This is accounted for by the fact that some Battns come from a County where Anti-vaccination spirit is rife.

September 1915

Sept 1. Motored to Headquarters R.E. Witham accompanied by D.A.D.M.S. & held medical Board on 18 men in that area. Sent (originally) motor Ambulance to Headquarters 3rd Army for bedding etc of the A.D.M.S. 3rd Army for disinfection when carried out return same at once. (The A.D.M.S. 3rd Army on week end leave was reported to be suffering from Diphtheria the precautions taken.

Sept 2. Visited (& accompanied by D.A.D.M.S.) Oaklands Hospital. Inspected the Stabling, Wagons, Hospital & other details & consulted with the O.C. of the 2nd & 3rd Field Ambulances on many points. Owing to hurried orders for 1/ist. Surtie attached to the 2/3rd R.F.A. Brigade Ingatestone to proceed overseas on the 1st inst, detailed Lt. Hutchinson R.A.M.C. attached to the 2nd Field Ambulance for duty with the 2/3rd R.F.A. Brigade at Ingatestone until their move to Epping & then to remain at Ingatestone in Medical Charge of the 2/1st R.F.A. on their arrival.

3rd. Held Medical Boards in accordance with orders of G.O.C. on the following:
Capt. Rose 1/4th Oxon & Bucks L.I.
Lt. Savory 2/1st Signal Co R.Es.
Lt. Pratty A.V.C. also Capt Whitehouse with a view of his proceeding overseas.

Sept 3rd (continued) Attended at 2/30pm a lecture on Rations by Major Whitehouse in accordance with South Midland Division Orders.

Sept 4th Motored to Epping Camp & held Medical Boards on drafts from the 2/4th & 2/6th Gloucester Bns & A.S.C. Board consisted of myself as President, Major Hayten R.A.M.C. Lieut. Moore. R.A.M.C. Lieut. Hawcett. R.A.M.C. Lieut. Graydon. R.A.M.C. These 3 Lieutenants attending with their respective drafts.

Interviewed the G.O.C. with regard to the question of Reports of Medical Boards forwarded him for perusal not being received by the O.Cs of the Units concerned, who had complained to the Brigadier-Commanders as to cause of delay. Wrote to A.D.M.S. 3rd Army for a ruling on the procedure of forwarding reports of Medical Boards, namely:- whether the A.D.M.S of the Division in accordance with instructions from both Central Force & Southern Command, to send them direct to War Office & Central Force or whether they were to be sent by the A.D.M.S. to the G.O.C for transmission in accordance with Central Force Order 320. dated March 3rd 1915.

Sept 5th Sunday.

Sept 6th Motored to Chelmsford and:-

1. Interviewed C.R.A on several details concerning examination of Officers & Men under his Command.
2. Interviewed D.O.R.E re: Cookhouse at Oaklands Hutment papering & whitewash kitchens & alteration of W.C. at Oaklands House.
3. Interviewed O.C 1st & 3rd Field Ambulances on several points.
4. Called on Clerk of Chelmsford Hospital Conjoint Board concerning Messrs Wenley's bill for Furniture supplied to "Kenilworth" Infectious Hos.

Sept 7th Re visited Oaklands Hospital met the G.O.C & the D.O.R.E. Several details of the utmost importance requiring urgent attention were presented to him. Afterwards inspected the kitchens and Oaklands Hutments which also requires serious attention. All these details were referred to the D.O.R.E. for action. Granted sick leave of 7 days to Major Hayten D.A.D.M.S. ~~Army~~ owing to continued feverish chill. Arranged by telephone with the D.A.D.M.S. 3rd Army to visit Boreham House to-morrow. Held Medical Board on Lieutenant Scott-Sunderland under orders of the G.O.C. Board consisted of myself as President, Captain Gilbert D.S.O. Lieutenant Graves R.A.M.C. 9th Bn Royal Warwick Regiment.

Sept 8th Attended with the General Staff a Field Day of 184 Infantry Brigade at Hatfield Peverell. Major Willmott D.A.D.M.S. also attended. Was present afterwards at the Generals Conference on the days work.
In afternoon attended Lecture on "Notes from the Front" by Lt.Col. Burroughes C.M.G. General Staff 61st (S.M.) Division.

Sept 9th Proceeded by Motor to Tillingham with Capt Roucher R.A.M.C. to hold Medical Board on 37 men of the R.E. reference to their being either retained for Home Service or returning to 1st Line.

Sept 10th At 3.0 pm received a most urgent telephone message from the 182nd Infantry Brigade that a Man in the Provisional Battalion at Goldhanger was very seriously ill. Urgent Orders for the Medical Officer from the 6th R War Regt Maldon to visit him at once who reported the man was only poorly with a Cold, Inflamed Eye & a Boil.

10th At 7.30 pm received a telephone message from Danbury that the man at Maldon, Regiment & name unknown had Enteric Fever & was to be transferred & A. Motor Ambulance was immediately sent out to Maldon & telephonic communication took place with the Great Baddow Infectious Hospital & Civil Hospital for his admission which these Institutions stated they could not carry out till next morning. The man was brought in that night to an Isolated Room at Oaklands & sent the following morning to the Great Baddow Infectious Hospital.
It transpired that this man had been in the 2/1 A.D. Hospital for nearly 2 weeks & the M.O. only telephoned to say that "Wydals Test" confirming the disease had only just arrived. It was therefore an error on his part through a misunderstanding of his telephone that the man was moved. The Divisional Sanitary Officer was ordered to fully investigate this case which he found to be a Corporal in 7th Worcesters who evidently contracted the Disease at Bisley & not at Maldon & every

detail as referred by Military Authorities has been carried out in such cases.

12th Sunday.

11th Visited Barnham with Captain Boucher R.A.M.C. & held a Medical Board on 17 men of the 2nd S. M. Home Service Field Co R.E.

13th Nil.

14th Held Medical Board at Oaklands Hospital Chelmsford on 2 men of Signal Co R.E. & one man (Glos) R.F.A. Bde & on Pte Smith Super6 Norfolk Regt, now attached to 3/6 Bn Essex Regt by special orders from 3rd Army.

Interviewed Medical Officer of Oaklands Hospital Lady Commandant re Cases, also Lt McMasters W.D. Land Agent re Danbury Mission Hall & Kenilworth.

Received letter from D.A.D.M.S. asking for 14 days Sick Leave.

The D.A.D.M.S. 3rd Army inspected 2nd Field Ambulance at Epping. Was unable to attend same owing to breakdown of Motor.

15th Visited Gt Baddow Hutment with Div. San. Officer & inspected the Drainage & the Dirty condition in which the whole Camp was left the previous day by the 2/4th S. M. (Glos) Bde. R.F.A. & consulted with the Medical Officer i/c of the Brigade.

Motored to Great Baddow & interviewed the Brigadier-General 182 Infantry Brigade re Vaccinations & various other subjects. Visited the 2/7th Bn R. Warwick Regiments Danbury Hutments & interviewed the O.C. & the M.O. on Cases for Medical Board.

16th Attended G.O.C.'s conference at 4.30pm

17th Nil.

18th Visited Oakland Hospital. Interviewed O/c Barracks re "Kenilworth Hospital Returns.

Lieut. Potter R.A.M.C. reported himself for duty from Colchester to relieve Lt Appleton recalled for Overseas Duty.

Interviewed O/c 2/4th R. Berks re Pte Lewis. V.A.D. being readmitted into Hospital.

19th Sunday.

20th Visited in conjunction with my Divisional Sanitary Officer the Camp at Chipping Ongar for "Details" of 1,000 men 1st London Territorial Division. Met in consultation the O.C. & the C.M.O. Dr Wilson (whom I have appointed M.O. i/c of same & gave the fullest detailed accounts as to all duties

20th to be carried out. Wrote full details to 3rd Army of all Medical arrangements that I have made for this Camp.
Visited Epping Camp, held a Medical Board on Lt Sprcat 1/7th Warwick Regiment.
Board consisted of Col. W. Hull Pres.
Lt. Col. Craig.
Lt Moore.
Inspected in conjunction with the D.S.O. Transport Lines of this Camp & their Latrines & Kitchens both of which I found in a dirty unsatisfactory condition.

21st Inoculation (Anti-typhoid) of members on Divisional Staff commencing this day at Boreham House.
Held Medical Board on Lt O'Flynn RAMC attached to R.F.A. interviewed Lieut. Hey RAMC R.F.A. Hord Brigade.
Visited Oaklands Hospital inspected same accompanied by Capt Richardson DADMS.
Afterwards proceeded with him to Baddow Hutments inspected the Drainage & Sanitary Arrangements in conjunction with D.S.O. & his Sanitary Clerk & M.O. of the Brigade Duty Capt Machio

22nd Attended the "Brigade Tactical Exercises" of 184 Inf. Bde. 3rd Field Ambulance taking part in the exercises from 10.0 am to 2-0 pm
Exercises extending over the areas of Boreham & Hatfield Peverelle.

23rd Attended Brigade Tactical Exercises of 182 Infantry Brigade in which the 1st Field Ambulance took part.
Accompanied by Major Willmott DADMS 3rd Army Central Force from 9-30 am till 2 o pm.
Interviewed the G.O.C. on various subjects. At 4-30 pm attended Conference of G.O.C. at Boreham House.

Sept 25th Under Orders of Central Force, through the 3rd Army, I proceeded to Clacton-on-Sea & arranged to hold Medical Boards on Provisional Battalions in the 7th Prov Brigade at Clacton on Sea, Frinton on Sea & Wivenhoe.

" 26th Interviewed the G.O.C. 7th Provisional Brigade & made all necessary arrangements to hold the various Boards in his Brigade. Also held a consultation with the D.A.D.M.S. 3rd Army Central Force who was at Clacton-on-Sea on duty for the day. Interviewed the President of the Travelling

Sept 26th (contd) Medical Board made all arrangements with him as to conducting the various Boards in the South Midland Divisional area.

Sept 27th At Clacton-on-Sea in a Room lent the Board by the 107th Provl Battalion, held Medical Board on
1. 107th Prov: Batta. 96 Imperial Service men.
2. 82th " " 83 " " "
Total 179

In addition, by order of the Brigadier-General Commanding 7th Provisional Brigade held a Medical Board on Lieut. W. J. Marshall 29th Provisional ~~Brigade~~ Battalion, 7th Provisional Brigade & forwarded the report of the Board in triplicate to the G.O.C. of the 7th Provisional Brigade. The Board consisted of myself (Col W. H. Hull) as President
Major Cozfield R.A.M.C.T.
Captain Myre R.A.M.C.T.

Sept 28th Attended the Board at Clacton-on-Sea (with same Members) and examined the 107th Provisional Battalion 114 Imp Ser. men
98th " " 183 " " "
Total 297 " " "

Sept 29th Attending at Clacton-on-Sea (with same Members) & examined 240 of the 82nd Provisional Brigade.

Sept 30th Examined at Clacton-on-Sea 51 Imp Ser. men of the 82 Provisional Battalion. Proceeded to Frinton-on-Sea and examined at the Headquarters of the 108th Provisional Battalion 43 men.

Precis.

There is nothing special to report during this month. The percentage of sickness in the Division is very small. Both inoculation & vaccinations are being carried out successfully, but slowly. Training with the 3 Field Ambulances is being satisfactory carried out & I note a marked improvement in the work during the last month.

October 1915.

Oct 1st. Examined at Frinton-on-Sea the 108th Provisional Battalion of 1 Officer & 75 N.C.O's & men. Total 76. The Board consisted of Col. W.H. Bull & Major Corfield.

Oct 2nd. Proceeded to Ivenhoe & examined 29th Provisional Batt., 166 Imperial Service Men.

Oct 4th. Examined at Ivenhoe 173 of the 29th Provisional Battalion. Left Ivenhoe after the Board & arrived at Headquarters at 5-15 pm reporting myself to Headquarters.

Oct 5th. Visited Oaklands Hospital & inspected same with the D.A.D.M.S 3rd Army. Attended an inspection of the 1st & 3rd Field Ambulances at Oaklands with D.A.D.M.S. 3rd Army.

Oct 6th. Motored to Brentwood accompanied by the Divisional Sanitary Officer & the billeting Officer of the 3rd Field Ambulance together with Major Corfield acting for the O.C. & inspected the London County Schools Rose Valley & made all arrangements for these Schools being taken over by the 2/3rd Field Ambulance as soon as the Gloster & Worcester Bde are under orders to take up their billets there.

Oct 8th. Interviewed the Secretary Chelmsford Conjoint Hospital Board re: Fees for Military Typhoid Patients to be admitted into Great Baddow Infectious Hospital:
Visited Oaklands Hospital & inspected the Infectious Tents. Held a Medical Board on Colonel W.K. Ludlow Commanding 184th Infantry Bde. Held a standing Board on Lieut. Webb. A. C. Dept. as to fitness for serving overseas. He was placed in Category 1.
The Board consisted of
Col. W. H. Bull, President.
Lt. Col. Rogers. }
Major Corfield } 3rd H.A. Members

Oct 9th. Proceeded on special leave by order of G.O.C. to Frinton-on-Sea leaving there early Monday morning, proceeded direct to London in accordance with Central Force letter to attend Exhibition of "Fracture Apparatus" etc at No 1 Wimpole Street returning to Headquarters 6-30pm.

~~Oct 12th.~~

Oct 11th In accordance with Divisional Orders that the Division were to occupy the existing trench line, Weybridge to Chipping Hill from Tuesday 12th to Wednesday evening the 13th inst, made all arrangements with the 3 Field Ambulances issued operation orders accordingly.

Oct 12th Proceeded to inspect the troops in the trenches accompanied by Major Wilmot. D.A.D.M.S. 3rd Army & Major Horton D.A.D.M.S. 61st (S.M.) Div.

1. Visited the whole of the trenches occupied by the 1/4th Oxon & Bucks Light Infantry together with their Headquarters at the Mills (North East of Hatfield Rn. G. E. R. of Map). The Oxon & Bucks L.I. had selected a good sight for their Headquarters & had made most satisfactory Sanitary arrangements. Their Regimental Aid Post was on the ground floor of the mill, a suitable & well selected room already prepared by the Regimental Stretcher Bearers. This Unit was unaccompanied by a M. O. (he being a C. M. P. remained with the details at Headquarters. This Unit had no R. A. M. C

Water Duty Men

attached & no one understood how to work their Filter Water Cart, consequently Water had been placed in it, direct from the well. This well however was pure water which supplied the house. I at once detailed 2 Water Duty Men from the 1/4th Bn Royal Berks to act as temporary Water Duty Men to this Unit during the period of remaining in the trenches.

At 5-30 pm that day attended Conference of G. O. C. at Hatfield Priory.

Oct 13th Proceeded with the D.A.D.M.S. 3rd Army & Major Horton D.A.D.M.S. 61st (S.M.) Division to temporary Headquarters of the Division (Hatfield Priory) to receive instructions.

2. Inspected 2/2nd Field Ambulance and Worcester Battns in Hatfield Priory Park.

Found Sanitary & all arrangements in the 183rd Infantry Brigade were most satisfactory. O.C. 2nd Field Ambulance reported as follows:-

1. "On the march from Epping to" "Chelmsford, the Sanitary" "Squad of the various Units"

(1915) Octr.

"dug latrines at their halting
"places."
"He found a pair of mules were"
not sufficient for the Water Cart
(when filled with Water) & heavy
Ambulance Wagon, & stated that
4 Mules for such a heavy load
was required. About 9 men of
the Worcester Regiment fell out on
the march from sore feet & detailed
reports would follow. He also
required shaft harness for his
Maltese Carts.

3. Visited the 3rd Field Ambulance
Hatfield Green, found the O.C.
had selected a suitable field
& pitched an Operating Tent & 3
Bell Tents. He made the following
report.

1. "Was unable to bring his
Maltese Carts having no shaft
harness."

2. "A pair of Mules were not
sufficient for his heavy
Ambulance Wagons, or Water
Cart when filled with
Water.

3. That, his Officers had no
riding horses, regardless
of same having been indented
for, more than once. He was
unable to furnish me with

a "Marching in State" from the
Battalions in the Brigade as to
men falling out, same not having
arrived.

4. Visited Headquarters of the
184th Infantry Brigade & of the
R. F. A. both at the same
farm at Wickham Bishops,
& found all Medical Arrangements
quite satisfactory.

5. Visited Advanced Dressing
Station of 3rd Field Ambulance
in field & Building opposite
Wickham Bishops Church, Major
Corfield in Command. All arrangements
were satisfactory.

6. Visited Headquarters of the
6th Glosters Regiment at Broomfield
Farm, found arrangements
satisfactory. First Aid Post
was established here with
Regimental Stretcher Bearers.
There was no Medical Officer,
(same being a civilian remaining
with details) had only 2 Water
Duty men, the other being kept
by the C.M.O at Headquarters.

6. Visited Headquarters of 4th
Royal Berks in field opposite
Little Braxted, where Regimental
Aid Post was established.
The Medical Officer who had

recently joined is not conversant with his duties, had sent back by train 9 men with sore feet, 11 with Cholic & 1 who had fallen out giddy. He was not aware of the duties of a Field Ambulance hence his mistake.

7. Visited Headquarters of the Bucks Battalion at St. Totham where the Medical Officer had established a Regimental Aid Post in the Wesleyan Chapel Schools & the details in this Battalion were carried out in a most highly satisfactory manner. visited & inspected their trenches.

8. Visited Langford Grove, Headquarters of 1/2 Infantry Brigade & consulted with Officers of the Divisional Staff. In this Brigade the Regimental Aid Posts were as follows.

1/6th Warwicks St Totham Schools
1/5th Warwicks South East corner of Southwood North of letter "Y" in Heybridge.
1/7th Warwicks at "The Sun" Broad Street Green.
1/8th Warwicks close to the 1st letter "T" in Totham Hill.

9. Visited Advanced Dressing Station of the 1st Field Ambulance at Langford in a Field & old Barns opposite the Mill. All arrangements had been ~~most~~ carefully & thoughtfully carried out ~~& everything was most~~ in a satisfactory manner.

10. Visited Ulting Hall, Headquarters of the 1st Field Ambulance. arrangements made were most satisfactory, Operating Tent being ~~all~~ properly laid out & all details have evidently been carefully studied.

11. Visited the Divisional Collecting Stn. at Danbury where again, details had been well arranged under the Command of Capt Moore (attached to the 3/1 Field Ambulance.) Visited the 1/1st Field Ambulance Hospital in Danbury. The DADMS 3rd Army C. F. expressed himself very satisfied, with ~~the manner in which~~ all details, all medical & sanitary arrangements, & considered the Field Ambulances had made Great Strides during the last few months.

1915

Oct 14 Held a medical Board ~~on~~ by order of the G.O.C. upon the following officers:–
Capt. Holtzapfell 7th Bn London Regt.
Major Dunscombe 1st S.M. R.F.A
Lt Lawson A.S.C
Lieut Warner 7/8 Bn Worcester Regt
The Board consisted of
Col W. Hull A.D.M.S. President
Major Hayton D.A.D.M.S.
Captn McLamahan R.A.M.C. T
Attended conference of G.O.C at 4.30pm at which the operations of the two preceding days were discussed.

Oct. 15 Motored to Tillingham held Medical Board on 16 men of the 1st S.M. Home Service Field Co R.Es
The Board consisted of
Col W. Hull A.D.M.S.
Capt McLamahan R.A.M.C. T
Dr Barrett M.O. i/c Troops
Held medical board on Captn McLamahan R.A.M.C. T 3rd Field Ambulance
Board consisted of
Col W. Hull A.D.M.S.
Major Hayton D.A.D.M.S.

Oct 16 Major Wilmot A.D.M.S. 3rd Army held Medical Board at Oaklands.

Oct 18. Visited Maldon 7/8th & 5/8th Bn Royal Warwick Regiments. Interviewed M.Os & gave demonstration on the New Water Carts. Inspected Camp which was most clean & well cared for.
Visited V.A.D. Hospital Maldon, found it expanded to 60 beds for benefit of Wounded from the Front.
3.0pm Visited Oaklands, attended Demonstration of Water Cart for all R.A.M.C. Water Duty men as ordered & addressed the men on their duties.
Interviewed O.C's. 1st & 3rd Fd. Ambulances
Major Hayton D.A.D.M.S. Held Medical Board at Oaklands.

Oct 19. Attended the ~~moves~~ manœuvres of South Midland Division ordered by 3rd Army
1. Proceeded to the New Headquarters. Witham House Witham which became my Headquarters until 12.0 on the 20th inst.
Visited in conjunction with the D.S.O the 1st Field Ambulance who had established their Headqrs & Dressing Station at Brick Hall Farm St Witham & their Advanced Dressing Stn at Inworth School.
2. Visited Headquarters of 182nd Infantry at Inworth Stn
3. Visited Tiptree where the 182nd Infantry Brigade were billeted for the night.

1915

& inspected the Schools. Interviewed the Head of the Police with reference to Water Supply & Drainage of the Village.
14. Motored on to Kelvedon. Interviewed the Brig-Commanding 184 Infantry Brigade at the Public Rooms Kelvedon, also interviewed the 3/3rd Field Ambulance who had just arrived & were being billeted in the town, making the Schools their Divisional Dressing Sta. Issued orders at Hatfield Peverel that it would be the Divisional Collecting Station
20th. The D A D M S arrived at Headquarters Witham House to carry on duty during my absence. Visited the 3/3rd Field Ambulance at Kelvedon, arranging with them in accordance with orders already issued to proceed to Hatfield Green where they would establish their Divisional Dressing Station, their Advanced " Station to be at the Schools Witham. Motored on to Brick Hall Farm & inspected the 3/1st Field Ambulance who were just leaving their new Station ~~at~~ Langford were they where to establish a Dressing

Oct 21

Station in accordance with orders already issued.
Visited their ~~Dress~~ Advanced Dressing Station at Faworth Schools. Then proceeded to Boreham House which, at 12 o'clock was established as the new Headquarters. In the afternoon visited Oaklands Hospital, reference to admissions of cases of Measles & interviewed orderly i/c Thresh's Disinfector.
Interviewed the O i/c Barracks with reference to taking a House for such cases of Measles etc. Afterwards motored with the D.S.O. & inspected the new Dressing Sta of the 3/3 Field Ambulance at Kelvedon where they had established the Divisional Dressing Station.
Afterwards visited Langford the new Headquarters of the 3/1st Field Ambulance returning to Headquarters at 6. 30 p.m.
Oct 21st Attended Conference of G O C at 4 - 20 p.m
Oct 22 Visited O i/c Barracks re disinfection of 3027 Pte

1915 Octr

Oct 22	Infected Blankets at Ongar Visited Oaklands, Interviewed Commandant & also interviewed C.R.A Held Medical Board on Lieuts. Spreat, Toby & Solomon
Oct 23.	Visited Oaklands Hospital & interviewed C.R.A.
Oct 24th	Sunday
25th	Proceeded to London to attend a Naval & military meeting of the British Medical Association
	Called upon the Clerk to the Conjoint Hospital Boards re: "Kenilworth" apcs.
26th	Drawing up reports with the D. S. O. in connection with Great Baddow Sewage scheme.
Oct 27.	Attended a lecture in Chelmsford by G. O. C on Court Martials & preparations of evidence.
Oct 28.	Visited Oaklands Hospital & arranged details with the O, Cs. of the 1st & 2nd Fd Ambs
Oct 29.	Attended the operations of the 183rd Infantry Brigade at Mount Nessing & visited Headquarters of the 2/3 Fd Ambulance at Brentwood
Oct 30th	~~Sat.~~ Granted week end Leave
Oct 31st	Sunday. to Major Hoyten to proceed Home on urgent Professional Business

1915 ~~[illegible]~~ October

Precis for October 1915.

Was absent from Headquarters during the 1st few days of October holding Medical Boards in the 7th & 8th Provisional Brigades as ordered by Central Force, returning on the evening of 4th having examined 1227 men, of whom 643 were recommended for duty overseas, 94 temporarily unfit, 476 recommended for Home Service & 14 for discharge. Owing to troops moving from Camps into Billets the Div. San. Officer has visited the various centres of ~~men~~ new billets & reported satisfactorily on them. The 3rd Field Ambulance have taken the L.C.C. Schools Brentwood which comfortably accommodates the Unit. As there is an outbreak of Scarlet Fever in Great Baddow, I recommended that the 2/3rd. S. M. Bde. R.F.A. should not be billeted in that village, they were consequently told off to Writtle Village, where the accommodation was sufficient. Attended the Divisional Operations & made a thorough inspection of their Sanitary & other arrangements, which on the whole had been well carried out. ~~Finding~~ Found the 2/4 Bn. Oxon & Bucks L. I. without R.A.M.C. Water Duty men, told off at once two men for duty from another Batn.

October 1915

The Field Ambulance had selected suitable sites for their Divisional Dressing Station, advanced Dressing Stations & practical work was given them with "Imaginary Accidents". It was reported that 2 Mules were not sufficient to draw a Watercart (when full of water) on heavy ground or up hill; same remark applied to Field Ambulance Wagons.

In one unit a team of 4 Mules pulled the Watercart.

One Field Ambulance was still without Riding Horses for Officers, but these have now been supplied.

It was noted that the M.O's arranged for the Brigade marching from Epping to the Trenches that the Regimental Sanitary Squads dug small latrines for the men when they halted.

In order that the R.A.M.C. Water Duty Men should be thoroughly conversant with the uses of the New Watercarts, I held a Class at Oaklands & requested the various M.O's to attend a practical demonstration.

Medical Boards on 6 Officers have been held during the month & the D.A.D.M.S. 3rd Army & of this Division have held Boards on all men to be transferred from present to Provisional Units (or for discharge).

Met the D.D.M.S. C.F. at Epping & inspected the whole Camp accompanied by the Sanitary Officer C.F. & D.A.D.M.S. 3rd Army & also by the Brigade Commander. The Camp was found in a clean condition & gave the D.D.M.S. every satisfaction. The Horsfall destructor had not been used for destruction of faeces & a special report was to be called for on the subject.

Received instructions to disinfect 3027 lice infected blankets for the London Division at Ongar with the O i/c Camp Barracks made arrangements for same, but owing to the limited means at my disposal (only one Thresh's Disinfector for the whole Division) the process would be slow.

Under instructions from C.F. visited, with most of the M.O's in the Division.

October 1915

The Surgical Exhibition at London of Splints & many other new appliances now used at the front.

The Division has been very free from sickness, no serious cases being recorded. Several cases have been admitted into the Hospital, but mostly of a minor nature, a number being admitted only for transfer to Cambridge Hospital for operation.

The Sanitation of the District is good, the question of connecting the drainage of Gt Baddow Hutments with the main village drains is under consideration.

The work done during the month by the Field Ambulances has been good & both the DADMS 3rd Army & myself notice a great improvement.

My shortage of Medical Officers becomes greater now that 3 Home Service M.O's are transferred to the Provisional Brigade & have not yet been replaced, hence I am compelled to call in CMP's.

November 1915

Nov 1	Was notified at 11-30 am by O.C. 1st Field Ambulance of a Case of small Pox at Oaklands. ~~[illegible]~~ Gave instructions for consultation to verify Diagnosis. Ordered Div San.O. to take immediate action. Visited Oaklands myself, verified the Diagnosis. Made every detailed arrangements required in such cases. Visited 2/2 SM Bde R.F.A. Gt Baddow Hutments from whence the case was sent. Ordered segregation of one Hut & all occupants. Ordered them to be vaccinated, recommended Brigade to be confined to Barracks pending sanction of G.O.C. Duly notified 3rd Army, Central Force War Office & GOC 61st (S.M.) Division. Sent a very full report in quadruplicate to 3rd Army.
Nov 2	Visited Oaklands. Met DADMS 3rd Army & 3rd Army consulting Dentist. Met GOC at Hospital. Inspected arrangements for disinfection which were to be carried out. Interviewed O i/c Barracks at his Headquarters. Attended a lecture on Venereal Diseases by Mr E.G. Turner F.R.C.S.
Nov 3rd	"Nil"
Nov 4th	The 2/1st & 2/2nd Field Ambulances attended "Brigade Tactical Exercises" at Danbury & East

Hanningfield with their Respective Brigades. Visited the conference of the G.O.C. in the afternoon. Interviewed Captn. Cohen, Surgeon Dentist with reference to Dental Cases in this Division.

Nov 5th Held Medical Board at "Oaklands" on drafts from various units. Total N.C.O.s & men 66. Officers 6.
The Board consisted of
Col. W. H. Hull. President
Major Boyten }
Captn. Moore } Members.
Captn. Smith-Ward. }

Nov 6th Proceeded to London to interview by appointment the D.D.M.S. C.F. & also called up the D.D.M.S. Eastern Command, interviewed also at C.F. Colonel Thomas A.D.C.T. re:- Transport Sections of Field Ambulances becoming attached to A.S.C.

Nov 7th Sunday.

" 8th Held a Medical Board at Danbury at 10.30 am on 22 N.C.O.s & men from Units in the 182nd Infantry Brigade.

Nov 9th Met D.A.D.M.S. 3rd Army Central Force at Headquarters & proceeded with him to Headquarters of the 2/1st Beds Yeomanry, interviewing the O.C., Adjutant, & Medical Officer. Proceeded with the M.O. to the village of Hatfield Peverelle inspected some of the billets, especially the best kind & the worst kind & in each case found 2 men sleeping per bed & in a similar ~~bed~~ house found 3 in a small room, recommended in each case 2 only should be in those rooms.
The Div. San. Off. visited Great Baddow Hutments & made arrangements regarding their overcrowding. He found a large number of men suffering from the effects of recent vaccination & several men were laid up with influenza.

Nov 10th Motored into Chelmsford and interviewed D.i/c Barracks, re: Hospital Equipment for the 3rd Field Ambulance. Called on D.O.R.E. reference to repairs to L.C.C. Schools Brentwood not having received attention. Called at Hospital & interviewed O.C.s 1st & 2nd Field Ambulance. Interviewed O.C. 2/2nd S.M. Bde. R.F.A. re condition of roads etc in his Hutment.

November 1915

Nov 11th Held Medical Board by special order of G.O.C. on 19 men of the 2/7th Bn Royal Warwick Regt. whose ages were under 19. The Medical Board consisted of:-
Colonel W.H. Bull.
Major Hoyten.
Lieut Dee.
Attended Conference of G.O.C. at 11-30 p.m.

Nov 12th Interviewed G.O.C. with the Divisional Sanitary Officer with reference to Drainage at Great Baddow Hutments.
Interviewed Surgeon Captain Baker with reference to extended leave of absence owing to Haemorrhagic Retinitis just discovered.

Nov 13th Held Medical Boards on:-
Lieut Quayle 2/1st Bucks Battn
2nd " Bingham 2/4 London Battalion
Lieut. Evans 2/5 Bn R. War Regt.
A "Standing Medical Board on "Captn. Hammond 2/4th Bn Royal Berks & Sgt Andrews 2/5th Gloster Regiment. Also a special examination officer Butler 2/4th S.W.(Bdr). R.H.A. for transfer to Flying Corps & granted certificate in accordance with Army Order 360/1912 (December).

Nov. 16th Absent. (at Euston Hall on duty) returning 5-4 pm.

Nov. 17. The new ADMS. 3rd Army. C.F. and DADMS 3rd Army C.F. called at 11am & remained until 2 pm. Discussed & arranged many details. Visited (with them) the Oaklands Hospital & interviewed O/Co. 1st & 2nd Field Ambulances.

Nov. 18. Attended Conference of G.O.C. at 10am. Under special orders of G.O.C., held Medical Board & medically examined Headquarters Staff, Staff & Commanding Officers of 184th Infantry Brigade, R.F.A. Brigade, Bedfordshire Yeomanry, A.S.C. and 2nd Field Ambulance. Total 24. The Medical Board consisted of
Colonel W.H. Bull
Major Hoyten.
Held Medical Board on :-
Lieut. Kalker. 1/1st S.M.D. C.C.
& a Medical Board on :-
Sgt. Solomon 2/4 Bn. Glos. Regt.

Nov. 19. Visited Brentwood 9-30am & in conjunction with Lieut. Col. Rogers, medically examined Colonel Sir John Barnsley & his Staff & O.Cs. of Brigade, including Lieut. Col. Rogers. Examined also at Boreham House :-

Nov. 19. Colonel Lyons. Colonel Williams C.R.E. Lt. Col. Law. A.A. & Q.M.G. Major Burbush. C.C. R.G.A Major Mackie. R.A.M.C.T. & Major Hoyten. R.A.M.C.T. Went on week-end leave until Monday.

Nov. 22. Returned from week-end leave.

Nov. 23. Motored to Chelmsford. Visited Oakland's & Kenilworth Hospitals & 2/4 Bn. Berks Regt. & with the M.O. inspected some of the small Billets & the Orderley Rooms & found A.F. B.178 not filled up in any of the Offices.

Nov. 24 Visited (in conjunction with Div. San. Officer) Headquarters 2/1st Bucks Bn. with reference to A.F. B178 not being filled in, O/c Barracks reference letter from 3rd. Army. re disinfection of the 302 Lice infected blankets - Ongar - also visited 2/6 & 2/8 Bns Royal Warwick Regts. Maldon & with M.O. inspected the Scabies cases at Workhouse & in empty house in Maldon. Inspected some Billets & interviewed the O.Cs on various subjects

Nov. 25. Attended G.O.Cs Conference 10am. Standing Medical Board on Major S.R. Field 2/4 S.M. (How) Bde. R.F.A & on 2nd Lieut A.F. Holiday. 2/4 Bn Oxon. & Bucks. L.I. (Members of Board) ADMS & DADMS.
Visited (with Div. San. Officer) Headquarters & Billets of 5th Glosters. & 2/4 Bn. Oxon. & Bucks L.I. & interviewed O.Cs.. Found no A.F. B178 at Orderly Room, Oxon & Bucks L.I., but same were being prepared:, found same with 2/5 Glosters only partly completed. Called on Clerk Joint Hospital Committee re bill for Kenilworth A/c.

Nov 26. Visited, with D.S.O., & inspected 2/2 & 2/3. S.M. Bde, R.F.A & interviewed, O.Cs; found A.F. B178 fairly well filled up.

Nov. 27 Visited (with Div. San. Officer) (How.) Bde R.F.A. Hutments, Writtle. Found camp clean, Kitchen well attended to & no waste refuse in tub. Saw 5 Large Bread & Currant puddings made out of wasted Bread.
Visited Headquarters, Mec. Transport, A.S.C, Broomfield Road. 36 men & 2 Officers living in House. Rooms clean & sanitation good. Refuse tub (36 Gallon Tub) practically full of good food, principally Bread, Pudding, & fresh Vegetables, none of which should have been rejected, also 2 tin pails full of vegetables, much of which was too good to be rejected as refuse.
Visited Headquarters A.S.C. Henry Street. Kitchen well kept but in small Refuse Bin, Bread wasted

Nov 27 which should have been used.
Reported same to G.O.C. (on return at 1 o.c.) & at 3 pm met G.O.C. with O.C. A.S.C. on the subject. Drew up extra return (giving dates) re Lieut. O'Flynn.

Nov 29. Held Medical Boards, Danbury on 26 men.

President.	ADMS.
Members:–	DADMS.
	Lieut Dee RAMC.

& at Chelmsford on 85 men.

President	ADMS.
Members:–	Lt. Col. Craig &
	DADMS.

Nov 30. Medical Board held at Brentwood on 42 men.

Members.	DADMS.

Capt. Hamill, Sanitary Officer, Central Force, visited Boreham & accompanied by ADMS. & Div. San. Officer visited Smallpox Hospital & investigated the case sent there on 1st inst. It would appear now, that this was not "true" Small-pox but a disease of an infective nature, which simulates Small-pox, but a technical term cannot be applied to it. The man was vaccinated on 13th inst very successfully, which, with present scientific knowledge, proves

Nov. 30 it was not "true" Small-pox.
Visited Gt. Baddow Hutments, 2/2 S.M. Bde. R.F.A. & 2/4 S.M. Bde RGA R.F.A. with the C.F. Sanitary Officer & the Div. San. Officer, found rubbish bin in latter Hutment had some wasted Bread & food thrown away – called attention of O.C. to same in writing.
Gave evidence before Court of Enquiry at A.S.C. (Hd. qrs, Div. Transport) upon waste of food found in swill tub on 27th inst.

Precis for the Month

On the 1st instant a case of small-pox was reported at "Oaklands", sent in (as a suspicious "throat" to be watched) from 2/2 S.M. Bde., R.F.A., Great Baddow Hutment. Five R.A.M.C.T. M.Os. with experience of that disease were ordered to see the case, & all unanimously diagnosed "undoubted small-pox". Case was sent to Small-Pox Hospital, & every precaution taken, and duly notified to 3rd Army, C.F. & W.O. During the third week the man was successfully re-vaccinated. Local Gov. Board asked for a Wassermann's test to be taken, suggesting it to be a case syphilis. The result was, however, "Negative". At end of month consulted with Sanitary Officer, Central Force, and Div. Sanitary Officer & arrived at the conclusion, it was a case of an "infective nature" "simulating small-pox" but- "not to be found in the nomenclature of diseases". During the month, have, in accordance with special orders, medically examined all Commanding Officers, & Staff Officers, & held Standing Medical Boards on 269 N.C.Os & men. Result:- Category "A" 92, Category "B" 39, Category "C" 135 Category "D" 3. These figures cannot be considered satisfactory, but the number of men who have been enrolled as "Medically fit", yet on examination found "Unfit" speaks for itself.

"Oaklands" Hospital has had a "Recreation Hut" erected on the grounds for Convalescent cases, & is a great boon. The work at the Hospital (under Major Mackie) is making steady & satisfactory progress, & the Engineers are by degrees carrying out the work of removing old wall papers, & colour washing the rooms, etc., etc., Inclement weather has compelled me to ask for a "covered place" for cases of scabies, as the Hospital Marquees, having no heating apparatus, are getting too cold & wet.

Inoculation percentages gradually increase. Owing to the alarm of small-pox, a large number rushed to be vaccinated, including the whole staff at "Oaklands" Hospital.

I have interviewed, & am giving all possible assistance to the new Divisional Dental Surgeon, but experience has conclusively shown me that my original recommendation of a Dentist for this Division (or area) would save the country hundreds of pounds, & have again recommended it for serious consideration.

Under orders from C. F., a lecture on Venereal Disease was given by Mr. E. B. Turner, F.R.C.S. (London)

Since my last report, the 2/1st Beds. Yeomanry have joined this Division, billeted at Hatfield Peverell, & I have made all the necessary arrangements for supply of medical equipment & have interviewed the O.C.

Another class of chiropody has been formed to train & qualify men for units that did not comply with last Divisional Order to attend the last course of instruction.

The question of connecting up Great Baddow Hutment Drainage with the village main drain, has received considerable attention, owing to the occasional faulty condition of present system.

The London Details Division, Ongar Camp, has been much troubled with

vermin, & I was called upon to disinfect 3.027 lice infected blankets in Thresh's Disinfector, which (under severe pressure) has been carried out, & a Board will be held over them prior to being sent away.
During the month I have visited a large number of the Units, inspecting billets, & found the houses & bedrooms clean & well kept, but in a large majority of cases two men were sleeping together in full sized beds.
At the Orderly Rooms, investigated the A. F. B178, which in nearly every instance were either not filled in at all, or most incompletely so. A Divisional Order (No 678, dated 10.11.15) called upon O.Cs. to give this matter their attention.
Again I call attention to the unnecessary waste of food. On inspecting "Swill tubs" & "recepticle bins" a large amount of bread, meat, & vegetables were found wasted. Potatoes are peeled far too thickly. In my opinion, potatoes are far better boiled in their jackets, this saves both waste & labour, & is by far the most pleasant way to eat them.
At the Headquarters, Mechanical Transport, the waste of food was so great that I made a special report on same, & a Board of Enquiry was held at which I gave evidence.
The training of the Field Ambulances continues satisfactory, & Weekly Programmes are drawn out for their guidance - an improvement in the work is noted. It is still most unsatisfactory being so short of Medical Officers, & I find since winter has set in, the C. M. Ps. are not over inclined to offer their services, owing to heavy pressure of work in their own private practices.

December

Nov. Transfer of Transport to A.S.C.

Dec 1st. Sent D.A.D.M.S. (owing to temporary indisposition of Div. San. Off) to Oaklands & report on Scabies marquee.

Dec 2nd. Attended G.O.C's conference. Held Medical Board on Capt. W. J. Cade A.V.C, Lt. B. R. Jack Cyclist Co & 2nd Lieut Holmes 7/4th Bde. R.F.A. (How). Interviewed Mr Leslie Moore A.R.I.B.A. & examined him for commission in Royal Engineers of this Division. - Motored to Headquarters 1/4th Bn Oxon & Bucks & inspected medical equipment & called for report. Visited Oaklands Hospital & interviewed O.Cs. 2/1st & 2/2nd Field Ambulance. Inspected Scabies Marquees & held Board on case of Hemiplegia

Dec

sent in from Essex Reserve Battalion.
Was notified by M. O. Beds Yeomanry that 4 cases severe (one fatal) of diphtheria in Hatfield Peverel, gave instructions notified D. S. O.

Dec 3rd Visited Workhouse with view of renting Infectious (disused) Hospital for Scabies, called on Clerk re same.
Inspected ~~Detent~~ Detention Ward at Workhouse - found all most satisfactory; called at Oaklands.

Dec. 4th. Visited Witham and examined 10 men R.E. who had had teeth extractions and placed in subsistence allowance; all cases were genuine. O.C., 2/3rd. Field Ambulance interviewed me re no supply of blinds to L.C.C. Schools where his unit is billeted. Visited Headquarters, Bedfordshire Yeomanry and interviewed M.O. re diphtheria in the village; found every precaution had been taken by him, and he was in daily communication with M.O.H.

Dec. 5th. Sunday.

Dec. 6th. Visited Oaklands and interviewed O.C., 2/1st. and 2/2nd. Field Ambulance, and examined case of [illegible] (about to be removed to Colchester in charge of a M.O.) Visited Orderly Room, R. Berks. Regt. re 3 letters just received connected with their unit.

Dec. 7th Visited at Brentwood, 3rd. Field Ambulance Hospital; Headquarters 183rd. Infantry Brigade, 2/4th. and 2/6th. Glos., and 2/7th. and 2/8th. Worc. Orderly Rooms and consulted with O.C.'s and M.O.'s; inspected A. F. B. 178; found them

1915

most incomplete.

Dec. 8th. Motored to Headquarters, 3rd. Army, C. F., and interviewed A.D.M.S. on many important matters.

Dec. 9th. Granted 7 days Sick Leave to the Divisional Sanitary Officer for influenza.

Dec. 10th. Owing to case of Diphtheria at Writtle, sent D.A.D.M.S. to investigate same. Sent M.O's. from Field Ambulance to ~~to~~ help to examine Recruits at Essex Depôt, Chelmsford. Visited Oaklands and Civil Hospital.

Dec. 11th. Visited 2/1st. S. Mid. Bde. R.F.A., Ingatestone. Consulted with Adjutant in absence of O.C.; found A. F. B. 178 partly filled up, but none signed. Inspected empty house & empty old sorting office. Found empty house dirty & badly kept. Swill tub, 14" of good thick slices of bread fit for puddings.
Found Sorting Room overcrowded, very dirty. No swill tub, all refuse being pitched on field.
Found large accumulation of manure in Yard of Crown Hotel"

" 12th Interviewed O.C. 2/1st Bucks Bn at his Headquarters re M.O. joining his Battn. on 13th instant.

Dec 13. Visited Hatfield Peverel, met M.O. 2/1st Beds Yeo. & visited some of his billets found no fresh cases of Diphtheria

Dec 1915

Dec 13. Contd among the civilians all cases had been removed to Infectious Hospital, & their houses properly fumigated.
Held Medical Board on Surg-Captain Baker, & 1 man (ea) of the following Units, 2/4th Bde (H) R.F.A., 2/3 Field Amb, 2/6th East Surrey Regt.
D.O.R.E. having removed top boards (under eaves of Hutments) created far too great draft & cold. Recommended G.O.C. to have one side replaced in each hut.

Dec 14. Lieut. J.E.S. Wilson R.A.M.C.T. reported himself for duty with 2/1st Bucks Bn, with effect from 13/12/15, pending gazetting.
D.A.D.M.S. proceeded on 3 days leave. Visited H'qtrs, 2/1st Bucks Bn, & M.O's. Inspection Room.
Interviewed Captn. McHannahan, R.A.M.C.T. - visited "Oaklands" Hosptl, & interviewed O.C. 2/1st Field Ambulance & Dr. Platts.

Dec. 15. Held Medical Board at "Oaklands" on 11 men R.E's. Board A.D.M.S. President, Lieut. Col. Craig, Captn. Moore.
Interviewed A.A.Q.M.G. re Q.M. Captn. Kimpton's accounts before leaving 2/1st S.M. Field Amb, & arranged meeting with A.A. & Q.M.G. on same, with O.C. - Q.M., & Staff Sergt. of 2/1st S.M. F. Amb.
Sent Captn McHannahan, R.A.M.C.T. to Beds. Yeo, their M.O. being ill.

Dec 16th Attended G.O.C's. Conference 10 A.M.
Visited H'qtrs. 2/1st Beds. Yeo. & interviewed the M.O., ill in bed with Influenza.
Arranged for R.A.M.C.T. M.O's. to replace C.M.P's under 3rd Army instructions:- Capt Hulbert reported return from sick leave.

Dec 17th Held medical Board on 3 R.E. men. Board consisted of A.D.M.S. & Div. San. Officer.

" 18th

" 20th Held a Medical Board on one man 2/6th Bn. Glos. Regt. at Oaklands. ~~On Board~~ also at Brockham House 2nd Lieut. Girdler on 2nd Lieut Walker 2/4th Berks for Commission in Regulars - (On Board A.D.M.S. Lt Col Craig & Major Mackie). New G.O.C. Major General Allison joined the Division.

Dec 22nd D.A.D.M.S. proceeded on 5 days leave. Visited Oaklands and met G.O.C. there. Interviewed Optician (Mr Boatman) re Ophthalmic duties in accordance with War Office letter 4/1 Gen Number/3999 (A.M.D. 3) dated 17-12-15.
Consulted with G.O.C. re Transport Sec. of R.A.M.C to A.S.C.

Dec 23rd Visited 2/2 Field Ambulance Hos. at Danbury found all very satisfactory

Dec — 1915

Dec 23rd (contd) Afterwards visited 2/7th Warwicks Hutments. Surrounding ground & some of roads in very bad state.
Held Medical Board (ADMS & O C 2/2 Field Amb.) on 2nd Lieut. Pollack 2/7th S.M. (Mtd) Bde. R.F.A. for admission as Pilot in Flying Corps.

Dec 24th Div. San. Off. went on leave till 26th inst. Received wire from S.M.O. 183rd Inf. Bde. Brentwood of sudden death of man 2/6th Glos Regt. wired him to carry out Kings Regs. para 1873.

Dec 25th Xmas Day.

Dec 26th DADMS & Div. San. Officer returned from Leave.

Dec 27th Wired S.M.O. 183rd Infantry Brigade to represent me at inquest on late Pte Yates. 4-30 pm this day at Brentwood. Verdict at inquest "Natural Causes".

Dec 28th Visited Oaklands Hospital & arranged with O.C. 2/1st S.M. F. Amb. for
10.15. attendance (with his witnesses) at the Court on Enquiry being held under S.M.O. orders to meet at 10. am.
12 noon Interviewed Mr Bacon Clerk to the Joint Hospitals re Kenilworth.
Visited Hatfield Peverel, interviewing M.O. i/c 2/1st Beds Yeomanry. Found no more cases of Dyphtheria among civilians
2.10 pm. Visited 2/5 & 2/7th Bn Royal Warwicks

Dec 28th at Danbury Hutments interviewing their M.O.s.
3.30 pm Visited 2/8 Royal Warwicks at Maldon interviewing their M.O.s. seeing empty House of Scabies (only Cases)
Called at Hdqrs. C.R.A. & interviewed Brigade Major.
Received notice that Travelling Medical Board would visit this Division on 3rd January next. Issued notices.

Dec 29th Interviewed Lt. Col. Craig re (secret) Composite Bde assembling 31st inst.

Dec 30th Attended G.O.C.s Conference at 10-0 am.
10.45 am. Visited Brentwood interviewed the Officers 3rd Field Ambulance & attended the instruction (in Field Ambulance work) which was being carried on.

" 31st A Composite Board assembly at Cold Norton for which I issued full instructions for ~~attendance~~ attendance of 2/2 Field Ambulance (in accordance with secret orders) & placed details in hands of D ADMS who took over duty from me this day, I having obtained sanction from G.O.C. to proceed Home on leave (on urgent Private matters) subject to being immediately recalled in case of emergency.

1916 — January

January 1st to 5th.	On leave with sanction of G.O.C., 61st. (S.M.) Divn.
Jan. 6th.	Routine Work.
" 7th.	Routine Work
" 8th.	Routine Work.
" 9th.	Sunday – Routine Work.
"	9. p.m. Received report from BACTERIOLOGIST, COLCHESTER "No Meningo Cocci are to be found in sample of cerebro-spinal fluid sent on 8th. inst"
Jan. 10th.	10.30 a.m. Visited OAKLANDS HOSPITAL and HUTMENTS and found large fatigue parties sweeping road and removing mud. Visited KENILWORTH HOSPITAL
	12.0 Called at A.S.C. Headquarters re Emergency Boxes which the M.O. had taken to his combined Inspection Room.
	2.30 p.m. Held Medical Board at Boreham House on SURGEON CAPTAIN BAKER, 2/1st. Bucks. Bn. by order of G.O.C. 61st (S.M.) Div.
	5.30 p.m. Held Medical Board on Clerks in office of A.D.M.S., also on the A.P.M's, O.O's., A.V.C's Clerks and on the CAMP COMMANDANT.
Jan. 11th.	9.30 a.m. Received report from COLCHESTER that the culture of spinal fluid in suspected case of C.S.M. was "negative".
	10.30 a.m. to 12.15 p.m. A.D.M.S., 3rd. ARMY interviewed me and we discussed many details.
	2.15 p.m. Interviewed O/c BARRACKS re barrows and shovels and brushes for men making new road at OAKLANDS HUTMENTS + HOSPITAL.
	2.40 p.m Inspected Hd. Qrs. Div. Train A.S.C. – found swill tubs containing "Refuse only". Inspected HD.QRS.

Jan 1916

Jan. 11th. (contd.)	HUTMENTS, HENRY ST., A.S.C. found bins with a very large amount of wasted good bread, and picked out an amount representing at least two large loaves (leaving much behind), also three good legs of lean meat, and the refuse which should not have been thrown away. There was a tendency to waste too much of the good leaves of the greens.
	Found paths round Hutments were being made, but – the State of the road in Horse Lines was "Deplorable"
	3.30 p.m. Visited OAKLANDS. The O.C. 2/1st. F. Ambce. had spent much labour on making up the roads.
Jan. 12th.	2.30 p.m. Visited H.QRS. 2/1st. & 2/2nd. F. Amb^ces. and inspected the Q.M's Books – found same well kept.
	5.0 p.m. Held Medical Board on Clerks in Hd. Qrs. Staff Offices.
Jan. 13th.	9.15 a.m. Held Medical Board on two subalterns R.E.
	10.0 a.m. Visited BRENTWOOD – 2/3rd S.M. Fd. Amb^ce. Hospl. and the Unit (at work) together with their H.Qrs. Interviewed O.C. and examined Books of Q.M. – found same well kept.
	Interviewed Captn. OSBORNE, M.O. 2/6 Bn. R. War. R.
	3.0 p.m. Interviewed M.O. i/c 2/1st. Beds. Yeo. Arranged with S.M.O. 8th. Prov. Bde. for Medical Attendance on Cyclist Co. (61 S.M.D.) Just transferred to BURNHAM.
Jan. 14th.	10 a.m. CAPTN. BOOME, RAMC.T. 1/1st. F. Amb^ce. 48th. Divn. reported himself for duty at

Jan

1916

Jan. 14th. (Contd.)	OAKLANDS HOSPITAL, being Boarded for "Light Duty".
	~~10.15 a.m. Held Medical Board at DANBURY on 2 Chaplains and 12 men 2/5th. Bn. R. War. R., 3 men of 2/1st. Yeo., and 2 men of F. Co. R.E.~~
	10.15 a.m. Held Medical Board on 2/Lieut QUAYLE 2/1st. Bucks. Bn. by order of G.O.C.
	11.0 a.m. Held Medical Board at DANBURY on 2 Chaplains and 12 men 2/5th Bn. R. War. R., 3 men of 2/1st. Yeo. and 2 men of F. Co. R.E.
	2.30 p.m. Held Medical Board at OAKLANDS on 7 Chaplains and One man of 2/2 Fld. Amb^ce. Interviewed O.C. 2/4th Bn. R. Berks. Regt. re examination of Officers.
Jan. 15th.	10.30 a.m. Held Standing Medical Board – S.M.D. Order 52/16 – on Officers of 2/1st. & 2/2nd Field Ambulances at OAKLANDS.
Jan. 16th.	Sunday. – Routine Work.
Jan. 17th.	10.15 a.m. Held Standing Md. Bd. on Officers A.S.C. & A.V.C. & on 4 officers 2/5 Bn. R. War. R. at H.Qrs. A.S.C.
	~~12.30 p.m.~~ Held Standing Medical Bd. on Officers – 2/4th. Bn. Oxford & Bucks. L.I. at their Hd.Qrs. BROOMFIELD. ~~2/4th. Bn. R. Berks. Regt. & one man with V.D.H. at Berks. H.Qrs.~~
	12.30 p.m. to 4 p.m. Visited Oaklands Hospital and interviewed O.C., 2/1st. S.M. Field Ambulance.
Jan. 18th.	10.15 a.m. Held Standing Medical Bd. on Officers 2/4th. Bn. R. Berks. R. & one man with V.D.H. at Berks. Hd. Qrs.
	2.15 p.m. Held Standing Medical Bd. on Officers 2/5th. Bn. Glos. Regt. at their Hd.Qrs. Temp. Lieut. A.J. Leitch R.A.M.C. reported himself as Dental Surgeon for Chelmsford Area. (Authority CR/CF 16888 M df- 2/1/16)
Jan. 19th.	2.30 p.m. Attended Lecture on Poisonous Gases by
Jan. 19th. (Contd.)	Prof. Major Starling, R.A.M.E. at Millbank R.A.M. College (Authority – CR/CF. 21067 M df- 10/1/16.)
Jan. 20th.	10.15 a.m. Held Standing Medical Board on Officers 2/1st Bucks. Bn. & Officers Signal Co. R.E., at Hd.Qrs. SPRINGFIELD.
	2.15 p.m. Held Standing Medical Board on Officers R.E. & A.S.C. at Hd.Qrs. WITHAM.
	6.0 p.m. Held Standing Medical Board on Officers Divisional H.Qrs. Staff at BOREHAM HOUSE
Jan. 21st.	10.15 a.m. Held Standing Medical Board on Officers 2/6th. Bn. R. War. R. & Officers 2/2 F. Amb. at MALDON.
	2.15 p.m. Held Standing Med. Bd. on Officers 2/8th Bn. R. War. R. at their Head Qrs. at MALDON.
	Visited the MALDON V.A.D. Hospital.
Jan. 22nd.	10.30 a.m. Held Standing Med. Bd. on Officers 2/1 Beds. Yeo. at HATFIELD PEVEREL.
	12 o/c Held Standing Med. Bd. on Officers Cyclist Coy. 61 S.M.D. at HATFIELD PEVEREL
	2.30 p.m. Visited OAKLANDS HOSPITAL and interviewed O.C. i/c Hospital.
Jan. 23rd.	Sunday – Routine Work.
Jan. 24th.	10. a.m. Held Standing Med. Bd. on Officers, 2/5th. Bn. R. War. R. at DANBURY.
	12.15 p.m. Held Standing Med. Bd. on Officers Head Qrs. 182nd. Infy. Bde. at DANBURY.
	2.15 p.m. Held Standing Med. Bd. on Officers 2/7th. Bn. R. War. R. at DANBURY.
	4.30 p.m. Called at Hd.Qrs. R.F.A. and arranged for Med. Bd. for Officers of the Bde.
Jan. 25th.	8.30 a.m. Held Standing Med. Bd. on Officers 2/4th. Bn. Glos. Regt. at BRENTWOOD.

Jan

Jan. 25th. 12 o/c Held Standing Medical Board on Officers 2/3rd. S.M. Field Ambce. at BRENTWOOD.

2.0 p.m. Held Standing Medical Board on Officers 2/6th. Bn. Glos. Regt. at BRENTWOOD.

4.30 p.m. Visited & inspected 2/3rd. Field Ambulance Hospital at BRENTWOOD.

Jan. 26th. 8.30 a.m. Held Standing Medical Board on Officers 2/7th. Bn. Worc. Regt. at BRENTWOOD.

12 o/c. Held Standing Med. Board on Officers 2/8th. Bn. Worc. Regt. at BRENTWOOD.

2.45 p.m. Held Standing Medical Board on Officers A.S.C. at BRENTWOOD.

Jan. 27th. 10.15 a.m. Held Standing Medical Board on 2/2nd. & 2/3rd. R.F.A. Bdes. & R.G.A. at HeadQrs. Gt. BADDOW Rd.

2.15 p.m. Held Standing Medical Board on Officers 2/4 SM(How) Bde, 2/3rd. R.F.A. Bde. & HdQrs. Staff Gt. BADDOW Rd.

Jan. 28th. 10.30 a.m. Held Standing Medical Board on Officers 2/1 R.F.A. Bde. at HdQrs., INGATESTONE. Ordered Div. San Officer to proceed to R.A.M. College, Millbank to attend lectures "on Poisonous Gases" on 29th. & 30th. inst. in accordance with orders from C.F. sent by 'phone through A.D.M.S., 3rd. Army.

Called at OAKLANDS HOSPITAL & interviewed O.C. 2/1st S.M. Fd. Ambce.

9.0 a.m. Was notified by O.C. 2/3rd. F. Ambce. he had closed Hospital for week owing to outbreak of one case of diphtheria. I sent Formalin Spray & Solution with special orderly

1916 Jan & Feb

Jan. 28th. and orders to carry out all required precautions & notified at once Div. San. Officer

Jan. 29th. Routine Work.

Jan. 30th. Sunday – Routine Work.

Jan. 31st. 10 a.m. Proceeded to LONDON to interview – by request – D.D.M.S., C.F., at whose request and orders I then proceeded to W.O. and interviewed Staff Officer to D.G.

February

1st — Routine work —

2nd 2-30 pm Visited Oaklands' Hospl. & interviewed the O/c also O.C. 2/1st F. Ambce. re further accommodation for cases of Scabies brought into Div: by new Drafts.

3rd 2/4 Bn. Glos. Regt. being ordered to Southend, instructed Capt. Fawcett to accompany Bn. & ordered O.C. 2/3rd F. Ambce. to supply Medical Officer for 2/8th Worc Regt. whilst Capt. Fawcett also had under his charge

3 pm Interviewed by A.D.M.S. 3rd Army – on several details

2-30 pm The O. 2/1 [illegible] interviewed me on — " —

" 4th 10 am to 4 pm. Held Standing Med: Board. (S.M.D. orders 52/16) at Oaklands' on 40 Officers who were absent from other Boards. (Owing to Leave or Sickness) –

" 4 pm Visited Oaklands Hospital —

" 5th 9-30 am Proceeded to Buntingford to Hold Med: Boards & make Med: Arrangements for Hants Heavy Batteries now under this Div:

" 10 am Major Hoyten DADMS. held Board at Oaklands on men, under W.O. wire – between ages of 18 & 41 who had not signed A.F.E. 624.

" 6th Sunday =

" 7th Proceeded from London to Harlow to Hold Med: Board on 2/2nd C. of Lond: Yeo: & examined & inspected their Med: arrangements & billets – returning by train to Chelmsford. 5-10 pm.

Feb 1916

Feby 8th 10-am Held Med: Board – under orders D.D.M.S. – at Oaklands Hospl on Capt. Boome – R.A.M.C. T. – D.D.M.S. proceeded home on Pte business: 5 days leave granted by G.O.C. –

" 9th 9-45 am Visited (with Div: San Officer) Brentwood – Interviewed Brigadier. 183 Inf: Bde re Scabies in the Bde (brought in by the new drafts) Visited the 3. Amb. Hosp. & accompanied by O.C. 2/3rd. F Amb. inspected a house taken for treatment of Scabies. found all arrangements satisfactory. Except the baths. which were too small – indents for larger ones ordered to be submitted at once – found all clothing, bedding &c was being sent for disinfection to Billericay Union = Inspected empty house taken by A.S.C. arrangements satisfactory –

" 10th 10. am Visited (with Div: San: Officer) Danbury – Inspected 2/2 F Amb. Hosp – Maldon – interviewing O.C. 2/8th Wars R. & M.O. – Inspected Scabies Hospl & Hd Qrs & Med: Inspection Room 2/2nd S.M. F Amb. & the O.C. –

3 pm attended lecture on noxious gases & treatment by Lt Pring R.E. at Chelmsford –

" 11th 9-40 am Visit H Qrs. 2/4th R Herts Regt & held Med Board on 13 men – also on one man 2/4 S.M./How/ Bde R.F.A. –

10-50 am Visited H Qrs 2/1st Herts Bn & held Med Board on 89 men to 4-30 pm sent up for drafts –

" 12th 10-45 am Held Standing Med: Board on 48 men in 2/1 Herts Yeo. at Hatfield Peverell – Held (10 am) Med: Board on Lt Cark – A.V.C. 6 pm D.D.M.S. reported himself from leave

" 13th Sunday –

" 14th 12 pm Visited Detention Bks at Chelmsford Workhouse. found everything satisfactory but large room in (female) casualty ward had all windows closed – ordered proper ventilation to be given at once –

2.45 pm Held Standing Med: Board on Sapper Alder 3rd Lond. Army Troops Sig: Co. R.E. –

Feby 14th Contd 3-pm Held Med: Board on Surgeon Captn Walker 2/1 Herts Bn and Lieut: Holmes 2/4 S.M. (How) Bde R.F.A.: Interviewed

4 pm Captain Watkins A.S.C.

" 15th 10 am Proceeded to Burnham on Crouch & Held Med Board on men of 2/8th (Cyclist) Bn Essex Regt and Cyclist Co. 61 S.M.D.

3-45 pm Held Med: Board at Witham on men of R.E. –

" 16th 9-30 am Visited Oaklands Hospl with Div: San: Officer. and exam a suspicious case of C.S.M. which Lumbar Puncture had been done & fluid sent Colchester for exam: –

10-30 am Held Med: Board at Broomfield on men of 2/4th Yorks Off: & Hunts L I. –

4 pm Interviewed Secty Essex Red Cross Society –

10-30 pm Recd by wire report from Bacteriologist – Colchester that the spinal fluid sent did not contain C.S.M. Cocci –

" 17th – 9.30 am Proceeded to Maldon & held Medical Board on Drafts 2/6 Bn R Wars Regt commencing 10.30 am & upon Drafts 2/8 Bn R Wars Regt commencing 2-15 pm

" 18th – 9. am Proceeded to Brentwood & held Med Board on drafts of 2/7th & 2/8th R Wors Regt & 2/6 Bn Glos Regt till 4-40 pm – Interviewed H Qrs 183 Inf: Bde

" 19th – 9.30 am Held Med: Board at Boreham House on 3 men A.S.C.

" 20th Sunday (Routine Work)

" 21st. Monday Proceeded to Danbury held Medical Board on drafts from 2/5th & 2/7th Bns R. War Regt. and 2/1st S.M. Bde R.F.A. Called at Oaklands Hospital visited some of the Wards. DADMS returned from his tour to Flanders at 3.40 pm, proceeded with Headquarters Staff to Cholderton, Salisbury Plain.

February 1916.

22nd 9.15am Proceeded by motor to Southend & held medical Board on 10 men 2/1st Home Service Field Company R.E. at their Headquarters and afterwards on one private of 9th Provisional Battalion at the V.A.D. (Glen) Hospital.

3.45 pm Held medical Board on Detention Barracks' Officers (Chelmsford).

4.30pm Visited Oaklands Hospital, interviewed M.O. i/c & saw the most serious cases.

23rd Handed over to the ADMS 65th Division, personally conducting him over Oaklands, Kenilworth, and Scarres Hospitals (Chelmsford), and the Detention Barracks

24th Routine Work.

25th Reported myself to DDMS Southern Command, and received instructions for my new appointment.

2.0pm Reported myself at Headquarters, Cholderton.

26th Routine Work

27th Sunday.

28th 11-44AM Lt Col: J. Young M.D. RAMC. O.C. 1/3rd S.M. F Amb. 48th Div: Reported himself as ADMS. of this Division & I commenced handing over to him my duties.

29th 10am Motored to Ludgershall & Reported myself (with Col: Young as my Successor) to ADMS. Salisbury Plain: Visited the Three Field Ambulances at No 1 Camp. Perham Down, and handed same over to my Successor. 3pm Reported my departure to the G.O.C. & Completed handing over my duties to Col: Young.

H H Bull

C. Roberts 29-2-16

1916 March.

1st 10.30a.m. Colonel BULL having left this morning I took over the duties of A.D.M.S of this Division.
Routine duties in office.

2nd 2.30p.m. to 6p.m. Accompanied by D.A.D.M.S walked to BULFORD and inspected billets and sanitary arrangements of hutments occupied by A.S.C and 2/1st R.F.A.
Instructed Capt. GROVES RAMCT to make frequent inspection & supervision of same.

3rd 10.30A.M. Interviewed G.O.C. with reference to appointment of O.C 2/3rd Fd Amb.
2.30p.m. Standing Medical Board Consisting of A.D.M.S. (President) D.A.D.M.S & Capt BOOME RAMCT (members) held on Lieut. A.J.M. BRAMELD 2/7th R. WARWICK REGT.
3.30p.m Interviewed Major SHELLARD 2/4 GLOS. REGT.

4th 11a.m. Interviewed O.Cs. 2/1st. 2/2nd & 2/3rd Field Ambulances and instructed them with reference to War Diaries.
6p.m Capt. HULBERT RAMCT Div. San. Off having completed handing over at CHELMSFORD rejoined Headquarters.

5th 12 noon. Interviewed member Travelling Medical Board.
Today I completed 21 years service in the Volunteer & T. Forces

6th Routine duties.

7th Do.

8th 10am. Interviewed the G.O.C. with reference to number of men to be sent for examination by Travelling Medical Board.
10.30 a.m Proceeded by motor car to Hdqrs 2/2nd S.M. Fd Amb. PERHAM DOWN and held Standing Medical Board (Consisting of myself, D.A.D.M.S & Capt BOOME RAMCT) on 30 Officers of various units.
3.15pm returned from above duty.

March 1916

March 9th 10.30 a.m. Accompanied by D.A.D.M.S. motored to PERHAM DOWN and held medical Board on men of 2/5 WARWICKS at Hdqtrs. that unit.

1 p.m. Proceeded to TIDWORTH and at

2.15 p.m. held medical Board on men of 2/6 & 2/8 WARWICKS.

6.30 p.m. Returned to Headquarters where I found that CAPT. DAVISON R.A.M.C.T. had arrived with complete SANITARY SECTION.

Interviewed CAPT. DAVISON and afterwards the G.O.C. with reference to position of CAPT. HULBERT who has hitherto been carrying out the duties of DIV. SAN. OFFICER.

March 10th 10 a.m. Inspected the SANITARY SECT. on parade and examined their equipment and appliances.

D.A.D.M.S. proceeded to LONDON on leave for the day.

CAPT. HULBERT proceeded on 7 days leave.

March 11th. 10.30 a.m. Proceeded to TIDWORTH and held ~~Stand~~ medical Board on men of 2/4th GLOSTERS.

4 p.m. By appointment interviewed the G.O.C. with reference to vacancies for Officers of Field Ambulances & regimental units.

March 12th Routine duties.

Forwarded & recommended to G.O.C. application of Capt. HULBERT for transfer as Divisional Sanitary Officer 65th Division.

March 13th 10 a.m. Accompanied by Major HOYTEN, proceeded to TIDWORTH & held medical Board on men of 2/6th 2/8th Worcesters. Returned 3.15 p.m.

March 14th 9.45 a.m. Accompanied the G.O.C. & staff on Billeting exercise in area comprising the villages of

QUARLEY, AMPORT, EAST CHOLDERTON, THRUXTON FYFIELD and KIMPTON. Reports handed to Director at WEYHILL Church at 1.15 p.m.

Returned 3 p.m.

March 15th 2.30 p.m. Walked to BULFORD: interviewed CAPT GROVES.

March 16th 10.30 a.m. Accompanied by D.A.D.M.S. motored to PERHAM DOWN where I had arranged to inspect the three Field Ambulances on parade at 11 o'clock, a telephone message having been sent to Lt. Col CRAIG the senior officer of the three units to that effect last evening asking him at the same time to convey my orders to the O.Cs the two other units. On arrival I found the 2/1st & 2/2nd Fd Ambulances ready for inspection but no sign of the 2/3rd nor of Lt. Col. ROGERS. After inspecting the former two units I sent for Lt. Col. ROGERS and enquired why my orders conveyed to him through Lt Col. CRAIG had not been carried out in respect of his unit. He admitted that he had received the verbal order from Lt Col. CRAIG but offered the excuse that he did not act because he "was awaiting confirmation of the telephone message by letter." I told him that in future when I sent an order verbally or otherwise to him through a senior – or ~~for that~~ officer I expected that order to be obeyed.

March 17th Wrote to the Secretary Warwickshire T.F. Assocn. with reference to C.C.S. requesting information as to the stage at which the formation of this unit has reached and the names & professional qualifications of Officers as well as that of the Officer nominated for Command.

2 p.m. Accompanied the G.O.C. & Lt Col. Sir HEREWARD WAKE

to PERHAM DOWN where the G.O.C. inspected the three Field Ambulances on parade in full marching order with Transport.

March 18th Routine duties: proceeded to LONDON by train on short leave; the D.A.D.M.S acting on my behalf.

" 19th Sunday: returned from LONDON by 5.50 pm Waterloo.

" 20th 11.30 The D.A.D.M.S proceeded to PARKHOUSE Camp to investigate case of C-S-F: No. 5280 Pte SELWOOD 2/4 R. BERKS admitted to MILITARY HOSP. TIDWORTH.

2.30 p.m. Proceeded to SALISBURY for interview with D.D.M.S SOUTHERN COMMAND on various matters concerning the Medical Services of the Division;

March 21st 10.am. Accompanied by D.A.D.M.S. proceeded by motor to PERHAM DOWN and formed Standing Medical Board Composed of myself as President the D.A.D.M.S & Capt BOOME RAMCT as members for examination of 69 Officers of various units.

March 22nd 11.a.m Interviewed Lieut SMITH M.O. 2/6 GLOSTERS with reference to death of No 4271. Pte E. PERKS of the 2/7th WORCESTER REGT.

Remainder of day routine duties

March 23rd 10.am Conferred with Div. San. Off. with reference to routine methods to be carried out in connection with Cases of C.S.M. and other infectious diseases.

" 24th Routine duties.

" 25th 10.30 am: Capt. H.N BURROUGHES R.A.M.C.T. reported for duty with the 2/1st S.M. Fd. Amb.

" 26th Routine Duties

" 27th Routine Duties:

5.30 p.m. attended meeting of "B" Mess, held at Manor Horse Farm, with reference to arrangements for starting Mess.

March 28th 10.am. Proceeded to TIDWORTH and formed Standing Medical Board - with Capt. DAVISON DIV. SAN OFF for examination of 5 men of 2/6 and 40 of the 2/8 R. WARWICKS.

2 p.m. The same Board proceeded to PERHAM DOWN and examined 34 men of the 2/7th R. WARWICKS and one man R.F.C. A Great blizzard with snow all day.

Mar 29th 10 am Proceeded to PERHAM DOWN and formed Standing Medical Board - with the D.A.D.M.S. - for examination of 29 men of the 2/7th R. Warwicks

2.30 pm. Proceeded to PARKHOUSE CAMP and formed Standing Medical Board - with the D.A.D.M.S - for examination of 29 men of the 2/1st Bucks. Batt. and 11 men of the 2/4th Oxfords + Bucks L. I.

March 30 Routine duties.

2 pm. Interviewed member of Travelling Medical Board who desired arrangements to be made for examination of men, but owing to the recent Gale telephonic & telegraphic Communication has been cut off for the past two days and this was not possible.

5.30 pm Attended meeting of "B" mess & arranged details.

March 31st 10 am The D.A.D.M.S. proceeded to LONDON for the day.

12 noon. Interviewed two members of the Travelling Medical Board and afterwards made arrangements for all men for examination by this Board to attend at CANDAHAR BARRACKS, TIDWORTH, at 10 a.m. tomorrow

April 1916.

April 1st 12 noon. Interviewed member of Travelling Medical Board
Routine duties.

April 2nd Sunday: routine duties.

" 3rd Routine duties: interviewed Capt. BANNERMAN M.O. i/c 2/4th OX. & BUCKS L.I. and advised him on some matters.

" 4th 10.15 A.M. Proceeded with the D.A.D.M.S to PERHAM DOWN and held Standing Medical Board on 79 men of the 2/5th 2/6th 2/7th & 2/8th R. WARWICKS.
2.30 p.m. Visited Field Ambulances at PERHAM DOWN and informally inspected huts & transport lines.
10 a.m. Had interview with the G.O.C. with reference to vaccination of drafts entitled to one months leave of absence; arranged for vaccination of same to proceed at once.

" 5th 10 a.m. Proceeded with the D.A.D.M.S. to PERHAM DOWN where with Capt BOOME RAMC.T. and officers and I held Standing Medical Board on 46 Officers from various units of the Division. With the D.A.D.M.S. I also held medical Board on Capt. BOOME & Capt GROVES, RAMC.T.
4 p.m. Visited with Capt BURROUGHES, BEDLAM HILL and inspected the "dug-out" dressing station constructed there by the 2/1st S.M. Fd. Amb.

" 6th Routine duties: A.D.M.S. in LONDON re new Dress Regulations.

" 7th 11.30 a.m. Interviewed Lieut WILSON R.A.M.C.T. with reference to transfer to R.A.M.C. (temporary).
2 p.m. The D.A.D.M.S. proceeded on 14 days special leave.

" 8th 11 a.m. Held medical Board on Major SIMCOX under authority of G.O.C. in C. Southern Command.
11.30 a.m. Held Standing Medical Board on 4 Officers [illegible].

April 1916.

April 9th 12 Noon. Proceeded with A.D.V.S to PERHAM DOWN and inspected the horses of the three Field Ambulances stationed there.
9 p.m. Received telegram from "PRACTICIAN SALISBURY" informing me that 31 RAMC. Officers would report for duty with the Division on the 12th inst.

April 10th Routine duties.

" 11th 10.15 a.m. Proceeded to TIDWORTH and held - with Major CORFIELD 2/3 S.M. FD. AMB. as member - Standing Medical Board on one man of the 2/6 GLOS. REGT. and one man of the 61st DIV. TRAIN.
Had arranged for board on 24 N.C.O.s & 34 men of the 2/5th GLOS. REGT and a number of men of the 2/7th WORCESTERS but was informed that these men had all proceeded on their final 5 days leave.
2.30 p.m. Proceeded with the DIV. SAN OFF (Capt DAVISON) to BULFORD and inspected kitchens & mess rooms of all Artillery units quartered there.

April 12th Interviewed Twenty three Officers R.A.M.C. from General Hospitals at BRISTOL, OXFORD, BIRMINGHAM, DEVONPORT & PORTSMOUTH and disposed of them to Field Ambulances and Regimental Units to Complete fill up vacancies.

April 13th Routine duties. Interviewed Major MACKIE 2/1st S.M. Fd. Amb.

" 14th Routine duties. This afternoon Capt DAVISON Div. San. Off proceeded on five days final leave. Capt HIRST R.A.M.C.T. 2/1st S.M. FD. AMB acting on his behalf.
3 p.m. Interviewed Capt. WILKINSON with reference to his transfer from 2/7 R. WARWICK REGT to 2/2 S.M. Fd. Amb and duly posted him to that Unit.

April 1916.

April 15th 10.30 a.m. Proceeded to No. 1 Camp PERHAM DOWN and formed Standing Medical Board with Major CORFIELD and Capt NIXON both of the 2/3rd S. M. Fd Amb as members, for examination of 18 R.A.M.C officers recently joined, and 2nd Lieut BRYANT 2/1st R.F.A.

April 16th Sunday. Routine duties.

" 17th 10.30 a.m. With Capt HIRST as member, held Standing Medical Board on Col. PEYTON 2/7 Worcesters.

11 a.m. Proceeded to TIDWORTH and interviewed Capt. WOOD, R.A.M.C. Ear & Throat Specialist Officer, Officers Hosp. Tidworth with reference to Capt. WETTON R.A. DIV. AMM. COL. with a view to submitting this officer to examination by Standing Med. Board as to his fitness for service overseas. Found Capt. WETTON had left the Hospital and was informed he had proceeded on 7 days sick leave.

" 18th 8.30 a.m. Accompanied the G.O.C. on Field Exercises of 184th Infy. Bde.

4.30 p.m. Interviewed nine Officers R.A.M.C who reported to me for duty with the Division. Posted these officers to vacancies in Field Ambulances and Regimental Units.

19th 7.30 a.m. Attended Divisional Route March.

20th 10.15 a.m. With Major CORFIELD & Capt NIXON as members formed Standing Medical Board at PARKHOUSE CAMP and examined 6 officers & 66 men of various units of the 184th Infy. Bde.

21st 2.45 p.m. Accompanied the G.O.C. to PARKHOUSE CAMP (GOOD FRIDAY) where we met Maj. General SIR FRANCIS HOWARD KCB, CMG

April 1916

who inspected men physically unfit in the various units of the 184th INFTY. BDE. D.A.D.M.S returned from leave.

Apl 22nd 10.15 a.m. Proceeded by motor to PARKHOUSE CAMP where with Major HOYTEN and Capt NIXON RAMC as members I formed Medical Board for examination of Brigadier General Hon C.G. FORTESCUE, 184th INFTY BDE, and Major CAPP his Brigade Major.

Afterwards interviewed Lieut. WILSON RAMC with reference to case of Diphtheria in this Camp.

April 23rd (Easter Sunday) 10.45. Proceeded by motor to CANDAHAR BARRACKS, TIDWORTH accompanied by D.A.D.M.S and the O.C. SAN. SECTION where I held a Conference of Regimental Med. Officers

April 24th Routine duties.

" 25th A.D.M.S proceeded on five days final leave.

" 26 DADMS met all Officers in Medical Charge Units and gave an instructional lecture on their duties. Routine work.

" 27 Proceeded to Candahar Barracks and held a Medical Board on all Officers in Medical Charge Units and other Officers.

28 Divisional Operations.

" 29 Routine work

" 30 Routine work. A.D.M.S returned from leave.

May 1916.

May 1st. 10.30 a.m. Held standing medical Board for examination of two men of 2/4th GLOSTERS.

11 a.m. Interview with Lt. Col. STEPHENS R.A.M.C.T with reference to C.C.S.

11.30 a.m. Capt E.H. WOOD R.A.M.C reported for duty with the D.C.L.I. & was granted four days leave before taking up his duties.

2.30 p.m. Visited PERHAM DOWN and interviewed O's C. 2/1st & 2/2nd Field Ambulances. Afterwards proceeded to PICKFORD HILL where the 2/3rd Fd Amb. was carrying out field operations and interviewed the O.C. & Capt NIXON with reference to making arrangements for treatment of Scabies cases under this Fd. Amb. at PERHAM DOWN.

May 2nd. 10 a.m. Accompanied by D.A.D.M.S. proceeded to TIDWORTH & formed Standing medical Board for examination of men of the 2/4th & 2/6 GLOSTERS & 2/8 WORCESTERS: Examined altogether 107 men of whom about 60% were found medically unfit to proceed for service abroad.

May 3rd. 10 a.m. Accompanied by D.A.D.M.S. proceeded to TIDWORTH and formed Standing medical Board for examination of a number of men of the 2/5th GLOS. 2/4 OX & BUCKS L.I. & 2/4 R. BERKS. Regt. 84 in all of whom 34 were placed in Category "A".

Today received a telegram from SOUTHERN COMMAND to the effect that the 2/1st S.M. C.C.S. is now altogether under the orders of G.O.C. 61st DIVISION.

May 4th. 10 a.m. Held medical Board on 1 N.C.O. of DIV. MOUNTED POLICE

11 a.m. Held Conference with D.A.D.M.S., DIV. SAN OFF and Capt NIXON R.A.M.C.T 2/3 S.M. Fd Amb. with reference to establishing a Scabies Hosp. at PERHAM DOWN.

May 5th. 11.30 a.m. H.M. THE KING inspected the Division on BULFORD FIELD.

May 1916

May 5th. Lieut Manuel R.A.M.C. reported for duty – under orders of Southern Command – with the 2/1st S.M. Fd Amb. to replace Capt WAY transferred to Home service.

Lieut. WOOD E.H. R.A.M.C reported for duty with the D.C.L.I. on his return from leave.

May 6th. 10.30 a.m. Held medical Board on two officers 2/4 R. BERKS Regt. and 1 Officer 2/4 Oxford & Bucks L.I.

May 7th. Routine Work.

" 8th. 8.30 a.m. Proceeded by motor to WHITCHURCH to take part in three days Field Exercises: Visited in course of the evening the billets of the 3 Field Ambulances, at HURSTBOURNE TARRANT; ST. MARY BOURNE and HURSTBOURNE PRIORS respectively.

The D.A.D.M.S and DIV. SAN. OFF remained for duty at CHOLDERTON.

9th. 9 a.m. Proceeded by motor to ANDOVER and visited later with A.A. & Q.M.G. the billets of the Fd. Ambulances.

10th. 5.15 A.M. Accompanied by the A.A. & Q.M.G. proceeded to MONXTON where the Headquarters for the day were established. The Field exercises for today included an attack on QUARLEY HILL etc: all three field Ambulances were employed under their respective Infantry Brigades. Operations ceased about mid day.

During these exercises a very large number of men 150-200 men per day fell out on the march almost every one of whom were suffering from sore feet. They wore their overseas boots which they had previously worn for a week or 10 days some weeks ago after which they had been returned to stores from which they were withdrawn just before proceeding on these exercises – with somewhat disastrous results.

May 1916

May 11th. 10.15 a.m. Proceeded to BULFORD and with Major MACKIE R.A.M.C.T. 2/1st (S.M.) FD AMB. and Major WATERHOUSE RAMCT 2/2nd (S.M.) FD. AMB. as members formed Standing Medical Board for examination of Officers of the Casualty Clearing Station and 4 men of the DIV. AMM. COL and 1 man of the 2/1st (S.M.) R.F.A.

12.30 p.m.: Inspected kitchens, latrines, mess rooms, baths etc. of the 2/4 R.F.A. & DIV. AMM. COL.

3.30 p.m. Visited FIELD AMBULANCES at PERHAM DOWN and inspected Scabies Hospital there.

May 12th. Routine duties:

5 p.m. Attended Conference of the G.O.C. Division at BHURTPORE BARRACKS TIDWORTH to discuss the operations of 8th 9th & 10th inst.

May 13th. Routine duties: 10 a.m. Conference of all Reg. M.Os with reference to examination of weary men in their respective units →

" 14th. DO. (Sunday)

" 15th. Proceeded to PERHAM DOWN and with D.A.D.M.S. 10.30 a.m. formed Standing Medical Board for examination of one officer 2/5 R. War. Reg. one off. 2/4 R. Berks Regt. 28 men 2/6 R. War. Reg. 5 men 2/5 R. War. Reg: 5 men 2/4 R. Berks: 2 men 1/3 3rd Co. R.E.: 3 men 2/5 Glosters: 4 men 2/4 Ox. & Bucks. 9 men 2/8 R. War. Reg.

3 p.m. Interviewed Lt Col. STEPHEN with reference to certain matters concerning the 2/1st C.C.S

6.30 p.m. Four Officers R.A.M.C. reported for duty to complete establishment of Division. Of these one Lieut POOLE was found medically unfit and an officer to replace him was applied for.

May 16th. 9 a.m. Lieut V. C. Innes R.A.M.C. reported for duty and was posted to 2/5 Glos. Regt. vice Lieut Graydon medically unfit for service overseas.

May 1916

May 17th. 10.30 a.m. Held Standing Medical Board for examination of Lieut. TOVEY 61st DIV. TRAIN and Lieut. SPREAT 2/7th WORCESTERS.

2.30 p.m. Medical Board on 1 man 2/3 S.M. FD AMB.

May 18th. 2 p.m. Proceeded to PERHAM DOWN and inspected the 2/1st (S.M.) C.C.S on parade.

3 p.m. Conference of all Officers of Field Ambulances and C.C.S. The A.D.M.S. addressed them on the work of Field Ambulances at the Front and some points in dealing with large numbers of wounded in action.

5.30 p.m. Interview with a Sergt. from Army Pay Department with reference to matters concerning 1/3 S.M. Fd Amb.

May 19th. Routine duties.

" 20th. 10 a.m. Held standing medical Board at CANDAHAR BKS. TIDWORTH for examination of Major GROUNDS and men of

21st. drafts recently sent to the Division.

21st. D.A.D.M.S. held Medical Board on draft of 40 men recently sent to the Division.

22nd. 9 a.m. Held standing Med. Bd. on Major CAPPER 2/5 R.War Regt.

Headquarters of Division proceeded overseas.

Intact.

War Diary. AUGUST 1915. A.D.M.S. 61(S.M.) Div.

August. 1915.

2nd. Sent D.A.D.M.S. to hold Boards at Maldon and Danbury.

3rd. Visited "Oaklands" and inspected Hospitals. Held Board (by order of G.O.C.) on Capt. Rose 1/4th Battn. Oxon and Bucks L.I. (wounded on 11th of May) at Oaklands: called on O i/c Barracks re-Lt. Col. Craig's Camps Claims. 6 p.m. attended G.O.C's conference re- arrangements for Lord Kitchener's inspection on the 6th inst.

4th. Sent D.A.D.M.S. with D.A.& Q.M.G. to Hylands re arrangements for the 6th inst. Visited Oaklands Hospital and motored toIngatestone to interview Dr. Sterling Hamilton re acting as Medical Officer i/c 2/3rd Royal Field Artillery Brigade. Interviewed Dr. Denning, Epping re attendance on troops at Epping –

5th. Visited Oaklands (Hospital and Marquees), sent D.A.D.M.S. with D.A.& Q.M.G. to Hylands with Divisional Sanitary Officer to make sanitary arrangements for inspection on the 6th inst.

6th. The Secretary of State for War (Lord Kitchener, K.G.) inspected 2/1st South Midland Division in Hylands Park at 11-0a.m., At 3 p.m. held a Medical Board on Capt. Cheshire 28th Provisional Battalion, and Lieut. Large 1/7th Royal Warwickshire Regiment. Interviewed Major Howard R.A.M.C.(T). now in charge of Provisional Units at Colchester.

7th. Visited Oaklands and held consultation with O.C's., Interviewed Dr. Smith in Chelmsford re taking commission as M.O. i/c6th Gloster regt., Held consultation with G.O.C.

8th. Arranged for Medical Board on Lieut. Austin 1/8th War. Regt. on 16th inst., but just received wire from S.C. to send his Documents to Military Hospital, Warwick.

9th. 2nd Lieut. Solomon (2/7th War. Regt.) presented himself for a Medical Board, but same had been held over him in London on 2 nd inst. Reported same to G.O.C.

Visited Oaklands Hospital, re application for more Hospital Eqipment and fully went into the matter with O. C's 2nd & 3rd Field Ambulances and Lady Commandant.

The G.O.C. came in at same time and went over the Hospital.

Aug 10th. Visited Oaklands Hospital.

Aug 11th. Proceeded early in the morning to Epping Camp accompanied by the D.A.D.M.S. and held Medical Board on 129 men.

Aug 12th. Held Medical Board on Captain Hague, Attended the G.O.C'S Conference at 4-30 p.m.

Visited Oaklands Hospital. Interviewed O.C. Army Service Corps, Re :- Supply of Manure of Field Ambulance Stables to Master of Workhouse.

Aug 13th. Held Medical Exercises with 2nd & 3rd Field Ambulances at Ingatestone. A.D.M.S. 3rd Army was present and inspected the various Advanced Dressing Stations & Divisional Dressing Stations.

Lieut. Appleton R.A.M.C. reported himself from Colchester was attached to 4th Bn. Royal Berks Regiment and Army Service Corps for duty -

Aug 14th. Interviewed the Clerk to the Board of Guardians with reference to use of Baths & Disinfector for cases of Itch at Workhouse.

Aug 16th. Under instructions from 3rd Army visited Central Force who requested me to interview the D.G. A.M.S. at WAR OFFICE.

Aug 17th. Surgeon-General Culling A.D.M.S. 3rd Army Central Force called at Headquarters and introduced to the Divisional Staff his successor Colonel Morgan. He himself proceeding as D.D.M.S. Central Force. They inspected Oaklands Hospital. They also inspected the The Infectious Tents, the Field Ambulance Hutments and Stables.

Aug 18th. Proceeded with D.A.D.M.S. to Maldo n and Danbury holding Medical Boards.

Aug 19th. Held Medical Boards with Major Hoyten and Lieut. Col. Craig at Oaklands on 2 Officers and 2 men of the Army Service Corps, 2 men of the 3rd Field Ambulance and on 6 patients in Oaklands Hospital.

Held consultation with O. C's. of the 2nd & 3rd Field Ambulances.

Interviewed Major Warwick R.A.M.C., at present doing duty at Colchester Military Hospital, re:- being attached to the 2nd. Field Ambulance of this Division.

Attended G. O. C's. Conference at 4-30 p.m.

Aug 20th. It being reported to me that Pte, Keeley of the 8th Gloster Regt. who was recommended by a Medical Board on the 8th instant for discharge through Mental Deficiency was showing symptons of loss of Control over his actions, I accordingly visited their Headquarters, (interviewed the O.C.) and ordered him to Oaklands Hospital with a guard to be furnished by the Battalion for strict observation. Strictest orders were given to the Medical Officer to carefully watch the case and report to me his condition in the evening . At 7-30 p.m. O.C. 3rd Field Ambulance informed me by telephone that the man was perfectly quiet and docile, and that, so far, it only appeared to be a case of Mental Deficiency.

Aug 21st. Held Boards at Maldon (with Lt. Col. Rogers and Surgeon-Captain Fowler) visited Witham and consulted with C.R.E. Under orders from Central Force the following Officers reported themselves for duty, and were posted to :-

Lieutenant Flegg R.A.M.C. R.F.A. (Howitzer) Brigade, and
R.G.A. Great Baddow.

Lieutenant Lavertine, R.A.M.C. 2/3rd R.F.A. Bde. Ingatestone.

Aug 22nd. Lieutenant Hutchinson R.A.M.C. 2nd. Field Ambulance Chelmsford.

Lieutenant Graydon. R.A.M.C. 1st. Field Ambulance. Epping.

Aug 23rd. Met the A.D.M.S. 3rd Army and proceeded with him and his Staff Officer and Divisional Sanitary Officer of 61st(South Midland) Division to inspect the following Units etc:—

Danbury 4th Bn. Gloster Regiment.
2nd Field Ambulance Hospital
6th Bn. Gloster Regiment.

Maldon. 7th Bn. Worcesters Regiment.
8th Bn. Worcesters Regiment.

and V.A.D. Hospital Riverscourt.Southminster, 1/8th Bn. (ESSEX) Cyclist Regiment., including Medical Inspection Room.

Burnham-on-Crouch. Headquarters of the 83rd Provisional Battalion and V.A.D. Hospital Burnham.

A Board was held at Oaklands Hospital on Lieut. Samuels 2/3rd R.F.A.. Board consisted of Lt. Col. Craig, Lt. Col. Rogers and Major Hoyten

Aug 24th. Held a Medical Board on Lt. Col. Ash 2/8th Bn. R. Warwick Regiment under orders of G.O.C. Proceeded to Southend with the D.A.D.M.S. and held Medical Board on 41 men 28th Provisional Battalion, and interviewed the O.C. on several details.

Aug 25th. Medical Board held at Oaklands Chelmsford on several small drafts from different Units.

Aug 26th. Visited Epping Camp with the D.A.D.M.S. and held Medical Boards on drafts from the 5th, 6th, 7th, & 8th Battalions Royal Warwick Regiments, on 1st Field Ambulance, and the 2/1st. S.M.R.F.A. & R.E'S. Attended G.O.C's Conference at 4-30 p.m.

Aug 27th. Held Medical Board on 2nd Lieut. Large 1/7th Royal Warwick Regiment. Interviewed Quartermaster Captain W.H.Kimpton transferred from 1st South Midland Field Ambulance to Colchester (Provisional Battn)

Met A.D.M.S. 3rd Army and with his Staff Officer, and the Divisional Sanitary Officer, visited & inspected Oaklands Hospital & Hutments and the Hutments at Writtle (2/2nd R.F.A.) Great Baddow Road (R.G.A. Hutments at Great Baddow, 2/4th (Howitzer) Brigade R.F.A. and Henry Street Chelmsford (Army Service Corps). The Medical Officer 2/2nd R.F.A. (at Writtle) had engaged the small Mission Hall as a Medical Orderly Room and told off part of it with 4 beds for cases of extreme emergency. The whole arrangements are well carried out.

Aug 28th. Sent the D.A.D.M.S. to interview the O.C's Field Ambulances at Oaklands with regard to horses and mules about to be supplied to the three (3) Field Ambulances.

Aug 29th (Sunday) "NIL"

Aug 30th. Interviewed D.O.R.E. respecting the unsatisfactory state of the Kitchens at Oaklands Hutment which had not yet received attention and which had been unfavourably reported upon, for <u>many weeks past</u> by the A.D.M.S. 3rd Army, the D.S.O, and myself.

Aug 31st. In conjunction with Lieut. Col. Rogers and Major Hoyten, held Medical Boards at Oaklands Hospital. Interviewed Capt. Burroughs Medical Officer i/c 1/8th Essex (Cyclists) Battalion. at Baddow.

PRECIS.

WAR DIARY FOR AUGUST 1915.

During the last month the Division has been very free from sickness no serious case occuring for many weeks.

A Transport Man in 2/5th Bn. Royal Warwick Regiment was killed at Epping Camp being thrown from a mule which kicked him, causing fracture of the skull.

Oaklands Hospital under new arrangements (made with the Essex Red Cross Society) has shown considerable improvement, but some of the Wards require urgent attention in the shape of distempering, floor planing etc, and until same is done and unhealthy wall paper removed it will never have the appearance of an"up-to-date Hospital", this however the authorities decline to do. The Sanitation in the Division is most satisfactory & receives the constant attention of the Divisional Sanitary Officer. The Hutments are well cared for & kept clean, but the roads & approaches should receive the immediate attention of the authorities before the approaching winter. This has several times been prominently brought before the notice of the D.O.R.E.

The training of the Field Ambulances continues very satisfactory and now they are receiving their full complement of Horses, and proper (military) Harness has just been delivered. During this month Central Force has detailed 5 R.A.M.C. Medical Officers for temporary duty, but the shortage of Medical Officers is still serious and will become more so when those for Home Service only, are transferred to Home Service Battalions. I fear this shortage will remain until the War Office fixes their pay at the "same rate" as those joining the New Army. A large number of Medical Boards have been held during the month, and a fair percentage of Recruits are found under age. Inoculations have made decided progress during the last month, but a few units are still showing a low percentage. This is accounted for by the fact that some Battalions come from a County where Anti-Vaccination spirit is rife.

[illegible]
COLONEL.
ASSISTANT DIRECTOR OF MEDICAL SERVICES.
61 (SOUTH MIDLAND) DIVISION.

[illegible] Farm
Chelmsford
2-IX-15.

ARB
2-9-15

War Diary. September 1915.
@&@&@&@&@&@&@&@&@&@&@&@&@

Sept 1st. Motored to Headquarters Royal Engineers Witham, accompanied by D.A.D.M.S. & held a Medical Board on 18 men in that area. Sent (~~originally~~ urgently) Motor Ambulance to Headquarters 3rd Army for bedding etc of the A.D.M.S. 3rd Army, for disinfection and when carried out, returned same at once. (The A.D.M.S. 3rd Army on week-end leave was reported to be suffering from Dyptheria, hence the precautions taken)

Sept2nd. Visited (accompanied by D.A.D.M.S.) Oaklands Hospital. Inspected the Stabling, Wagons, Hospital, and other details and consulted with the O.C. of the 2nd & 3rd Field Ambulances on many points. Owing to hurried orders for Lieutenant Lavertine attached to the 2/3rd R.F.A. Brigade Ingatestone, to proceed overseas on the 1st instant, detailed Lieut. Hutchinson R.A.M.C. attached to the 2nd Field Ambulance for duty with the 2/3rd R.F.A.Brigade at Ingatestone, until their move to Epping and then to remain at Ingatestone in Medical Charge of the 2/1st. R.F.A. Brigade on their arrival.

Sept 3rd. Held Medical Board, in accordance with orders of the G.O.C, on the following:-

Captain Rose 1/4th Oxon & Bucks Light Infantry.
Lieut. Savory 3/1st. Signal Company Royal Engineers.
Lieut. Batty A.V.C. also Captain Whitehouse, with a view

to proceeding overseas. Attended at 2-30 p.m. a Lecture on Rations by Major Whitehouse in accordance with South Midland Division Orders.

Sept 4th. Motored to Epping Camp and held Medical Boards on drafts from the 2/4th & 2/6th Gloucester Battalions & Army Service Corps. Board consisted of myself as President, Major Hoyten D.A.D.M.S.

Lieut. Moore R.A.M.C.
Lieut. Fawcett. R.A.M.C.
Lieut. Graydon. R.A.M.C.

these Three Lieutenants attending with their respective drafts.

Interviewed the G.O.C. with regard to the question of Reports of Medical Boards forwarded him for perusal, not being received by the O.C's of the Units concerned, who had complained to the Brigadier-Generals as to ~~cause of~~ delay. Wrote to the A.D.M.S. 3rd ARMY for a ruling on the procedure of forwarding reports of Medical Boards namely:-
" whether the A.D.M.S. of the Division (in accordance with instructions from both Central Force, And Southern Command) should send them direct to

War Office & Central Force, or whether they were to be sent by the A.D.M.S. to the G.O.C. for transmission in accordance with Central Force Order 320 dated March 3rd 1915.

Sept 6th. Motored into Chelmsford, and:-

1. Interviewed C.R.A. on several details concerning examination of Officers & Men under his Command.

2. Interviewed D.O.R.E. re:- Cookhouse at Oaklands Hutment, Papering and whitewashing kitchens and alteration of W.C. at Oaklands House.

3. Interviewed O.C. 1st. & 3rd Field Ambulances on several points.

4. Called on Clerk of Chelmsford Hospital Conjoint Board concerning Messrs Wenley's bill for Furniture suplied to "Kenilworth" Infectious Hospital.

Sept 7th. Visited Oaklands Hospital, met the G.O.C. and the D.O.R.E.. Several details of the utmost importance requiring urgent attention were presented to him. Afterwards inspected the Kitchens & Oaklands Hutments which also required serious attention. All these details were referred to the D.O.R.E. for action. Granted sick leave of 7 days to Major Hoyten D.A.D.M.S. owing to continued feverish chill. Arranged by telephone with the D.A.D.M.S. 3rd Army to visit Boreham House to-morrow. Held Medical Board on Lieutenant Scott-Sunderland under orders of the G.O.C. Board consisted of myself as President, Captain Hulbert. Divisional Sanitary Officer & Lieutenant Graves R.A.M.C. 2/8th Battalion Royal Warwickshire Regiment.

Sept 8th. Attended with the General Staff a Field Day of the 184th Infantry Brigade at Hatfield-Peverelle . Major Wilmot D.A.D.M.S. 3rd Army also attended. Was present at the Generals Conference discussing the days work. In afternoon attended lecture on "NOTES FROM THE FRONT" by Lieutenant Colonel Burroughs. C.M.G. General Staff, 61st. (South Midland) Division.

Sept 9th. Proceeded by Motor to TILLINGHAM with Captain Boucher R.A.M.C., and held Medical Board on 37 men of the Royal Engineers with reference to their being either retained for "HOME SERVICE" or returned to 2/1st Line.

Sept 10th. At 3-30 p.m. received a most urgent telephone message from the 182nd Infantry Brigade that a man in the Provisional Battalion at Goldhanger was very seriously ill. Sent Urgent orders for the Medical Officer of the 6th Battalion Royal Warwick Regiment Maldon to visit him at once, who reported the man was "very poorly" with a cold, inflamed eye & a boil.

Sept 10th. At 7-30 p.m. received a telephone message from DANBURY that a ~~the~~ man at Maldon, (Regiment and name unknown) had ENTERIC FEVER and was to be transferred. A Motor Ambulance was immediately sent out to Maldon and telephonic communication took place with the Great Baddow Infectious Hospital, and the CIVIL HOSPITAL for his admission, which these institutions stated, "they could not carry out till next morning." The man was broght in that night to an Isolated room at "Oaklands" & sent the following morning to the Great Baddow Infectious Hospital. It transpired that this man had been in the V.A.D. Hospital for nearly two (2) weeks and the Medical Officer only telephoned to say that " WYDAL'S TEST" confirming the disease, had ~~only~~ just arrived. It was therefore an error on his part (through a misunderstanding on his telephone, that the man was moved.) The Divisional Sanitary Officer (was ordered to fully investigate the case ~~which~~ & found he ~~was found to be~~ a Corporal in the 7th Worcester Regiment who evidently contracted the disease at Bisley and not at Maldon, ~~and~~ every detail (as ~~referred~~ requiring by Military ~~Authorities~~ regulations) had been carried out in ~~such~~ this case.

Sept11th. Visited Burnham with Captain Boucher R.A.M.C.(T) and held a Medical Board on 17 men of the 2nd South Midland Home Service Field Company Royal Engineers.

Sept 14th. Held Medical Board at Oaklands Hospital Chelmsford on 2 men of the Signal Company Royal Engineers and one man (Howitzer) Brigade R.F.A. and on Private Smith, Super. Coy. Norfolk Regiment, now attached to the 2/6th Battalion Essex Regiment by special orders from 3rd Army. Interviewed Medical Officer of Oaklands Hospital and Lady Commandant Re; Cases, also Lieut. MacMasters W.D. Land Agent re Danbury Mission Hall & Kenilworth Infectious Hospital. Received letter from D.A.D.M.S. asking for 14 days leave. The D.A.D.M.S. 3rd Army inspected 2nd. Field Ambulance at Epping. Was unable to attend same, owing to breakdown of Motor.

Sept15th. Visited Great Baddow Hutment with Divisional Sanitary Officer and inspected the drainage & the dirty condition in which the whole

Camp was left the previous day by the 2/4th S.M.(Howitzer) Bde. R.F.A. and consulted with the Medical Officer in charge of the Brigade. Motored to ~~Great Baddow~~ Danbury and interviewed the Brigadier-General 182 Inf. Bde. re:- Vaccination and various other subjects. Visited the 2/7th Battalion Royal Warwick Regiment Danbury Hutments & interviewed the O.C. and the Medical Officer re cases for Medical Board.

Sept 16th. Attended G.O.C's Conference at 4-30 p.m.

Sept 17th. NIl.

Sept 18th. Visited Oaklands Hospital. Interviewed OFFICER i/c Barracks re; Kenilworth Hospital Returns.

Lieut. Potter R.A.M.C. reported himself for duty from Colchester to relieve Lieutenant Appleton recalled for Overseas Duty.

Interviewed Officer i/c 2/4th Royal Berks, ordered Pte, Lewis V.D.H. to be re-admitted into Hospital.

Sept 20th. Visited , inconjunction with my Divisional Sanitary Officer, the Camp at CHIPPING ONGAR "DETAILS" of 1,000 men 1st London Territorials,

Met in consultation the O.C. and the C.M.P, Dr.Wilson (whom I have appointed Medical Officer i/c of same and the gave the fullest detailed accounts as to all duties to be carried out.) Wrote full details to 3rd Army of all Medical arrangements that I have made for this Camp.

Visited Epping Camp, held a Medical Board on Lieut,Spreat 2/7th Warwick Regiment . Board consisted of Colonel W.H.Bull President.

Lieut. Colonel Craig.) MEMBERS.
Lieut. Moore.)

Inspected, inconjunction with the Divisional Sanitary Officer, Transport Lines of this Camp and their Latrines & Kitchens, both of which I found in a dirty and unsatisfactory condition.

Sept 21st. Inoculation (ANTI-TYPHOID) of members on Divisional Staff commencing this day at Boreham House.

Held Medical Board on Lieut.O'Flynn R.A.M.C. attached to the R.E'S. Interviewed Lieut. Flegg R.A.M.C. attached to R.F.A.(Howitzer) Brigade. Visited Oaklands Hospital and inspected same accompanied by Captain Richardson D.A.&Q.M.G. Afterwards proceeded with him to Great Baddow Hutments, and inspected the drainage & sanitary arrangements inconjunction with the DIvisional Sanitary Officer and his Clerk and Medical Officer of the Brigade (Surgeon-Captain Mackie).

Sept 22nd. Attended the "Brigade Tactical Exercises" of the 184th Infantry Brigade, the 3rd Field Ambulance taking part in the exercises, from 10-0 a.m. to 2-0 p.m. Exercises extending over the areas of Boreham & Hatfield Peverell.

Sept 23rd. Attended "Brigade Tactical Exercises " of 182nd Infantry Brigade in which the 1st. Field Ambulance took part. Accompanied by Major Wilmot D.A.D.M.S. 3rd Army Central Force from 9-30 a.m. to 2-0 p.m. Interviewed the G.O.C. on various subjects. At 4-30. p.m. attended Conference of G.O.C. at Boreham House.

Sept 25. Under Orders of Central Force (through the 3rd Army,) I proceeded to Clacton-on-Sea and arranged to hold Medical Boards on Provisional Battalions in the 7th Provisional Brigade at Clacton-on-Sea, Frinton-on-Sea and Wivenhoe.

Sept 26th. Interviewed the G.O.C. 7th Provisional Brigade and made all necessary arrangements to hold the various Boards in his Brigade. Also held a consultation with the D.A.D.M.S. 3rd Army, Central Force who was at Clacton-on-Sea on duty for the day. Interviewed the President of the " Travelling Medical Board " and made all arrangements with him for conducting the various Boards in the South Midland Divisional area.

Sept 27th. At Clacton-on-Sea (in a room lent the Board by the 107th Provisional Battalion,) held a Medical Board on the 107th Provisional Battalion (96 Imperial Service Men) 82nd Provisional Battalion (83 Imperial Service Men.) Total 179.

In addition, by order of the Brigadier-General Commanding 7th Provisional Brigade, held a Medical Board on Lieut. W. J. Marshall, 29th Provisional Battalion, 7th Provisional Brigade, and forwarded the report of the Board in triplicate to the G.O.C. of the 7th Provisional Brigade. The Board consisted of [redacted] (Colonel. W.H.Bull. A.D.M.S.) [redacted] President.

Major Corfield. R.A.M.C.(T).

Captain Wyne. R.A.M.C.(T).

Sept 28th. Attended the Board at Clacton-on-Sea (with same members) and examined:- 107th Provisional Battalion. 14 Imperial Service Men.
28th Provisional Battalion. 283 Imperial Service Men.
TOTAL. 297.

Sept 29th. Attended at Clacton - on- Sea (with same members) and examined 240 Imperial Service Men of the 82nd Provisional Brigade.

Sept 30th. Examined at Clacton-on-Sea 51 Imperial Service Men of the 82nd. Provisional Battalion. Proceeded to Frinton-on-Sea and examined at the Headquarters, 108th Provisional Brigade. 43 Imperial Service Men.

@:@:@:@:@:@:@:@:@:@:@:@:@:@:@:@:@:@

H H Bull -

COLONEL.

ASSISTANT DIRECTOR OF MEDICAL SERVICES.

61 (SOUTH MIDLAND) DIVISION.

R.A.M.C

Was absent from Headquarters during the first few days of October holding Medical Boards in the 7th & 8th Provisional Brigades as ordered by Central Force, returning on the evening of the 4th, having examined 1227 men, of whom 643 were recommended for duty overseas, 94 temporarily unfit, 476 recommended for Home Service & 14 for discharge.

Owing to troops moving from Camps into Billets the Divisional Sanitary Officer has visited the various centres of new billets and reported satisfactorily on them.

The 3rd. Field Ambulance have taken the London County Council Schools, Brentwood, which comfortably accommodates the Unit.

As there is an outbreak of Scarlet Fever in Great Baddow, I recommended the 2/3rd. South Midland Brigade Royal Field Artillery should not be billeted in that village, they were consequently told off to Writtle village where the accommodation was sufficient. Attended the "Divisional Operations" and made a thorough inspection of their Sanitary & other arrangements, which, on the whole had been well carried out. Found the 2/4th Oxon & Bucks L.I. without R.A.M.C. Water Duty Men, told off at once 2 men for duty from another Battalion.

The Field Ambulance had selected suitable sites for their Divisional & Advanced Dressing Stations, and practical work was given them with " IMAGINARY ACCIDENTS". It was reported that 2 Mules were not sufficient to draw a Water Cart (when full of water) on heavy ground or up hills, same remark applied to Field Ambulance Wagons. In one Unit a team of 4 Mules pulled the Water Cart. One Field Ambulance was still without "RIDING HORSES" for Officers, but these have now been supplied.

It was noted that the Medical Officers arranged (in the Brigade marching from Epping to the Trenches) for the Regimental Sanitary Squads to dig small latrines for the men when they halted.

In order that the R.A.M.C. Water Duty Men should be conversant with the uses of the New Water Carts, I held a class at

Oaklands and requested the various Water Duty Men and Medical Officers to attend a Practical Demonstration.

Medical Boards on Officers (6) have been held during the month, & the D.A.D.M.S. 3rd Army & of this Division have held Boards on all men to be transferred from present to Provisional Units (or for discharge).

Met the D.D.M.S. CENTRAL FORCE at Epping & inspected the whole Camp, accompanied by the Sanitary Officer Central Force & D.A.D.M.S. 3rd Army and also by the Brigade Commander.

The Camp was found in a clean condition & gave the D.D.M.S. every satisfaction.

The Horsfall destructor had not been used for destruction of fæces and a special report was to be called for on the subject.

Received instructions to disinfect 3,027 lice-infected blankets from the London Divisional Camp at Ongar & with the Officer i/c Barracks made arrangements for same, but owing to the limited means at my disposal (only one Thresh's disinfector for the whole Division) the process will be slow.

Under instructions from Central Force, visited, with most of the Medical Officers in the Division " THE SURGICAL EXHIBITION " in London, of splints and many other new appliances now used at the FRONT.

The Division has been very free from sickness, no serious cases being recorded. Several cases have been admitted into the Hospital, but mostly of a minor nature, a number being admitted only for transfer to Cambridge Hospital for operations.

The Sanitation of the District is good, the question of connecting the drainage of Great Baddow Hutments with the main village drains is under consideration.

The work done during the month by the Field Ambulances has been good and both the D.A.D.M.S. 3rd Army & myself notice a great improvement.

My shortage of Medical Officers becomes greater, as now three (3) Home Service Medical Officers are transferred to the Provisional Brigade & have not yet been replaced, hence I am compelled to call in Civil Medical Practitioners.

Boreham House.
Chelmsford.
6. XI. 15.

W. W. Bull
COLONEL,
ASSISTANT DIRECTOR OF MEDICAL SERVICES,
61 (SOUTH MIDLAND) DIVISION.

CONFIDENTIAL

Instructions regarding War Diaries and Intelligence Summaries are contained in F. S. Regs., Part II. and the Staff Manual respectively. Title Pages will be prepared in manuscript.

WAR DIARY

~~WAR DIARY~~ or ~~INTELLIGENCE SUMMARY~~

(Erase heading not required.)

R.A.M.C.
61st S.M. DIVISION.

Army Form C. 2118

NOVEMBER, 1915.

Place	Date	Hour	Summary of Events and Information	Remarks and references to Appendices
Head Quarters. 61st (S.M.) Division. Boreham House - Chelmsford	1915 November		On the 1st instant a case of small-pox was reported at "Oaklands", sent in (as a suspicious throat" to be watched) from 2/2nd S.M. Bde., R.F.A., Great Baddow Hutment. Five R.A.M.C.T. M.Os. with experience of that disease were ordered to see the case, and all unanimously diagnosed "undoubted small-pox". Case was sent to Small Pox Hospital, and every precaution taken, and duly notified to 3rd Army, C.F., and W.O.	
			Durig the 3rd week the man was successfully re-vaccinated. Local Gov. Board asked for a Wassermann's test to be taken, suggesting it to be a case of syphilis. The result was, however, "NEGATIVE". At end of month consulted with Santary Officer, Central Force, and Div. Sanitary Officer, and arrived at the conclusion it was a case of an "infective nature" "simulating small-pox"-but-"not to be found in the nomenclature of diseases".	
			During the month, have, in accordane with special orders, medically examined all Commanding Officers, and Staff Officers, and held Standig Medical Boards on 269 NC.Os. and men, Result:- Category "A" 92, Category "B" 39, Category "C" 135, Category "D" 3 these figures cannot be considered satisfactory, but the number of men who have been enrolled as "Medically fit", yet on examination found "Unfit" speaks for itself.	
			"Oaklands" Hospital has had a "Recreation Hut" erected on the grounds for Convalescent cases, and is a great boon. The work at the Hospital (under Major Mackie) is making steady and satisfactory progress, and the Engineers are by degrees carrying out the work of removing old wall papers, and colour washing the rooms, etc., etc.,	
			Inclement weather has compelled me to ask for a "covered place" for cases of scabies, as the Hospital Marquees, having no heating apparatus, are getting too cold and wet.	
			Inoculation percentages gradually increase. Owing to the alarm of small-pox, a large number rushed to be vaccinated, including the whole staff at "Oaklands" Hospital.	
			I have interviewed, and am giving all possible assistance to the new Divisional Dental Surgeon, but experience has conclusively shown me that my original recommendation of a Dentist for this Division (or area) would save the country hundreds of pounds, and have again recommended it for serious consideration.	
			Under orders from C.F., a Lecture on Venereal Disease was given by Mr. E. B.Turner,F.R.C.S. (London).	
			Since my last report, the 2/1st Beds. Yeomanry have joined this Division, billeted at Hatfield Peverell, and I have made all the necessary arrangements for supply of medical equipment, and have interviewed the O.C.	

1875 Wt. W593/826 1,000,000 4/15 J.B.C. & A. A.D.S.S./Forms/C. 2118.

Army Form C. 2118

Instructions regarding War Diaries and Intelligence Summaries are contained in F. S. Regs., Part II. and the Staff Manual respectively. Title Pages will be prepared in manuscript.

~~WAR DIARY~~

or

INTELLIGENCE SUMMARY

(Erase heading not required.)

Place	Date	Hour	Summary of Events and Information	Remarks and references to Appendices
	1915 November		Another class of chiropody has been formed to train and qualify men for units that did not comply with last Divisional Order to attend the last course of instruction. The question of connecting up Great Baddow Sailment Drainage with the village main drain, has received considerable attention, owing to the occasional faulty condition of present system. The London Details Division, Ongar Camp, has been much troubled with vermin, and I was called upon to disinfect 3,027 lice infected blankets in Thresh's Disinfector, which (under severe pressure) has been carried out, and a Board will be held over them prior to being sent away. During the month I have visited a large number of the Units, inspecting billets, and found the houses and bedrooms clean and well kept, but in a large majority of cases, two men were sleeping together in full sized beds. At the Orderly Rooms, investigated the A.Fs. B.178, which in nearly every instance were either not filled in at all, or most incompletely so. A Divisional Order (No.678, dated 10.11.15.) called upon O.C's. to give this matter their attention. Again I call attention to the unnecessary waste of food. On inspecting "Swill tubs" and "recepticle bins" a large amount of bread, meat, and vegetables were found wasted. Potatoes are peeled far too thickly. In my opinion potatoes are far better boiled in their jackets, this saves both waste and labour, and is by far the most pleasant way to eat them. At the Headquarters, Mechanical Transport, the waste of food was so great that I made a special report on same, and a Board of Enquiry was held at which I gave evidence. The training of the Field Ambulances continues satisfactory, and Weekly ~~Training~~ Programmes are drawn out for their guidance - an improvement in the work is noted. It is still most unsatisfactory being so short of Medical Officers, and I find since winter has set in, the C.M.P's. are not over inclined to offer their services, owing to heavy pressure of work in their own private practices. W H Bull COLONEL, ASSISTANT DIRECTOR OF MEDICAL SERVICES, 61(SOUTH MIDLAND) DIVISION.	

Confidential –

War Diary of

The A.D.M.S. 61st (S.M.) Division

From 1st December 1915 to 31st December 1915 –

(Volume 2)

Instructions regarding War Diaries and Intelligence Summaries are contained in F. S. Regs., Part II. and the Staff Manual respectively. Title Pages will be prepared in manuscript.

WAR DIARY

or

~~INTELLIGENCE SUMMARY~~

(Erase heading not required.)

Army Form C. 2118

Place	Date	Hour	Summary of Events and Information	Remarks and references to Appendices
HEADQUARTERS.	Dec 1st.	2-30 p.m.	Sent D.A.D.M.S. to OAKLANDS HOSPITAL to report on present conditions of Hospital Marquees used for cases of Scabies and Vermin.	
61st.S.M.D.	" 2nd.	10 a.m.	Attended conference of G. O. C.	
Boreham House,	" "	11.30.	Held Medical Board on CAPTAIN W.J.CADE. A.V.C., LIEUT. B.B.JACK. CYCLIST COMPANY and 2nd LIEUT J.HOLMES 2/4th Bde. R.F.A. (HOW) under orders of G.O.C. 61st.(South Midland) Division.	
	do.	3p.m.	Visited Headquarters 2/4th BN. OXON & BUCKS L.I. and inspected Medical & Surgical Panniers and rest of equipment in M.O.Inspection Room.	
CHELMSFORD.			Medical Officer 2/1st. BEDS YEOMANRY notified me (on phone) that 4 cases of Dyphtheria (one fatal) among civilians was reported to him by M.O.H. HATFIELD PEVEREL. Informed Divisional Sanitary Officer and ordered investigation & necessary action.	
ESSEX.	3rd.	10.30. a.m.	Visited CHELMSFORD WORKHOUSE and inspected their disused "Infectious Building" with view of renting same for use of Scabies and verminous cases, as the Hospital Marquees were getting too wet & cold for the cases at OAKLANDS.	
	4th.	11-0 a.m.	Examined 10 men at WITHAM (R.F's) who were placed on subsistence owing to extraction of many teeth.	
			O.C. 2/3rd Field Ambulance interviewed me re. non supply of blinds for the L.C.C.SCHOOLS BRENTWOOD where the Unit under his Command was billeted- took action.	
	do	12 noon.	Visited Headquarters, 2/1st. BEDS YEOMANRY HATFIELD PEVEREL and interviewed M.O. re.- the out-break of Dyphtheria in civilians.	
	5th.		----- SUNDAY-------	
	6th	11.a.m.	Visited OAKLANDS HOSPITAL recommended a case of hemiphlegia sent in from Super.Co. Essex Regt. be sent to Colchester Military Hospital in Motor Ambulance under care of M.O. & Orderlies. Visited Headquarters 2/4th BATTALION ROYAL BERKS REGT. in New London Road.	
	7th	10 a.m.	Motored to BRENTWOOD & visited 2/3rd. S.M.Field Ambulance Hospital. Headquarters 2/4th & 2/6th Battn. Gloucester Regiment & interviewed in each case the O.C's and the M.O's. Found (in all cases) A.F. B178 not filled properly on page 1.	
	8th.	11.30.	Motored over to HEADQUARTERS, 3rd ARMY C.F. to interview A.D.M.S. 3rd ARMY on various matters	
	9th.		Granted with sanction of G.O.C. 7 days sick leave to Div. San. Officer.	
	10th.	9.30am.	Receiving notice of case of Dyphtheria at Writtle. Sent D.A.D.M.S. at once to investigate & report. It occured in a man 2/4th Bde (How) R.F.A. who had recently been on leave & undoubtedly caught it at his home. He was removed to a Civil Infectious Hospital & all precautions were carried out.	

1875 Wt. W593/826 1,000,000 4/15 J.B.C. & A. A.D.S.S./Forms/C. 2118.

Army Form C. 2118

WAR DIARY

or

~~INTELLIGENCE SUMMARY~~

(Erase heading not required.)

Instructions regarding War Diaries and Intelligence Summaries are contained in F. S. Regs., Part II. and the Staff Manual respectively. Title Pages will be prepared in manuscript.

Place	Date 1915 DEC.	Hour	Summary of Events and Information	Remarks and references to Appendices
HEADQUARTERS, 61st.(S.M.) Division. Boreham House CHELMSFORD. ESSEX.	11th	10a.m.	Visited 2/1st. S.M.Bde. R.F.A. INGATESTONE. Found an empty House & empty old "Sorting Office" badly kept and dirty. In swill tub found a quantity of bread thrown away. In yard of "Crown Hotel" ground there was a large collection of manure not removed. Notified C.R.A. for immediate action to be taken.	
	12th.	12.45 p.m.	Called at HEADQUARTERS, 2/1st. BUCKS BATTALION re. Lieut. Wilson R.A.M.C.T. being attached for duty vice. Surg-Captn Baker who now is recommended for Home Service & ordered on Sick Leave with eye trouble.	
	13th.	10.45 a.m.	Visited HATFIELD PEVEREL & in conjunction with M.O. 2/1st.BEDS. YEOMANRY., visited many of the Billets. There had been no further cases of Dyphtheria in the village.	
	13th.	7 p.m.	Held consultation with G.O.C. respecting the cold state of Hutments ~~for~~ through removing top boards for cross ventilation.	
	14th.	2 p.m.	Lt. J.E.S.Wilson R.A.M.C.T. reported himself for duty with the 2/1st. Bucks Battalion with effect from the 13th inst.	
		3 p.m.	Visited OAKLANDS HOSPITAL.	
	15th.	11a.m.	Held Standing Medical Board(AT OAKLANDS INSPECTION ROOM) on 11 men of R.E's. Board consisting of Colonel W.H.Bull, A.D.M.S. 61st.(S.M.) Division; Lt. Col. Craig, R.A.M.C.T. O.C. 2/2nd S.M.Field Ambulance & Captain Moore R.A.M.C.T. 2/2nd. S.M.Field Ambulance.(Members.)	
	15th.	6p.m.	Owing to accounts of the late Quartermaster (Hon. Captn Kimpton) 2/1st. S.M.Field Ambulance not being considered satisfactory, interviewed A.A.&Q.M.G. & ordered present O.C., Q.M. & Q.M.S. of that Field Ambulance to attend.	
	16th	10.45. a.m.	Visited HEADQUARTERS, 2/1st.BEDS YEOMANRY & owing to M.O. being ill with Influenza, detailed Captain McLannahan R.A.M.C.T. (Home Service Officer 2/3rd Field Ambulance) for duty.	
	16th.	10a.m.	Attended Conference of G.O.C.	
	17th	10.30 a.m.	Held Medical Board on 3 men R.E's . Board consisting of Col. W.H.Bull, A.D.M.S. President & Major, W.J.Hoyten D.A.D.M.S. Member.	
	19th.		------------SUNDAY----------	
	20th.	10.30 a.m.	Held Medical Board by order of G.O.C. on 2nd Lieut. Girdler 83rd Provisional Battalion, also on 2nd Lieut. Walker 2/4th Battalion Royal Berks(for commission in Regular Forces) Board:- Col.W.H.Bull A.D.M.S.(President.) Lt.Col.Craig O.C. 2/2nd S.M.Field Ambulance & Major Mackie R.A.M.C.T. 2/1st. S.M.Field Ambulance(Members.)	
	22nd.		Consulted with G.O.C. re. Transport Sections of Field Ambulances R.A.M.C. to A.S.C.T.F.	
	22nd.	10.45 a.m.	Visited OAKLANDS. Interviewed (in CHELMSFORD) an Optician (Mr Boatman F.S.M.C.) re Ophthalmic duties, in accordance with W.O.letter 24/Gen No./3999 (A.M.D.3.) dated 17.12.1915.	

1875 Wt. W593/826 1,000,000 4/15 J.B.C. & A. A.D.S.S./Forms/C. 2118.

Instructions regarding War Diaries and Intelligence Summaries are contained in F. S. Regs., Part II. and the Staff Manual respectively. Title Pages will be prepared in manuscript.

WAR DIARY

or

~~INTELLIGENCE SUMMARY~~

(Erase heading not required.)

Army Fo[rm]

Place	Date	Hour	Summary of Events and Information	Remarks and references to Appendices
HEADQUARTERS, 61st.S.M. Division. Boreham House CHELMSFORD, ESSEX.	1915 DEC. 23rd.	11a.m.	Held Medical Board(Col. W.H.Bull A.D.M.S. (President,) Lt.Col. Craig, R.A.M.C.T. O.C. 2/2nd S.M. Field Ambulance (Member) on 2nd. Lieut. Pollack 2/4th S.M.(HOW) Bde. R.F.A. for admission as "Pilot" in Flying Corps.	
	23rd.	3p.m.	Visited in conjunction with Divisional Sanitary Officer 2/2nd. South Midland Field Ambulance Hospital Danbury, finding every detail satisfactory, also visited No.1 DANBURY HUTMENTS 2/7th Royal Warwick Regiment. The surrounding ground, and some of the Roads, were in a very bad state. (This condition of grounds and roads of Hutments in Division has been reported upon).	
	24th	5 p.m.	Received wire from S.M.O. 183rd Infantry Brigade BRENTWOOD that a man 2/6th Bn. Gloster Regiment had been found dead in his Billet sent him wire to see Kings Regs. para. 1873. were carried out (strictly.)	
	25th		----------- CHRISTMAS DAY ---------	
	26th		----------- S U N D A Y -----------	
	27th		Received 'phone from S.M.O. 183rd Infantry Brigade, that post-mortem had been held on man who died on 24th inst & that Inquest would be held 4-30 p.m. Instructed him to attend & Represent me at Inquest. VERDICT phoned me "NATURAL CAUSES".	
	28th	10.15 a.m.	Visited Oaklands Hospital. Arranged with O.C. 2/1st. S.M.Field Ambulance to attend Court of Enquiry at CHELMSFORD on 29th inst. 10 a.m. and take all witnesses with him.	
	28th	11.15 a.m.	Interviewed Secretary CHELMSFORD (CIVIL) Conjoint Hospital Board re "Kenilworth accounts" Visited HATFIELD PEVEREL & interviewed M.O.i/c 2/1st. BEDS YEOMANRY & ascertained that no further cases of Dyphtheria had occurred among the civil population of village.	
	28th	2.15 p.m.	Visited HUTMENTS at DANBURY of 2/5th & 2/7th Royal Warwicks Regiments and interviewed the M.O.	
	28th	5.30 p.m.	Visited 2/6th & 2/8th Battn Royal Warwicks Regts. and interviewed the M.O. Inspected House for Scabies, only 5 cases remaining .	
	28th.		Received notice that Travelling Medical Board would visit this Division on 3rd January, 1916. Issued notices accordingly.	
	29th	10a.m.	Interviewed O.C. 2/2nd. S.M.Field Ambulance re. SECRET COMPOSITE ~~BOARD~~ Bde. Assembly for 31st inst.	
	30th.	10a.m.	Attended G.O.C's. Conference.	
	30th	10-45 a.m.	Visited BRENTWOOD & interviewed all the Officers 2/3rd South Midland Field Ambulance and attended instructions (Field Ambulance Work) which were being carried out by the unit.	

1875 Wt. W593/826 1,000,000 4/15 J.B.C. & A. A.D.S.S./Forms/C. 2118.

Army Form C. 2118

WAR DIARY

or

~~INTELLIGENCE SUMMARY~~

(Erase heading not required.)

Instructions regarding War Diaries and Intelligence Summaries are contained in F. S. Regs., Part II. and the Staff Manual respectively. Title Pages will be prepared in manuscript.

Place	Date	Hour	Summary of Events and Information	Remarks and references to Appendices
	1915. DEC.			
HEADQUARTERS, 61st.S.M. DIVISION. BOREHAM HOUSE CHELMSFORD ESSEX.	31st.	10.20. a.m.	A Composite Bde Assembly at "COLDNORTON", In accordance with secret orders, I gave secret instructions for attendance of 2/2nd. South Midland Field Ambulance, and placed details in hands of D.A.D.M.S. who took over duty from me this day, I having obtained sanction from G.O.C. to proceed home on leave on urgent private matters,(subject to being immediately recalled in case of emergency).	[illegible]

Headquarters,
Boreham House,
Chelmsford.
DECEMBER 31st, 1915.

[illegible signature]
COLONEL.
ASSISTANT DIRECTOR OF MEDICAL SERVICES,
61st. (SOUTH MIDLAND) DIVISION.

1875 Wt. W593/826 1,000,000 4/15 J.B.C. & A. A.D.S.S./Forms/C. 2118.

Confidential —

War Diary of

— A.D.M.S. — 61st (S.M.) Division —

— From — 1st January 1916 to 31st January 1916 —

— Volume 2 —

Head Quarters — [illegible] House.
Chelmsford —

Instructions regarding War Diaries and Intelligence Summaries are contained in F. S. Regs., Part II. and the Staff Manual respectively. Title Pages will be prepared in manuscript.

WAR DIARY
or
INTELLIGENCE SUMMARY
(Erase heading not required.)

Army Form C. 2118

Place	Date 1916	Hour	Summary of Events and Information	Remarks and references to Appendices
Head Quarters	January 1st to 5th	--	on Leave with sanction of G.O.C. 61st (S.M.) Division	AHS
61st (S.M.) Div.	" 6th	—	Routine work	AHS
Hoslam House	" 7th	—	Routine work	AHS
Chelmsford	" 8th	—	Routine work	AHS
Essex.	" 9th	Sunday	Routine work	AHS.
		9pm	Recd. Report from BACTERIOLOGIST... COLCHESTER. "No Meningo Cocci are to be found in sample of cerebro-spinal fluid sent on 8th inst."	
	" 10th	10.30am	Visited OAKLANDS HOSPITAL & HUTMENTS & found large fatigue Parties sweeping Roads and Removing mud. — Visited KENILWORTH HOSPITAL.	
	"	12 o/c	Called at A.S.C. HQrs re Emergency Boxes whilst the M.O. had taken to his combined Inspection Room.	AHS
	"	2.30pm	Held Medical Board at BOREHAM HOUSE on SURGEON-CAPTAIN BAKER 2/1st BUCKS Bn. by order of G.O.C. 61st S.M. (Div.)	
	"	5.30pm	Held Medical Board on Clerks in Office of A.D.M.S. also on the A.P.M.; O.O.; A.V.C.; Clerks and on the CAMP COMMANDANT.	
	" 11th	9.30am	Recd. Report from COLCHESTER that the culture of spinal fluid in suspected case of C.S.M. was "negative".	
	"	10.30am	A.D.M.S. 3rd ARMY interviewed me & we discussed many details.	AHS
	"	to 12.15pm	Interviewed O. i/c BARRACKS re Barrows & Shovels & trucks for men making new road at	
	"	2-15pm	OAKLANDS HUTMENTS & HOSPITAL.	

1875 Wt. W593/826 1,000,000 4/15 J.B.C. & A. A.D.S.S./Forms/C. 2118.

Army Form C. 2118

Instructions regarding War Diaries and Intelligence Summaries are contained in F. S. Regs., Part II. and the Staff Manual respectively. Title Pages will be prepared in manuscript.

WAR DIARY
or
INTELLIGENCE SUMMARY
(Erase heading not required.)

Place	Date 1916	Hour	Summary of Events and Information	Remarks and references to Appendices
H. Qrs 61st S.M. Div ~~Aukland House.~~ CHELMSFORD	Jany 11th	2-40 pm	Inspected H Qrs Div. Train A.S.C. – found swill tubs containing "Refuse only" – Inspected H Qrs Hutments – Henry St., A.S.C. – found tins with a very large amount of wasted good bread – & picked out an amount representing at least two large loaves / leaving much behind, also three good lbs of lean meat – & other refuse which should not have been thrown away – there was a tendency to waste too much of the good leaves of the Greens – found Paths round Hutments were being made, but – the state of the Road in Horse lines was "deplorable"	[initials]
"		3-30 pm	Visited OAKLAND's – the O.C. 2/1st F. Amb: had spent much labour on making up the Road –	
"	12th	2-30 pm	Visited H. Qrs 2/1st & 2/2nd F. Ambces & inspected the Q.M.'s Books – found same well kept –	[initials]
"		3 pm	Held Medical Board on Clerks in H. Qrs Staff Offices –	
"	13th	9-15 am	Held Med: Board on two Subalterns. R.E. –	[initials]
		10 am	Visited BRENTWOOD – 2/3rd S. M. F. Amb. Hospl. & the Unit (at work) together with their H. Qrs. Interviewed O.C. and exam'd Books of Q.M. found same well kept – Interviewed Capt. OSBORNE – M.O. 2/6th R. Wars Regt.	
"		3 pm	Interviewed M.O. i/c 2/1 Herts Yeo. – for medical attendance on Cyclist Co (61st S.M.D) just arranged with S. M.O. 8th Prov: Bde – transferred to ~~Burnham~~	
"	14th	10 am	CAPT. BOOMER R.A.M.C. 1/1st F. Ambce 48th Div: reported himself for duty at OAKLANDS HOSPL. being Boarded for "Light Duty" –	[initials]

1875 Wt. W593/826 1,000,000 4/15 J.B.C. & A. A.D.S.S./Forms/C. 2118.

Instructions regarding War Diaries and Intelligence Summaries are contained in F. S. Regs., Part II. and the Staff Manual respectively. Title Pages will be prepared in manuscript.

WAR DIARY
or
INTELLIGENCE SUMMARY
(Erase heading not required.)

Army Form C. 2118

Place	Date 1916	Hour	Summary of Events and Information	Remarks and references to Appendices
H Qrs. 61st S.M. Div BOREHAM HOUSE CHELMSFORD.	Jan 14th	10-15am	Held Med: Board on 2/Lieut QUAILE 2/1st Herts Bn by order of G.O.C. —	
	"	11am	Held Med: Board at DANBURY on 2 Chaplains & 12 men 2/5th Bn R War Regt 3 men of 2/1 Rev. & 2 men of ?.C. R.E. —	[illegible]
	"	2-30pm	Held Med: Board at OAKLANDS on 7 Chaplains & one man of 2/1st F. Ambce. interviewed O.C. 2/4th R Berks Regt re exam: of Officers. —	
	15th	10.30am	Held Standing Med: Board — S.M.D. order 5-2/16 — on Officers of 2/1 & 2/2 F. Ambces at OAKLANDS	[illegible]
	16th		Sunday — Routine work — — —	[illegible]
	17th		Held Standing Med: Board — on Officers A.S.C. & A.V.C. & on 4 Officers 2/5th Bn R War Regt at HQrs A.S.C. —	[illegible]
		10.15am	— Ditto — 2/4th Bn Oxford & Bucks L.I. at their H.Qrs. BROOMFIELD —	
		12.30pm to 4pm	Visited Oaklands Hospl. & interviewed O.C. 2/1 S.M.F. Ambce — — —	
	18th	10-15am	Held Standing Med: Board on Officers — 2/4 Bn R Berks Regt & one man with V.D.H. at Herts H.Qrs —	[illegible]
		2-15pm	— Ditto — 2/5th Bn Glos Regt at their H.Qrs — — —	
	"		Temp. Lieut: A.J. Leitch. RAMC. reported himself as Dental Surgeon for Chelmsford Area — — —	authority CR/C7168884 d/7.1.16
	19th	2.30pm	attended Lecture on Poisonous gases by Prof. Major Starling RAMC. at Millbank RAM College — authority:	CR/C7.21067 d/14.1.16
	20th	10-15am	Held Standing Med: Board on Officers 2/1 Bucks Bn & Officers Signal Co. R.E. at H Qrs SPRINGFIELD —	[illegible]
	"	2-15pm	— Ditto — R.E. & A.S.C. at H.Qrs WITHAM.	[illegible]
	"	6pm	— Ditto — on Officers Divisional H Qrs Staff at BOREHAM HOUSE —	
	21st	10-15am	— Ditto — 2/6th Bn R War Regt & Officers 2/2 F. Ambce at MALDON —	[illegible]
	"	2-15pm	Ditto 2/8th " at their H.Qrs also at "	
	"		Visited the MALDON V.R.D. Hospital —	

1875 Wt. W593/826 1,000,000 4/15 J.B.C. & A. A.D.S.S./Forms/C. 2118.

Instructions regarding War Diaries and Intelligence Summaries are contained in F. S. Regs., Part II. and the Staff Manual respectively. Title Pages will be prepared in manuscript.

WAR DIARY
or
INTELLIGENCE SUMMARY
(Erase heading not required.)

Army Form C. 2118

Place	Date 1916	Hour	Summary of Events and Information	Remarks and references to Appendices
H. Qrs 61. S. M. Div	Jany 22nd	10.30am	Held Standing Medical Board on Officers. 2/1 Bed Yeo. at HATFIELD PEVEREL.	
		12 o/c	Do. Do. Cyclist Co. 61 S M D Do.	[illegible]
BOREHAM HOUSE.	"	2.30pm	Visited OAKLAND'S HOSPl. & interviewed O.C. i/c Hospl.	
	"23rd	—	Sunday — Routine work	[illegible]
CHELMSFORD.	"24th	10 am	Held Standing Med: Board on Officers. 2/5 Bn. R. Wars Regt. at DANBURY	
	"	12-15pm	Do. Do. Head Qrs. 182 Inf: Bde. Do.	
	"	2-15pm	Do. Do. 2/7th Bn. R. Wars Regt. Do.	[illegible]
	"	4.30pm	Called at H. Qrs. R.F.A. & arranged for Med: Board for Officers of the Bdes.	
	"25th	8.30am	Held Standing Med: Board on Officers. 2/4 Bn. Glos Regt. at BRENTWOOD	
	"	12 o/c	Ditto Do. 2/3rd S. M. F. Ambce. Ditto	[illegible]
	"	2pm	Ditto Do. 2/6th Bn. Glos Regt. Ditto	
	"	4-30pm	Visited & inspected 2/3rd F. Ambce. Hospl.	Ditto
			2/7th Bn. Wors Regt. Ditto	
	"26th	8.30am	Held Standing Med; Board on Officers 2/8th Bn. Wors Regt. Ditto	[illegible]
	"	12 o/c	Ditto A. S. C. Ditto	
	"	2-45pm	Ditto 2/2 & 2/3 R.F.A. Bdes. & R.F.A. at H. Qrs. Gt. BADDOW ROAD	
	"27th	10-15am	Ditto 2/4 S.M. How Bde. 2/3 R.F.A. Bde. & H. Qrs. Staff Do.	[illegible]
	"	2-15pm	Ditto 2/1st R.F.A. Bde. at H. Qrs. INGATESTONE	
	"28th	10-30am	Ordered Div: San: Officer to proceed to R.A.M. College Millbank to attend Lectures "on Poisonous gases" on 29th & 30th inst. in accordance with orders from C. F. sent by phone through A.D.M.S. 3rd Army	
	"		Called at OAKLANDS HOSPl. & interviewed O. C. 2/1 S.M. F. Ambce.	[illegible]
	"	9. am	Was notified by O.C. 2/3rd F. Ambce. he had closed Hospl. for week owing to outbreak of one case of Diphtheria & ~~Sent Formalin Spray & Solution~~ with Special Orderly, & orders to carry out all reqd. precautions & notified at once Div: San: Officer	

Instructions regarding War Diaries and Intelligence Summaries are contained in F. S. Regs., Part II. and the Staff Manual respectively. Title Pages will be prepared in manuscript.

WAR DIARY
or
INTELLIGENCE SUMMARY
(Erase heading not required.)

Army Form C. 2118

Place	Date 1916	Hour	Summary of Events and Information	Remarks and references to Appendices
H. Qrs 61st S. M/Div.	January 29th	—	Routine work — — — — —	HHM
BOREHAM HOUSE.	" 30th	Sunday.	Routine work — — — — —	HHM
CHELMSFORD.	" 31st	10 am	Proceeded to LONDON to interview — by Request — DDMS. C.F. at whose request & orders I then proceeded to W.O. & interviewed Staff Officer to D.G. — — — — —	HHM

Head Quarters 61st S. M/Division —
Borham House,
Chelmsford
31 – 1 – 16.

HHBull
COLONEL
ASSISTANT DIRECTOR OF MEDICAL SERVICES
61 (SOUTH MIDLAND) DIVISION.

1875 Wt. W593/826 1,000,000 4/15 J.B.C. & A. A.D.S.S./Forms/C. 2118.

MAY 1916.

A.D.M.S. 61st DIVISION.

Instructions regarding War Diaries and Intelligence Summaries are contained in F. S. Regs., Part II. and the Staff Manual respectively. Title Pages will be prepared in manuscript.

WAR DIARY
or
INTELLIGENCE SUMMARY
(Erase heading not required.)

Army Form

ADMS 61 Div
Vol 1

Place	Date 1916	Hour	Summary of Events and Information	Remarks and references to Appendices
LE HAVRE	May 23rd	7.30 a.m.	The Headquarters Staff of the 61st S.M. Division having left CHOLDERTON, WILTS on the afternoon of May 22nd and proceeded via SOUTHAMPTON — LE HAVRE arrived at the latter port at 7.30 a.m. on the 23rd	Reference Map FRANCE Sheet No. 36a Scale 1-40.000
		10.30 a.m.	Reported arrival to D.A.Q.M.G. Base and also to A.D.M.S. HAVRE.	
Do.	May 24th	6 pm	Left LE HAVRE by train.	
St. VENANT	May 25th	3.30 p.m.	Detrained BERGUETTE: proceeded by motor car to ST. VENANT the Headquarters of the Division 2/1st S.M. Fd. Amb. proceeded by march route to VERTE BOIS	
Do.	May 26th	11 a.m.	Reported arrival to D.D.M.S. XIth Corps. by whom I was instructed to arrange with A.D.M.S. 39th Division to take over the buildings occupied by the 134th Fd. Amb. at ROBECQ for the use of the 2/3rd Field Amb. of this Division and also to arrange with A.D.M.S. 35th Division to take over buildings occupied by a Fd. Amb. of that Div. at CALONNE sur la LYS for the use of the 2/2nd Fd. Amb.	
Do	May 27th	10.30 a.m.	Proceeded by motor car to AIRE and reported arrival to D.M.S. 1st Army.	
		11.30 a.m.	Visited 137th Fd. Amb at ROBECQ with reference to arrangements for taking over. 2/2nd Fd. Amb. reported arrival at GONNEHEM	
Do	May 28th		Routine Duties.	
		3 pm	D.A.D.M.S XIth Corps called with reference to one or two matters.	
		midnight	2/3rd Fd. Amb. arrived at BUSNES	

1875 Wt. W593/826 1,000,000 4/15 J.B.C. & A. A.D.S.S./Forms/C. 2118.

Army Form C. 2118

Instructions regarding War Diaries and Intelligence Summaries are contained in F. S. Regs., Part II. and the Staff Manual respectively. Title Pages will be prepared in manuscript.

WAR DIARY
or
INTELLIGENCE SUMMARY
(Erase heading not required.)

Place	Date 1916	Hour	Summary of Events and Information	Remarks and references to Appendices
ST. VENANT	May 29th.	9.30	Proceeded by motor car to GONNEHEM to instruct O.C. 2/2nd Fd. Amb. with reference to his move to CALONNE. Thence to BUSNES to instruct O.C. 2/3rd Fd. Amb. with reference to his move to ROBECQ.	Reference Map FRANCE Sheet No 36? Scale 1-40,000
		3 p.m	attended Div. Hdqtrs. to meet G.O.C. 1st ARMY	
DO.	May 30th		Routine Duties.	
		3.30 p	The 2/2nd Fd. Amb. moved to CALONNE sur la LYS, and reported arrival there.	
DO	May 31st	11 a.m	The 2/3 Fd. Amb moved to ROBECQ and reported arrival there.	
		2.30 p.m	Proceeded by motor car to LESTREM to discuss with A.D.M.S. 35th Division arrangements for attachment of 2/2 Fd. Amb. for training. Returned via La GORGUE where I visited and inspected Baths and Laundry under supervision of Capt JAMES 14th Gloster Regt.	

James Young

COLONEL.
ASSISTANT DIRECTOR OF MEDICAL SERVICES
61st (SOUTH MIDLAND) DIVISION

1875 Wt. W593/826 1,000,000 4/15 J.B.C. & A. A.D.S.S./Forms/C. 2118.

19

Vol 2

3911

Confidential

War Diary

A.D.M.S. 61st Division

June 1916.

June/16

Instructions regarding War Diaries and Intelligence Summaries are contained in F. S. Regs., Part II. and the Staff Manual respectively. Title Pages will be prepared in manuscript.

WAR DIARY
or
INTELLIGENCE SUMMARY
(Erase heading not required.)

Army Form C. 2118

Place	Date	Hour	Summary of Events and Information	Remarks and references to Appendices
St VENANT.	1/6/16	10. A.M.	Baths opened by O.C. Sanitary Section for Headquarters at 10. A.M. and all other Units at St VENANT. (P.4.a.10.4)	Reference Map. France Sheet. 36A. Scale. 1-40,000
"	1/6/16	3.15 p.m.	Proceeded to LE VERTBOIS (K.26.a.7.8) and inspected Sanitary and all other arrangements of 2/1st S.M. FIELD AMBULANCE.	
"	2/6/16		Routine work.	
"	3/6/16		Routine work.	
"	4/6/16		Routine work.	
"	5/6/16		Inspected 2/3rd S. M. FIELD AMBULANCE at ROBECQ (P.23.b.8.8.) and gave instructions regarding Sanitary and other arrangements. Instructed O.C. 2/3rd S.M. Field Ambulance to have the baths put into repair immediately and to put same into use with least possible delay.	
	6/6/16		Proceeded to CALONNE (Q.3.c.6.2.) and inspected Sanitary and other arrangements of 2/2nd S.M. FIELD AMBULANCE and suggested various improvements.	
	7/6/16		Routine work.	
	8/6/16		Routine work	
	9/6/16		Proceeded to Hd Qrs. 11th Corps (W.16.a.7.6.) to attend D.D.M.S. Conference.	
	10/6/16		Ordered D.A.D.M.S to proceed to LA GORGUE (L.35.b.4.6.) and interview A.D.M.S. 38th DIVISION previous to taking over from him on 13th inst.	
	11/6/16		Routine work.	

1875 Wt. W593/826 1,000,000 4/15 J.B.C. & A. A.D.S.S./Forms/C. 2118.

3921

Instructions regarding War Diaries and Intelligence Summaries are contained in F. S. Regs., Part II. and the Staff Manual respectively. Title Pages will be prepared in manuscript.

WAR DIARY
or
INTELLIGENCE SUMMARY
(Erase heading not required.)

Army Form C. 2118

Place	Date	Hour	Summary of Events and Information	Remarks and references to Appendices
LA GORGUE	12/6/16	10.A.M.	Proceeded to LA GORGUE (L.35.b.4.6) with 61st S.M Division and took over Medical Administration of area previously occupied by 38th Division & now occupied by 61st Div. Took over Headquarters of A.D.M.S. 38th Division as my Headquarters. Notified D.D.M.S CORPS of arrival & position, and positions of 1st. 2nd. 3rd Field Ambulances. Baths & Laundry opened at LA GORGUE. (L.35.b.0.7)	
	13/6/16		Inspected 3rd Field Ambulance at LA GORGUE (L.35.b.9.9) also CORPS REST STATION and SKIN DEPÔT at MERVILLE (K.29.d.2.9) run by 2nd FIELD AMBULANCE.	
	14/6/16		Proceeded to Headquarters Corps (W.16.a.7.6) on instructions from D.D.M.S. 11th CORPS.	
	15/6/16		Inspected 2/2 Field Ambulance MERVILLE (K.29.d.2.9) and 2/1st Field Ambulance at LA GORGUE. (L.35.b.6.2) Examined 5 men unfit for duty to be sent to Base.	
	16/6/16		Examined 4 men unfit for duty. Inspected 2/2 S.M. Field Ambulance at MERVILLE (K.29.d.2.9.) also MOBILE VETERINARY SECTION LA GORGUE	
	17/6/16	10.A.M.	Inspected Baths and Laundry at LA GORGUE (L.35.b.0.7) with D.A.Q.M.G. 61st S.M. DIVISION.	
	"	3.p.m.	Proceeded to A.D.S. LAVENTIE (G.34.c.6.3.) of 2/1st Field Ambulance and inspected same, also COLLECTING POST EAST of LAVENTIE and R.A. POSTS at RED BARN (M.6.d.2.0.) and HUGUEMONT. (M.12.c.3.4.)	
	18/6/16	10.A.M.	Inspected 2/3rd Field Ambulance.	
	"	3.p.m.	Visited Advanced Dressing Station of 3rd Field Ambulance at GREEN BARN (M.27.d.5.2) and R.A. POSTS at EBENZEER FARM (M.34.b.5.9½.) STIRLING CASTLE (S.4.d.4.10) and MOGGS HOLE. (M.35.c.5.6.)	
	19/6/16		Routine work.	
	20/6/16		Routine work.	

1875 Wt. W593/826 1,000,000 4/15 J.B.C. & A. A.D.S.S./Forms/C. 2118.

393

Army Form C. 2118

Instructions regarding War Diaries and Intelligence Summaries are contained in F. S. Regs., Part II. and the Staff Manual respectively. Title Pages will be prepared in manuscript.

WAR DIARY
or
INTELLIGENCE SUMMARY
(Erase heading not required.)

Place	Date	Hour	Summary of Events and Information	Remarks and references to Appendices
LA GORGUE.	21/6/16		Inspected CORPS REST STATION MERVILLE (K.29.d.2.9) also CHATEAU DEMON at MERVILLE (K.22.d.5.3) which is to be opened as OFFICERS REST STATION.	
	22/6/16		Inspected 1st and 3rd Field Ambulances (L.30.b.6.2) (L.35.b.9.9) LA GORGUE. A.D.S of 3rd Field Ambulance at LA FLINQUE (M.10.c.7.1). Collecting post L'EPINETTE FARM (M.16.d.6.6) and R.A.P. at WINCHESTER HOUSE (M.23.a.3½.1)	
	23/6/16		Routine work.	
	23/6/16	5 pm	Attended Lecture on Gas.	
	24/6/16		Inspected 1st & 3rd (L.34.b.6.2) (L.35.b.9.9) Field Ambulances with D.D.M.S. CORPS at LA GORGUE	
	25/6/16		Routine Work.	
	26/6/16		Visited CORPS REST STATION (K.29.d.9.9), SKIN DEPÔT (K.34.d.8.8) and OFFICERS REST STATION (K.22.d.5.3) MERVILLE and 1st Field Ambulance LA GORGUE. (L.34.b.6.2)	
	27/6/16		Routine work	
	28/6/16		Routine work	
	29/6/16		Visited A.D.S LA FLINQUE (M.10.c.7.1) and GREEN BARN (M.27.d.5.2) and BATHS at CROIX BARBEE (M.26.c.8.3)	
	30/6/16		Proceeded to LAVENTIE (M.4.d.0.6) to see if another suitable place for A.D.S. could be obtained. No other suitable place available.	

James [illegible] Colonel
A.D.M.S. 61st Divn.

3/7/16

3942

61

July/16

Volume 3.

Vol 3

War Diary

A.D.M.S. 61st Division.

July 1916.

Instructions regarding War Diaries and Intelligence Summaries are contained in F. S. Regs., Part II. and the Staff Manual respectively. Title Pages will be prepared in manuscript.

WAR DIARY
or
INTELLIGENCE SUMMARY
(Erase heading not required.)

Army Form C. 2118

Place	Date	Hour	Summary of Events and Information	Remarks and references to Appendices
LA. GORGUE	1 7/16		Inspected A.D.S. at LAVENTIE. G.34.c.6.3 Inspected A.D.S. at LA.FLINQUE. M.10.c.7.1.	Map references Square 36 S.W. L.35.b.4.6
"	2 7/16		Routine work.	
"	3 7/16		Inspected 1st & 2nd Field Ambulances with D.D.M.S. 11th Corps	
"	4 7/16		Routine work.	
"	5 7/16		Routine work.	
"	6 7/16		Visited A.D.S. at LA FLINQUE M.10.c.7.1 and GREEN BARN M.27.d.5.2 and baths at CROIX BARBEE. M.26.c.8.3	
		3 p.m.	Attended Conference D.D.M.S. 11th Corps at HINGES W.6.a.2.8. and arranged for certain alterations in Medical arrangements.	
"	7 7/16		Routine work.	
"	8 7/16		Routine work.	
"	9 7/16		Visited 1st Field Ambulance. L.34.b.6.2.	
"	10 7/16		Visited Main Dressing Station of 3rd Field Ambulance at VIEILLE CHAPELLE. R.34.a.9.9. Auxiliary Dressing Station at ZELOBES. R.26.d.10.4. Collecting Post at KING GEORGES POST. X.5.d.5.2 Baths at LESTREM. R.8.b.10.8.	
"	11 7/16		Attended presentation of parchment certificate for gallantry to Pte Packer. 3rd Field Ambulance by G.O.C. 61st Division. Conference of O.C. 3 Field Ambulances.	
"	12 7/16		Visited billets of 6th Warwicks at RIEZ BAILLEUL. M.7.d.5.5.	
"	13 7/16		Visited 1st Field Ambulance. L.34.b.6.2. Corps Rest Station. MERVILLE. K.29.d.2.9. Officers Rest Station MERVILLE. K.22.d.5.3 and Corps Skin Depot. REGNIER LE CLERCQ. K.34.d.8.8.	

1875 Wt. W593/826 1,000,000 4/15 J.B.C. & A. A.D.S.S./Forms/C. 2118.

396J

Instructions regarding War Diaries and Intelligence Summaries are contained in F. S. Regs., Part II. and the Staff Manual respectively. Title Pages will be prepared in manuscript.

WAR DIARY
or
INTELLIGENCE SUMMARY
(Erase heading not required.)

Army Form C. 2118

Place	Date	Hour	Summary of Events and Information	Remarks and references to Appendices
LA GORGUE	14/7/16		Routine work. Attended conference with DDMS. 11th Corps at HINGES. W.16.a.2.8.	L.35.b.4.6
"	15/7/16		Routine work.	
"	16/7/16		Routine work.	
	17/7/16		Routine work. Visited 1st Field Ambulance at LA GORGUE L.34.b.6.2. and 3rd Field Ambulance LA GORGUE. L.35.b.9.9., also A.D.S. LAVENTIE G.34.c.6.3. Lieut R. M. McMINN R.A.M.C. reported for duty and was posted to 3rd Field Ambulance.	
"	18/7/16		Visited Corps Rest Station. MERVILLE. K.29.d.2.9.	
"	19/7/16		Operations in which 61st Division took part.	See Appendix I
"	20/7/16			
"	20/7/16		Inspected collecting Post at LAVANTIE EAST. M5c7.9. and R.A.Ps at RED HOUSE M.6.d.2.0. and HOUGOMONT. M.12c.3.4. with D.A.D.M.S. 1st ARMY.	
"	21/7/16		G.O.C. 1st Army & G.O.C. Corps visited and inspected 1st Field Ambulance. L.34.b.6.2.	
"	22/7/16		Routine duties.	
"	23/7/16		Attended Conference held by D.D.M.S 11th Corps HINGES. W.16.a.2.8. Inspected 1st Field Ambulance.	
	24/7/16		Held conference with all Regimental M.Os.	
	25/7/16		Attended Conference at DHQ. L.35.b.4.6 with officers "Q" Branch. Inspected Corps Rest Station MERVILLE. K.29.d.2.9. & Corps Skin Depôt REGNIER LE CLERCQ. K.34.d.8.8.	
	26/7/16		Routine duty.	

1875 Wt W593/826 1,000,000 4/15 J.B.C. & A. A.D.S.S./Forms/C. 2118.

Army Form C. 2118

Instructions regarding War Diaries and Intelligence Summaries are contained in F. S. Regs., Part II. and the Staff Manual respectively. Title Pages will be prepared in manuscript.

WAR DIARY
or
INTELLIGENCE SUMMARY

(Erase heading not required.)

Place	Date	Hour	Summary of Events and Information	Remarks and references to Appendices
LA GORGUE.	27/7/16		Visited LAVENTIE. G.34.c.6.3 with O.C. Sanitary Section to inspect billets etc	L.35.b.4.6
	28/7/16	5.30pm	Attended address on "Pyrexias of Unknown origin" by Capt McNEE and Capt GALLOWAY.	
	29/7/16		Routine duties	
	30/7/16		Routine work.	
	31/7/16		2nd Field Amb took over main & A.D.S. at LA GORGUE L.34.b.6.2 and LAVENTIE G.34.c.6.3 and 1st Field Ambulance took over Corps Rest Station K.29.d.2.9. Corps Skin Depôt K.34.d.8.8. and Officers Rest Station. MERVILLE. K.22.d.5.3	
			Visited Corps Rest Station. K.29.d.2.9.	

James Young
COLONEL
ASSISTANT DIRECTOR OF MEDICAL SERVICES
61st ~~SOUTH MIDLAND~~ DIVISION.

1875 Wt. W593/826 1,000,000 4/15 J.B.C. & A. A.D.S.S./Forms/C. 2118.

3985

399J

Appendix 1. Operations July. 19th 1916.

On July 18th the following extract from 61st Divisional Orders No 31 were received.

" The operations detailed in 61st Div Orders Nos 28 + 29 for the 17th July will be carried out as therein detailed on 19th July. The hour of Zero will not be earlier than 11. A.M."

In view of the above order the medical arrangements as detailed in Appendix 2 were drawn up and circulated to Os. C. 1st and 3rd Field Ambulances; one copy was sent to D.H.Q and approved.

The personnel of the 1st and 3rd Field Ambulances was augmented by the following:

Captain KING and Lieut WALES of the 94th Field Ambulance 31st Div reported for temporary duty and were posted to the 1st Fd Ambulance.

Lieuts J.B. ALEXANDER and J.C. BLACKMORE of the 93rd Fd Ambulance 31st Division reported for temporary duty and were posted to the 3rd Field Ambulance.

Captain BANNERMAN and one Bearer Sub Division of the 2nd Fd Amb reported for temporary duty and were posted to 1st Fd Ambulance.

Captain MOORE and one bearer Sub Division of the 2nd Fd Ambulance reported for temporary duty and were posted to 3rd Fd Ambulance.

All the arrangements worked perfectly and without a single hitch. At no period was the accommodation strained and the evacuation from the Main Dressing Stations and the Divisional Collecting Station, where the slighter cases were dealt with, was most efficiently carried out by the No 2 Motor Ambulance Convoy and No 13 Motor Ambulance Convoy respectively.

By nine A.M on the 20th, I was able to report that the whole of the trenches were clear of wounded.

The total number of wounded dealt with was 977 including 46 Officers.

James Glover[?]

COLONEL.
ASSISTANT DIRECTOR OF MEDICAL SERVICES
61st ~~SOUTH MIDLAND~~ DIVISION.

Appendix ii.

4005
SP

S E C R E T.

MEDICAL ARRANGEMENTS.

MAIN DRESSING STATIONS.	IST. FIELD AMBULANCE.	LA GORGUE.	L.34.b.6.2.
	3RD. FIELD AMBULANCE.	LA GORGUE.	L.35.b.9.9.
ADVANCED DRESSING STATION.		LAVENTIE.	C.34.c.6.3.
COLLECTING POST.		LAVENTIE EAST.	M.5.c.7.9.
REGIMENTAL AID POSTS.		RED HOUSE.	M.6.d.2.0.
		HOUGOMONT.	M.I2.c.3.4.

In addition to the above, it is proposed to utilise the DIVISIONAL THEATRE. LA GORGUE, for sitting and walking cases.

The personnel for this will be found by the O.C. 3RD. FIELD AMBULANCE.

One additional Officer, and twelve Stretcher Bearers will be detailed for duty at each of the Regimental Aid Posts.

At the Collecting Post, the personnel will be:- One Officer and eight men.

In addition, fifty Staretcher Bearers will be detailed for duty, with twenty wheeled stretchers, working between Regimental Aid Posts, and Advanced Dressing Station.

At the Advanced Dressing Station, it is proposed to utilise a Barn, and, if necessary, the Goods Shed at the RAILWAY STATION, LAVENTIE, for walking and slightly wounded cases.

There will be available, I4 Deasey Motor Ambulances, and 4 Ford Ambulances. - Two of these cars will be retained at the Main Dressing Stations, for the evacuation of urgent cases.

Empty cars will travel to LAVENTIE by road crossing RAILWAY and LA BASSEE ROAD, and loaded cars will return to Main Dressing Station by NOUVEAU MONDE and ESTAIRES.

Evacuation of wounded from trenches, will be by GREAT NORTH ROAD, and STRAND to RED HOUSE and HOUGOMONT respectively.

The fullest possible use will be made of the GREAT NORTHERN and GREAT CENTRAL tramlines.

18.7.16

@@@@@@@@@@@@@@@@@@@@@@@@@@@

James Jones
COLONEL
ASSISTANT DIRECTOR OF MEDICAL SERVICES
61st (SOUTH MIDLAND) DIVISION.

No1 Copy to H.Q. 61st Div
No2 " O.C. 1st Fd Amb
No3 " " 3rd " "
No4 " Filed in War Diary

Volume 4.

Aug. 1916.

Vol 4

War Diary. August 1916.
A.D.M.S. 61st Division

4015

Instructions regarding War Diaries and Intelligence Summaries are contained in F. S. Regs., Part II and the Staff Manual respectively. Title Pages will be prepared in manuscript.

Army Form C. 2118

WAR DIARY
or
INTELLIGENCE SUMMARY
(Erase heading not required.)

Map References. Sheet. 36a S.W.

4021

Place	Date	Hour	Summary of Events and Information	Remarks and references to Appendices
LA GORGUE L.35.b.4.6	1/8/16		Visited Advanced Dressing Station LAVENTIE (G.34.c.6.3) and LA FLINQUE (M.10.c.7.1) and Regimental Aid Posts at EPINETTE FARM (M.16.d.6.6.) and WINCHESTER HOUSE. (M.23.a.3½.1)	
"	2/8/16		Inspected 2nd Field Ambulance (L.34.b.6.2) and 3rd Field Ambulance LA GORGUE (L.35.b.9.9)	
"	3/8/16		Visited Corps Rest Station MERVILLE (K.29.d.2.9), Officers Rest Station MERVILLE (K.22.d.5.3) and Skin Depôt at REGNIER LE CLERC. (K.34.d.8.8)	
"	4/8/16		Routine Duties.	
"	5/8/16		Routine Duties.	
"	6/8/16		Attended Church Service on 2nd Anniversary of Declaration of War at BETHUNE	
"	7/8/16		Visited Corps Rest Station MERVILLE (K.29.d.2.9) and Skin Depôt REGNIER LE CLERC (K.34.d.8.8). Lieutenant NASE R.A.M.C. reported for duty with this Division	
	8/8/16		Visited 2/2nd Field Ambulance (L.34.b.6.2) and 2/3rd Field Ambulance LA GORGUE (L.35.b.9.9).	
"	9/8/16		Routine Duties.	
"	10/8/16		Inspected 1st Field Ambulance MERVILLE (K.29.d.2.9)	

1875 Wt. W593/826 1,000,000 4/15 J.B.C. & A. A.D.S.S./Forms/C. 2118.

Army Form C. 2118

Instructions regarding War Diaries and Intelligence Summaries are contained in F. S. Regs., Part II. and the Staff Manual respectively. Title Pages will be prepared in manuscript.

WAR DIARY
or
INTELLIGENCE SUMMARY
(Erase heading not required.)

Map references. Sheet 36A S.W.

Place	Date	Hour	Summary of Events and Information	Remarks and references to Appendices
LA GORGUE	11/8/16		Inspected 2/2nd (L.34.b.6.2) & 2/3rd (L.35.b.9.9) Field Ambulances LA GORGUE.	OK
"	12/8/16		Routine Duties.	OK
"	13/8/16		Visited Corps Rest Station MERVILLE (K.29.d.2.9)	OK
"	14/8/16		Routine Duties.	OK
"	15/8/16		Routine Duties.	OK
"	16/8/16		Inspected 2nd Field Ambulance. LA GORGUE (L.34.b.6.2)	OK
"	17/8/16		Routine Duty	OK
"	18/8/16		Visited 2/2nd Field Ambulance, (L.34.b.6.2) 2/3rd Field Ambulance (L.35.b.9.9). LA GORGUE and Corps Rest Station MERVILLE (K.29.d.2.9)	OK
"	19/8/16		Routine duties.	OK
"	20/8/16		Visited A.D.S. LAVENTIE (G.34.c.6.5) and R.A.Ps at RED HOUSE (M.6.d.2.0) and HOUGOMONT. (M.12.c.3.4)	OK
"	21/8/16		Routine Duties.	OK
"	22/8/16		Routine Duties.	OK

403J.

1875 Wt. W593/826 1,000,000 4/15 J.B.C. & A. A.D.S.S./Forms/C. 2118.

Instructions regarding War Diaries and Intelligence Summaries are contained in F. S. Regs., Part II. and the Staff Manual respectively. Title Pages will be prepared in manuscript.

WAR DIARY
or
INTELLIGENCE SUMMARY
(Erase heading not required.)

Army Form C. 2118

Map reference Sheet 36A. S.W.

Place	Date	Hour	Summary of Events and Information	Remarks and references to Appendices
LA GORGUE. L.35.b.4.6.	23/8/16		Visited Corps Skin Depôt REGNIER LE CLERC (K.34.d.8.8) • Corps Rest Station MERVILLE (K.29.d.2.9)	
"	24/8/16		Routine duties.	
"	25/8/16		Routine duties.	
"	26/8/16		Inspected transport of 3 Fd Ambulances with O.C. Divisional Train.	
"	27/8/16		Routine duties.	
"	28/8/16		Routine duties.	
"	29/8/16		Routine duties.	
"	30/8/16		Visited A.D.S. LAVENTIE (G.34.c.6.3) • R.A.Ps at RED HOUSE (M.6.d.2.0) and HOUGOMONT. (M.12.c.3.4)	
"	31/8/16		Visited Corps Rest Station (K.29.d.2.9) • Officers Rest Station (K.22.d.5.3).	

James Young
Colonel
A.D.M.S. 61st Division

1875 Wt. W593/826 1,000,000 4/15 J.B.C. & A. A.D.S.S./Forms/C. 2118.

4045
EB

Sept. 1916

Vol 5

Confidential

War Diary.

A.D.M.S. 61st Division

Period. 1 - 30th September 1916.

Volume 5.

4051

Instructions regarding War Diaries and Intelligence Summaries are contained in F. S. Regs., Part II. and the Staff Manual respectively. Title Pages will be prepared in manuscript.

WAR DIARY
or
INTELLIGENCE SUMMARY
(Erase heading not required.)

Map reference
Sheet 36A. SW

Army Form C. 2118

4061

Place	Date	Hour	Summary of Events and Information	Remarks and references to Appendices
LA GORGUE L.35.b.4.6.	1/9/16		Visited R.A.P. RED HOUSE (M.6.d.2.0) and HOUGOMONT. (M.12.c.3.4)	
"	2/9/16		Routine Duties.	
"	3/9/16		Inspected 1st Field Ambulance. (G.34.c.6.3). Corps Rest Station MERVILLE (K.29.d.2.9) and 2/2nd Field Ambulance LA GORGUE. (L.34.b.6.2).	
"	4/9/16		Visited Officers Rest Station MERVILLE (K.22.d.5.3)	
"	5/9/16		Routine Duties	
"	6/9/16		Routine Duties	
"	7/9/16		Routine Duties.	
"	8/9/16		Inspected 1st Field Ambulance (K.29.d.2.9) & accompanied G.O.C. in inspection of RED HOUSE (M.6.d.2.0)	
"	9/9/16		Routine Duties.	
"	10/9/16		Routine Duties.	
"	11/9/16		Inspected 2nd Field Ambulance. (L.34.b.6.2). 3rd Field Ambulance. (L.35.b.9.9)	
"	12/9/16		Routine Duties.	
"	13/9/16		Visited A.D.S. LAVENTIE (G.34.c.6.3) & R.A.P. RED HOUSE (M.6.a.2.0)	
"	14/9/16		Visited Corps Rest Station MERVILLE (K.29.d.2.9). Skin Depot REGNIER LE CLERC (K.34.d.8.8) & Officers Rest Station BUSNES (P.26.)	
"	15/9/16		Routine Duties	

1875 Wt. W593/826 1,000,000 4/15 J.B.C. & A. A.D.S.S./Forms/C. 2118.

Army Form C. 2118

Instructions regarding War Diaries and Intelligence Summaries are contained in F. S. Regs., Part II. and the Staff Manual respectively. Title Pages will be prepared in manuscript.

WAR DIARY
or
INTELLIGENCE SUMMARY
(Erase heading not required.)

Map reference Sheet 36ᵃ. S.W.

Place	Date	Hour	Summary of Events and Information	Remarks and references to Appendices
LA GORGUE L.35.b.4.6.	16/9/16		Inspection of all Field Ambulances, Advanced Dressing Stations & Sanitary Section by D.M.S. 1st ARMY.	[initials]
"	17/9/16		Routine Duties.	[initials]
"	18/9/16		D.A.D.M.S. proceeded on 10 days Leave. 12.0 A.M.	[initials]
"	19/9/16		Routine Duties.	[initials]
"	20/9/16		Routine Duties.	[initials]
"	21/9/16		Visited Corps Rest Station MERVILLE (K.29.d.2.9.) Officers Rest Station MERVILLE (K.22.d.5.3) & Skin Depôt REGNIER LE CLERC (K.34.d.8.8)	[initials]
"	22/9/16		Visited A.D.S. LAVENTIE (G.34 c.6.3) & R.A.P. RED HOUSE (M.6 d.2.0)	[initials]
"	23/9/16		Visited Corps Rest Station MERVILLE (K.29.d.2.9)	[initials]
"	24/9/16		Routine Duties.	[initials]
"	25/9/16		Inspected 2/2 Field Ambulance (L.34.b.6.2). 2/3rd Field Ambulance (L.35.b.9.9)	[initials]
"	26/9/16		Visited GREEN BARN. A.D.S (M.27.d.5.2)	[initials]
"	27/9/16		Routine Duties	[initials]
"	28/9/16		Routine Duties.	[initials]

4071

1875 Wt. W593/826 1,000,000 4/15 J.B.C. & A. A.D.S.S./Forms/C. 2118.

Army Form C. 2118

Instructions regarding War Diaries and Intelligence Summaries are contained in F. S. Regs., Part II. and the Staff Manual respectively. Title Pages will be prepared in manuscript.

WAR DIARY
or
INTELLIGENCE SUMMARY
(Erase heading not required.)

Map reference Sheet 36A SW.

Place	Date	Hour	Summary of Events and Information	Remarks and references to Appendices
LA GORGUE L.35.b.4.6.	29/9/16		DADMS returned from Leave.	
			Lieut ANDERSON RAMC. reported for duty with 2/2nd Field Ambulance.	
	30/9/16		Inspected 2/3rd Field Ambulance (L.35.b.9.9) & Corps Rest Station MERVILLE. (K.29.d.2.9).	

James Young
Colonel
ADMS 61st Division

4081

1875 Wt. W593/826 1,000,000 4/15 J.B.C. & A. A.D.S.S./Forms/C. 2118.

Oct. 1916

140/17/88

O.D.M.S. 61st Div.

4091

Instructions regarding War Diaries and Intelligence Summaries are contained in F. S. Regs., Part II. and the Staff Manual respectively. Title Pages will be prepared in manuscript.

WAR DIARY
or
INTELLIGENCE SUMMARY
(Erase heading not required.)

Army Form C. 2118

ADMS 61 D
Vol 6

Place	Date	Hour	Summary of Events and Information	Remarks and references to Appendices
La Gorque.	1 10/16		Routine Duties.	
	2 10/16		Routine Duties. A.D.M.S. proceeded on 10 days leave.	
	3 10/16		Inspected 2nd Field Ambulance.	
	4 10/16		Lieut Deacon R.A.M.C proceeded to 31st Division for duty under orders of D.D.M.S. XI Corps.	
	5 10/16		Lieut O'Meara returned to duty from the 31st Division and posted to duty with the 2/4 R. Berks.	
	6 10/16		Routine Duties. Visited General Gordon at Officers Rest Stn Hazbrouke.	
	7 10/16		Routine Duties.	
	8 10/16		Inspected 2/2 Field Amb.	
	9 10/16		Routine Duties.	
	10 10/16		Inspected 2/3 Field Amb.	
	11 10/16		Routine Duties.	
	12 10/16		Routine Duties. A.D.M.S. returned from leave.	
	13 10/16		Routine Duties.	
	14 10/16		Inspected 2/2 and 2/3 Field Ambulances	
	15 10/16		Routine Duties.	
	16 10/16		Routine Duties	
	17 10/16		Routine Duties.	
	18 10/16		Routine Duties	

4101

1875 Wt. W593/826 1,000,000 4/15 J.B.C. & A. A.D.S.S./Forms/C. 2118.

Instructions regarding War Diaries and Intelligence Summaries are contained in F. S. Regs., Part II. and the Staff Manual respectively. Title Pages will be prepared in manuscript.

WAR DIARY
or
INTELLIGENCE SUMMARY
(Erase heading not required.)

Army Form C. 2118

Place	Date	Hour	Summary of Events and Information	Remarks and references to Appendices
La. Gorgue.	19 10/16		Routine Duties.	
	20 10/16		Inspected 2/2 and 2/3 Field Ambulances	
	21 10/16		Routine Duties.	
	22 10/16		Routine Duties.	
	23 10/16		Inspected 2/1 Field Ambulance	
	24 10/16		Routine Duties	
	25 10/16		Routine Duties	
	26 10/16		Routine Duties.	
	27 10/16		Attended Medical Board on Capt Marshall. Merville.	
	28 10/16		Closed Office at La. Gorgue. 12 noon. Opened Office at St. Vennant. 1 pm.	
			Moved with Division from La. Gorgue. to St. Vennant.	
St. Vennant.	29 10/16		Inspected 2/1 and 2/3 Field Ambulances.	
	30 10/16		Inspected 2/2 Field Ambulance	
	31 10/16		Routine Duties.	

[illegible]

Colonel.

A.D.M.S. 61st Division

4113

1875 Wt. W593/826 1,000,000 4/15 J.B.C. & A. A.D.S.S./Forms/C. 2118.

Nov. 1916

S/

140/1849

Confidential

Vol 7

War Diary.

ADMS 61st Division

Period. 1st 30th November 1916

Volume 7.

Instructions regarding War Diaries and Intelligence Summaries are contained in F. S. Regs., Part II. and the Staff Manual respectively. Title Pages will be prepared in manuscript.

WAR DIARY
or
INTELLIGENCE SUMMARY
(Erase heading not required.)

Army Form C. 2118

Map references Hazebrouck 5ª 1/100000 Lens XI. 1/100000 Sheets

Place	Date	Hour	Summary of Events and Information	Remarks and references to Appendices
St VENANT.	1.11.16		Routine duties.	
	2.11.16		Moved with 61st Division to CHELERS. Closed office at St VENANT 8.0 A.M. opened office CHELERS at 11.0 A.M. Captain W.H. DAVISON. RAMCT. OC Sanitary Section removed to No 32. C.C.S. Sick.	
CHELERS	3.11.16		Routine duties	
"	4.11.16		Division moved to ROLLECOURT.	
ROLLECOURT.	5.11.16		Routine duties	
	6.11.16		Division moved to FROHEN LE GRAND. Capt. VICKERS. RAMCTC reported for duty from No 2 Stationary Hospital, ABBEVILLE to relieve Capt. MARSHALL. RAMCT. 2/2nd Field Ambulance.	
FROHEN LE GRAND	7.11.16		Major W.J. HOYTEN. RAMCT. DADMS 61st DVN evacuated sick to No 19. C.C.S. Visited 2/2 Field Ambulance at VILLERS HÔPITAL	
	8.11.16		Visited 2/1st Field Ambulance at NEUVILLETTE.	
	9.11.16		Visited 2/3rd Field Ambulance at BOFFLES.	
	10.11.16		Routine duties. CAPT. W.H. DAVISON. RAMCT. O.C. Sanitary Section returned from No. 32. C.C.S.	
	11.11.16		Visited 2/1st Field Ambulance at NEUVILLETTE. Capt MARSHALL. RAMCT. proceeded to ABBEVILLE for duty.	
	12.11.16		Bearer divisions of 2/1st Field Ambulance. 2/2 Field Ambulance & 2/3 Fd Ambulance proceeded to BERTRANCOURT, FORCEVILLE and HEDAUVILLE respectively.	
	13.11.16		Routine duties.	
	14.11.16		Routine duties.	
	15.11.16		Moved to BERNAVILLE. Capt. T.H.P. BREEN. RAMC. reported for duty as DADMS	

1875 Wt. W593/826 1,000,000 4/15 J.B.C. & A. A.D.S.S./Forms/C. 2118.

Instructions regarding War Diaries and Intelligence Summaries are contained in F. S. Regs., Part II. and the Staff Manual respectively. Title Pages will be prepared in manuscript.

WAR DIARY
or
INTELLIGENCE SUMMARY
(Erase heading not required.)

Army Form C. 2118

Map reference. Hazebrouck 5a 1/100000. Lens XI. 1/100000.

Place	Date	Hour	Summary of Events and Information	Remarks and references to Appendices
FROHEN LE GRAND	16.11.16		Moved to CANAPLES.	
	17.11.16		Moved to CONTAY	
CONTAY	18.11.16		Routine duties in office	
	19.11.16		Routine duties in office	
	20.11.16		Conferred with A.D.M.S. 18th Division regarding the taking over of Dressing Stations held by his Field Ambulances	
	21.11.16		Visited A.D.M.S. 19th Div. with reference to taking over from 59th Fd Amb.	
	22.11.16		Divisional Headquarters moved to BOUZINCOURT. Captain D.T. EVANS R.A.M.C. reported for duty.	
BOUZINCOURT	23.11.16		Routine duties in office	
	24.11.16		Routine duties in office. Captain ROBSON. RAMC. reported for duty.	
	25.11.16		Visited A.D.S. at DONNETS POST, Headquarters of Main Dressing Station at CABSTAND and water supplies at CRUCIFIX CORNER.	
	26.11.16		Attended conference at office of D.D.M.S. II CORPS.	
	27.11.16		Visited FORCEVILLE in company with O.C. 2/2 Field Ambulance & Major FOSTER. RAMCT. 2/2 Field Ambulance. with a view to the construction of a CORPS SCABIES DEPOT.	
	28.11.16		Routine duties in office	
	29.11.16		Routine duties in office. CAPT CORNELIUS. R.A.M.C. reported for duty.	
	30.11.16		Routine duties in office	

Samuel Young[?] Colonel
A.D.M.S. 63rd Division

Dec. 1916

S/

140/1898

Confidential

Vol 8

War Diary.

A. D. M. S. 61st Division

December 1916.

Volume 8.

Instructions regarding War Diaries and Intelligence Summaries are contained in F. S. Regs., Part II. and the Staff Manual respectively. Title Pages will be prepared in manuscript.

WAR DIARY
or
INTELLIGENCE SUMMARY
(Erase heading not required.)

Reference Map 57° S.E

Army Form C. 2118

Place	Date	Hour	Summary of Events and Information	Remarks and references to Appendices
BOUZINCOURT	Dec 1st		Routine duties in office. Reported to DDMS 4th Corps JJPB	JJPB
	2		Attended meeting at No 4. C.C.S. VARENNES with reference to formation of 5th Army Medical Society. Visited & inspected 2/3 Field Ambulance at VARENNES. JJPB	
	3		Attended conference at DDMS 4th Corps JJPB	
	4		Routine duties. JJPB	
	5		ADMS evacuated to No 4 C.C.S. Lt Col CRAIG OC 2/2 Field Ambulance evacuated to No 4 C.C.S. JJPB	
	6		Routine duties in office. JJPB	
	7		Routine duties in office JJPB	
	8		Visited 2/1 Field Ambulance at AVELUY POST JJPB	
	9		Visited 2/2 Field Ambulance at FORCEVILLE. JJPB	
	10		Visited 2/1 Field Ambulance at AVELUY POST. JJPB	
	11		Visited RED CROSS CORNER X9b5.4. found that part of dugout accomodation had been blown in by shellfire and that the post had been partially abandoned. As it is possible to bring cars up to X4 a 6.9 just behind the CEMETRY DRESSING STATION R34c4, there does not seem much to be gained by maintaining personnel at RED CROSS CORNER. This appears to be a registered spot as it is constantly shelled – Also visited CEMETRY DRESSING STATION. weather wet and cold. JJPB.	

1875 Wt. W593/826 1,000,000 4/15 J.B.C. & A. A.D.S.S./Forms/C. 2118.

Army Form C. 2118

Instructions regarding War Diaries and Intelligence Summaries are contained in F. S. Regs., Part II. and the Staff Manual respectively. Title Pages will be prepared in manuscript.

WAR DIARY
or
INTELLIGENCE SUMMARY
(Erase heading not required.)

Place	Date	Hour	Summary of Events and Information	Remarks and references to Appendices
BOUZINCOURT	12		Routine duties JJPB	
	13		Routine duties JJPB	
	14		Routine duties JJPB.	
	15		Routine duties JJPB	
	16		Routine duties JJPB	
	17		DADMS attended Sanitary conference at IV Corps Sanitary Sections are now to be attached to areas and not to move with Divisions unless latter move out of the Army area JJPB.	
	18		Lt.Col. CLAYTON reported his arrival and assumed the duties of A.D.M.S. DADMS carried out routine inspection of convalescent company and visited 2/1st Field Ambulance - weather very cold. J.J.P.B	
	19		ADMS inspected 2/2nd and 2/3rd Field Ambulances. Some difficulty is being experienced in getting the medical units to pay due attention to sanitary arrangements especially at detached posts - weather very cold. JJPB	
	20		ADMS inspected 2/1st Field Ambulance at AVELUY POST - There is now accomodation here for sixty stretcher cases. JJPB.	
	21		DADMS visited 2/1st Field Ambulance - weather warmer but wet JJPB	

1875 Wt. W593/826 1,000,000 4/15 J.B.C. & A. A.D.S.S./Forms/C. 2118.

Instructions regarding War Diaries and Intelligence Summaries are contained in F. S. Regs., Part II. and the Staff Manual respectively. Title Pages will be prepared in manuscript.

WAR DIARY
or
INTELLIGENCE SUMMARY
(Erase heading not required.)

Army Form C. 2118

Place	Date	Hour	Summary of Events and Information	Remarks and references to Appendices
BOUZINCOURT	22		Routine duties JFPB.	
"	23		Routine duties JFPB	
"	24		ADMS inspected 2/2nd and 2/3rd Field Ambulances JFPB.	
"	25		Xmas Day - Routine duties J.F.P.B	
"	26		Routine duties. DADMS visited Divisional Baths J.F.P.B.	
"	27		Routine duties JFP.B	
"	28		Routine duties JFPB.	
"	29		DADMS visited 2/1st Field Ambulance JFPB	
"	30		O.C. 2/1st Field Ambulance reported that dugouts at POZIERES CEMETRY had been very seriously damaged by shell fire and were leaking badly. It was decided to move the Advanced Dressing Station to a point on the ORVILLERS-ROAD. J.F.P.B	
"	31		DADMS accompanied by OC 2/1st Field Ambulance selected a site for a new temporary Advanced Dressing Station at X3 a 8.8. RE to proceed with work at once. J.F.P.B	

[signature] Colonel.
1.1.17 ADMS 61 Division

1875 Wt. W593/826 1,000,000 4/15 J.B.C. & A. A.D.S.S./Forms/C. 2118.

S

Vol 9

Confidential

War Diary

of

ADMS 61st Division

From January 1st 1917 To January 31st 1917

(Volume 9)

Army Form C. 2118

Instructions regarding War Diaries and Intelligence Summaries are contained in F. S. Regs., Part II. and the Staff Manual respectively. Title Pages will be prepared in manuscript.

WAR DIARY
or
INTELLIGENCE SUMMARY
(Erase heading not required.)

Place	Date	Hour	Summary of Events and Information	Remarks and references to Appendices
BOUZINCOURT	1		Routine duties JJPB.	
	2		DADMS visited GRAVEL PIT (R27 c. cent) to see if there was any possibility of moving the ADS from DANUBE TRENCH (R32 c 84) to this place. There is no accomodation available at the moment. GRAVEL PIT and AVELUY POST are now connected by telephone and it was decided to abandon DONNETT'S POST X7 c.0.8. and to bring cars up from AVELUY POST on receipt of a telephone message. JJPB	
	3		Routine duties JJPB	
	4		Routine duties JJPB	
	5		DADMS visited 1st Field Ambulance JJPB	
	6		ADMS & ~~DA~~ visited 2/3rd Field Ambulance at VARENNES JJPB.	
	7		Routine duties JJPB	
	8		DADMS visited ADS at DANUBE TRENCH and RAP at GRAVEL PIT. No anti gas solution at ADS. SSO communicated with also Divisional Gas Officer JJPB	
	9		Routine duties JJPB	
	10		Orders recieved that 182 Infantry Brigade would carry out a raid on morning of 11th inst in connection with operations by XIII Corps and 11th Division on left of this Division. All spare ambulances attached to 2/1st Field Ambulance. Posts on rt. sector doubled. Wheeled stretchers posted at TULLOCH'S CORNER extra officer [illegible] to 2/1st Field Ambulance JJPB	

1,000,000 4/15 J.B.C. & A. A.D.S.S./Forms/C. 2118.

Instructions regarding War Diaries and Intelligence Summaries are contained in F. S. Regs., Part II. and the Staff Manual respectively. Title Pages will be prepared in manuscript.

WAR DIARY
or
INTELLIGENCE SUMMARY
(Erase heading not required.)

Army Form C. 2118.

Place	Date	Hour	Summary of Events and Information	Remarks and references to Appendices
BOUZINCOURT	11		DADMS visited HQ 182 Infantry Brigade at 8 AM to enquire as to casualties. No information available. DADMS visited ADS on ORVILLERS ROAD at 11.30 AM found that touch was not being maintained with the regimental aid post. This had been moved about 1000 yards forward into Desire Trench and no notification had been sent either to ADMS or ambulance. DADMS visited DESIRE TRENCH found 14 wounded cases in deep dugout no steps being taken to get them away. RAMC bearers sent up evacuation completed 1 AM. JFPB	
	12		Operation orders* drafted for move of Division to Rest Area. JFPB	*Appendix I
	13		DADMS 18th Div called to arrange details of relief. Instructions as to handing over* issued to Field Ambulances.	*Appendix II
	14		Routine duties JFPB	
	15		Move of Division to rest area commenced - 2/1st Field Ambulance moved to VAL DE MAISON 2/2nd Field Ambulance to PUCHEVILLERS JFPB	
MARIEUX	16		Div HQ moved to MARIEUX - 2/3rd Field Ambulance to BEAUQUESNE Lt. Col. MOXEY O.C. 2/3rd Field Ambulance admitted to Hospital. JFPB.	
BERNAVILLE	17.		Div H.Q. moved to BERNAVILLE 2/1st Field Ambulance moved to VACQUERIE 2/2nd Field Ambulance moved to GEZAINCOURT 2/3rd Field Ambulance to LE MEILLARD. JFPB.	

18 Wt. W593/8 4/15 J.B.C. & A. A.D.S.S.

Instructions regarding War Diaries and Intelligence Summaries are contained in F. S. Regs., Part II. and the Staff Manual respectively. Title Pages will be prepared in manuscript.

WAR DIARY
or
INTELLIGENCE SUMMARY
(Erase heading not required.)

Army Form C. 2118

Place	Date	Hour	Summary of Events and Information	Remarks and references to Appendices
BERNAVILLE		18	Div HQ remained at BERNAVILLE. 2/1st Field Ambulance moved to HANCHY 2/2nd Field Ambulance to LE PLOUY 2/3rd Field Ambulance to CONTEVILLE. Great difficulty with motor transport of 2/3rd Field Ambulance - All Deasys broken down. This type of car appears to be most unsuitable for hard work on bad roads. JFPB.	
BRAILLY		19	Div HQ moved to BRAILLY 2/1st Field Ambulance to GUESCHART 2/2nd Field Ambulance to DOMVAST 2/3rd Field Ambulance to L'ABBAYE D'AIMONT FME. ADMS reported to DDMS II Corps JFPB.	
		20	Apart from temporary unfit men carried in ambulances for the march 248 men were admitted and evacuated to CCS for the period 15th-20th both inclusive DADMS visited 2/3rd Field Ambulance JFPB	
		21	DADMS visited 2/1st Field Ambulance JFPB	
		22	ADMS visited 2/2nd and 2/3rd Field Ambulances JFPB.	
		23	Routine duties JFPB	
		24	ADMS visited 183 Bde billets and interviewed medical officers JFPB.	

1875 Wt. W593/826 1,000,000 4/15 J.B.C. & A. A.D.S.S./Forms/C. 2118.

Instructions regarding War Diaries and Intelligence Summaries are contained in F. S. Regs., Part II. and the Staff Manual respectively. Title Pages will be prepared in manuscript.

WAR DIARY
or
INTELLIGENCE SUMMARY
(Erase heading not required.)

Army Form C. 2118

Place	Date	Hour	Summary of Events and Information	Remarks and references to Appendices
BRAILLY	25		ADMS visited billets occupied by 184 Brigade - and interviewed the medical officers attached to battalions - There is an almost complete want of sanitary appliances throughout the area. Practically nothing was left by the outgoing division JJPB	
"	26		Thresh Disinfector partially broken down. Considerable amount of pediculosis in Division. One thresh quite insufficient for dealing with amount of material requiring disinfection in a division. JJPB	
"	27		Instructions received for LT NASE to proceed to No 3 Canadian Stationary Hospital for duty LT FAIRFAX 2/2nd Field Ambulance detailed to 2/5th Glosters JJPB.	
"	28.		ADMS visited the Artillery Area and the 2/1st Field Ambulance JJPB.	
"	29		Warning order received for further move of Division JJPB.	
"	30		Routine duties JJPB	
"	31		ADMS visited RA-HQ and also NOYELLES where 4th Berks are billetted JJPB	

[signature] Col.
ADMS 61st Div

1875 Wt. W593/826 1,000,000 4/15 J.B.C. & A. A.D.S.S./Forms/C. 2118.

Appendix 1.

SECRET

Appendix 1

Copy No 8 13 Jan Y 17.

61 Division RAMC Order 1208

1 The 61st Division (less artillery) will be relieved by the 18th Division (less artillery) on January 15th and January 16th and will move to the MARIEUX AREA.

2 Advance parties from incoming units will arrive as follows
For 2/1 Field Ambulance from 55 Fd Amb on evening 13th
For 2/2 Field Ambulance from 55 Fd Amb on morning 14th
For 2/3 Field Ambulance from 56 Fd Amb on morning 15th

3 All details of the relief of personnel in the forward area will be arranged between O.C. 2/1 Field Ambulance and O.C. 54 Field Ambulance

4 Separate instructions will be issued as to handing over patients and stores

5 The Field Ambulances less motor transport will move in accordance with attached march table

6 The Sanitary Section will not move with the Division. It will remain in the area, attached to the 18 Division for a period of one week.

7 On arrival in the MARIEUX AREA Field Ambulances will be distributed as follows

GROUP	UNIT	BDE AREAS
182 Bde Group under GOC 182 Bde	1st F Ambulance	RUBEMPRE-LA-VICOGNE
183 Bde Group under GOC 183 Bde	3rd F Ambulance	BEAUQUESNE
184 Bde Group under GOC 184 Bde	2nd F Ambulance	PUCHEVILLERS

Maps showing limits of Bde Areas have been issued.

8 Distances of 500 yds between Field Ambulances and units in front will be maintained on the march into the MARIEUX AREA

9 A.D.M.S. Office will close at 12 noon on 16th Jan at W7 b 2.7 BOUZINCOURT and will reopen at same hour at MARIEUX.

Whiter Clayton Col.
ADMS 61 Div.

January 13th 1916

Copies to 1st 2nd + 3 F Ambs 1-2 2 War Diary 8-9
61 Div Q 4 1 DDMS IV Corps 10
ADMS 18 Div 5
1 File 6-7

No	Date	Unit	From	To	Route	Remarks
1	Jany 15	1st F Amb	AVELUY POST	VAL DE MAISON	BOUZINCOURT HEDAUVILLE VARENNES. HARPONVILLE	To follow a Batt of 183 Bde from huts at W 10 C 2·7 be clear of HEDAUVILLE by 12·15 pm
2	Jany 15	2nd F Amb	FORCEVILLE	PUCHEVILLERS	VARENNES HARPONVILLE	F Amb join 184 Bde at VARENNES.
3	Jany 16	3rd F Amb	VARENNES	BEAUQUESNE AREA	LEALVILLERS ARQUEVES	To follow 3 C Div Trn To be clear of VARENNES by 12 NOON

Appendix 2.

Instructions as to Handing Over and Moving out and March.

706/17/17

1. Personnel of incoming units will work with personnel of this Division for 24 hours before handing over takes place.
2. Units will hand over and obtain receipts for all stores in excess of mobilization equipment and additions made to same by G.R.Os or A.R.Os.
3. Attention is directed to paras 1.d.e and para 4 of 61st Div. No Q.823/15 dated 10/1/17 to paras 4.5.6 61st Division G.C 96/2 dated 11/1/17 and to 61 Div No Q 823/15 dated 12/1/17, which have been circulated.
4. The patients at FORCEVILLE will be handed over to 54 Field Ambulance by order of D.D.M.S. IV Corps.
5. All patients left behind will be rationed for the day of relief and the following day. Fuel fuel rations for patients will be handed over.
6. Motor transport will start four hours after the ambulances have moved off and will follow the route traversed by their Brigade Group to pick up any men who may have fallen out.
7. While the Division is on the march Field Ambulances will compile as soon as possible each day and forward to this office a list of men by units who although not regularly admitted do not march the distance but are carried in the ambulances.
8. Sick on line of march may be evacuated direct to C.C.S. at GEZAINCOURT, VARENNES and PUCHEVILLERS.
9. A table showing supply arrangements during the march is being circulated.
10. Daily states will be rendered in the usual way, books being closed before the commencement of each day's march.
11. Instructions for the Rest Area will be issued.

W. Hutton Clayton Colonel

ADMS 61 Division

13/1/17

Feb. 1917

140/986

Vol 10

Confidential

War Diary

of

A.D.M.S. 61st Division

From February 1st 1917 To February 28th 1917.

(Volume. 10)

1

Army Form C. 2118

Instructions regarding War Diaries and Intelligence Summaries are contained in F. S. Regs., Part II. and the Staff Manual respectively. Title Pages will be prepared in manuscript.

WAR DIARY
or
INTELLIGENCE SUMMARY
(Erase heading not required.)

Place	Date	Hour	Summary of Events and Information	Remarks and references to Appendices
BRAILLY	1		Warning order issued to Field Ambulances to be prepared to march to an adjoining area (one day's march) on 4th. Message received from Supply Column that DEASEY AMBULANCES were about to be replaced with DAIMLERS from No 6 MAC. This will probably lead to some improvement in the general state of the motor transport of the Ambulances. Instructions asked for from IV Corps as to disposal of ordinary sick and scabies cases on move of Division. Ordinary sick likely to need more than a few days treatment are to be sent to 57th DIV. REST-STN. OUVILLE scabies cases to IV Corps scabies station CAOURS J.F.P.B	
"	2		IV Corps notified that there were 24 cases requiring transfer to CAOURS by MAC. DIV Operation Orders for march received 61st Div to pass under administration of Fourth Army from 12 noon on 5th inst Message received that 61st DIV Sanitary Section would rejoin Division on Feb 6th. Though there is much to be said for placing Sanitary Sections in areas and leaving them there for considerable periods. I think the system of Divisional Sanitary Sections is preferable. In this area three separate sanitary officers have charge of different parts of the divisional area. This leads to much waste of time and I think to loss of efficiency. If sanitary sections must have permanent areas the actual boundaries should be altered so as to correspond with boundaries	

1875 Wt. W593/826 1,000,000 4/15 J.B.C. & A. A.D.S.S./Forms/C. 2118.

Instructions regarding War Diaries and Intelligence Summaries are contained in F. S. Regs., Part II. and the Staff Manual respectively. Title Pages will be prepared in manuscript.

WAR DIARY
or
INTELLIGENCE SUMMARY
(Erase heading not required.)

Army Form C. 2118

Place	Date	Hour	Summary of Events and Information	Remarks and references to Appendices
BRAILLY	2		of areas occupied by divisions JJPB.	
"	3		Message received from IV Corps that all evacuation overseas was temporarily suspended and that evacuation to CCS was to be curtailed as much as possible only serious cases being sent. RAMC Orders* (Appendix I) issued for move. Ambulances to be grouped for purposes of move as follows 182 Brigade Group 2/1st Field Amb. 183 Brigade Group 2/2nd Field Ambulance 183 Brigade Group 2/3 Field Ambulance. DADMS visited new area. There will be accomodation for about 200 sick at L'ETOILE (2/3rd Field Ambulance) for about 25 sick at BUSSUS BUSSUE (2/2nd Field Ambulance) and for about 100 at VAUCHELLES-LES-QUESNOY. Proposed to transfer about 40 sick to OUVILLE and carry about 50 JJPB	* APP I
"	4.		2/2nd Field Ambulance moved to BUSSUS-BUSSUE. 2/3rd Field Amb to L'ETOILE. The first seven DAIMLER ambulances arrived and were distributed three to 2/1st Field Ambulance two each to the others. 308 Brigade R.F.A. is being broken up three batteries are remaining behind and not moving with Division. Capt THOMSON RAMC.T. transferred to 2/1st Field Ambulance and CAPT MACDONALD RAMC (TC) left behind to look after the batteries. JJPB.	

1875 Wt. W593/826 1,000,000 4/15 J.B.C. & A. A.D.S.S./Forms/C. 2118.

Instructions regarding War Diaries and Intelligence Summaries are contained in F. S. Regs., Part II. and the Staff Manual respectively. Title Pages will be prepared in manuscript.

WAR DIARY
or
INTELLIGENCE SUMMARY
(Erase heading not required.)

Army Form C. 2118

Place	Date	Hour	Summary of Events and Information	Remarks and references to Appendices
LONG	5		DIV H.Q. moved to LONG. 2/1st Field Ambulance to VAUCHELLES-LES-QUESNOY. Instructions received from Fourth Army that ordinary sick and sick officers were to be transferred to No 2 NEW ZEALAND STATIONARY HOSPITAL AMIENS. infectious cases to HEILLY. Message received from ADMS 63rd (RN) Division that two officers under his command were detailed for duty with this Division but that there were no trains running and he had no transport available. Agreed to send motor ambulance to collect officers. JFPB	
"	6.		Considerable difficulty is being experienced with water supply owing to very severe frost. All water carts are frozen and chlorination is very difficult to carry out. ADMS visited 2/1st Field Ambulance. OC. San Sec reported his arrival. An unbroken frost has now continued for 22 days. JFPB	
"	7		LTS B.B. METCALFE and J. YOUNG reported their arrival and were posted to the 2/3rd Field Ambulance for duty. Instructions received from Fourth Army that ordinary sick and officers were to be sent to ABBEVILLE and infectious cases to TREPORT JFPB	
"	8		ADMS visited 2/3rd Field Ambulance. JFPB.	

Instructions regarding War Diaries and Intelligence Summaries are contained in F. S. Regs., Part II. and the Staff Manual respectively. Title Pages will be prepared in manuscript.

WAR DIARY
or
INTELLIGENCE SUMMARY
(Erase heading not required.)

Army Form C. 2118

Place	Date	Hour	Summary of Events and Information	Remarks and references to Appendices
LONG	9		61st Div Warning Order for move to line received. It is proposed to move all transport and mounted personnel by road and all dismounted personnel by train two days afterwards - This will involve closing the Ambulances two days before RAMC personnel moves - and will leave most of the Division without water carts for two days - This matter represented to G.O.C. - JJPB -	
"	10		61st Div Order No 71 received. RAMC warning order issued* Instructions asked for from IV Corps as to disposal of scabies cases JJPB -	*App 2
"	11		~~RAMC Order No 10 issued~~ - Instructions received from IV Corps that scabies cases are to be taken with the Division on the move - ADMS visited Fourth Army H.Q. DADMS visited IV Corps H.Q. Corps want to put two Field Ambulances into HARBONNIERS and one into GUILLACOURT JJPB	
"	12		ADMS visited 2/1st Field Ambulance - RAMC Order No 10* issued - 61st Div Order No. 72 received - The Divisional front will be from GENERMONT to CHAULNES WOOD and will be taken over on 16th 17th 18th from the French 124th Division JJPB	*App 3

Instructions regarding War Diaries and Intelligence Summaries are contained in F. S. Regs., Part II. and the Staff Manual respectively. Title Pages will be prepared in manuscript.

WAR DIARY
or
INTELLIGENCE SUMMARY
(Erase heading not required.)

Army Form C. 2118

Place	Date	Hour	Summary of Events and Information	Remarks and references to Appendices
LONG	13		2/3rd Field Ambulance personnel moved to A Staging Area - Transport of 2/1st Field Ambulance moved. J.F.P.B	
GUILLAUCOURT	14		Div. HQ moved to GUILLAUCOURT - ADMS and DADMS visited the Medecin Divisionnaire of 124th French Division to discuss taking over medical arrangements - It was decided to visit the various posts starting at 6.30 AM on 15th J.F.P.B	
	15		French posts visited - The French work their evacuation with fewer men than we do, and make a great point of relays of stretcher bearers. The 124th Regiment in the DENIECOURT Sector had developed an excellent form of trench stretcher carried on the shoulders of bearers, and it was arranged that a specimen of this should be left behind. It was decided to take over as they stood the French posts in accordance with tracing* J.F.P.B	*App 4
	16		RAMC order No. 11* issued 2/3rd Field Ambulance moved to HARBONNIERES and established its headquarters in HOSPICE at this place. Accomodation about 100 patients. It was decided to use HARBONNIERES as a main dressing station and make the 2/2nd Field Ambulance responsible for the advanced dressing stations and the front line. J.F.P.B	*App 5.

Instructions regarding War Diaries and Intelligence Summaries are contained in F. S. Regs., Part II. and the Staff Manual respectively. Title Pages will be prepared in manuscript.

WAR DIARY
or
INTELLIGENCE SUMMARY
(Erase heading not required.)

Army Form C. 2118

Place	Date	Hour	Summary of Events and Information	Remarks and references to Appendices
GUILLAUCOURT	17		2/2nd Field Ambulance took over left sector of line (evacuation through DENIECOURT on night 16th-17th without event. French informed us that they did not wish to be relieved in rt sector until morning 18th. All villages so far seen are in a most filthy condition. Latrine accomodation is absent or inadequate - refuse of all sorts is strewn about and ground generally is very foul. French Divisions have a special "water officer" which appears to be a good system. Their water examinations for villages in the back areas are very complete chemically but they do not seem to do any bacteriological examinations and information about the forward area is very scanty. J.F.P.B.	
HARBONNIERES	18.		Div HQ moved to HARBONNIERES. 2/2nd Field Ambulance to VAUVILLERS. Taking over medical arrangements in the forward area completed. Wheeled stretcher carriers indented for urgently. Congratulatory letter written to Medecin Divisionnaire 126th Division on excellent state of area handed over for purpose of supporting entente. J.F.P.B	
	19.		DADMS visited SANITAS advanced dressing station. Forward relay posts have not been provided with stretchers to hand over to regimental bearers who bring down cases. This matter remedied J.F.P. Breen	

1875 Wt. W593/826 1,000,000 4/15 J.B.C. & A. A.D.S.S./Forms/C. 2118.

Army Form C. 2118.

Instructions regarding War Diaries and Intelligence Summaries are contained in F. S. Regs., Part II. and the Staff Manual respectively. Title pages will be prepared in manuscript.

WAR DIARY
or
INTELLIGENCE SUMMARY.

(*Erase heading not required.*)

Place	Date	Hour	Summary of Events and Information	Remarks and references to Appendices
HARBONNIERES	20		Enquiries made as to position of nearest Red Cross Depot with view to getting Divisional Rest Station at GUILLAUCOURT fitted up when it is occupied by 2/1st Field Ambulance on 28th inst. Nearest Depot in Fifth Army Area at HEM. JJPB.	
"	21.		DADMS inspected accomodation at the CHATEAUX - GUILLAUCOURT - There is good accomodation here for about 100 patients. It is proposed to treat scabies cases here. One case of trench foot occurred yesterday and three to-day - The conditions in the front line are extremely bad but insufficient use seems to be made of thigh gum boots. JJPB	
"	22		Fifteen cases of trench foot to-day - JJPB	
"	23		Twenty one cases of trench foot. Almost all cases have not worn gum boots. JJPB	
"	24		Fifty nine cases of trench foot - Col CLAYTON ADMS proceeded on three weeks leave - Lt Col MACKIE O.C. 2/1st Field Ambulance appointed to act during his absence JJPB	
"	25.		CAPT SCOTT RAMC reported his arrival to assume command of 2/3rd Field Ambulance - RAMC Order No. 12* issued - 33 cases of trench foot JJPBrem	*App 6

Instructions regarding War Diaries and Intelligence Summaries are contained in F. S. Regs., Part II. and the Staff Manual respectively. Title pages will be prepared in manuscript.

WAR DIARY
or
INTELLIGENCE SUMMARY.
(Erase heading not required.)

Army Form C. 2118.

Place	Date	Hour	Summary of Events and Information	Remarks and references to Appendices
HARBONNIERES	26.		Routine duties - weather cloudy but fine J.F.P.B	
"	27.		DADMS visited Advanced Dressing Station DENIECOURT - no copy of code calls yet in use at this place although telephone has been installed - Officer in charge instructed to ask for these immediately - J.F.P.Brun.	
"	28.		Copy of instructions for purification of water by French method with extract of Javel (Sodium hypochlorite) received. This appears excellent for stationary water points but would probably lead to neglect of chlorination in moving warfare the water duty men being accustomed to having the chlorination done for them automatically - During the month the average daily percentage of sick admissions was 0'32 and the percentage of sick evacuations 0'23 J.F.P.B	

P.E. Mackie. Lt. Col.
for Colonel. A.D.M.S.
61st DIVISION.

A5834 Wt. W4973/M687 750,000 8/16 D. D. & L. Ltd. Forms/C.2118/13.

Appendix 1

Secret 61st Div. Move Order No 9 — Copy No. 10

1. The 61st Division (less R.E. and Pioneers) will march to the AILLY-LE-HAUT - CLOCHER - LONG area on the 4th and 5th Feb.

2. The Field Ambulances will be grouped as follows and will move under the orders of the Group Commanders

182 Brigade	183 Brigade	184 Brigade
2/1st Fd Amb	2/2 Fd Amb	2/3 Fd Amb

3. Maps showing the limits of Brigade areas are being issued.

4. All billet and training stores will be dumped by 2/1st 2/2nd Fd Ambs under area group arrangements in accordance with following table, at existing R.E. Dumps on day preceding move. A list will be prepared in duplicate of all stores handed in and receipt taken from storeman in charge, one list being left with him, other forwarded to this office.

2/1st Field Amb	2/2 Fd Ambulance
GUESCHART	ARGENVILLERS

5. The 2/3 Fd Ambulance will hand over all billet stores to a representative of 11th Division on morning of 4th inst. Careful receipts in duplicate will be taken and copy forwarded to this office.

6. A table showing supply arrangements and extra transport allotment has been circulated.

7. Separate instructions as to disposal of patients are being issued.

8. ADMS Office will close at BRAILLY on 5th Feb at 11.30 am and will re-open at same hour at LONG.

Colonel
ADMS 61 Division

3/2/17.

Copies to 61st Div Q — 2nd Army [illegible]
DDMS [illegible] — [illegible]
182 183 184 Bdes
2/1 2/2 2/3 Fd Ambces

Appendix 2

Secret. 61st Div RAMC Warning Order. Copy No 6

1. The arrangements for the move of the Medical units will probably be as on attached table.
2. The dismounted personnel and transport will move under Brigade Group arrangements. A Medical Officer will accompany the transport of each Field Ambulance.
3. Motor ambulances will not move with the rest of the transport. Separate instructions with regard to them will be issued.
4. The 2/3rd Field Ambulance will close for the reception of sick at 6 pm on 10th. All sick sent for admission after this hour will be transferred either to 2/1 Field Ambulance or to C.C.S.
5. The 2/2 Field Ambulance will close for the reception of sick at 6.0 pm on the 11th. All sick sent for admission after this hour will be transferred either to 2/1 Field Ambulance or C.C.S.
6. The 2/1 Field Ambulance will remain open until 8.0 AM on 15th. A minimum of medical equipment blankets etc, will be retained by the 2/1 Field Ambulance and will be transported by lorry to the "C" Staging Area.
7. Separate instructions with regard to Scabies cases will be issued.

8. Acknowledge.

W. Hunter Crompton Colonel
ADMS 61 Division

February 10th 1917. Issued at 5 0 pm.

Copies to - 1. 61 Div Q'
2. 3. 4. 182 183 184 Bdes.
5. 6. War Diary
7. 8. 9. 1st 2nd 3rd Fd Ambs

Date	Unit	Road or Train	From	To	Route
11th	2/3 Field Ambulance Transport	Road	VILLERS-SOUS AILLY AREA	ARGOEUVES ST SAUVEUR	N of SOMME
12th	2/2 Field Ambulance Transport.	Road	AILLY LE-HAUT CLOCHER AREA	ARGOEUVES ST SAUVEUR.	N of SOMME
13th	2/3 Field Ambulance Personnel	Train	VILLERS-SOUS AILLY AREA	A Staging AREA	Entrain LONGPRÉ
13th	2/1st Field Ambulance Transport	road	BELLANCOURT AREA	ARGOEUVES ST SAUVEUR	N. of SOMME
14th	2/2 Field Ambulance Personnel	Train	AILLY-LE-HAUT CLOCHER AREA	B. Staging Area.	Entrain at PONT REMY.
15th	2/1 Field Ambulance Personnel	Train	BELLANCOURT AREA.	C Staging Area.	Entrain at PONT REMY

Appendix 3

Secret

Copy No 9

61st Div RAMC ORDER No 10

1 The arrangements for the move of the medical units laid down in 61st Div Warning Order dated 10/2/17 are confirmed.

2 Scabies cases will be taken with the Division into the new area. The O.C. 2/1st Field Amb will accommodate these cases from evening of 12th when they will be transferred from 2/3rd Field Amb until morning of 15th when he will be responsible for their transport to the new area.

3 Instructions as to motor transport are issued herewith

4 A plan of the staging areas is attached.

5 The nearest C.C.S to the staging Areas is No 21 at CORBIE (LA NEUVILLE)

6 ADMS' Office will close at LONG at 11·30am on 14th and will reopen at that hour at GUILLACOURT

7 Acknowledge

12/2/17.

W Wilson Clayton Colonel
ADMS 61st Div

Issued at 12 noon 12/2/17
Copies to 1, 61 Div Q
2-4 182, 183 184 Bdes
5-7 1. 2. 3 F Amb
8-9 War Diary

Instructions as to Motor Transport.

1. The O.C. 2/3 Field Ambulance will detail one Daimler car to report to 306th Bde R.F.A. at ERONDELLE by 5. pm on 11th.

2. The O.C. 2/2 Field Ambulance will detail one Daimler car to report to 307 Bde R.F.A. at LIERCOURT by 5.0 pm on 12th.

3. The O.C. 2/3 Field Ambulance will detail one Daimler car to be attached to 2/1st Field Ambulance from evening of 12th for transport of scabies cases.

4. The remainder of 2/3 Field Ambulance Motor Transport will proceed to A Staging Area on 13th and report to O/c horse transport.

5. The O.C. 2/2 Field Ambulance will detail two Daimler cars for duty at DIV H.QRS. at 8.30 am. on 14th

6. The remainder of the motor transport of 2/2 Field Ambulance will proceed to B. Staging Area on 14th and report to O/c horse transport.

7. The O.C. 2/1 Field Ambulance after satisfying himself that the present area is clear will dispatch all motor transport under his Command, with exception of that required for scabies cases, to C. Staging Area on 15th. The destination of the scabies cases will be notified to him later.

8. A motor lorry will report to O.C. 2/1st Field Ambulance at 6.0 pm on 14th.

J.F.P. Breen
Capt
for Col. ADMS 61 Div

12/2/17.

Appendix 4

Appendix 5.

Secret. 61st Div RAMC Order No 11. Copy No. 9

1. The 2/3rd Field Ambulance will move from Camp 101 "A" Staging Area to HARBONNIERES (HOSPICE) on 16th inst and will be ready for reception of sick and wounded by 4.0pm.

2. The 2/2nd Field Ambulance will take over the medical arrangements of the LEFT SECTOR from the Divisional Ambulance of 124th French Division on night 16th + 17th. The O.C. 2/2 Field Ambulance will be responsible for the motor ambulance service of this sector from 8.0 A.M. on 17th.

3. The 2/2nd Field Ambulance will take over the French Medical arrangements of the RIGHT SECTOR on night 17th - 18th and will be responsible for the motor ambulance service of this sector from 8.0 A.M. on 18th.

4. The 2/2 Field Ambulance will move to HARBONNIERES and ~~[illegible]~~ VAUVILLERS on 18th and must be clear of "B" Staging area by 9.30 a.m. on that date.

5. Further orders will be issued as to 2/1 Field Amb.

6. Scabies cases will be treated by the 2/1 Fd. Ambulance.

7. Evacuations of sick and wounded as soon as the Ambulances have left the Staging areas will take place as follows. Sick to GAILLY. Wounded to BRAY.

8. Map references for French Medical Posts to be taken over are sent herewith.

9. Acknowledge.

Issued at 3.0pm Feb 16th 1917.

W. Clayton Colonel
ADMS 61 Div.

Copies: No 1. 61 Div. Q.
Nos 2-4. 182. 183. 184 Bdes.
Nos 5-6. 306. 307 Bdes R.F.A.
No 7. Medecin Divisionnaire 124th Div.
Nos 8-9 War Diary
Nos 10-12 2/1 2/2 2/3 Field Ambs
No 13. Sanitary Section

Reference ROSIERES Combined
1/40000

LEFT SECTOR (DENIECOURT - ABLAINCOURT)

Advanced Dressing Station DENIECOURT M.36.c.9.2

Relay posts for bearers T.1.a.2.2 T.1.d.2.4. S.4.c.8.2. S.27.3.1.

Motor ambulances kept at M.30.c.2.4 near ESTREES and HERLEVILLE

RIGHT SECTOR (PRESSOIRE - KRATZ)

Advanced Dressing Station SANITAS S.15.a.1.9

Relay posts for bearers S.16.a.2.8 S.16.a.9.0. (B. SERPENTIN)
S.16.c.3.8 X.28.b.3.6

Motor ambulances kept at HERLEVILLE and TOUR CARRE.
X.28.b.3.6

Secret

Amendment to R.A.M.C. Order No 11

Copy No 9

Para 4 Delete "HARBONNIERES and"

J F P Breen Capt
for Col. ADMS 61 Dvn

17.2.17.

Copies. 1. 61 Dvn. Q.
2-4. 182. 183. 184 Bdes. R.F.A
5-6. 306. 307. Bdes. R.F.A
7 Medicin Divisionaire 12th Dvn
8-9 War Diary
10-12 2/1 2/2 2/3 Fd Ambs.
13 Sanitary Section

Appendix 6

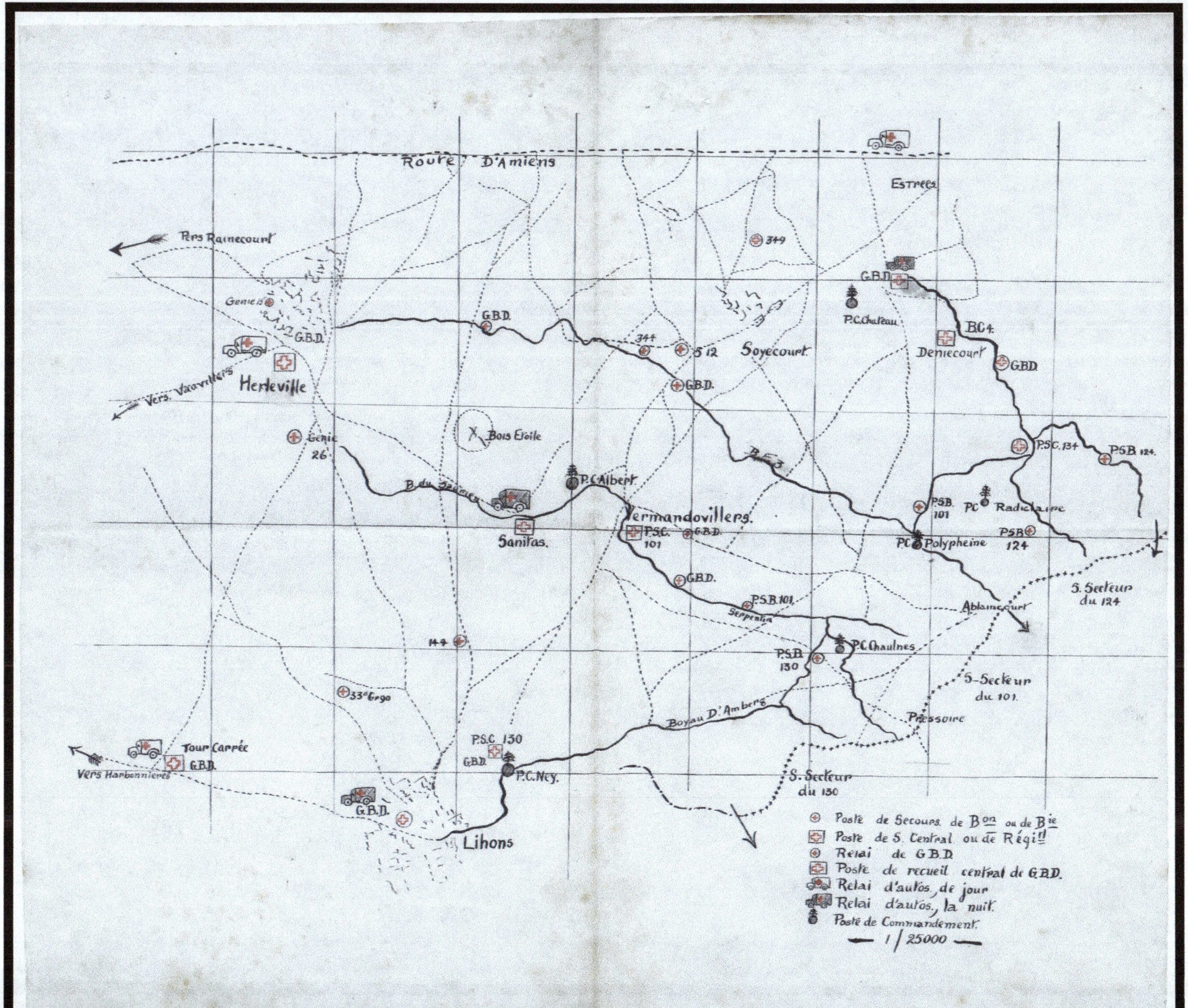

Roure D'Amiens
Estrees
Vers Rainecourt
Vers Vauvillers
Herleville
G.B.D.
Genie
Genie 26
Bois Etoile
B. du Sanitas
Sanitas
P.C. Albert
Vermandovillers
P.S.C. 101
G.B.D.
344
512
Soyecourt
349
P.C. Chateau
B.C.4
Deniecourt
P.S.C. 134
P.S.B. 124
P.S.B. 101
PC Radiclaire
PC Polypheine
P.S.B. 124
Ablaincourt
S. Secteur du 124
P.S.B. 101
Serpentin
P.S.B. 130
P.C. Chaulnes
S. Secteur du 101.
Pressoire
Boyau D'Amberg
P.S.C. 130
P.C. Ney
S. Secteur du 130
147
33e Grgo
Tour Carrée
Vers Harbonnieres
Lihons
Poste de Secours de Bon ou de Bie
Poste de S. Central ou de Régit
Relai de G.B.D.
Poste de recueil central de G.B.D.
Relai d'autos, de jour
Relai d'autos, la nuit.
Poste de Commandement.
1/25000

SECRET Copy No 13

61st Div Sanit. Order No 15

1 The 2/1 Field Ambulance will move from MARCELCAVE to GUILLACOURT (CHATEAUX) on 26th.

2 It will be ready for the reception of sick by 2 p.m. on that date.

3 Acknowledge.

G.W. Meakins Lt Colonel
for ADMS 61 Division

25/7

Copies No 1 61 Div Q.
2-4 182-3-4 Inf Bdes
5-6 306. 307 Bdes R.F.A
7-9 2/1st 2/2nd 2/3 Fd Ambs
10 Sanitary Section
11 D.D.M.S. 4th Corps
12 61st Div Supply Col
13.14 War Diary

Mar. 1917

S

Vol XI

140/2037

Confidential

War Diary of the

A.D.M.S. 61st Division

From:- March 1st 1917.
To:- March 31st 1917.

Volume No: 11.

Army Form C. 2118

WAR DIARY
or
INTELLIGENCE SUMMARY
(Erase heading not required.)

Instructions regarding War Diaries and Intelligence Summaries are contained in F. S. Regs., Part II. and the Staff Manual respectively. Title Pages will be prepared in manuscript.

Place	Date March	Hour	Summary of Events and Information	Remarks and references to Appendices
HARBONNIERES	1.		Germans raided trenches in T14 a (Ref Trench map VERMANDOVILLERS 62c S.W. 3) held by 2/4th Oxford and Bucks in early morning. About twenty wounded many with bombs. Considerable difficulty experienced in getting lying cases away - found impossible to do so in daylight owing to state of communication trenches. JFPB	
	2.		ADMS attended conference at H.Q. III Corps. French method of trench foot prophylaxis and treatment by washing with camphorated soap and powdering with talc and camphor to be adopted immediately. Arrangements made for two officers to proceed to HQ 1st Division to see system in action - JFPB	
	3.		DDMS III Corps visited Divisional HQ in connection with a confidential matter and also about accomodation for walking wounded cases. Second large hut at HARBONNIERES allotted by Division for hospital purposes. JFPB.	
	4		DADMS visited H.Q. 1st DIVISION at CHUIGNOLLES with reference to French method of trench foot prophylaxis also for Baths at CHUIGNES JFPB	
	5.		DADMS visited HQ 182 Inf. Brigade at VERMANDOVILLERS with reference to accomodation for foot washing - ADMS agreed to take over organisation of baths at HARBONNIERES JFPB -	

1875 Wt. W593/826 1,000,000 4/15 J.B.C. & A. A.D.S.S./Forms/C. 2118.

Army Form C. 2118.

Instructions regarding War Diaries and Intelligence Summaries are contained in F. S. Regs., Part II. and the Staff Manual respectively. Title pages will be prepared in manuscript.

WAR DIARY
or
INTELLIGENCE SUMMARY.
(Erase heading not required.)

Place	Date	Hour	Summary of Events and Information	Remarks and references to Appendices
HARBONNIERES	6		ADMS arranged to take over control of Divisional Baths and adapt same for foot washing scheme. DDMS IV Corps called reference use of Daimler cars in Front Area. M.T. department anxious to use Ford cars and horse ambulances to the exclusion of heavier cars which they find difficult to keep on the road owing to difficulty in obtaining spare parts. I consider this a completely wrong point of view the whole object of motor transport being to evacuate wounded from the front line as quickly and comfortably as possible. JJPB.	
	7.		Alterations in Divisional Baths proceeded with. DADMS visited 2/1st Field Ambulance. JJPBreen.	
	8.		DADMS visited LIHONS accompanied by O.C. 2/2nd Field Ambulance with reference to taking over medical posts from 35th Division 61st Division is taking over extra frontage as far as LIHONS CHAULNES ROAD to the South. It was arranged to take over the Advanced Dressing Station in LIHONS and two posts in front of this. Letter to DDMS II Corps protesting against restrictions in the use of Daimler ambulances JJPB.	

A5834 Wt W4973/M687 750,000 8/16 D. D. & L. Ltd. Forms/C.2118/13.

Instructions regarding War Diaries and Intelligence Summaries are contained in F. S. Regs., Part II. and the Staff Manual respectively. Title pages will be prepared in manuscript.

WAR DIARY
or
INTELLIGENCE SUMMARY.
(Erase heading not required.)

Army Form C. 2118.

Place	Date	Hour	Summary of Events and Information	Remarks and references to Appendices
HARBONNIERES	9		Telephone message received from DDMS IV Corps that use of DAIMLER cars might be left to the discretion of O.C. Field Ambulance clearing the line. O.C. 2/2nd Field Ambulance informed. Information received from DIV.H.Q. that gas shells containing hydrocyanic acid had been used by Germans on Russian Front and would probably be shortly used on the Western Front. Letter sent to DDMS IV Corps with reference to quantities of various ingredients required for French method of trench foot prophylaxis. On assumption that 9.000 men would use powder daily and that 9000 men would have a footbath every five days the quantities required per week would be Talc - 970 lbs camphor 30 lbs borax 30 lbs soap 175 lbs JJPB.	
"	10		Message received from DIV H.Q. that LT. COL. PICHARD RAMC T.F. appointed ADMS 61st DIVISION. At present commanding 24th Field Ambulance. DADMS visited FRAMERVILLE to inspect progress of work at bathing establishment there - no progress being made by RE. CRE communicated with. JJPB.	
"	11		Routine duties. JJPB	

A5834 Wt. W4973/M687 750,000 8/16 D. D. & L. Ltd. Forms/C.2118/13.

Instructions regarding War Diaries and Intelligence Summaries are contained in F. S. Regs., Part II. and the Staff Manual respectively. Title pages will be prepared in manuscript.

WAR DIARY
or
INTELLIGENCE SUMMARY.
(Erase heading not required.)

Army Form C. 2118.

Place	Date	Hour	Summary of Events and Information	Remarks and references to Appendices
HARBONNIERES	12		Lt Col PICKARD reported his arrival and assumed duties of ADMS - DDMS IX Corps visited Divisional H.Q. also 2/1st Field Ambulance. J.F.P.B.	
"	13.3.17		Visited A.D.S. at DENIECOURT & "SANITAS", also Adv. H'dqrs of 2nd/2nd Fd Amb'ce at HERLEVILLE. D.M.S. Fourth Army telephoned message to have body of man who died at No. 8 Post (T.14.a.) on 11th to be taken to No. 40 C.C.S. for examination. Note 2 patients suffering from shell gas were evacuated there on 11th.	RP
"	14.3.17		Inspected 2nd/1st Fd Amb & Divl. Rest Stn. at GUILLAUCOURT. The scabies cases are in a barn & not classified, another billet which will allow of this is to be taken over.	RP
"	16.3.17	9.30am	Visited ADS at LIHONS, relay posts in CAIN & IRIS trenches, & R.A.P. in TRIANGULAR WOOD. Visited Baths at HARBONNIERES. They are now in working order, the kits being ironed, men bathing, & their feet being washed with camphor, borax, & potash soap (trench foot treatment)	RP
"	16.3	7pm	61st Div. opern order No. 79 received, ordering a bombardment at various points of the line & a raid at T.14.a.4.0 — in conjunction with French attack S. of AMIENS-ROYE road	RP

A5834 Wt. W4973/M687 750,000 8/16 D. D. & L. Ltd. Forms/C.2118/13.

Instructions regarding War Diaries and Intelligence Summaries are contained in F. S. Regs., Part II and the Staff Manual respectively. Title Pages will be prepared in manuscript.

WAR DIARY
or
INTELLIGENCE SUMMARY
(Erase heading not required.)

Place	Date	Hour	Summary of Events and Information	Remarks and references to Appendices
HARBONNIERES	17.3.17	1.0pm	Conference of C/Os Fd Ambs N of SOMME In consequence of withdrawal of Germans & successful attack of French S. of AMIENS – ROYE road, & it being probable the Germans are retiring before this front, issued RAMC operation order no. 13 (App. 1.)	
"	"	2.30 pm	61st Divn Op. ord. 78 cancelled	
"	18.3.17	7.0 am	Received 61st Div. op. ord. no 80, detailing advance to line CHAULNES – MARCHLEPOT – T.16.c.9.1. On this issued RAMC op. orders no. 14. (App. 2.)	
		8.0pm	Went at 2.0pm to HERLEVILLE (2nd/2nd Fd Ambce), thence to ABLAINCOURT, chose A.D.S. & ordered 2nd/2nd to take possession. Went to LIHONS & TOUR CARRÉ, found 2nd/1st established there. Posts &c are as follows:– 2nd/1st (Rt Bgde area) RAP (8th Worcesters) A.6.c.9.2 (Rosière sheet) ADS (CHAULNES) A.5.c.1.7 " Brr. Relay Post A.3.b.2.4 " (LIHONS) ADS S.26.c.3.7 " TOUR CARRÉ (Hdqrs Fd Amb) X.28.b.3.4 " 2nd/2nd (Lt Bgde area) ADS (ABLAINCOURT) S.18.d.1.1 " Horse Waggon Post S.16.a.9.8 " Brr. Relay " S.16.d.9.5 " Car (Ambce) " (SANITAS) S.8.c.9.5 " Hdqrs Fd Amb. (HERLEVILLE) S.1.a.3.7 "	

1875 Wt. W593/826 1,000,000 4/15 J.B.C. & A. A.D.S.S./Forms/C. 2118.

Instructions regarding War Diaries and Intelligence Summaries are contained in F. S. Regs., Part II. and the Staff Manual respectively. Title Pages will be prepared in manuscript.

WAR DIARY
or
INTELLIGENCE SUMMARY
(Erase heading not required.)

ADMS - 61st Dvn

Army Form C. 2118

Place	Date	Hour	Summary of Events and Information	Remarks and references to Appendices
HARBONNIERE	19.3.17 - Contd		Wells have been found in CHAULNES	
			1) A.4.d.4.3 – 10 ft deep. Requires 1 measure of bleaching powder. Contains no arsenic. Windlass broken.	
			2) A.5.c.0.4 – Covered in, pump broken, therefore could not be tested. Other wells are either dry or partly filled with rubbish.	
			Sanitary work. 5 men of Sanitary Section to go to billet in CHAULNES on ~~18~~ 19.3.17 for work there & in forward area. Latrine buckets stored at TOUR CARRÉ.	RP
"	19.3.17	8.0pm	Operation Order No 15 issued.	(vide app. 3.)
			There has been no fighting W. of SOMME in this area. ADS.s have been formed by 2nd/1st Fld Amb at PERTAIN D.9.d.2.2.	
			" 2nd/2nd " " " MARCHLEPOT T.21.d.4.4.	
			The only road forward at present is from VERMANDOVILLERS to CHAULNES. The 2nd/1st ~~Fld~~ Ambce have at CHAULNES 1 Ford car, 1 limber g.s. 1 maltese cart, at PERTAIN 1 limber g.s. waggon	RP
"	20.3.17		Visited DENIECOURT, MARCHÉLEPOT, OMIÉCOURT, PERTAIN, CHAULNES	
			ROADS	
			ADS at MARCHELEPOT in German dugouts in railway embankment. Good	
			" at PERTAIN in ruined house, best obtainable	RP

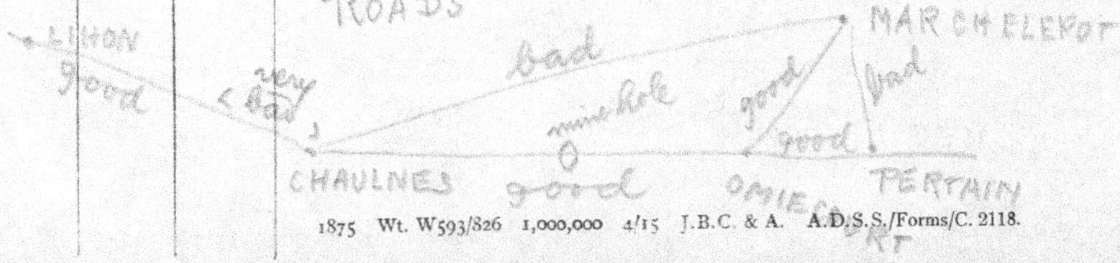

Instructions regarding War Diaries and Intelligence Summaries are contained in F. S. Regs., Part II. and the Staff Manual respectively. Title pages will be prepared in manuscript.

WAR DIARY
or
INTELLIGENCE SUMMARY.
(Erase heading not required.)

ADMS - 61st Divn

Army Form C. 2118.

Place	Date	Hour	Summary of Events and Information	Remarks and references to Appendices
HARBONNIERES	21.3.17		No change in positions of ~~Fd~~ Ambs. ~~Have~~ emptied Divl. Rest Stn & Scabies hospital at GUILLAUCOURT, lest we advance. Cases at 2nd/3rd ~~Fd~~ Amb at HARBONNIERES are only kept if ~~~~ they are likely to recover in 48 hours - App 4.	for R.P. [illegible]
			To day a ~~Daimler~~ FORD car reached MARCHELEPOT via VILLERS CARBONNEL. A DAIMLER car reached PERTAIN via CHILLY.	
			The 2nd/1st ~~Fd~~ Amb have now billets at PERTAIN, taken by pack & limber	for R.P. [illegible]
			A large no. of wells in forward area have been examined for chlorination ~~& ...~~ poisons	
"	22		Lt Col Pickard ADMS admitted to 2/3rd Field Ambulance suffering from concussion scalp wound and broken fingers. Lt-Col Mackie assumed the duties of ADMS. O.C. San Sec instructed to proceed as quickly as possible with the examination of water supplies east of the canal JTPB.	

A5834 Wt. W4973/M687 750,000 8/16 D. D. & L. Ltd. Forms/C.2118/13.

Instructions regarding War Diaries and Intelligence Summaries are contained in F. S. Regs., Part II. and the Staff Manual respectively. Title pages will be prepared in manuscript.

WAR DIARY
or
INTELLIGENCE SUMMARY.
(*Erase heading not required.*)

Army Form C. 2118.

Ref. FRANCE – AMIENS 1:100.000.

Place	Date	Hour	Summary of Events and Information	Remarks and references to Appendices
HARBONNIERES	1917 MAR. 23rd		Reports received on condition of wells arranged, tabulated & circulated to units concerned.	
			Inspected 1st F.A. posts at LIHONS. CHAULNES. & PERTAIN with D.A.D.M.S. & proceeded to BETHENCOURT in FORD AMBULANCE to prospect possible evacuation routes & state of roads.	
			Having found site of former German Hospital at BETHENCOURT – almost entirely destroyed. applied to "G" & "Q" 61st DIV. for permission to take over this place for a Fld. Amb. in event of a forward move.	[illegible]
			A.D.M.S. Sanitation. B.E.F. visited area.	
	MAR. 24th		D.D.M.S. IV. CORPS. visited area & inspected 1st FLD. AMB. at TOUR CARRÉ with D.A.D.M.S.	
			Lt. Col. H.N. BURROUGHES – O.C. 2nd FLD. AMB. reported back from leave of absence.	[illegible]
			Officers & men of 1st & 2nd FA's in touch with units E. of SOMME.	
	MAR. 25th		visited forward area with D.A.D.M.S. to see how roads were progressing towards completion.	[illegible]
			Preliminary orders received regarding approaching forward move of Division and warning order issued to FLD. AMB's. Arrangements begun for fresh disposition of the ambulances when moved.	
	MAR. 26th		Visited & inspected roads & bridges up to & beyond the SOMME & prospected for possible sites for the FLD. AMB's. at ATHIES. FALVY. PARGNY. CROIX MOLIGNEAUX. and on return after consultation with "Q" & "G" decided to place the three FLD. AMB's. as follows.	[illegible]

A5834 Wt. W4973/M687 750,000 8/16 D. D. & L. Ltd. Forms/C.2118/13.

Instructions regarding War Diaries and Intelligence Summaries are contained in F. S. Regs., Part II. and the Staff Manual respectively. Title pages will be prepared in manuscript.

Army Form C. 2118.

WAR DIARY
or
INTELLIGENCE SUMMARY.

Ref. FRANCE – AMIENS 1/100.000. + Sheets. 62C, 66D – 1/40.000.

(*Erase heading not required.*)

Place	Date	Hour	Summary of Events and Information	Remarks and references to Appendices
HARBONNIERES	1917. MAR. 26th contd.		1st FLD. AMB. at BETHENCOURT with an Advanced Collecting Post at MOLIGNEAUX. 2nd FLD. AMB. at ATHIES with a Collecting Post at MONTECOURT & an Advanced Dressing Station at TERTRY 3rd FLD. AMB. at PARGNY. O.C. San. Sec. reports that wells at all these places will be labelled after testing today.	[initials]
	MAR. 27th		DADMS. with O.C. 2nd FLD. AMB. visited forward area & selected sites for Advanced Dressing Station at TERTRY – Collecting Post at MONTECOURT – to be used until Evacuation routes are well established – and main dressing station at ATHIES. Satisfactory positions selected but great difficulty of access to ATHIES until temporary road repairs effected as all roads entering have been badly mined.	
			R.A.M.C. order No. 16. with march table & sketch maps attached, issued at 12 noon to the Field Ambulances etc. Reports received that preparations are well in hand for the move and that all posts working satisfactorily.	vide app. No. 5 [initials]
			Report on forward wells received from the DIV. San. Office. Forwarded to "Q" 61st DIVN. for circulation.	
	MAR. 28th		DADMS. visited A.D.M.S. 35th DIV. to arrange for attendance & collecting of casual sick left in our area by Field Ambulances of 35th DIVN. O.C. 3rd FLD. AMB. instructed to leave behind one M.O. and 2 Nursing orderlies with one car to do the routine work involved – Appendix 6 Visited 1st FLD. AMB. Posts & inspected their new premises at BETHENCOURT. LIHONS – CHAULNES Road open today for traffic. 61st DIV. order received for ADMS. Office to move on 29th to GUIZANCOURT. E. of SOMME CANAL. R.A.M.C. order No. 17. issued. v. appendix. No. 6	[initials]

A5834 Wt. W4973/M687 750,000 8/16 D. D. & L. Ltd. Forms/C.2118/13.

Instructions regarding War Diaries and Intelligence Summaries are contained in F. S. Regs., Part II. and the Staff Manual respectively. Title Pages will be prepared in manuscript.

WAR DIARY
or
INTELLIGENCE SUMMARY
(Erase heading not required.)

Army Form C. 2118

Map. Reference.
FRANCE. Sheets. 62c & 66D
1/40,000.

Place	Date	Hour	Summary of Events and Information	Remarks and references to Appendices
GUIZANCOURT	1917. MAR 29th		61st DN. H.Q. moved to GUIZANCOURT. 3rd FLD. AMB diverted to FALVY owing to an ~~administrative~~ Redistribution.	
			Warning from "G" 61st DIV. that active operations are to be undertaken this evening.	
			Arranged for 2nd FLD. AMB. to send out a forward party & relays of bearers to be in forward position in time. Visited 1st FLD. AMB. at BETHENCOURT & arranged for temporary increase in accommodation in marquees. Visited 2nd FLD. AMB. at ATHIES & inspected their arrangements.	
			D.A.D.M.S. prospected forward line as far as E of POEUILLY & found hut suitable for Advanced Dressing Station there with Relay Post in VRAIGNES WOOD. Arrangements completed when information received that operations postponed for 24 hours.	
			G.O.C. 61st DIV. held Conference with reference to these & proposed subsequent operations on this front.	T.W.L.
	MAR. 30th		Arrangements made yesterday confirmed & extended. O.C. all three FLD. AMB's seen personally informed of all details. Evacuation arranged to BETHENCOURT & clearance from there by M.A.C. Serious & urgent cases to NESLE to 91st FLD. AMB. which is to act as a temporary C.C.S. with one extra Surgeon on staff detailed for duty there by D.D.M.S. IV CORPS.	
			R.A.M.C. order No. 18. issued – (V. app. No. 7	
			D.D.M.S. IV CORPS visited H.Q.	
			Visited all 3 FLD. AMB's & went over Evacuation route. Roads on the whole satisfactory & all personnel & horse & motor ambulances etc in position by 6 p.m.	
			Operations postponed till 7.45 p.m.	T.W.L.

1875 Wt. W593/826 1,000,000 4/15 J.B.C. & A. A.D.S.S./Forms/C. 2118.

Instructions regarding War Diaries and Intelligence Summaries are contained in F. S. Regs., Part II. and the Staff Manual respectively. Title Pages will be prepared in manuscript.

WAR DIARY
or
INTELLIGENCE SUMMARY
(Erase heading not required.)

Army Form C. 2118

Map. Reference.
FRANCE. Sheets 62C & 66D
1/40.000.

Place	Date	Hour	Summary of Events and Information	Remarks and references to Appendices
GUIZANCOURT.	1917. MAR. 31st		D.A.D.M.S. visited and inspected POEUILLY and VERMAND with the adjoining roads and the Country round. Selected site for an Advanced Dressing Station at both places when necessary. Visited 1st FLD. AMB. at BETHENCOURT. Good constructional work going on. Accommodation ready for over 100 patients and by tonight marquees sufficient for 150 will be ready.	
		2.30pm.	Instructions received from "G" 61st DIV. that operations of considerable importance are in prospect N.E. of VERMAND on an early date.	
			2nd FLD. AMB. ordered to move forward from ATHIES to establish an Advanced Dressing Station at POEUILLY to evacuate casualties from new front.	
			R.A.M.C. order No. 19 issued.	Vide appendix No. 8
			Saw O.C. 2nd FLD. AMB. personally & went over all details with him as to probable present and future course of operations.	[initials]

G. E. Mackie
Lt. Col. R.A.M.C. T.
for COL. A.D.M.S. 61st DIVISION.

1875 Wt. W593/826 1,000,000 4/15 J.B.C. & A. A.D.S.S./Forms/C. 2118.

APPENDIX 1.

SECRET. 61st Division R.A.M.C.Order No 13. Copy No. 13

1. The III Corps to the North has commenced to Advance.- the French are advancing South of the ALBERT - ROYE ROAD. The 182 and 183 Brigades are pushing out patrols towards MARCHELPOT and HYENCOURT-LE-GRAND.

2. The O.C. 2/2nd Field Ambulance will establish his Headquarters at HERLEVILLE.

3. A second M.O. will be sent to DENIECOURT and SANITAS and will be responsible for keeping in touch with the regimental M.Os of the Battalions cleared by those A.D.Ss

4. The personnel at all posts in front of DENIECOURT and SANITAS will be doubled.

5. The O.C. 2/3rd Field Ambulance will arrange to take over the line of evacuation from TRIANGULAR WOOD through BOYEAU CAIN to LIHONS, and the cellar formerly used as an A.D.S. in LIHONS. The O.C. 2/2nd Field Ambulance will continue to be responsible for the remainder of the front.

6. All cases will be evacuated direct to HARBONNIERES from both sectors of the front.

7. The O.C. 2/1st Field Ambulance will send one tent subdivision to TOUR CARRE and will prepare this place to act as a Main Dressing Station in the event of a further advance.

8. The 2/1st Field Ambulance less half a tent subdivision will be prepared to move at 4 hours notice.

9. All above dispositions will be carried out forthwith.

10. If it becomes necessary to establish walking wounded stations, they will be situated at DENIECOURT, HERLEVILLE, and TOUR CARRE. TOUR CARRE will be staffed by the 2/1st Field Ambulance, DENIECOURT and HERLEVILLE by the 2/2nd Field Ambulance.

11. Acknowledge.

[signature]
Colonel.
A.D.M.S. 61st Division.

17/3/17.

Copies to:-
No 1. 61st Div. Q.
2. D.D.M.S. IV Corps.
3-5. 2/1. 2/2. 2/3. Fd Ambs.
6-8. 182. 183. 184 Bdes.
9-10. 306. 307 Bdes.R.F.A.
11. C.R.E.
12-13. War Diary.

APPENDIX 2.

COPY No

SECRET.

R.A.M.C. OPERATION ORDER No 14.

TACTICAL POSITION. 1. Advance of French to South of Fourth Army is meeting with practically no opposition.

2. The 3rd and 4th Corps will send forward detachments towards the RIVER SOMME.

3. The Division will advance (A) To Line CHAULNES - HIRNCOURT-LE-GRAND - MARCHELEPOT. (B) Patrols will be pushed forward to line BERSAUCOURT - PERTAIN- LICOURT. The advance from present line will begin at 9.0.a.m.today.

MOVES OF FD AMBS. The Operation Order No 13 is cancelled and the following substituted.

(A). The 2/1st Field Ambulance less half a tent sub division will establish Headquarters at TOUR CARRE and will send forward a bearer sub division under an officer, with a view to establishing an advanced dressing station at CHAULNES. They will detach another medical officer to report to Brigade Headqrs RIGHT BRIGADE, to test any wells west of the line CHAULNES- MARCHELEPOT in the Brigade Area, both for metallic poisons and chlorination purposes. Touch must be kept with Battalions by means of stretcher squads, the most forward of which will keep with the Regimental M.O.

(B). The 2/2nd Field Ambulance will move to HERLEVILLE as soon as possible. It will establish an Advanced Dressing Station at ABLAINCOURT and about T.8.c.5.9. (where good regimental aid post already exists). An M.O. will report to Left Brigade Headquarters, with a view to testing water in LEFT BRIGADE AREA, west of CHAULNES-MARCHELEPOT Line, as detailed above. Touch will be kept with Regimental M.Os as described under (A).

(C). The 2/3rd Field Ambulance will remain in HARBONNIERES and will evacuate all cases not likely to recover in 48 hours.

(D). O.C.Sanitary Section will assist in water testing in the CHAULNES AREA.

COMMUNICATIONS. 4. The Os.C. of the 2/1st and the 2/2nd Field Ambs and the O.C.Sanitary Section will send reports as soon as possible upon the water supply of the district West of the Line CHAULNES- MARCHELEPOT. All information concerning the tactical position which they learn must at once be communicated to this office which will remain at HARBONNIERES.

TIME. These operations will be carried out immediately on receipt of this order.

ACKNOWLEDGE.

Issued at 9.45.a.m.

R Pickard Colonel.

18/3/17.

A.D.M.S. 61st Division.

Copies to
1. 61st Div.Q.
2. D.D.M.S. IV Corps.
3-5. 2/1. 2/2. 2/3. Fd Amb.
6-8. 182. 183. 184 Bdes.
9-10. 306. 307 Bdes.R.F.A.
11. Sanitary Section.
12-13. War Diary.

APPENDIX 3

Copy No. 12

SECRET.

61st Division.R.A.M.C.Order No 15.

TACTICAL POSITION 1. The country in the IV Corps Area up to the SOMME between CANIZY and EPENANCOURT is said to be clear of Germans, except for small parties. The 3rd and 4th Corps will continue their march to the line of the SOMME on the 19th.

AREAS. 2. Divisional Boundaries are SOUTH - CHAULNES-BERSAUCOURT - DRESLINGCOURT- ROUY LE GRAND- (exclusive) NORTH Present Boundary MARCHELEPOT (inclusive) EPENANCOURT (inclusive). The Division will take up a line MESNIL ST NICAISE MORCHAIN - LICOURT, with outposts on the Line ROUY LE GRAND- EPENANCOURT.
Boundaries between Brigades are PERTAIN - MENCHAIN- FONTAINE LES PERGAU road (inclusive to 183rd Brigade).

MEDICAL ARRANGEMENTS. 3. If possible, line of evacuation of cases from both Brigades will be through CHAULNES.
(a). The 2/1st Field Ambulance will establish an Advanced Dressing Station as far forward as PERTAIN if this is possible. They will keep on their present A.D.S. at CHAULNES as a bearer relay post and depot for stores. They will collect from the RIGHT BRIGADE.
(b). The 2/2nd Field Ambulance will establish an Advanced Dressing Station at MARCHELEPOT, retaining the present A.D.S. at ABLAINCOURT as a bearer post and depot for stores. They will collect from the LEFT BRIGADE.
The A.D.S. at DENIECOURT will be retained with a minimum of personnel for local sick for the present.
(c). 2/3rd Field Ambulance will remain at HARBONNIERES . All cases collected from the Forward AREA will be sent there, except urgent cases which may be sent direct to C.C.S. nominal rolls of these being sent to the 2/3rd Field Ambulance.
Reports of posts formed, their capacity, proposed lines of evacuation, sites of relay posts, water supply, etc must be forwarded as soon as possible to the A.D.M.S. Office.

COMMUNICATIONS. 4. A.D.M.S. Office remains at HARBONNIERES.
5. Acknowledge.

R. Richard
Colonel.
A.D.M.S. 61st Division.

19/3/17.
Issued at 10.15.a.m.

Copies to 1. 61 Div.Q.
2. D.D.M.S. IV Corps.
3-5. 2/1. 2/2. 2/3.F.Amb.
6-8. 182. 183. 184 Bdes.
9-10. 306, 307 Bdes.R.F.A.
11. Sanitary Section.
12-13. War Diary.

APPENDIX 4

SECRET.

Copy No 13

61st Divisional R.A.M.C. Operation Orders No 16.

1. Advanced Dressing Stations are established at PERTAIN(E.9.d.2.2.) and MARCHELEPOT (T.21.d.9.9.)

2. Divisional Rest Station.
All cases which will not recover in 48 hours will be evacuated to C.C.S. on 20/3/17. No other cases will be sent to Divisional Rest Station
On 22/3/17 the tent subdivision will join main party at TOUR CARRE.
Scabies.
Scabies cases will be returned to duty on 21/3/17. A nominal roll will be kept of all those not cured, so that they may be treated later. No more Scabies cases will be admitted to Field Ambs at present.

3. Stores.
The O.C. 2/1st Field Ambulance will choose a site, preferably at PERTAIN but not further forward, where he will store tents and other material for a Dressing Station. He will take there four marquees which will be handed over by the Sanitary Section lorry at TOUR CARRE.

4. Acknowledge.

Colonel.
20/3/17. A.D.M.S. 61st Division.

Issued at 10.0 AM

Copies to 1. 61 Dvn.Q.
2. D.D.M.S. IV Corps.
3-5. 2/1. 2/2. 2/3. Fd Ambs.
6-8. 182. 183. 184 Bdes.
9-10. 306. 307 Bdes.R.F.A.
11. Sanitary Section.
12-13. War Diary.

APPENDIX 5

SECRET. COPY No:

61st Division R.A.M.C. Order No: 16.A

Ref: Maps - France 62c and 66d 1/40,000

1. The 61st Division will advance to the line BEAUVOIS (exclusive) to about Q.23 central. The 32nd Division will be on the right; the 59th Division will be on the left.

2. The 2nd Field Ambulance will establish a Main Dressin Station at ATHIES and will have an Advanced Dressing Station at TERTRY with Collecting Post at MONTECOURT.

3. The posts at DENIECOURT and SANITAS at present staffe by the 2nd Field Ambulance will be vacated by 3 p.m. on the 28th and the post at MARCHELPOT by 10 a.m. on the 29th.

4. The 1st Field Ambulance will establish a Dressing Station at BETHENCOURT. It will also establish a post in MOLIGNEAUX.

5. The posts at present occupied by the 1st Field Ambulance will be vacated as follows -

LIHONS by 3 p.m. on the 28th
CHAULNES by 4 p.m. on the 28th
PERTAIN by 7 p.m. on the 28th.

6. The 3rd Field Ambulance will establish its headquarters in PARGNY.

7. The moves mentioned above will take place in accordan with the attached table.

8. Os.C. Field Ambulances will be responsible for providing their own guides.

9. Casual sick remaining in back area will be dealt with under arrangement with A.D.M.S., 35th Division.

10. Acknowledge.

Issued at 12 noon 27th of March 1917.

G.W. Mackie
Lieut:Colonel.
Actg A.D.M.S., 61st Division.

Copies to No:1. 61st Div "Q"
2. 61st Div "G"
3. D.D.M.S., IV Corps.
4. A.D.M.S., 32nd Div:
5. A.D.M.S., 59th Div:
6-8. 1st, 2nd, 3rd, Fd. Ambs.
9-11. 182-3-4 Inf: Bdes:
12-14. 306.307.157. Bdes: R.F.A.
15. C.R.E.
16. 61st Div: Train.
17. 61st Div: Supply Column.
18-19. War Diary.

APPENDIX 5

SECRET.

MARCH TABLE ISSUED WITH R.A.M.C. ORDER NO: 16.

DATE.	UNIT.	FROM.	TO.	REMARKS
28.3.17	1st Field Amb:	TOUR CARRE	BETHENCOURT	Not to cross MORCHAIN-LICOURT line before 7.30 p.m. on 28th
28.3.17	2nd Field Amb:	HERLEVILLE	ATHIES	
29.3.17	3rd Field Amb.	HARBONNIERES	PARGNY	End of column to be clear of MORCHAIN-LICOURT line by 12 noon on the 29th.

- -

APPENDIX 6.

SECRET COPY NO:- 19.

61st DIVISION R.A.M.C. ORDER NO:- 17. 28.3.17

1. The Divisional Sanitary Section will move to CROIX MOLIGNAUX on the 29th and will be clear of the line MORCHAIN - LICOURT by 12 Noon.

2. The A.D.M.S. Office will close at HARBONNIERES at 9 a.m. and will reopen at the same hour at GUIZANCOURT.

3. The Officer Commanding 2/3rd Field Ambulance will leave behind one Medical Officer and one orderly to see the sick of the details remaining in the area. He will also send back a Motor Ambulance on the 30th instant, which will be at the disposal of the officer left. Sick will be evacuated to the 107 Field Ambulance. ROSIERES.

[signature]
Lieut:Colonel.
Acting A.D.M.S., 61st Division.

March 28th 1917.

Copies to :-
No:1 "G"
2 "Q"
3 D.D.M.S., IV Corps.
4-6 1st,2nd,3rd Field Ambs.
7-9 182,183,184 Inf:Bdes:
10-12 306,307,157 Bdes:RFA
13 C.R.E.
14 O.C.Sanitary Section
15 Town Major. HARBONNIERES.
16 Claims Office
17 Salvage Officer
18-19 War Diary

APPENDIX 7

SECRET. COPY NO:

61st DIVISION R.A.M.C. OPERATION ORDER NO:18. March 30th 1917

1. An attack on the village of SOYECOURT will be carried out by the 182nd Brigade this evening.

2. The attack will be carried out by the 8th Warwicks. This battalion will deploy east of POEUILLY and advance from there at 6.15 p.m.

3. The O.C. 2/2nd Field Ambulance will establish a post in VRAIGNES WOOD. Q.27a. by 2 p.m. and will transport all stores necessary for forming an advanced dressing station to this place.

4. An Advanced Dressing Station will be formed in POEUILLY at Q.28.b.8.0. by 6 p.m. personnel and equipment being moved by the side road through Q.27b - Q.28a.

5. Evacuation will be carried out by wheeled stretcher to crater at Q.26.b.5.6. thence by horse ambulances to crater at P.30.d.2.6. and from there by motor ambulance to ATHIES, or BETHENCOURT, at discretion of O.C. 2/2nd Field Ambulance.

7. Sixty stretcher bearers will be available at POEUILLY and a further 20 will be in reserve at TERTRY.

8. Acknowledge.

Issued at 11.30 a.m.

J.P. Brown
Captain.
for Colonel A.D.M.S. 61st Division

Copies to:-
No:1. "G"
2. "Q"
3. D.D.M.S. IVth Corps.
4-6. 182,183,184 Inf.Bdes.
7-8. 307,308 Bdes R.F.A.
9. C.R.E.
10. A.D.M.S., 32nd Division.
11. A.D.M.S., 35th Division.
12-13. War Diary.

APPENDIX 8

SECRET. COPY NO: 17

61st DIVISION R.A.M.C. OPERATION ORDER NO: 19.

1. The 2/2nd Field Ambulance will move to TERTRY on April 1st and will establish a Main Dressing Station at this place by 12 noon.

2. All tentage will be taken to TERTRY in sufficient time to permit of it being pitched by 12 noon.

3. The section equipment of two sections, all medical comforts, and all stretchers, must be at TERTRY by 12 noon.

4. The present Advanced Dressing Station at POEUILLY will be expanded and one section will be stationed there.

5. Sufficient details should be left at ATHIES to take charge of stores left behind. These must be taken to TERTRY as soon as possible.

6. All wheeled stretchers held by the 2/2nd Field Ambulance are to be sent to POEUILLY.

7. If necessary the O.C. 2/2nd Field Ambulance may evacuate to 2/1st Field Ambulance at ENTHENCOURT.

8. Acknowledge.

G. Mackie
Lieut:Colonel.
Acting A.D.M.S., 61st Division.

Issued at 7 p.m. 31/3/17.

Copies to :-
No: 1. "G"
2. "Q"
3. D.D.M.S., IVth Corps.
4-6. 1,2,3, Field Ambs.
7-9. 182,183,184 Inf. Bdes.
10-11. 306,307 Bdes R.F.A.
12. 61 Div: Train.
13. 61 Div Supply Column.
14. C.R.E.
15. A.D.M.S., 32nd Division.
16. A.D.M.S., 59th Division.
17-18. War Diary.

CONFIDENTIAL.

WAR DIARY.

of the

A.D.M.S. 61st DIVISION.

for the month of APRIL 1917.

VOLUME No. 12.

In the Field.
May 3rd, 1917.

Instructions regarding War Diaries and Intelligence Summaries are contained in F. S. Regs., Part II. and the Staff Manual respectively. Title pages will be prepared in manuscript.

WAR DIARY *or* INTELLIGENCE SUMMARY.

(*Erase heading not required.*)

Map Reference. FRANCE Sheets. 62C 62B 66D

Army Form C. 2118.

Place	Date	Hour	Summary of Events and Information	Remarks and references to Appendices
GUIZANCOURT	1917. APRIL 1st		Visited TERTRY to prospect site for 2nd FLD. AMB. to which they moved this morning arriving about 11a.m. Went on to POEUILLY. Advanced Dressing Station there is in a large corrugated iron shed evidently used by German Cavalry & left intact by them. Eastern gable is obvious from the German position & possibly a mark. Selected new site under adjacent bank about 300yds E. of shed & advised O.C. 2nd FLD. AMB. to dig shelters there.	
			Sent San. Sec. motor lorry back to HARBONNIERES to fetch spare stretchers & blankets left there by 3rd FLD. AMB. These dumped at 1st FLD. AMB. at BETHENCOURT as Divisional Reserve.	
			Inspected 61st DIV. San. Sec. premises at CROIX MOLIGNEAUX.	
			Information received from "G" 61st DIV: of an attack by us along DIV. FRONT at 5a.m. April 2nd. D.A.D.M.S. inspected VERMAND & selected site for further advanced post to be occupied by the 2nd FLD. AMB. in advance of POEUILLY A.D.S.	
			Visited 3rd FLD. AMB. at FALVY – Saw O.C. & explained operations in detail. Warned him that his ambulance would be moved up to clear Right of line which is now divided in two by the River OMIGNON. Communication across which is at present doubtful.	
			Visited O.C. 1st FLD. AMB. & arranged for him to act as main Dressing Station for division & told him to supply extra blankets. stretchers. & Petrol regularly.	
			Sent San. Sec. Lorry to MARCHELPOT & ATHIES to collect marquees to be erected at TERTRY.	
			D.A.D.M.S. returned having found site for 3rd FLD. AMB. at TREFCON with Advanced Dressing Stn at VILLEVEQUE.	
			61st DIV. R.A.M.C. order No. 20 issued at 3.45p.m.	vide App. 1
				[illegible initials]

A5834 Wt. W4973 M687 750,000 8/16 D. D. & L. Ltd. Forms/C.2118/13.

Instructions regarding War Diaries and Intelligence Summaries are contained in F. S. Regs., Part II. and the Staff Manual respectively. Title pages will be prepared in manuscript.

WAR DIARY Map Reference – FRANCE –
or
INTELLIGENCE SUMMARY. Sheets – 62c. 62B. 66D.

(*Erase heading not required.*)

Army Form C. 2118.

Place	Date	Hour	Summary of Events and Information	Remarks and references to Appendices
	1917.			
GUIZANCOURT.	APRIL 2nd		With D.A.D.M.S. visited 2nd & 3rd FLD. AMBULANCES & inspected premises. Found evacuation of wounded proceeding smoothly and satisfactorily. Some delay in getting men back from actual line as infantry reported advancing. Circular car service from BETHENCOURT via PARGNY-FALVY-ENNEMAIN to TERTRY and back via MONCHY-LAGACHE & CROIX MOLIGNEAUX to BETHENCOURT – working well.	
			8 wounded Germans brought down. 1 died at VERMAND.	
			Inspected 3rd FLD. AMB. advanced dressing station at VILLEVEQUE & surrounding area. D.A.D.M.S. selected a further advanced post for this ambulance in chalk quarry at R.27.c.8.4. and a further post for 2nd FLD. AMB. in railway station at R.20.d.9.3.	
			R.A.M.C. order No. 21 issued. Special instructions received from G. 61st DIV: that our troops having attained their objective a further advance was in preparation. Urgent orders sent to 2nd & 3rd FLD. AMBULANCES to occupy their new posts without delay.	vide app. No. 2.
			D.D.M.S. IV CORPS visited H.Qrs. re Evacuations — [illegible] tentage etc.	[initials]
	APRIL 3rd		Field Marshal Sir Douglas Haig G.C.B. etc. Commander in Chief – visited divisional area.	
			3rd FLD. AMB. moved its H.Qrs to TREFCON & doubled its personnel at its forward posts.	
			Inspected 2nd FLD. AMB. at TERTRY and 1st FLD. AMB. at BETHENCOURT where there is now room for over 150 patients & a satisfactory system for receiving & clearing patients in considerable numbers if necessary.	
			Congratulatory message received by the Division from the Commander-in-Chief.	[initials]

A5834 Wt. W4973/M687 750,000 8/16 D. D. & L. Ltd. Forms/C.2118/13.

Instructions regarding War Diaries and Intelligence Summaries are contained in F. S. Regs., Part II. and the Staff Manual respectively. Title Pages will be prepared in manuscript.

WAR DIARY
or
INTELLIGENCE SUMMARY
(Erase heading not required.)

Army Form C. 2118

Map Reference
FRANCE
Sheets - 62c 62B & 66D.

Place	Date	Hour	Summary of Events and Information	Remarks and references to Appendices
GUIZANCOURT	1917 APRIL 4th		D.A.D.M.S. visited forward area and selected two sites for further Advanced Dressing Stations in case of a further advance on our divisional front. One at BIHECOURT - R.21.d.9.9. and one near MAISSEMY at R.22.b.5.4. Also another site for an advanced post in the BOIS d' HOLNON at R.35.d.5.5.	
			Saw O.C. 2nd FLD. AMB and explained situation in detail.	
			61st DIV. RAMC Operation order. No. 22 issued at 6p.m.	vide appendix - 3.
			Instructions received from G.O.C. 61st DIV. to place O.C. San. Sec. under arrest for failing to comply with an order on April 2nd re despatching San. Sec. Lorry to fetch stores.	Geo. Kr.
	APRIL 5th		Visited forward posts of 2nd FLD. AMB. as far as VERMAND. Found everything working satisfactorily though accommodation very limited and tents being used where possible.	
			Visited. 3rd FLD. AMB. Hd. Qrs & went over their line of evacuation as far as MARTEVILLE.	
			Saw Staff of 183rd INF. BDE. HD. QRS. at VILLEVEQUE & found arrangements understood & considered satisfactory in view of possible active operations this evening.	
			Telephoned D.D.M.S. Corps about M.A.Convoy possibilities & arranged that while our main evacuation centre would be 1st FLD. AMB. at BETHENCOURT. still it would be possible to have the convoy cars up to TERTRY by main N. Road through ESTRÉES en CHAUSSÉE in case of any congestion.	Geo. Kr.
			O.C. San. Sec. 61. DIV. Reprimanded by GOC-61.DIV. & released from arrest.	
	APRIL 6th		Information received that last night's operations were not carried out. So medical arrangements and dispositions remain the same until they have taken place. Special evacuation route scheme prepared & issued. Inspected all three Field Ambulances. D.D.M.S. IV CORPS called. Ordered by "Q" 61 DIV. to withdraw back area officer from HARBONNIERES.	vide app. 4 Geo. Kr.

Instructions regarding War Diaries and Intelligence Summaries are contained in F. S. Regs., Part II. and the Staff Manual respectively. Title pages will be prepared in manuscript.

WAR DIARY
or
INTELLIGENCE SUMMARY.
(*Erase heading not required.*)

Army Form C. 2118.

MAP REFERENCE.
FRANCE – Sheets
62c SE. 62B 66D.

Place	Date	Hour	Summary of Events and Information	Remarks and references to Appendices
GUIZANCOURT	1917. APRIL 6th Contd.		Information received from "G" 61st DIV. that tonights operations would include both Brigades – 184th on left and 183rd on Right. – Field Ambulances warned to prepare for roughly 150 casualties –	[illegible]
	APRIL 7th		D.A.D.M.S. visited forward area to see how evacuation of Casualties estimated at about ~~100 or~~ 150 was being carried out – Found their arrival from line rather slow. Otherwise arrangements good – Met D.D.M.S. IV CORPS by appointment at 1st FLD. AMB. at BETHENCOURT to discuss accommodation there and the question of Back area medical attendance – Visited 2nd FLD. AMB. and 3rd FLD. AMB. & inspected premises – Advanced Dressing Station of the 3rd FLD. AMB in BOIS d'HOLNON had been shelled in the night. Position had therefore been altered – One horse ambulance had been hit. 2 horses killed & orderly slightly wounded by small fragment in back – Not being evacuated from the ambulance. DIVISIONAL COMMANDER sent in a message of thanks & congratulation from BRIG.GEN. SPOONER G.O.C. 183rd INF. BDE. to O.C. 3rd FLD. AMB. and his officers NCOs & men for their excellent work. This message was duly conveyed to the ambulance concerned with congratulations from this Office	[illegible]
	APRIL 8th		150 extra stretchers drawn & issued to the Field Ambulances in the line. Instructions received from "G." 61st DIVn that operations would take place tonight on both sectors of our divisional front. & that as some of the posts to be attacked are held in strength casualties may be numerous – 61st D.R.A.M.C. Order No. 23. issued & Field Ambulance Commanders warned (vide appendix – 4) to be ready to deal with about 150 casualties from both sectors –	[illegible]

A5834 Wt. W4973 M687 750,000 8/16 D. D. & L. Ltd. Forms/C.2118/13.

Instructions regarding War Diaries and Intelligence Summaries are contained in F. S. Regs., Part II. and the Staff Manual respectively. Title pages will be prepared in manuscript.

WAR DIARY
or
INTELLIGENCE SUMMARY.
(Erase heading not required.)

MAP. Reference FRANCE. SHEETS. 62C 62B & 66D

Army Form C. 2118.

Place	Date	Hour	Summary of Events and Information	Remarks and references to Appendices
GUIZANCOURT	1917. APRIL.9th		Divisional Operations reported successful. All objectives gained on both fronts. 2nd Field Ambulance on left scarcely employed. 3rd FLD. AMB. on Right reports about 40 casualties in all. Evacuation working smoothly. M.A.C. cleared for first time direct from TREFCON.	
			Orders received from "G" 61st DIV. that this Division is to be relieved by 35th DIVn. March table for Brigades received. A.D.M.S. instructed to arrange Field Ambulance reliefs direct with A.D.M.S. 35th DIV.	
			A.D.M.S & D.A.D.M.S. 35th DIV. called at DIV. Hd Qrs & after discussion went round the area. Marquees & fixtures to be left in position.	
			After consulting D.D.M.S. IV Corps. arranged that 1st FLD. AMB. should remain at BETHENCOURT to look after 183rd INF. BDE. — area. ATHIES. ENNEMAIN. CROIX MOLIGNEAUX. 2nd FLD. AMB. should relieve 106th FLD. AMB. at OFFOY to serve 184th INF. BDE. area — HOMBLEUX. VOYENNES. OFFOY. CANIZY. 3rd FLD. AMB. to be relieved by 106th will move to 182nd INF. BDE. area. DOUILLY. QUIVIERES. ETREILLERS. VAUX. when a suitable site has been found.	
			Visited 2nd & 3rd FLD. AMB'S & acquainted O.C.'s with these preliminary arrangements pending the settlement in detail.	G.W.Che.
	APRIL.10th		Prospected sites at OFFOY for 2nd FLD. AMB. and at DOUILLY for the 3rd FLD. AMB: MATIGNY too badly destroyed to be of any use.	
			Met A.D.M.S. 35th DIVISION and arranged with him all details of move & as to handing over. Marquees stretchers etc. now in position in forward area. 61 D.R.A.M.C. order No. 24. issued.	(vide appendix No. 5) G.W.Che.

A5834 Wt. W4973/M687 750,000 8/16 D. D. & L. Ltd. Forms/C.2118/13.

Army Form C. 2118.

Instructions regarding War Diaries and Intelligence Summaries are contained in F. S. Regs., Part II. and the Staff Manual respectively. Title pages will be prepared in manuscript.

WAR DIARY or INTELLIGENCE SUMMARY.

(Erase heading not required.)

MAP REFERENCE – FRANCE SHEETS – 62C 62B 66D

Place	Date	Hour	Summary of Events and Information	Remarks and references to Appendices
GUIZANCOURT	1917 April		Visited and inspected 2/1st FLD. AMB. at BETHENCOURT & arranged for the opening of a SCABIES Hospital there as soon as possible – Difficulty in billetting all troops in new area, therefore again visited DOUILLY with D.A.D.M.S. & after consultation with "Q" 61. DIV. arranged premises for 2/3rd FLD. AMB.	
			2/2nd FLD. AMB. arrived at OFFOY & opened for reception of patients –	
			2/3rd FLD. AMB. arrived at DOUILLY & secured temporary accommodation to move into their billets tomorrow morning when 2/7 R. War. R. moves out –	
			O.C. 2/1st F.A. instructed to see G.O.C. 183rd INF. BDE. at ENNEMAIN to arrange direct evacuation of Brigade sick –	
			Orders received for move of 61st DIV. HQ as tomorrow to VOYENNES – & supplementary order on this issued to all units of change of location of A.D.M.S. office to that place –	[signature]
VOYENNES	12		Divisional H.Q. moved to VOYENNES – Col HOWKINS reported his arrival to assume duties of ADMS – Col HOWKINS and Lt. Col. MACKIE attended the conference of ADsMS at IV Corps HQ. J.T.P.B	
	13		DADMS visited 2/2nd Field Ambulance – Request received from IV Corps for one tent subdivision to report at LANGUEVOISIN to form an offshoot of 107 Field Ambulance.	
	14		Orders received from IV Corps to send one officer and the personnel of a tent subdivision – two marquees 200 stretchers and as many blankets	

A5834 Wt. W4973 M687 750,000 8/16 D. D. & L. Ltd. Forms/C.2118/13.

Instructions regarding War Diaries and Intelligence Summaries are contained in F. S. Regs., Part II. and the Staff Manual respectively. Title pages will be prepared in manuscript.

WAR DIARY
or
INTELLIGENCE SUMMARY.
(Erase heading not required.)

Army Form C. 2118.

Place	Date	Hour	Summary of Events and Information	Remarks and references to Appendices
VOYENNES	14		possible to LANGUEVOISIN to take over five German huts and form a Corps Rest Station in connection with 107 Field Ambulance NESLE. Request received from 32nd Division for loan of bearer subdivision to report at FORESTE as soon as possible. 2/3rd Field Ambulance detailed to find both these parties. Verbal instructions received from DDMS to send all available motor ambulances to NESLE to assist in the evacuation of cases to CCS. seven Daimlers and one Ford ambulance sent for this purpose. J.F.P. Brun	
	15		ADMS inspected 2/2nd Field Ambulance on early morning parade. DADMS visited main dressing station of 32nd Division at FORESTE. Bearers lent by 2/3rd Field Ambulance being returned to-night. Request for six wheeled stretcher carriers to be delivered to 105 Field Ambulance at TERTRY received from 35th Division. Lt. MANUEL MO i/c 2/7th WORCESTERS diagnosed diphtheria and evacuated to C.C.S. Verbal message received from DDMS IV Corps that motor ambulances sent to NESLE would be returned to-morrow afternoon. J.F.P.B.	
	16		ADMS inspected 2/3rd Field Ambulance and selected sites of bathing centres. Foden disinfector now working at 2/1st Field Ambulance BETHENCOURT J.F.P.B.	

Instructions regarding War Diaries and Intelligence Summaries are contained in F. S. Regs., Part II. and the Staff Manual respectively. Title pages will be prepared in manuscript.

WAR DIARY
or
INTELLIGENCE SUMMARY.
(Erase heading not required.)

Army Form C. 2118.

Place	Date	Hour	Summary of Events and Information	Remarks and references to Appendices
VOYENNES	17		ADMS & DADMS visited ADMS 32nd DIVISION to arrange preliminaries of taking over. orders having been received that 61st Div would relieve 32nd Div. JJPB.	
	18		DADMS visited new forward area and completed arrangements for relief of Field Ambulances with ADMS 32nd Division. RAMC Order No 25 issued. Case of CSM reported from 2/1st Bucks at OFFOY. OC mobile lab wired for contacts (4) isolated. JJPB.	App 6
	19		ADMS visited 2/3rd Field Ambulance. Special leave of 5 days granted to Capt STAFFORD RAMC att. 61st DAC. JJPB	
	20		DADMS visited 2/2nd Field Ambulance and also 2/1st Field Ambulance at BETHENCOURT. arrangements for treatment of scabies cases here are now complete JJPB.	
	21		ADMS visited 2/3rd Field Ambulance at FORESTE in new position and inspected bathing arrangements at GERMAIN where Divisional Baths are about to be erected. 2/2nd Field Ambulance moved to DOUILLY. DDMS III Corps visited Div H.Q. He proposes to make a Corps scabies station at BETHENCOURT under 1st Field Ambulance. JJPB.	

A5834 Wt. W4973 M687 750,000 8/16 D. D. & L. Ltd. Forms/C.2118/13.

Instructions regarding War Diaries and Intelligence Summaries are contained in F. S. Regs., Part II. and the Staff Manual respectively. Title pages will be prepared in manuscript.

WAR DIARY
or
INTELLIGENCE SUMMARY.
(Erase heading not required.)

Army Form C. 2118.

Place	Date	Hour	Summary of Events and Information	Remarks and references to Appendices
HOROIR	22		DIV HQ moved to HOROIR. ADMS drafted orders for foot washing arrangements. DADMS visited forward area - Water supply in FAYET unsatisfactory - Water being drawn from a rainwater cistern. JFPGreen -	
	23		DADMS visited aid post in S16b 4.6 (Sheet 62B) - There is practically no accomodation at this post - evacuation is carried out down the ROMAN ROAD by hand as far as SALENCY cross roads and thence by wheeled stretcher carriage to HOLNON JFPB.	
	24		ADMS visited foot washing establishment at GERMAINE and held conference with O's C ambulances. J.F.P.B.	
	25		Routine duties JFPB	
	26		ADMS attended conference at office of DDMS corps. "C" Solution to be indented for on a scale of 20 gallons per Division per month for spraying bodies. Orders received that Lt Col SCOTT Commanding 2/3rd Field Ambulance was to be relieved by Capt SCOTT WILLIAMSON from 1/3rd Field Ambulance and was to assume command of 106th Field Ambulance 35th Division. Capt SCOTT WILLIAMSON arrived J.F.P.B.	
	27		Orders received that 184 Brigade would carry out a raid on trenches from M36 cent to M30 b 5.6. at 4.30 AM on 28th. 2/3rd Field Ambulance warned JFPB. Lt Col Scott reported his departure. Capt SCOTT WILLIAMSON assumed command of 2/3rd Field Ambulance	

A5834 Wt. W4973 M687 750,000 8/16 D. D. & L. Ltd. Forms/C.2118/13.

Instructions regarding War Diaries and Intelligence Summaries are contained in F. S. Regs., Part II. and the Staff Manual respectively. Title pages will be prepared in manuscript.

WAR DIARY
or
INTELLIGENCE SUMMARY.

(Erase heading not required.)

Army Form C. 2118.

Place	Date	Hour	Summary of Events and Information	Remarks and references to Appendices
AUROIR	28		DADMS visited SAVY and ETREILLERS about 45 casualties in raid by 184 Brigade. Two men only reported as missing. – JFPB.	
	29		CAPT AGT FISHER RAMC.T. 2/3rd Field Ambulance awarded MC in recognition of his work at HOLNON WOOD during early part of ~~last~~ month. – JFPB.	
	30		Routine duties JFPB.	

C Hawkins
Colonel
ADMS 61 Div

A5834 Wt. W4973 M687 750,000 8/16 D. D. & L. Ltd. Forms/C.2118/13.

APP I

SECRET

COPY NO:- 15

61st Division R.A.M.C. OPERATION ORDER NO: 20.

1. The 61st Division will attack the line from North R.9. Central to South R.28.c.2.4. at 5 a.m. April 2nd. 184 Infantry Brigade will be N. of River OMIGNON and 183 Infantry Brigade S. of the river.

2. The O.C. 2/2 Field Ambulance will establish an Advanced Dressing Station at VERMAND about R.32.a.8.6. 2 Officers, one bearer sub-division and half a tent sub-division will be stationed here. Evacuation from this post will take place along road from R.25.d.6.6. to Q.30.c.1.6. and thence through CAULAINCOURT to TERTRY.

3. The Advanced Dressing Station at POEUILLY will remain open. 2 Officers one bearer sub-division, and half a tent sub-division will be stationed here. Evacuation will take place along POEUILLY - CAULAINCOURT road and thence to TERTRY.

4. There will be a bearer sub-division and two tent sub-divisions in reserve at TERTRY.

5. The O.C. 2/3rd Field Ambulance will establish a post at TREFCON and will station here 2 Officers, one tent sub-division and one bearer sub-division. Evacuations via cross roads at W.9.a.0.2. to TERTRY.

6. The O.C. 2/3rd Field Ambulance will establish an Advanced Dressing Station at VILLEVEQUE and will station here 2 Officers and one bearer sub-division. Evacuation via cross roads at W.18.a.8.8. to TREFCON.

7. O.C. 2/2nd Field Ambulance will arrange for evacuation of patients from TERTRY. to Main Dressing Station at BETHENCOURT.

8. One bearer sub-division from 2/3rd Field Ambulance and one bearer sub-division from 2/1st Field Ambulance will be held in readiness to move forward as reliefs if required.

9. Separate instructions about tentage and motor transport will be issued later.

10. Acknowledge.

F.E. Mackie.
Lieut Colonel.
Acting A.D.M.S., 61st Division.

Issued at 3.45 p.m. April 1st 1917.

Copies to :- No: 1. "G"
2. "Q"
3. D.D.M.S., IVth Corps
4-6. 1,2, 3, Field Ambs.
7-9. 182,183,184 Infantry Brigades.
10-11. 306, 307 Bdes. R.F.A.
12. C.R.E.
13. A.D.M.S., 32nd Division.
14. A.D.M.S., 59th Division.
15-16. War Diary.

SECRET.

Issued with R.A.M.C.OPERATION ORDER NO: 20. 1/5/17

INSTRUCTIONS REGARDING MOTOR TRANSPORT AND TENTAGE.

1. Officer Commanding 2/2nd Field Ambulance will station Cars as follows :- In VERMAND 2 Ford Ambulances about R.25.d.9.3. At Q.29.c.2.2. Two Daimlers. In CAULAINCOURT 2 Daimlers. In reserve at TERTRY one Daimler.

2. The Officer Commanding 2/3rd Field Ambulance will station cars as follows :- near TREFCON three Daimlers. At TERTRY at disposal of O.C. 2/2nd Field Ambulance one Daimler.

3. The Officer Commanding 2/1st Field Ambulance will place one Daimler at disposal of 2/2nd Field Ambulance at TERTRY.

4. Tentage will be erected by Officers Commanding Field Ambulances as follows:- (a) by O.C. 2/2nd Field Amb, at VERMAND - one Operating tent and one Bell tent. (b) by O.C. 2/3rd Field Ambulance at TREFCON - one Operating tent and two Bell tents. At VILLEVEQUE if possible two Bell tents. These dispositions to be complete by 4 a.m.

April 1st 1917.

F.W. Mackie

Lieut Colonel
Acting A.D.M.S., 61st Division.

APP 2

SECRET. COPY NO: 18

61ST DIVISION R.A.M.C. OPERATION ORDER NO: 21.
APRIL 2nd 1917

1. The infantry are now holding the general line R.4 central VADENCOURT (inclusive) MAISSEMY (inclusive) to R.36.c.

2. The O.C. 2/3rd Field Ambulance will establish a post to-night in the dug-out in crater at R.27.c.8.4. and will station there one officer, twenty men, and two wheeled stretchers. Touch will be maintained by the officer stationed here with the Medical Officers of troops in line south of the river and in support at VILLECHOLLES.

3. The officers at present stationed at VILLEVEQUE will maintain touch with the troops stationed at HARTEVILLE and ATTILLY.

4. The Officer Commanding 2/2nd Field Ambulance will establish a post at the station at R.20.d.9.3. and if necessary a second post in BIHECOURT in dug out at R.21.b.9.9. Two wheeled stretchers will be kept at R.20.d.9.3.

5. The post at present established near POEUILLY at Q.29.c.2.2. will remain open and will deal with any casualties evacuated through SOYECOURT.

2/3 6. The 2/3nd Field Ambulance will move to TREFCON on 3rd and will be fully open for reception of sick and wounded by 1 p.m.

7. Separate instructions have been issued as to routes available for evacuation, and as to distribution of transport.

8. Acknowledge.

Issued at 7.30 p.m. April 2nd 1917.

[signature]

Lieut:Colonel.
Acting A.D.M.S., 61st Division.

Copies to :-
No:1. "G"
2. "Q"
3. D.D.M.S., IVth Corps.
4-6. 182,183,184 Bdes.
7-9. 306,307,157 Bdes R.F.A.,
10. C.R.A.,
11. C.R.E.,
12-14. 1,2,3 Field Ambulances.
15. A.D.M.S., 32nd Division.
16. A.D.M.S., 35th Division.
17. A.D.M.S., 59th Division.
18-19. War Diary.

App 3

SECRET. COPY NO 17

1

61ST DIVISION R.A.M.C., ORDER NO: 22
Issued April 4th 1917.

1. The 61st Division will advance its line of resistance to approximately M.7.cent.M.33.d. (sheet 62B) This operation will be carried out on the night of April 5-6th.

2. The O.C. 2/2nd Field Ambulance will be prepared to establish an Advanced Dressing Station at BIHECOURT and to station there two officers and a bearer sub-division. The posts at the station R.20.d.8.3. and at VERMAND will remain open. Touch will be maintained with battalion in VADENCOURT.

3. The O.C. 2/3rd Field Ambulance will be prepared to establish an Advanced Dressing Station near MAISSEMY at R.22.b.5.4. and to station there one officer and a bearer sub-division less the 12 men already attached to the M.O. of the battalion at present holding this village, and half a tent sub-division. This Dressing Station to be established immediately the infantry move forward.

4. Evacuation from MAISSEMY will be carried out by horse Ambulance as far as the crater POST R.27.c.8.4. until the road through VILLECHOLLES is passable for motor ambulances. From CRATER POST cases will be evacuated by motor ambulance.

5. The O.C. 2/3rd Field Ambulance will establish a post in BOIS D'HOLNON at about R.35.d.8.5. and will station there one officer, a nursing Sergeant, three nursing orderlies and a bearer sub-division less the 12 men already attached to the M.O. of the Battalion. This Post to be established by 10 P.M. TO-NIGHT.

6. One N.C.O. and three nursing orderlies will remain at VILLEVEQUE with a supply of dressings and Medical Comforts.

7. Two Medical officers will be stationed at CRATER POST when these operations commence.

8. The O.C. 2/2nd Field Ambulance will attach one horse ambulance for duty with the 2/3rd Field Ambulance until further orders.

9. All available motor transport of 2/3rd Field Ambulance except two Daimler cars will work east of TREFCON.

10. Two horse Ambulance wagons will clear the MAISSEMY AREA, and two the BOIS D'HOLNON road, reinforced by cars as necessary.

11. Regimental Medical Officers will, whenever possible notify the O.C. Advanced Dressing Stations of the position of their Aid Posts.

12. The O.C. 2/1st Field Ambulance will hold his cars in readiness to clear cases from TERTRY and TREFCON to BETHENCOURT.

13. Small bearer parties for transhipment must be stationed at any points on the road that become unsuitable for loaded cars.

14. Acknowledge.

Issued at 6 p.m. April 4th 1917.

T.E. Mackie.

Lieut:Colonel.
Acting A.D.M.S., 61st Division.

Copies:-
No: 1. "G"
2. "Q"
3. D.D.M.S. IVth Corps
4-6. 1,2,3, Field Amb:
7-9. 182,183,184 Inf: Bdes:
10-12. 306, 307,157 Bdes R.F.A.
13. C.R.A.
14. C.R.E.
15. A.D.M.S., 59 Div:
16. A.D.M.S., 32 Div:
17-18. War Diary.

APP 4

SECRET. COPY NO: 18

61ST DIVISION R.A.M.C. ORDER NO: 23. 8/4/17.

1. There are indications that the enemy is retiring from ST QUENTIN.

2. The 182 Brigade will attack the trenches at the eastern end of FRESNOY-LE-PETIT and north of the village as far as the wood in M.21.c. this evening.

3. On the morning of 9th April the 182 Infantry Brigade will attack and capture the German front line trenches on HILL 120 from about M.21.a.3.7. through M.14.d. and c. to the HAISSEMY-BERTHAUCOURT road about M.14.a.4.8.

4. The Advanced Dressing Stations of the right section will remain as at present namely VILLECHOLLES and R.35.a.8.2. and will be staffed by the 2/3rd Field Ambulance.

5. Twelve stretcher bearers will be attached to each of the H.Qs. of the right and left batallions.

6. The O.C. 2/2nd Field Ambulance will detail one Daimler Ambulance to work under the orders of the O.C. 2/3rd Field Ambulance for 24 hours from 6 p.m. to-day.

7. Acknowledge.

Issued at 3.30 p.m.

J J P Breen

Captain D.A.D.M.S.,
for Colonel A.D.M.S., 61st Division.

Copies to:-
No: 1. "G"
2. "Q"
3. D.D.M.S., IV Corps.
4-6. 1-2-3 Field Ambulances.
7-9. 182,183,184 Brigades.
10-12. 306,307,157 Bdes. R.F.A.
13. C.R.A.
14. C.R.E.
15. A.D.M.S. 59th Div:
16. A.D.M.S. 32nd Div:
17. A.D.M.S. 35th Div:
18-19. War Diary.

APP No 5

SECRET COPY NO: 21

61st DIVISION R. . .C. ORD . NO: 24. April 10th 1917

1. The 61st Division is being relieved by the 35th Division and is going into reserve.

2. The 2/1st Field Ambulance will remain at BETHENCOURT, arrangements will be made there for the treatment of Scabies cases. The date on which cases may be sent will be notified later.

3. The 2/2nd Field Ambulance will, on relief by the 105th Field Ambulance, move to OFFOY and will establish its headquarters at the GENDARMERIE there by 7 p.m. on the 11th. The O.C. 2/2nd Field Ambulance will be responsible for collection of sick in the 184 Brigade area.

4. The 2/3rd Field Ambulance will, on relief by the 106th Field Ambulance, move to DOUILLY and will establish its headquarters there by 7 p.m. on the 11th. O.C. 2/3rd Field Ambulance will be responsible for collection of sick in 182 Brigade area.

5. The Os.C. 105th and 106th Field Ambulances will take over all Posts at present staffed by the 2/2nd and 2/3rd Field Ambulances and will be responsible for clearing both sectors of the line after 4 p.m. on the 11th, they will also deal with any sick from 184 Brigade in the TREFCON - MONCHY LAGACHE area and from 182 Brigade in MARTEVILLE - VILLEVEQUE area.

6. Advance parties of one officer and five other ranks will report to-night at TERTRY and TREFCON from 105 and 106 Field Ambulances.

7. A billeting party should be sent to DOUILLY to-morrow by 10 a.m.

8. Two Hospital marquees will be handed over at OFFOY by O.C. 105 Field Ambulance and one marquee may be drawn by O.C. 2/2nd Field Ambulance from 107 Field Ambulance at NESLE. Two hospital marquees will be handed over by O.C. 106 Field Ambulance to O.C. 2/3rd Field Ambulance, under arrangemets to be made direct.

9. The O.C. 2/2nd Field Ambulance will hand over 100 Stretchers to O.C. 105 Fi Ambulance, and will obtain a receipt.

10. All wheeled stretchers will be taken by units to the new area.

11. All Trench shelters will be handed over to incoming units and receipts obtained.

12. All transport temporarily attached by one ambulance to another will rejoin the Unit to which it belongs to-night.

13. The Sanitary Section will not move.

14. Acknowledge.

Issued at 4.30 p.m.

T.F.P. Breen Capt. for
Acting A.D.M.S., 61st Division.

Copies to :-
1. 61st Division "G"
2. 61st Division "Q"
3. D.D.M.S. IVth Corps.
4-6. 1,2,3,Field Ambulances.
7-9. 182,183,184 Bdes.
10-12. 306,307,157,Bdes R.F.A.
13. C.R.A.
14. C.R.E.
15. O.C. S.n Sec.
16. 61st Div.Train.
17. 61st Div.Sup.Col.
18. A.D.M.S.35th Division.
19. A.D.M.S. 32nd Division.
20. A.D.M.S. 59th Division.
21-22. War Diary.

App No 6

SECRET. COPY NO: 15

61st DIVISION R.A.M.C. ORDER NO: 25. April 18th 1917.

1. The 61st Division will relieve the 32nd Division on April 19th, 20th and 21st, in the right sector of the IVth Corps area.

2. The 2/1st Field Ambulance will remain at BETHENCOURT.

3. The 2/2nd and 2/3rd Field Ambulances will move in accordance with attached march table.

4. Details of handing over the Ambulance site at OFFOY will be arranged direct between O.C. 2/2nd Field Ambulance and O.C. 92nd Field Ambulance.

5. O.C. 2/2nd Field Ambulance will arrange to take over the Ambulance site at DOUILLY direct with O.C. 2/3rd Field Ambulance - relief to be complete by 10 a.m. on 21st.

6. O.C. 2/2nd Field Ambulance will arrange for the collection and treatment of sick from units of the Reserve Brigade at GERMAINE and BEAUVOIS after 10 a.m. on 21st.

7. 2/3rd Field Ambulance will collect sick from 184 Brigade in GERMAINE BEAUVOIS area from 11 a.m. on the 19th to 10 a.m. on the 21st.

8. The 2/3rd Field Ambulance will take over the Main Dressing Station of 32nd Division at FORESTE, and all advanced posts from the 92nd Field Ambulance. Relief to be completed by 12 noon on 21st. Advance parties will be sent by O.C. 2/3rd Field Ambulance as follows :-
by noon 19th - one officer and one bearer sub-division.
by noon 20th - one officer and 24 other ranks.
2 Ford Ambulances. 3 Daimler Ambulances. Party for checking stores.

9. The O.C. 2/2nd Field Ambulance will hand over two hospital marquees at OFFOY to O.C. 92nd Field Ambulance. The O.C.2/3rd Field Ambulance will hand over two hospital marquees at DOUILLY to O.C. 2/2nd Field Ambulance. The O.C. 2/3rd Field Ambulance will take over the hospital marquees at FORESTE from O.C. 92nd Field Ambulance.

10. The O.C. 2/3rd Field Ambulance will take over surplus stretchers and blankets etc from O.C. 92nd Field Ambulance.

11. All wheeled stretcher carriages will be taken into the new area. O.C. 2/2nd Field Ambulance will hand over all held by him to O.C. 2/3rd Field Ambulance.

12. M.A.C. Cars will evacuate from the Main Dressing Station.

13. Sick from 2/2nd Field Ambulance of 61st Division will be transferred to 2/1st Field Ambulance, and those of the 32nd Division and Corps troops transferred to 92nd ~~Division~~ Fld Ambulance on relief.

14. Ambulances will report when moves are completed.

15. The A.D.M.S., office will close at 10 a.m. on the 22nd and open at ~~AURIOR~~ AUROIR at same time.

16. Acknowledge.

Issued at 9 p.m.

J F P Breen
Captain,
for Colonel A.D.M.S., 61st Div:

Copies to :- 1.61st Div: "G"
2.61st Div: "Q"
3.D.D.M.S.,IVth Corps.
4.-6.1,2,3rd Field Ambs.
7 -9.182,183,184 Bdes:
10.C.R.E.
11.61st Div:Train
12.61st Div.Sup.Col.
13.A.D.M.S., 32nd Div:
14-15 War Diary.

SECRET.

DATE.	UNIT.	FROM.	TO.	REMARKS.
April 21st	2/2nd Field Ambulance.	OFFOY.	DOUILLY.	
April 21st	2/3rd Field Ambulance.	DOUILLY.	FORESTE.	

J J P Breen
Captain.
for Colonel A.D.M.S., 61st Division.

April 18th 1917.

Medical.

May 1917

S

CONFIDENTIAL

140/21 S.S.

Vol 13

WAR DIARY

of

A. D. M. S. 61 Div

From:- May 1st To:- May 31st 1917

VOLUME 13

June 1st 1917.

Instructions regarding War Diaries and Intelligence Summaries are contained in F. S. Regs., Part II. and the Staff Manual respectively. Title pages will be prepared in manuscript.

WAR DIARY
or
INTELLIGENCE SUMMARY.
(Erase heading not required.)

Army Form C. 2118.

Place	Date	Hour	Summary of Events and Information	Remarks and references to Appendices
AUROIR	MAY 1		ADMS inspected sanitary conditions at AUROIR accompanied by GOC 183 Brigade - JJPB	
	2		DADMS visited forward area and saw new site for relay post at S1 D45. 2/3rd Field Ambulance have been compelled to abandon relay post in village of HOLNON owing to heavy shelling. JJPB.	
"	3-7		ADMS carried out routine sanitary and general inspections arranged for opening of baths at ETREILLERS and issued circulars on care of feet and supply of medical comforts and dressings JJPB.	
"	8-9		Routine sanitary inspections visits to forward posts JJPB	
"	10		Conference at DDMS IV Corps JJPB	
"	11		Warning order received that Division was about to be relieved by 26th French Division JJPB	
"	12		ADMS held a conference with MEDECIN DIVISSONAIRE 26th French Division JJPB RAMC Order No 27 issued JJPB	*App I.
"	13		RAMC Order No 28 issued JJPB	*App II.
"	14		RAMC Order No 29 issued JJPB	*App III
"	15		ADMS visited MEDECIN DIVISIONAIRE 26th Div. also MESNIL ST NICAISE to which 1st FA moved on 13th JJPB	
VIGNACOURT	16		Div HQ moved to VIGNACOURT. 2/3rd Field Ambulance from DOUILLY to MESNIL ST NICAISE JJPB.	

A5834 Wt. W4973 M687 750,000 8/16 D. D. & L. Ltd. Forms/C.2118/13.

Army Form C. 2118.

Instructions regarding War Diaries and Intelligence Summaries are contained in F. S. Regs., Part II. and the Staff Manual respectively. Title pages will be prepared in manuscript.

WAR DIARY
or
INTELLIGENCE SUMMARY.
(Erase heading not required.)

Place	Date	Hour	Summary of Events and Information	Remarks and references to Appendices
VIGNACOURT	17-20		Move of Division to VIGNACOURT concentration area continued. RAMC Order No 30^x issued on 19th JTPB	App. IV
DOULLENS	21-		Div HQ moved to DOULLENS. 1st Field Ambulance to HEM 2nd to BRETEL 3rd to BEAUVAL. There appears to be a tendency on the part of Brigades to allot billeting accomodation for the personnel and transport of Field Ambulances only and leave out of consideration the possibility of there being patients to treat in addition JTPB.	
	22		Routine duties JTPB	
LE CAUROY	23		Div HQ moved to LE CAUROY ambulances BARLY - IVERGNY - SUS ST. LEGER JTPB	
	24		Div HQ moved to WARLUS ambulances DUISANS - BERNEVILLE - DAINVILLE JTPB.	
	25		Conference at office of DDMS VI Corps JTPB	
	26-8		Routine duties. preliminary order received that 61st Division would relieve 37th Division in the CAMBRAI ROAD sector of the line on June 1st-2nd "Arrangements for taking over Medical Arrangements of the 37th Div" * issued on 28th	* App V
	29		DADMS visited forward area - There is very fine accomodation	

Army Form C. 2118.

Instructions regarding War Diaries and Intelligence Summaries are contained in F. S. Regs., Part II. and the Staff Manual respectively. Title pages will be prepared in manuscript.

WAR DIARY
or
INTELLIGENCE SUMMARY.
(Erase heading not required.)

Place	Date	Hour	Summary of Events and Information	Remarks and references to Appendices
WARLUS	29		in MARLIERE CAVE. a large natural cavern with one entrance from the cellar of a house and a second artificial entrance constructed by the Germans down which it is possible to carry stretchers. The ventilation is however bad and the lighting at present insufficient J.F.P.B. RAMC Order no 31* ~~appendix~~ issued	* App VI
	30		Routine duties. A.D.M.S. visited H.Q. Divisional Artillery at OUTREBOIS J.F.P.B.	
	31		Routine duties. J.F.P.B.	

C Hawken
Colonel.
A, D, M, S., 61st, Div,

A5834 Wt. W4973 M687 750,000 8/16 D. D. & L. Ltd. Forms/C.2118/13.

Appendix I   War Diary

SECRET   Copy No. 9

61st.DIVISION ADMINISTRATIVE ORDER NO.27.

* *

The following arrangements will be made:-

(1) The sick etc will be disposed of as follows:-

(a) If not likely to be fit in two days- to 21 C.C.S.

(b) If likely to be fit in that period- conveyed by Ambulance.

(c) Scabies will be sent to Units.
The 2/1 Field Ambulance will convey materials (as much as possible) to new area.

(2) All equipment over Mobilisation Scale and G.R.O.419. will be sent to 21 C.C.S. commencing at once. Sanitary Section lorry and M.A.C. will assist 2/3 Field Ambulance.

(3) In forward area all non-expendable material will be returned, save minimum requirements to 2/3 Field Ambulance, at earliest moment.

(4) Wheeled Stretcher Carriages. These will be equally divided by O.C. 2/3 Field Ambulance (as far as tactical circumstances will permit) between the Field Ambulances.

(5) ACKNOWLEDGE.

Issued at 11 pm. 12/5/17.

[signature]

Colonel A.M.S.
A.D.M.S. 61st.Division.

Copies to :-

1. 61st.Div. "G"
2. 61st.Div. "Q"
3. 2/1 Field Amb.
4. 2/2 Field Amb.
5. 2/3 Field Amb.
6. D.D.M.S. 4th.Corps.
7. No.10.M.A.C.
8. 72nd.Sanitary Sec.
9 - 10 War Diary.

S E C R E T. War Diary Appendix II C O P Y No. 13

61st.DIVISION R.A.M.C. ORDER No.28.

-*-*-*-*-*-*-*-*-*-*-*-*-*-

1. The 2/1 Field Ambulance will collect on the 13th.instant, Convalescents of the 184 Infantry Brigade from the C.R.S. and keep them at MESNIL ST NICAISE till the Brigade moves. Those who can go will proceed with their Units. Those who are likely to be better in 48 hours will be left with succeeding Ambulance.

2. The men of other Units likely to be well in 24 hours will be sent from C.R.S., to 2/2 Field Ambulance: and then returned to Battalions etc.

3. The remainder of patients from C.R.S., will be evacuated to C.C.S.

4. Patients who are collected from forward area after the 12th.instant will be sent to 2/2 Field Ambulance: if likely to be well in 48 hours, and disposed of by them. If not likely to be fit in that time they will be sent to C.C.S., or to Ambulance at MESNIL ST NICAISE.

5. The 2/3 Field Ambulance will take in sick and wounded from the 14th.instant from forward area.

6. During moves each Field Ambulance will arrange to collect and treat sick of their associated Brigade Groups. Cases may be transferred to 21 C.C.S. Medical arrangements for new area will be notified later.

7. Daily State of Sick and wounded will be rendered to this Office by 10.am.

8. ACKNOWLEDGE.

C Howkins

Colonel A.M.S.
13/5/17. A.D.M.S.61st.Division.

Copies to :-

1. 2/1 Field Amb.
2. 2/2 Field Amb.
3. 2/3 Field Amb.

For information to :-

4. 61st.Div "A"
5. 61st.Div "Q"
6. D.D.M.S.
7. O.C. 91st.Field Amb.
8. O.C. 21 C.C.S.
9-11 182, 183, 184 Bdes.
12-13 War Diary.

Date.	Troops.	From.	To.	R.A.M.C. ATTACHED.	Probable date of entraining.	French.
May 13th	184 Inf: Bde:	GERMAINE area.	NESLE area.	2/1 Fd.Amb.	May 15th	
May 15 th.	182 Inf: Bde less 2 Battalions.	-do-	-do-	2/2 Fd Amb. less 1 Horse Ambulance.	May 17th	French Amb will take over at DOUILLY.
May 16th.	D.H.Q. and 2 Batts: 182 Inf:Bde:	-do-	-do-	1 Horse Amb: & Motor Amb:	May 17th	
May 17th	183 Inf: Bde.	-do-	-do-	2/3rd Fd Amb.	May 18th	French Amb will take over at FORESTE.

Appendix III

S E C R E T.

Copy No: 8

61st DIVISION R.A.M.C., ORDER No: 29.

* * * * * * *

(1) The Motor Ambulances attached to the 2/3rd Field Ambulance will rejoin their Units on morning of the 16th.

(2) The O.C. 2/2nd Field Ambulance will make arrangements to deal with any sick etc of D.H.Q. Group till arrival in "X" area

(3) Os.C. Field Ambulances will keep in touch with the Artillery Brigades and D.A.C. to which their Horse Ambulances are attached.

(4) On arrival in "X" area Ambulances will make medical arrangements with their associated Brigades until further orders.

(5) Cases can be evacuated to 21 C.C.S., New Zealand Stationary Hospital (AMIENS)

(6) The A.D.M.S., office closes at 9 a.m. on the 16th instant and opens at Divisional Headquarters VIGNACOURT at 3 p.m. same day.

(7) Sketch showing LONGUEAU and "X" area is attached.

(8) ACKNOWLEDGE.

Issued at 4.30 p.m. 14/5/17.

C Howkins

Colonel A.M.S.
A.D.M.S., 61st Division.

Copies to :-
1-3. 2/1,2/2,2/3 Field Ambs.
4. D.D.M.S. IVth Corps for information.
5. 61st Div "A" -do-
6. 61st Div "Q" -do-
7. C.R.A.
8-9. War Diary.

Appendix IV

SECRET COPY NO: *5*

61st DIVISION R.A.M.C., ORDER NO: 30.

1. The 61st Division (less Artillery) will move to the area NEUVILLETTE, BARLY, GEZAINCOURT, BEAUVAL, on the 21st May. There will be no move on the 22nd.

2. The Field Ambulances will remain grouped as at present and will collect sick from the Brigade Groups to which they are attached.

3. O.C., 2/2nd Field Ambulance will attach a Motor Ambulance to Headquarters Divisional Artillery by 4 p.m. on the 21st. This will be available for the collection of sick intho "E" area; and from the Medium and Heavy Trench Mortar Batteries at VIGNACOURT.

4. O.C., 2/1st Field Ambulance will arrange for an Ambulance to report to O.C., 1/5th D.C.L.I., by 6 p.m. on the 20th to follow the battalion on the march. O.C., 2/1st Field Amb., will collect sick from this Unit on arrival in new area.

5. Sick will be evacuated to No: 3 CANADIAN STATIONARY HOSPITAL DOULLENS.

6. The A.D.M.S., Office will close at VIGNACOURT at 10 a.m. and will reopen at DOULLENS at the same hour.

7. ACKNOWLEDGE.

Issued at 10 p.m. 19/5/17.

C. Hoskins

Colonel A.M.S.
A.D.M.S., 61st Division.

Copies to :-

1. 2/1st Field Ambulance.
2. 2/2nd Field Ambulance.
3. 2/3rd Field Ambulance.

4 -5. War Diary.

For information:

6. 61st Division "Q"
7. D.D.M.S., IVth Corps.
8. 182 Infantry Brigade.
9. 183 Infantry Brigade.
10. 184 Infantry Brigade.
11. C.R.E.
12. C.R.A.
13. 61st Div.Supply Column.
14. 1/5 D.C.L.I.

S E C R E T.   *Appendix V*

MEDICAL ARRANGEMENTS FOR 61st DIVISION ON RELIEVING 37th DIVISION.

LINE.	The present LINE runs from O.8.a.8.8. to O.14.c.3.0.
DISPOSITION OF AMBULANCES	2/1st Field Ambulance Headquarters at TILLOY. Will form the Advanced Dressing Station, and provide personnel for Bear[er] Posts.
	2/2nd Field Ambulance at HOPITAL ST JEAN. ARRAS. and will form the Main Dressing Station.
	2/3rd Field Ambulance in reserve at HOPITAL ST JEAN. ARR[AS] and will collect sick from Reserve Brigade.
ADVANCED DRESSING STATION.	The Advanced Dressing Station will be formed by the 2/1st Field Ambulance at TILLOY (PRINZ RUPPRECHT STRASSE) about N.31.b.2.6.
BEARER POSTS	One bearer sub-division will be at each post. There are two Bearer Posts in advance of the Main Dressin[g] Station. They are situated at N.11.a.7.7. in some gun pi[ts] and at N.17.d.3.4. HARLIERE CAVE.
REGIMENTAL AID POSTS	Two Regimental Aid Posts N.12.c.7.4. and N.18.d.5.5.
EVACUATION.	(1) To M.D.S., Cars can come up the ARRAS-CAMBRAI ROAD as far as one derelict tank and along the WANCOURT ROAD a[s] far as the Observation Post on left side of road going o[ut] Exact map reference of these points not yet known. From LEFT Regimental Aid Post cases are carried to the gun pits, and thence by wheeled stretchers to the tank wh[ere] they are placed on cars. Total carry about 2,000 yards. From RIGHT Regimental Aid Post cases are carried to HARLIERE CAVE and thence by wheeled stretchers to the Observation tree. Total carry about 2,500 yards.
	(2) From M.D.S., by Motor ambulance convoy.
MAIN DRESSING STATION	To be formed by 2/2nd Field Ambulance HOPITAL ST JEAN. RU[E] ST AUBERT. ARRAS. and will take in wounded and sick of Division.
MOTOR TRANSPORT.	15 Motor Ambulances will be kept at Advanced Dressing Station at TILLOY.
RELIEF.	Relief of line to be complete by 6 p.m. on 1st June. Relief of Main Dressing Station to be complete by 10 a.m. 1st June.
ADVANCE PARTIES.	For LINE by 4 p.m. on 30th May. For Main Dressing Station by 4 p.m. on 30th May.
HORSE LINES	To be on RACECOURSE. ARRAS.

J F P Breen
Captain.
for Colonel A.D.M.S., 61st Division

29/5/17.

SECRET. *Appendix VI* COPY NO: *14*

61ST DIVISION R.A.M.C., ORDER NO: 31

INTENTION. The 61st Division will take over the LINE from the 37th Division in the line on night of June 1/2.

MOVES. The 2/1st Field Ambulance will relieve the 48th Field Amb: at TILLOY by 6 p.m. on June 1st.

The 2/2nd Field Ambulance will take over the Main Dressing Station at HOPITAL ST JEAN. ARRAS. from the 49th Field Ambulance by 10 a.m. on June 1st.

The 2/3rd Field Ambulance will take over from the 50th Field Ambulance at HOPITAL ST JEAN ARRAS. by 10 a.m. on June 1st.

Details of relief to be arranged between Os.C. concerned.

ADVANCED PARTIES. Advanced Parties will be sent by all three Field Ambulances by 4 p.m. on the 30th.

MARCH TO new AREA. Os.C. Field Ambulances will arrange necessary medical attention for their associated Brigades during the march.

COLLECTION OF PATIENTS IN NEW AREA.

2/1st Field Amb:	Brigade in Line and Brigade in Support.
2/2nd Field Ambulance.	MAIN DRESSING STATION.
2/3rd Field Ambulance.	Brigade in Reserve. 2 Brigade Schools of 37th Division at ACHICOURT.

Issued at 8 p.m. 29/5/17.

C Hawkins

Colonel A.M.S.
A.D.M.S., 61st Division.

Copies to:- No1. 2/1 Fd.Amb.
2. 2/2 Fd Amb.
3. 2/3 Fd Amb.

4. 61st Div "G"
5. 61st Div "Q"
6. D.D.M.S.VIth Corps.
7-9. 182,183,184 Brigades.
10. C.R.A.,
11. C.R.E.,
12. 61st Div.Train.
13. 61st Div.Sup.Column.
14. A.D.M.S.37th Div.
15. A.D.M.S.29th Div.
16. A.D.M.S.14th Div.
17-18. War Diary.

) For information.

8

MEDICAL

Vol 14

June 1917

140/2279.

Confidential

War Diary (Medical)

of

A.D.M.S. 61st Division

From June 1st - 30th 1917.

Volume 14.

Instructions regarding War Diaries and Intelligence Summaries are contained in F. S. Regs., Part II. and the Staff Manual respectively. Title pages will be prepared in manuscript.

WAR DIARY
or
INTELLIGENCE SUMMARY.
(Erase heading not required.)

Army Form C. 2118.

Place	Date	Hour	Summary of Events and Information	Remarks and references to Appendices
June WARLUS	1		ADMS visited forward area and inspected aid posts and dressing stations. The various posts are not at present sufficiently marked and the evacuation routes would be extremely difficult to find at night. Three Field Ambulances moved. Forward area taken over by 2/1st Field Ambulance (see map App I). JJPB.	App. I
ARRAS.	2		Div. HQ moved to ARRAS JJPB	
	3-4		Routine duties. "GAS ALERT" ordered night of 4th considerable hostile shelling of the gun pits dressing station. JJPB.	
	5-7		Routine duties. ADMS visited forward area and inspected sanitary conditions. There are practically no sanitary arrangements at all. Shell holes are being used and the excreta is not being covered. Arrangements made to send up cresol tins with flyproof covers on a scale of 10 per battalion in the front line. More to be sent as soon as these installed. Orders received that Division would be relieved by 56th Division on 10-11th June JJPB.	
	8		RAMC Order No: 32 issued JJPB.	App II
	9		Routine duties. JJPB.	
	10-12		Div HQ moved to WARLUS 11th on completion of relief by 37th Div. ADMS proceeded on leave on 12th JJPB.	

A5834 Wt. W4973 M687 750,000 8/16 D. D. & L. Ltd. Forms/C.2118/13.

Army Form C. 2118.

WAR DIARY
or
INTELLIGENCE SUMMARY.
(Erase heading not required.)

Instructions regarding War Diaries and Intelligence Summaries are contained in F. S. Regs., Part II. and the Staff Manual respectively. Title pages will be prepared in manuscript.

Place	Date	Hour	Summary of Events and Information	Remarks and references to Appendices
WARLUS	13-23		Division at rest - nothing to note specially - Warning order received on 20th that Division (less artillery) would proceed on 21st 22nd 23rd to WILLEMAN FROHEN AREA the transport of each group to move one day ahead of dismounted personnel. Arrangements made for supply of water sterilizing tablets for use in waterbottles - as water carts would not be with units for about 24 hours - RAMC Warning order* issued on 20th and RAMC Order No 33* together with Extracts from Administrative Addendum issued on 21st - Div HQ moved to WILLEMAN on 23rd J.F.P.B.	App III App IV App V
	24.		New Divisional Area in extremely bad sanitary condition - practically all sanitary fixtures either broken or removed - no ablution benches - Supplies of timber &c asked for. J.F.P.B.	
	25-30		Division in rest area - Flyproof latrine covers obtained - timber and canvas for sanitary fixtures brought from MONDICOURT and AUXI-LE-CHATEAU ADMS issued tactical scheme for solution by O.C. Field Ambulances as part of Field Ambulance training - Arrangements made for tactical scheme for MOs attached to units. J.F.P.B.	

C. [signature]
COLONEL A.M.S.
A.D.M.S. 61st DIVISION

2353 Wt. W2544/1454 700,000 5/15 D. D. & L. A.D.S.S./Forms/C. 2118.

APPENDIX I

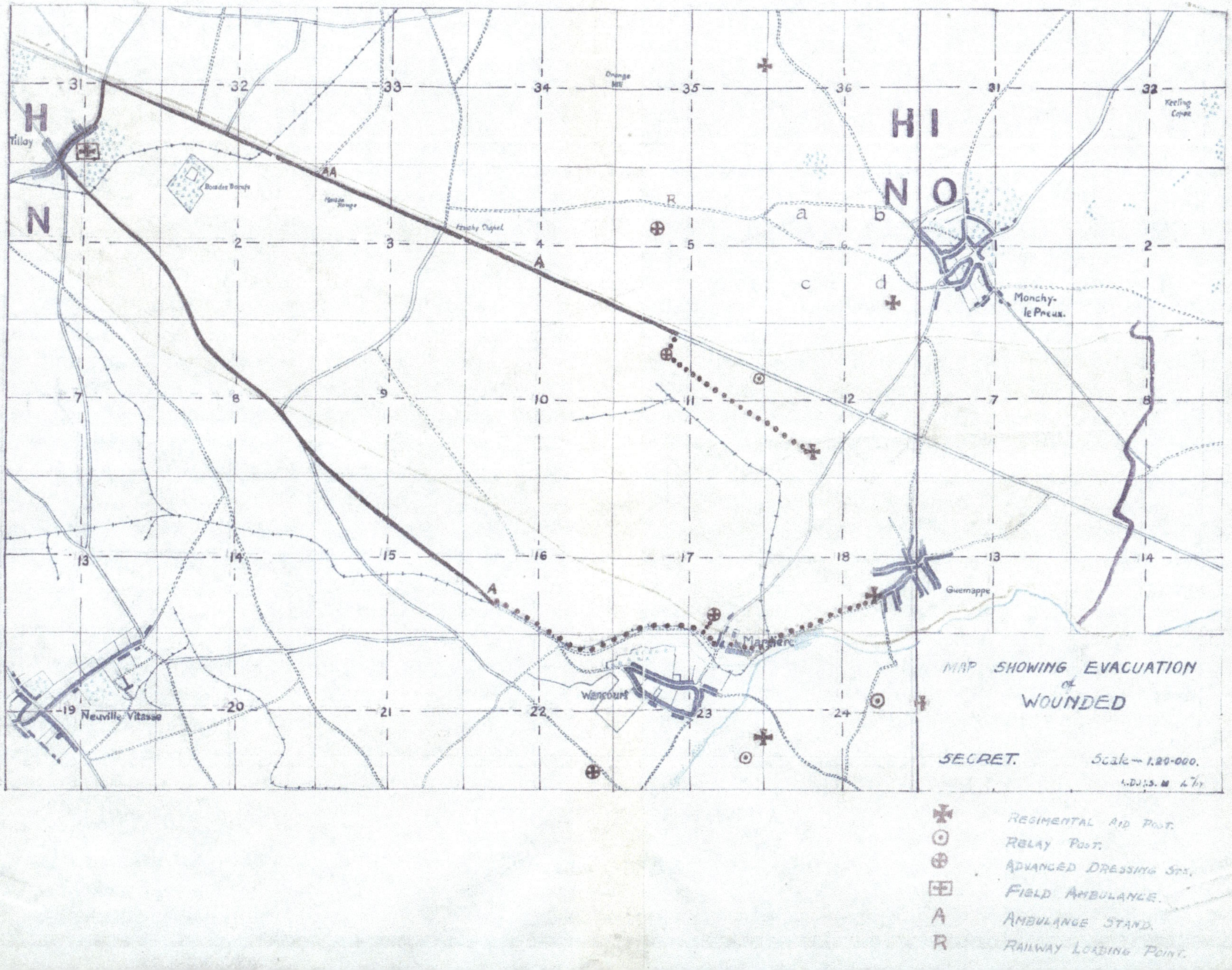

MAP SHOWING EVACUATION of WOUNDED
SECRET.
Scale – 1.20-000.
Tilloy
Neuville Vitasse
Wancourt
Guemappe
Monchy-le Preux.
Keeling Copse
Orange Hill
Feuchy Chapel
Bois des Boeufs
REGIMENTAL AID POST.
RELAY POST.
ADVANCED DRESSING STN.
FIELD AMBULANCE.
A AMBULANCE STAND.
R RAILWAY LOADING POINT.

APPENDIX 2.

S E C R E T

Copy No: 18.

61st DIVISION R.A.M.C., ORDER NO: 32.

Ref: Map 51B. 51C. Scale 1/40,000.

Intention. 1. The 61st Division (less Artillery) will be relieved on 10/11th June by 56th Division.

Relief of Medical Posts. 2. The Advanced Dressing Stations (N.17.d.22) and (N.11.a.7.6.) TILLOY (H.31.d.2.4.) Hopital St Jean, and Convent ARRAS will be taken over by day break June 11th. Details to be arranged between the Os.C. concerned.

Advance Parties. 3. Advance Parties will be sent on June 9th by 56th Division.

Materials. 4. Thomas Splint Outfits, blankets, and Stretchers etc at Medical Posts to be handed over to relieving Unit.

Moves. 5. The 2/1st Field Ambulance will be associated with the 184 Brigade Group.
The 2/2nd Field Ambulance will be associated with the 182 Brigade Group.
The 2/3rd Field Ambulance will be associated with the 183 Brigade Group.
March under Brigade orders, and will make medical arrangements in new area for their Groups.
The O.C., 2/1st Field Ambulance will arrange necessary Ambulance transport during march, for the 1/5 D.C.L.I.,

A.D.M.S. Office. 6. The A.D.M.S., Office will close at ARRAS at 10 a.m. on the 11th instant, and reopen at WARLUS at the same hour and date.

7. ACKNOWLEDGE.

Issued at 8 p.m. 8/6/17.

C Hawkins
Colonel A.M.S.
A.D.M.S., 61st Division.

Copies to:-
1-3. 2/1,2/2,2/3 Fd Ambs.
4. 61st Div: "G"
5. 61st Div: "Q"
6. D.D.M.S. VIth Corps.
7-9. 182,183,184 Brigades.
10. C.R.A.
11. C.R.E.
12. 61 Div Supply Col.
13. 61 Div Train.
14. 1/5 D.C.L.I.
15. 3a Sanitary Section.
16. 23rd Sanitary Section
17. Town Major ARRAS.
(4–17: For information.)
18-19. War Diary.

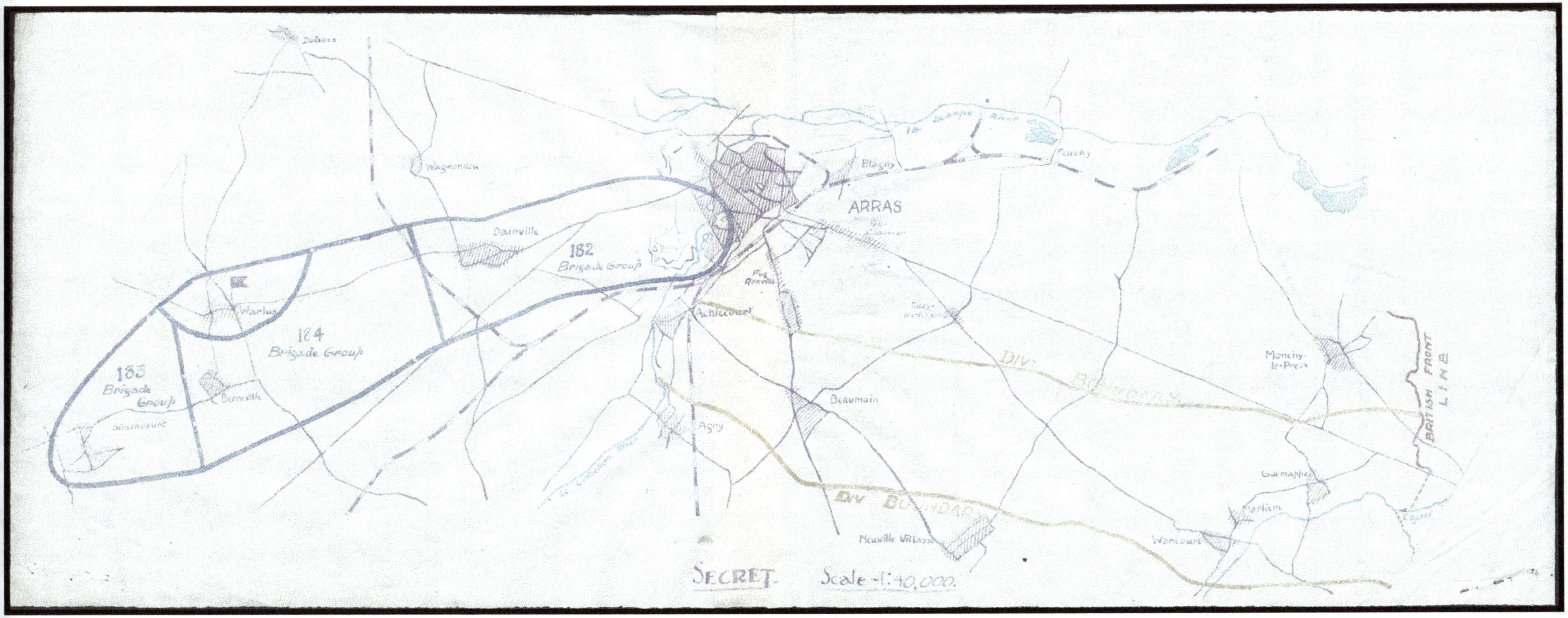
ARRAS
Blagny
Feuchy
La Scarpe River
Wagnonlieu
Dainville
182
Brigade Group
184
Brigade Group
183
Brigade Group
Warlus
Berneville
Simencourt
Duisans
Achicourt
Agny
Beaurain
Neuville Vitasse
DIV. BOUNDARY
DIV BOUNDARY
Monchy-le-Preux
Guemappe
Wancourt
BRITISH FRONT LINE
SECRET.
Scale 1:40,000.

S E C R E T

APPENDIX 3

2/1st Field Ambulance.
2/2nd Field Ambulance.
2/3rd Field Ambulance.

WARNING ORDER.

(1) The 61st Division (Less Artillery) will move on 21st 22nd and 23rd June to the area WILLEMAN WAVANS as shown below:-

21st. Transport 183 Brigade Group and transport 1/5 D.C.L.I.

22nd. Transport 182 - 184 Brigade Groups and transport 478 Field Company.

183 Brigade Group by train.
1/5 D.C.L.I. by Bus.

23rd. 184 Brigade Group and 478 Field Company by train.
182 Brigade Group by bus.

(2) Field Ambulances will move under orders of their Group Commanders.

(3) A Medical officer will accompany each Group of Brigade transport.

(4) O.C. 2/1st Field Ambulance will collect any sick from 478 Field Company at SIMENCOURT after departure of 2/3rd Field Ambulance.

(5) On arrival in the new Area Os.C. Field Ambulances will arrange for the collection of sick in the areas occupied by their Brigade Groups. O.C. 2/1st Field Ambulance will in addition collect sick in the VAULX AREA.

(6) O.C. 2/3rd Field Ambulance will arrange for collection of sick from 1/5 D.C.L.I. in VAULX Area until arrival of 2/1st Field Ambulance on 23rd.

(7) A tracing showing Brigade areas and staging area for transport is attached.

(8) No: 6 Stationary Hospital FREVENT is the nearest Hospital to the T. Area.

(9) ACKNOWLEDGE.

~~Issued at~~

F. W. Mackie

Lieut Colonel.
A/A.D.M.S., 61st Division.

20/6/18.

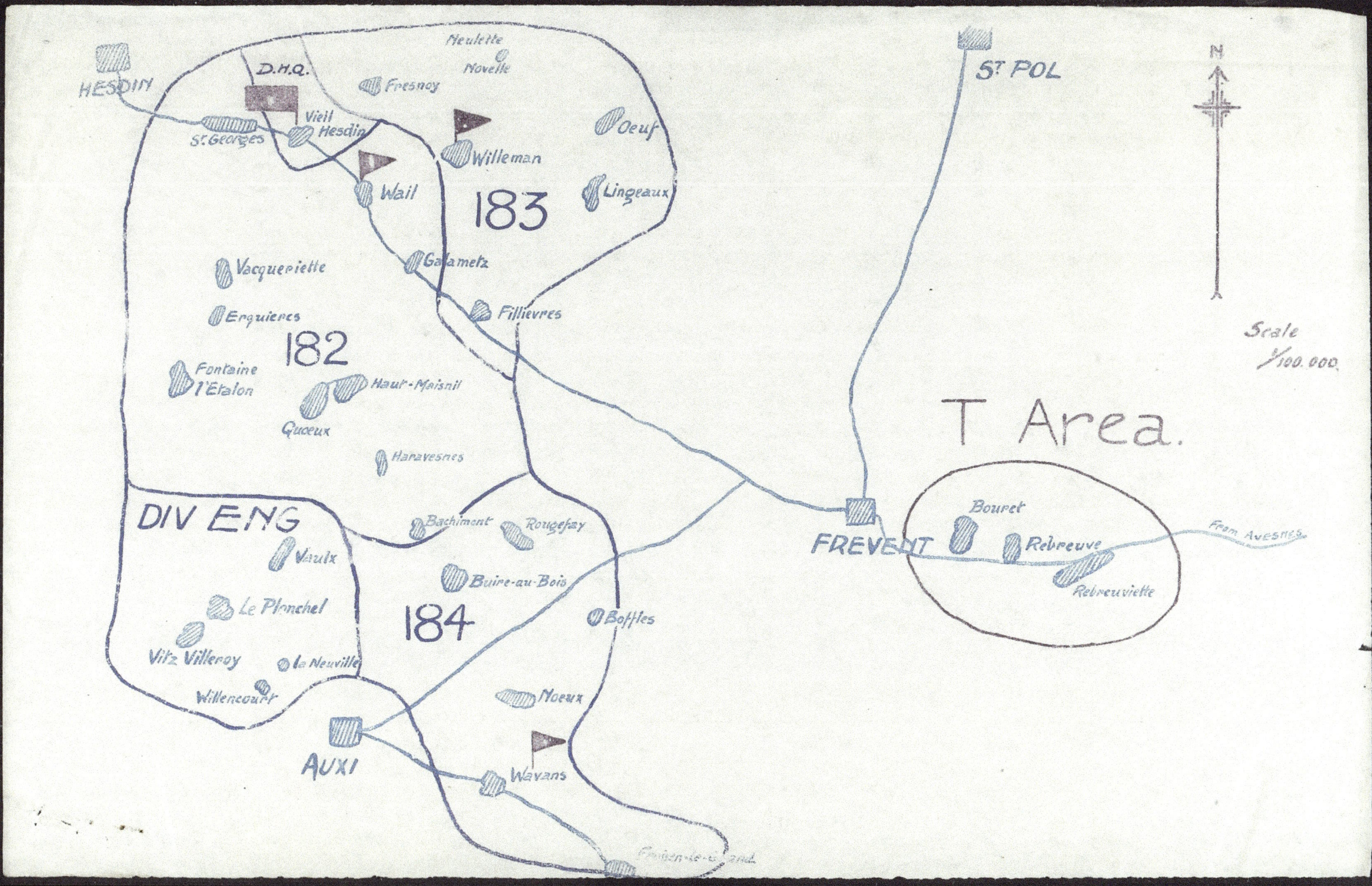
HESDIN
D.H.Q.
St. Georges
Vieil Hesdin
Fresnoy
Meulette
Novelle
Willeman
Wail
Oeuf
Lingeaux
183
Galametz
Vacqueriette
Fillievres
Erquieres
182
Fontaine l'Etalon
Haut-Maisnil
Quoeux
Haravesnes
DIV ENG
Bachimont
Rougefay
Vaulx
Buire-au-Bois
Le Plouchel
184
Boffles
Vitz Villeroy
La Neuville
Willencourt
Moeux
AUXI
Wavans
St POL
N
Scale 1/100,000
T Area.
FREVENT
Bouret
Rebreuve
Rebreuviette
From Avesnes

APPENDIX 4

SECRET. COPY NO: 12.

61st DIVISION R.A.M.C., ORDER NO: 33.

June 21st 1917.

1. The Division (less Artillery) will move by road and rail to the WILLEMAN - FROHEN AREA on 21st, 22nd, and 23rd June.

2. The Field Ambulances will remain grouped as at present, and will move under the orders of their Group Commanders.

3. Motor Transport will move under orders of Os.C. Field Ambulances.

4. On arrival in the new area Os.C. Field Ambulances will arrange to collect sick from their Group area.

5. O.C. 2/1st Field Ambulance will, in addition, collect sick from the Divisional Engineers Area.

6. All maps VIth Corps Area in possession of Field Ambulances will be retained.

7. The A.D.M.S., Office will close at WARLUS at 11 a.m. on June 23rd and reopen at the same hour at WILLEMAN.

8. ACKNOWLEDGE.

Issued at 1 p.m.

[signature]

Lieut: Colonel.
Acting A.D.M.S., 61st Division

Copies No: 1. 2/1st Field Amb.
2. 2/2nd Field Amb.
3. 2/3rd Field Amb.

4. 61st Div H.Q. "G"
5. 61st Div H.Q. "A"
6. D.D.M.S., VI Corps.
7-9. 182,183,184 Brigades.
10. C.R.E.
11. 1/5 D.C.L.I.
12-13. War Diary.
14. File.

For information.

S E C R E T APPENDIX 5

2/1st Field Ambulance.
2/2nd Field Ambulance.
2/3rd Field Ambulance.

EXTRACTS FROM ADMINISTRATIVE ADDENDUM TO 61ST DIVISION ORDER DATED 20/6/1917.

* * * * * *

1. ENTRAINMENT ORDERS.

Units will entrain in accordance with Table below.
G.Os.C. Brigade Groups will issue orders :-

(a) as to which units of their Group entrain on which of the two trains allotted to their Group.

(b) Route and rendezvous etc for troops entraining.

Date.	Unit.	Train No:	Entrain.	Time of departure.	Detrain.
22nd	1st portion 183 Bde Group.	1.	FOSSEUX locp. (Q.l.a.)	10 a.m.	HESDIN about 4 p.m.
22nd	2nd portion 183 Bde Group.	2.	-do-	11 a.m.	HESDIN about 4 p.m.
23rd	1st portion 184 Bde Group.	3.	-do-	10 a.m.	AUXI LE CHATEAU about 2 p.m.
23rd	2nd portion 184 Bde Group.	4.	-do-	11 a.m.	AUXI LE CHATEAU about 3 p.m.

2. All Water Bottles will be filled before departure.

3. Small advance parties from units of 182 - 184 Brigade Groups will be sent with the lorries conveying 1/5 D.C.L.I. to VAULX on June 22nd. All Advance Parties will carry rations for 22nd and 23rd with them.

4. O.C. Advance Parties in conjunction with detraining officers will be responsible for providing guides for units to new billets on arrival in the WILLEMAN area.

5. A Table showing Supply arrangements is attached.
Ambulances remain in same Supply Groups.
Transport columns will carry with them from present area rations for consumption on both days of their journey.

6. LORRIES. Six lorries will report to each Brigade Headquarters before 7 a.m. on day of departure of personnel, for the carriage of stores which have not been sent by horse transport to the new area.

7. EMBUSSING.

Orders to units proceeding by bus to be issued later.

8. REFITTING.

While the Division is in the WILLEMAN Area every effort is to be made to send in demands for equipment to complete re-fitting.

9. All tentage and other Stores which are area stores will be handed over to Town Majors, receipts obtained, and list of Stores sent to D.H.Q.,

10. LEAVE parties after June 23rd will proceed from ST POL at 1.30 p.m., a lorry will be detailed to carry leave men to ST POL Station.

11. ACKNOWLEDGE.

Lieut Colonel.
June 21st 1917. Acting A.D.M.S., 61st Division.

9 Vol 15

140/2292

MEDICAL.

WAR DIARY

OF

A. D. M. S., 61st. DIVISION

From:- July 1st 1917. To:- July 31st 1917.

VOLUME 15.

July 31st. 1917.

Army Form C. 2118.

Instructions regarding War Diaries and Intelligence Summaries are contained in F. S. Regs., Part II. and the Staff Manual respectively. Title pages will be prepared in manuscript.

WAR DIARY
or
INTELLIGENCE SUMMARY.
(Erase heading not required.)

Place	Date	Hour	Summary of Events and Information	Remarks and references to Appendices
	JULY			
WILLEMAN				
	3rd		DADMS. CAPT BREEN. TFP. evacuated to No 12 Stationary Hospital ST POL with simple fracture of left fibula due to accident. CAPT STOBIE. W. RAMC.T reported for temporary duty as DADMS. Conference of Medical Officers of 183 BDE at ADMS office to discuss a Tactical Exercise.	W.S.
	4th		MEDICAL BOARD held on SEVEN ASC officers re fitness for infantry. LIEUT STOWELL RAMC reported for duty from HAVRE and was posted to 2/1. S.M. FD AMB. Routine duties	W.S.

2353 Wt. W2544/1454 700,000 5/15 D. D. & L. A.D.S.S./Forms/C. 2118.

Instructions regarding War Diaries and Intelligence Summaries are contained in F. S. Regs., Part II. and the Staff Manual respectively. Title pages will be prepared in manuscript.

WAR DIARY
or
~~INTELLIGENCE SUMMARY.~~
(Erase heading not required.)

Army Form C. 2118.

Place	Date	Hour	Summary of Events and Information	Remarks and references to Appendices
	July			
WILLEMAN	5		ADMS visited 184 BDE HDQRS, also 2/5 GLOSTERS and 2/4 Roy. BERKS and inspected the sanitary arrangements and equipment. M.O's of 182nd BDE attended for conference & were taken by ADMS for map reading & given a tactical exercise	W.S.
"	6		ADMS visited 2/3 S. Mid Fd Amb. Routine duties	W.S.
"	7		M.O's of 184 Inf BDE attended a conference at ADMS office & were taken out & given a tactical exercise by the ADMS.	W.S.
"	8		R.F.A. began long march ~~yesterday~~ W.S. and two ambulances were detailed to proceed with them. Routine duties	W.S.
"	9		ADMS visited 17th Corps (formerly 6th Corps) rest station at WARLUS and arranged for the transfer of 41 patients belonging to 61st Div. to 2/2 S.M. Fd Amb at BACHIMONT.	W.S.

2353 Wt. W2544/1454 700,000 5/15 D. D. & L. A.D.S.S./Forms/C. 2118.

Army Form C. 2118.

Instructions regarding War Diaries and Intelligence Summaries are contained in F. S. Regs., Part II. and the Staff Manual respectively. Title pages will be prepared in manuscript.

WAR DIARY
or
INTELLIGENCE SUMMARY.
(Erase heading not required.)

Place	Date	Hour	Summary of Events and Information	Remarks and references to Appendices
	JULY			
WILLEMAN	10		61 Div. Sports. Routine duties.	WS
"	11		ADMS visited S. Bearers 2/5 Warwicks 2/8 Warwicks 2/1 Bucks 2/1 Fd Amb. 2/3 Fd Amb. Tactical Exercise with Lt Col BROUGH CMG. GSO 2 and OC's ambulances. a/DADMS. visited DSC & inspected Sanitary arrangements.	WS
"	12		ADMS. visited MO's 2/7 Worcs 2/4 Glos. 2/8 Worcs and inspected the Stretcher bearers. In the afternoon he visited No 6 Stationary Hospital at FREVENT a/DADMS visited M.O. 2/4 Glos.	WS
"	13		ADMS. visited stretcher bearers of 2/4 O.B.L.I. 2/5 Glos. 2/1 Bucks and 1/5 D.C.L.I.	WS
"	14		Conference of O.C. ambulances with ADMS with reference to competition for Regimental Stretcher bearers. Three (3) MO's from each ambulance with Sanitary NCO and 8 Regimental MO's with San. NCO with a/DADMS visited Sanitary Exhibition at No 12 Stationary Hosp. ST POL. Arrangement for remainder for next week	WS

2353 Wt. W2544/1454 700,000 5/15 D. D. & L. A.D.S.S./Forms/C. 2118.

Instructions regarding War Diaries and Intelligence Summaries are contained in F. S. Regs., Part II. and the Staff Manual respectively. Title pages will be prepared in manuscript.

WAR DIARY
or
INTELLIGENCE SUMMARY.
(Erase heading not required.)

Army Form C. 2118.

Place	Date	Hour	Summary of Events and Information	Remarks and references to Appendices
	July			
WILLEMAN	15		ADMS. visited 2/3 S M FD AMB. with reference to Stretcher bearers competition. notification received from 3rd Army of the appointment of CAPT. W.V. CORBETT 9th Cav. Fd Amb, to be DADMS. 61 DIV. vice CAPT T.F.P. BREEN. sick.	W.S.
"	16		ADMS. visited M.O. 2/8 Warwicks. M.O. 2/4 R. Berks & M.O. R.E. and saw a tactical Exercise carried out by O.C. 2/1st S.M. FD AMB. Another party of MO's from Division visited Sanitary Exhibit at St Pol.	W.S.
"	17.		CAPT CORBETT. W.V. 1st Cav. division reported for duty as DADMS. Routine duties	W.S.
"	18.		Conference at 11·30 AM to discuss Stretcher Bearers Competition, O's C. Fd. Amb's present. Routine duties. Weather turned wet.	W. Victor Corbett.
"	19.		Stretcher Bearers Competition, commenced 2·30 P.M. Results proved to be very satisfactory. Routine duties.	W.H.
"	20.		A.D.M.S. visited M.O. i/c 2/4 GLOSTERS & inspected their baths.	W.H.
"	21.		61st Division warning order received. A.D.M.S. visited 2/1 & 2/3 S.M. Field Amb's & arranged with the O's C same for the evacuation of their cases not fit to rejoin their units. W.H.	

2353 Wt. W2544/1454 700,000 5/15 D. D. & L. A.D.S.S./Forms/C. 2118.

Instructions regarding War Diaries and Intelligence Summaries are contained in F. S. Regs., Part II. and the Staff Manual respectively. Title pages will be prepared in manuscript.

WAR DIARY
or
INTELLIGENCE SUMMARY.
(Erase heading not required.)

Army Form C. 2118.

Place	Date	Hour	Summary of Events and Information	Remarks and references to Appendices
	July			
WILLEMAN	22.		A.D.M.S. + D.A.D.M.S. visited the 2/1 BUCKS + inspected a new draft of men for that Battn. For the purpose of the forthcoming move the Field Ambs. will move with their respective Brigade Groups. A.D.M.S + D.A.D.M.S. visited 2/7 WARWICKS. Weather improved - fine. W.H.	
"	23.		A.D.M.S. visited H.Q. of the three Brigades today also the 2/2 (S.M.) Fd. Amb. and O.C. 2/8 Worcesters. Routine duties. W.H.	
"	24.		182 Brigade moved today to FREVENT area [Map. Ref. LENS (sheet 11) 3.D.] prior to entraining. R.A.M.C. Administrative Instructions No 34 issued*. D.A.D.M.S visited 2/3 (S.M.) Fd. Amb which had arrived + billeted for tonight at SERICOURT [Map. Ref. LENS (sheet 11) 3.D.]. W.H.	* App. I.
WILLEMAN.	25.		D.A.D.M.S. visited 2/1 (S.M.) Fd. Amb. + found them prepared to move. A.D.M.S. visited entraining station at AUXI-LE-CHALEAU [Map Ref LENS. (sheet 11) 4.B.] + found the entraining of the 184 Brigade (Infantry) proceeding satisfactory. D.A.D.M.S. visited FREVENT + PETIT HOUVIN [Map. Ref. LENS (sheet 11) 3.D. + 3.D. respectively] the entraining stations of the 182 + 183 Brigades (Infantry). Satisfactory W.H.	
WILLEMAN.	26.		Divisional H.Q. closed at 9 A.M. W.H.	
ZEGGERS-CAPPEL.	26.		Divisional H.Q. opened 9 A.M. Move is being completed without any event of importance. Locations are as follows [Map Ref. HAZEBROUCK 5a in all cases] :- (1) 61st Divisional HQ + A.D.M.S offices ZEGGERS-CAPPEL. 2E.	

2353 Wt. W2544/1454 700,000 5/15 D. D. & L. A.D.S.S./Forms/C. 2118.

Instructions regarding War Diaries and Intelligence Summaries are contained in F. S. Regs., Part II. and the Staff Manual respectively. Title pages will be prepared in manuscript.

WAR DIARY
or
INTELLIGENCE SUMMARY.
(Erase heading not required.)

Army Form C. 2118.

Place	Date	Hour	Summary of Events and Information	Remarks and references to Appendices
	July		Cont:	
ZEGGERS-CAPPEL.	26		2/1. (S.M.) Fd Amb. at BROXEELE. 3.D. 2/2. (S.M.) Fd Amb. " RUBROUCK. 2.E. 2/3. (S.M.) Fd Amb. " 200yds S.E. of the F in PEENHOF. 2 E. A.D.M.S. + D.A.D.M.S. visited D.D.M.S. VIII Corps at ESQUELBECQ. 2F. + afterwards visited 2/2 (S.M.) Fd Amb. Move of Division nearly completed. [illegible]. The Division is now being administered by VIII Corps. W.K.	
"	27.		Move of Division completed. A.D.M.S. attended a conference of the Brigadiers + "G". Routine. A.D.M.S. visited 2/1 and 2/3 Fd Ambs. W.K.	
"	28.		A.D.M.S. attended lecture on "Shell Gas", given at D.H.Q. D.A.D.M.S. visited 183 Brigade Area + inspected sanitary conditions. Conference of O's C. Fd Ambs held at A.D.M.S. office re:impending operations. ~~Captain~~ A.L. ANTHONY reported from ENGLAD for duty + posted to 2/3 (S.M.) Fd Amb. W.K.	
"	29.		D.A.D.M.S. visited No 7 General Hospital + saw some of the new ("Mustard Shell") Gas cases. Routine. W.K.	
"	30.		A.D.M.S. visited D.D.M.S. VIII Corps; W.K.	
"	31.		D.A.D.M.S. visited 2/1 S.M. Fd Amb. + 184 Brigade area. Routine. W.K.	

C Hawkins
Colonel
A. D. M. S., 61st. Div.

2353 Wt. W2544/1454 700,000 5/15 D. D. & L. A.D.S.S./Forms/C. 2118.

Appendix I.

SECRET. COPY NO: 13.

R.A.M.C., ADMINISTRATIVE INSTRUCTIONS NO: 34

1. Motor Ambulances at Entrainment & Detrainment Stations.	Officers Commanding Field Ambulances will arrange for one motor ambulance to be at the entraining station whilst the troops of their associated Brigades entrain; and also to be at the detraining station during detrainment. Written instfuctions as to destination etc will be given to drivers of Ambulances proceeding to new area independently. One medical officer will remain attached to the Ambulance car doing duty at the above stations until the entrainment and detrainment is completed and will arrange evacuation of any urgent cases.
2. Motor Ambulances proceeding to new area.	Os.C., Field Ambulances will arrange that all Motor Ambulances except those on duty, join the Supply Column with sufficient petrol by 11 a.m. on the 25th to travel with the Supply Column to new area.
3. Medical arrangements in new area.	On arrival in new area Field Ambulances will collect and deal with the sick of their associated Brigades. All serious cases will be evacuated to the nearest Medical establishment pending further instructions.
4. Notification of Ambulance sites.	On arrival, the exact location and accomodation of premises to be utilised by Ambulances will be notified to the A.D.M.S., at Divisional H.Qrs.

5. ACKNOWLEDGE.

Issued at 10.30 a.m. 24/7/17.

W. Victor Corbett
Captain.
for Colonel A.D.M.S., 61st Div.

Copies to:-
1-3. 2/1,2/2,2/3 Field Ambs.,
4-6. 182,183,184 Infantry Bdes. For information.
7. 61st Division "G"
8. 61st Division "Q"
9. C.R.E.,
10. 61st Div: Train. 15.61st Div:Sup.Col.
11. 1/5 D.C.L.I.
12-13. War Diary.
14. File.

B.E.F.

SUMMARY OF MEDICAL WAR DIARIES OF 61st Div. 8th Corps.

5th ARMY. from 26.7.17.

19th Corps from August 15th.

5th Corps from Sept. 7th.

17th Corps III. ARMY from 18th Sept.

Western Front Operations - July - November 1917.

A.D.M.S. Col. C. Howkins.

D.A.D.M.S. - Capt. W.V. Corbett.

Summarised under the following headings:-

Phase "D" 1. Passchendaele Operations, "July- Nov.1917".

(a). Operations commencing 1/7/17.

(b). Operations commencing 1/10/17.
Canadians attacked Passchendaele, Oct.30th.
Canadians took Passchendaele, Nov 6th.

B.E.F.

61st Div. 8th Corps. 5th ARMY. WESTERN FRONT.
July-Aug., 1917.

A.D.M.S. Col. C. Howkins.

Div. transferred to 19th Corps.

PHASE "D" 1. Passchendaele Operations, July - Nov. 1917.

(a). Operations commencing 1/7/1917.

Headquarters at ZEGGERS - CAPPEL.

July 26th. Moves.) 61st Division arrived in 8th Corps Area
Transfer.)
from 6th Corps 1st ARMY.

2/1st S.M. F.A. at BROXEELE.

2/2nd S.M. F.A. at RUBROUCK.

2/3rd S.M. F.A. at PEENHOF.

B.E.F.

61st Div. 8th Corps. 5th ARMY. WESTERN FRONT. July-Aug. 1917.

A.D.M.S. Col. C. Howkins.

Div. transferred to 19th Corps.

PHASE "D" 1. Passchendaele Operations, July - Nov. 1917.

(a). Operations commencing 1/7/1917.

Headquarters at ZEGGERS - CAPPEL.

July 26th. Moves.) 61st Division arrived in 8th Corps Area
Transfer.)
from 6th Corps 1st ARMY.

2/1st (S.M.) F.A. at BROXEELE.

2/2nd (S.M.) F.A. at RUBROUCK.

2/3rd (S.M.) F.A. at PEENHOF.

Confidential

Medical

16

Vol 16

Aug 1917

140/2362

War Diary

of

A.D.M.S. 61st Division

From August 1st To August 31st 1917.

Volume 16.

~~Diaries Enclosed~~
~~2/1 Field Amb.~~
~~2/2 Field Amb.~~
~~2/3 Field Amb.~~

August 31st 1917.

~~Colonel~~
~~A.D.M.S.~~ 61 Div

Army Form C. 2118.

WAR DIARY
or
INTELLIGENCE SUMMARY.
(Erase heading not required.)

Instructions regarding War Diaries and Intelligence Summaries are contained in F. S. Regs., Part II. and the Staff Manual respectively. Title pages will be prepared in manuscript.

Place	Date	Hour	Summary of Events and Information	Remarks and references to Appendices
ZAGGERS CAPPEL.	Aug. 1st 1917.		A.D.M.S + D.A.D.M.S. visited XVIII + XIX Corps area, with a view to seeing the Medical arrangements during the present battle. Weather conditions extremely bad. W.H.	
..	2.		A.D.M.S + D.A.D.M.S. visited D.D.M.S. of XVIII + also of XIX Corps. Obtained copies of medical arrangements. Weather still very bad. W.H.	
..	3.		A.D.M.S. visited 2/1 S.M. Fd Amb. Routine duties. W.H.	
..	4.		D.D.M.S. VIII Corps visited A.D.M.S. 61 Div: D.A.D.M.S. visited 2/3 S.M. Fd Amb. + Battalions of the 184th Brigade. W.H.	
..	5.		Routine duties. Weather still very wet. W.H.	
..	6.		Capt. BERRY. W.A. (R.A.M.C. T.C.) reported from England + posted to 2/3 (S.M.) Fd Amb for duty. A.D.M.S. present at Tactical exercise of 182nd Brigade. D.A.D.M.S. visited 2/3 (S.M.) Fd Amb. + 183rd Brigade area. W.H.	
	7.		A.D.M.S. present at Tactical exercise of 183rd Brigade. Capt. WHATLEY. J.A. (R.A.M.C. T.C.) reported from England + posted to 2/1 (S.M.) Fd Amb for duty. W.H.	
..	8.		A.D.M.S. present at Tactical exercise of 184th Brigade. D.A.D.M.S. visited 2/2 (S.M.) Fd Amb. + 182nd Brigade area. A.D.M.S. visited D.D.M.S. VIII Corps + 2/3 (S.M.) Fd Amb. W.H.	
..	9.		Lieut. MILLER. S. (U.S. Army) reported from England + posted to 2/1 (S.M.) Fd Amb for duty. A.D.M.S. visited D.D.M.S. Sanitation W.H.	

2353 Wt. W2544/1454 700,000 5/15 D. D. & L. A.D.S.S./Forms/C. 2118.

Instructions regarding War Diaries and Intelligence Summaries are contained in F. S. Regs., Part II. and the Staff Manual respectively. Title pages will be prepared in manuscript.

WAR DIARY
or
~~INTELLIGENCE SUMMARY.~~
(Erase heading not required.)

Army Form C. 2118.

Place	Date	Hour	Summary of Events and Information	Remarks and references to Appendices
	August.			
ZAGGERS CAPPEL.	10.		A.D.M.S. visited D.D.M.S. Sanitation. Capt. RIDGWAY. from 2/3 (S.M.) Field Amb. reported for duty + instruction in A.D.M.S. office. D.A.D.M.S. visited 2/8 Worcesters. W.H.	
..	11.		A.D.M.S. visited 2/1. 2/2. 2/3. (S.M.) Fd Ambs. Warning order that division was about to move received. Routine duties. W.H.	
..	12.		D.A.D.M.S. visited 2/4 Berks inspected Sanitary arrangements. Routine duties. W.H.C.	See
..	13.		A.D.M.S. visited D.D.M.S. XIX Corps. Administrative Orders No 35 x + 36 + issued at 3 + 6 P.M respectively. W.H.	x. App I. + App II.
..	14		A.D.M.S. visited 2/2 (S.M.) Fd Amb. Administrative Instructions ⊙ issued 12 noon. Conference of O's C Fd Ambs at A.D.M.S office 2.30 P.M.	⊙ App III.
POPERINGHE	15.		Divisional move begun. 184th Brigade Group to WATOU No 1. area. 183rd Brigade Group to BRANDHOEK No 3 area. Divisional H.Q. to POPERINGHE. Alteration made in Medical arrangements as follows. The Tent division of the 2/1 S.M. Fd Amb. will proceed to MOATED FARM instead of the Tent division of the 2/3 S.M. Fd Amb. Move completed without event.	
			A.D.M.S. + D.A.D.M.S. visited A.D.M.S. 36 Division + after proceeded to C.M.D.S. Red Farm. (G5 d 2 5). A.D.M.S. attended conference of D.D.M.S XIX Corps.	
			Positioning of A.D.M.S. office 12 Noon. No 65, Rue de BOESCHEPE. POPERINGHE.	

2353 Wt. W2544/1454 700,000 5/15 D. D. & L. A.D.S.S./Forms/C. 2118.

Instructions regarding War Diaries and Intelligence Summaries are contained in F. S. Regs., Part II. and the Staff Manual respectively. Title pages will be prepared in manuscript.

WAR DIARY
or
INTELLIGENCE SUMMARY.
(Erase heading not required.)

Army Form C. 2118.

Place	Date	Hour	Summary of Events and Information	Remarks and references to Appendices
	August			
POPERINGHE	15.		Location of Medical units 9 P.M.	
			2/1 S.M. Fd Amb (1) H.Q. + Bearer Div: WATOU. (The Hospice) K4 b85. (Sheet 27).	
			(2) Tent Div: MOATED FARM H2 d73 (Sheet 28 N.W.)	
			2/2 S.M. Fd Amb. Taken over Corps Rest Station. HILLHOEK. L20 b64 (Sheet 27)	
			2/3 S.M. Fd Amb. not yet moved from ZEGGERS CAPPEL. W.L.	
"	16.		182nd Brigade group move into BRANDHOEK area No 1 completed. Location of 2/3 S.M. Fd Amb is Sheet 27 L13 d32 [MILL FARM]. RAMC Order No 37* issued at 5 P.M. W.L.C	* App IV
"	17.		A.D.M.S. visited A.D.M.S. 36 Division + D.D.M.S. XIX Corps. D.A.D.M.S visited 3/1 Fd Amb + H.Q. 183 Brigade. XIX Corps N.W.C.P. + M.D.S. O.C. 2/3 (S.M.) F.A. reported that his arrangements were complete to take over forward area from 109th Fd Amb. W.L.C	
"	18.		183rd Brigade moved up into the line night of 17/18: 2/3 (S.M.) Fd Amb have taken over from 109th Fd Amb. 2/3 (S.M.) Fd Amb: Headquarters are established at [illegible] G11. a central. (Sheet 28 N.W.) [illegible] A.D.M.S visited D.D.M.S. XIX Corps. A.D.M.S. office closed 3 P.M. W.L.C	
MERSEY CAMP	18.		D.H.Q. moved from POPERINGHE to MERSEY CAMP. H1 a55 (Sheet 28 N.W.) A.D.M.S. office opened 3 P.M. 2/1 S.M. Fd Amb. moved to G11. a. Central.	
[Sheet 28 N.W. H.1.]	19.		O.C. 2/1 (S.M.) Fd Amb. + O.C. 2/3 (S.M.) Fd Amb visited A.D.M.S. A.D.M.S. visited C.W.W.C.P. +	

2353 Wt. W2544/1454 700,000 5/15 D. D. & L. A.D.S.S./Forms/C. 2118.

Instructions regarding War Diaries and Intelligence Summaries are contained in F. S. Regs., Part II. and the Staff Manual respectively. Title pages will be prepared in manuscript.

WAR DIARY
or
INTELLIGENCE SUMMARY.

(Erase heading not required.)

Army Form C. 2118.

Place	Date	Hour	Summary of Events and Information	Remarks and references to Appendices
	Aug.			
MERSEY CAMP.	19.		A.D.S. Left C.M.D.S. closed. 2/3 SM. Fd Amb. H.Q. established Canal Bank A.D.S. [I.7.b.77]. W.K.	
	20.		184 Brigade taking over line from 183 Brigade. 2/1 SM. Fd Amb. has taken over XIX Corps C.W.W.C.P. VLAMERTINGHE MILL [Sheet 28. H8a99] + in addition MOATED FARM. [H2d73]. A.D.M.S. visited D.D.M.S. XIX Corps. + forward Area. W.K.	
"	21.		"Y" Day. Medical instructions 61 Div. issued*. Captain J.E.S. WILSON R.A.M.C. 2/1 Bucks wounded. D.A.D.M.S. visited XIX Corps W.W.D.S.; Left C.M.D.S. + transport lines of 2/3 (SM.) Fd Amb. A.D.M.S. visited C.W.W.D.S. + Reserve A.D.S. (Canal Bank) Front line taken over by the 184th Brigade from the 183rd Brigade. W.K.	* App. V.
"	22.		D.A.D.M.S. visited A.D.S. reserve A.D.S. C.W.W.D.S. + Motor Amb. Car Pool (Red farm). Zero 4.45 A.M. Wounded were coming in + at 8 A.M. when these points were visited "evacuation" was progressing without any trouble or congestion. A.D.M.S. visited A.D.S + C.W.W.D.S. Captain STOBIE W. RAMC slightly wounded + transferred for duty at C.W.W.D.S. Captain A. PRESSLIE R.A.M.C. sick. Captain G.L. WILKINSON sent to replace him in the 2/4 GLOSTERS. D.A.D.M.S. visited C.R.S. W.K.	
	23.		D.A.D.M.S. visited A.D.S + C.W.W.D.S. Evacuation of battle field progressing well. O.C. forward area hopes to have it completely cleared by this evening. The 200 Auxiliary Stretcher bearers.	

2353 Wt. W2544/1454 700,000 5/15 D. D. & L. A.D.S.S./Forms/C. 2118.

Army Form C. 2118.

WAR DIARY
or
INTELLIGENCE SUMMARY.
(Erase heading not required.)

Instructions regarding War Diaries and Intelligence Summaries are contained in F. S. Regs., Part II. and the Staff Manual respectively. Title pages will be prepared in manuscript.

Place	Date	Hour	Summary of Events and Information	Remarks and references to Appendices
MERSEY CAMP	Aug 23. (cont).		will be returned to their units this evening. The retaine 50 Stretcher Bearers are now required at 3 A.M. daily at the A.D.S. – A.D.M.S. visited C.N.W.D.S. – D.A.D.M.S. visited A.D.M.S. 15th Division. About 13 Casualties occurred today among the R.A.M.C. bearers of the 2/2 (S.M.) Fd. Amb. while on their way up to the A.D.S. as reliefs. W.H.C.	
"	24.		A.D.M.S. held a board on several men of Labour Group 38 to classify them P.B. men. A.D.M.S. visited A.D.S. C.M.D.S. C.W.W.D.S. D.A.D.M.S. on a board to classify 12th H.Q. A.S.C. into Class A or B. 183 Brigade moved into the line + relieved 184 Brigade. Captain F.J. CAHILL U.S.R. reported for duty + posted to 2/1 S.M. Fd Amb. W.H.	
"	25.		184 Brigade at Camp N. YPRES replaced by 182 Brigade. A.D.M.S. visited C.W.W.D.S. W.H.	
"	26.		Captain A. COLEMAN. RAMC reported slightly wounded. Positions of H.Q. Field Ambulances are 2/1 (S.M.) Fd Amb. C.W.W.D.S. (XIX Corps). H 8 a 9 9. (Sheet 28 N.W. 1/2000.) 2/2 (S.M.) " " C.R.S. (XIX Corps). L 20 b 6 4. (Sheet 27.) 2/3 (S.M.) " " Forward area. C 28 a 9 2. (Sheet 28 N.W. 1/20000.) A.D.M.S + Capt CAHILL (U.S.R.) boarded the Ordnance personnel for classification. Interviewed the R.M.O's who were in the recent operations. A.D.M.S. visited the XIX Corps W.W.D.S. also forward area. Weather turned very wet. W.H.	

Instructions regarding War Diaries and Intelligence Summaries are contained in F. S. Regs., Part II. and the Staff Manual respectively. Title pages will be prepared in manuscript.

WAR DIARY
or
~~INTELLIGENCE SUMMARY.~~
(Erase heading not required.)

Army Form C. 2118.

Place	Date	Hour	Summary of Events and Information	Remarks and references to Appendices
	Aug.			
MERSEY CAMP.	27.		A.D.M.S. visited A.D.S. & C.W.W.D.S. also C.M.D.S. Weather very bad. Routine duties. Zero 2 P.M. today. WH	
"	28.		D.A.D.M.S. visited A.D.S. Reserve A.D.S. C.W.W.D.S. & Car Pool (Red farm) found everything in order & evacuation of wounded progressing. The evacuation of wounded was of necessity slow on account of the muddy state of the ground. There was no congestion. Capt. W. H. CORNELIUS R.A.M.C. slightly wounded & remaining at duty. A.D.M.S. visited C.W.W.D.S.	WH
"	29.		D.A.D.M.S. sanitary inspection of C.W.W.D.S. 2/4 Ox & Bucks Camp & 2/1 Bucks Camps (Brandhoek area). Sanitary Officer visited A.D.M.S. A.D.M.S. visited forward area. Lieut-Col. SCOTT-WILLIAMSON. R.A.M.C. O.C. 2/3 Fd Amb & 14 Men reported missing. WH	
"	30.		D.A.D.M.S. inspected sanitary condition of 2/5 Glosters. visited C.W.W.D.S. A.D.M.S & D.A.D.M.S visited 2/4 Berks. D.A.D.M.S. inspected H.Q. 267 Employment Coy with a view to classification. A.D.M.S. visited XIX Corps & C.R.S. (2/2 S.M. Fd Amb) WH	
"	31.		A.D.M.S. visited forward area. 182nd Brigade relieved 183rd Brigade in the line. A.D.M.S. attended D.D.M.S. conference 11 AM. & visited C.W.W.D.S. Capt. A. PRESSLIE. R.A.M.C. evacuated sick. Capt. A.L. ANTHONY. R.A.M.C. reported wounded. W.V.C.	

C. Hopkins
Colonel
ADMS 61 Div

2353 Wt. W2544/1454 700,000 5/15 D. D. & L. A.D.S.S./Forms/C. 2118.

Appendix I

S E C R E T.

COPY NO. 7.......

61st DIVISION R.A.M.C. ADMINISTRATIVE ORDER NO 35.

1. The following moves will take place on the dates mentioned:-

183 Infantry Brigade on 15th August by train.
184 Infantry Brigade on 15th August ny train.
182 Infantry Brigade on 16th August by train.

2. All Transport will proceed by road.

3. Os.C.Field Ambulances will take steps to dispose of their sick forthwith.

4. ACKNOWLEDGE.

Issued at 3 p.m. August 13th 1917.

[signature]

Colonel A.M.S.

13/8/17.

A.D.M.S., 61st Division.

Copies to:-
(1) 2/1st Fld Ambulance.
(2) 2/2nd Fld Ambulance.
(3) 2/3rd Fld Ambulance.
(4) 61st Division "G" For Information.
(5) 61st Division "Q" For Information.
(6.7) War Diary.
(8) File.

Appendix II

SECRET COPY NO:- 12

61st DIVISION R.A.M.C., ORDER NO: 36.

(1) The 2/1st Field Ambulance will :-

(a) Move with the 184th Infantry Brigade Group on the 15th instant to the WATOU AREA.
(b) Take over from the detachment of the 46th Field Amb., at the HOSPICE, WATOU (K.4.b.85) Sheet 27.
(c) Open one Tent Sub-Division for reception and evacuation of local sick and wounded, and collect same.
(d) Send three clerks to the C.W.W.C.P., on "YZ" night.

(2) The 2/2nd Field Ambulance will :-

(a) Move with the 183rd Infantry Brigade Group (in place of the 2/3rd Field Amb.,) on the 15th instant to the HILLHOEK AREA.
(b) Send on an Advance Party to HILLHOEK (L.20.b.64) and take over from the 110th Field Amb., This will be accomplished by the morning of the 15th.
(c) Open three Tent Sub-Divisions and establish a Corps Rest Station - details to be arranged between Os.C. concerned.
(d) Hold the three Bearer Sub-Divisions ready to move off at any moment.
(e) Hold three horsed Ambulance wagons in readiness to reinforce the front if called upon to do so by the D.D.M.S.,

(3) The 2/3rd Field Ambulance will :-

(a) Move with the 182nd Infantry Brigade Group (in place of the 2/2nd Field Ambulance) on the 16th instant.
(b) Establish Headquarters at HILL FARM (L.13.d.32)
(c) Open three Tent Sub-Divisions at MOATED FARM (H.2.d.73) and be prepared to take in slightly sick and wounded as an accessory Walking Wounded Dressing Station, and work under the Officer Commanding, Corps Walking Wounded Dressing Station.
(d) Hold five large Motor Ambulances in readiness to reinforce the front if called upon to do so by the D.D.M.S.,
(e) Send two clerks to the Left C.M.D.S. on "YZ" night.

(4) ACKNOWLEDGE.

Issued at 6 p.m. August 13th 1917.

[signature] Corbett
for Colonel A.M.S.
A.D.M.S., 61st Division.

Copies to:-
1-3. 2/1st, 2/2nd, 2/3rd Fd.Ambs.,
4-6. 182, 183, 184 Infantry Bdes.,
7. 61 Div. "G" For information.
8. 61 Div. "Q" For information.
9. D.D.M.S., VIII Corps. "
10. D.D.M.S., XIX Corps. "
11. A.D.M.S., 36th Division.
12-13. War Diary.
14. File.

SECRET. *Appendix III* A.D.M.S.,No:955/5/M/17.
COPY NO:- *14*

61st DIVISION R.A.M.C., ADMINISTRATIVE INSTRUCTION

(1) HORSE TRANSPORT.

The 2/1st Field Ambulance will detail one Horse Ambulance to follow the Horse Transport of the 184 Infantry Brigade.

The 2/3rd Field Ambulance will detail one Horse Ambulance to follow the Horse Transport of the 182 and 183 Inf.Bdes. respectively. A Medical officer will be in charge of each Horse Ambulance.

(2) SICK DURING MOVE

The sick from the 182 Inf.Bde. will be collected etc by the 2/3rd Field Ambulance from 12 noon August 14th, during the move.

(3) SICK IN NEW AREA.

The 2/1st Field Amb., will collect sick etc from the 184 Inf.Bde.,

The 2/3rd Field Ambulance at MOATED FARM will collect sick etc from the 182 and 183 Inf.Bdes., and form a small reception Hospital. Cases not fit in 48 hours will be transferred to the Corps Rest Station (or Casualty Clearing Station, if necessary)

The 2/1st Field Ambulance will collect and treat sick from the 183 Inf.Bde. until the 2/3rd Field Amb arrive in new area. Os.C. Field Ambulances to arrange details.

(4) URGENT CASES OF SICKNESS ETC

Urgent cases of sickness will be sent to the nearest Medical Unit, and the A.D.M.S., notified if direct admission.

(5) ENTRAINING & DETRAINING

The 2/1st Fd.Amb., will arrange for a motor Ambulance to be at each DETRAINING station until the detraining is complete.

The 2/3rd Field Amb., will arrange for a motor ambulance to be at each ENTRAINING station till the entraining is complete.

A good Nursing Orderly to be with each Motor Ambulance.

(6) LOCATION.

A map is attached showing location of Medical Units in new area.

(7) ACKNOWLEDGE

Issued at 12 noon. 14/8/1917.

W. Victor Corbett.
Colonel A.M.S.
A.D.M.S., 61st Division.

Copies :-
1-3. 2/1, 2/2, 2/3 Fd.Ambs.,
4-6. 182, 183, 184 Inf.Bdes.,
7. 61 Div "G" For information.
8. 61 Div "Q" -do-
9. D.D.M.S.,VIII Corps -do-
10. D.D.M.S.,XIX Corps -do-
11. O.C.Train.
12. C.R.E. For information.
13. C.R.A., -do-
14-15. War Diary.
16. File.

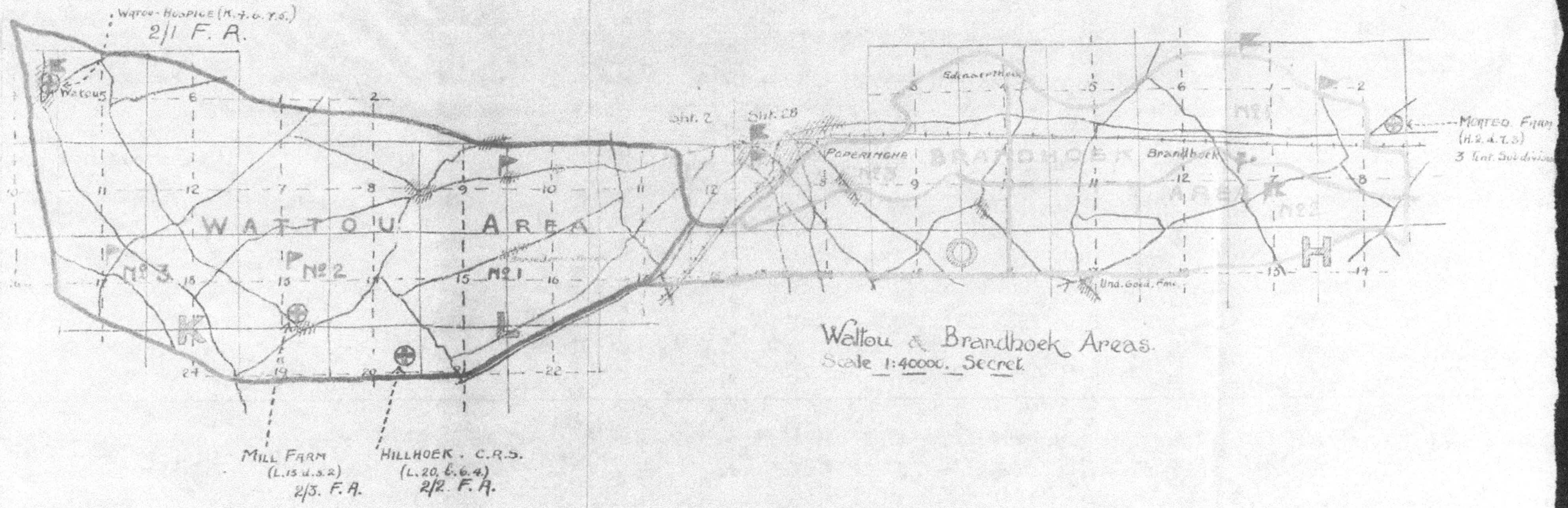

Watou-Hospice (K.4.c.7.5.)
2/1 F.A.
Watous
WATTOU AREA
No 1
No 2
No 3
Mill Farm
(L.13 d.5.2)
2/3. F.A.
Hillhoek. C.R.S.
(L.20, b.6.4.)
2/2. F.A.
Poperinghe
Brandhoek Area
Brandhoek
Morteo Farm
(H.2.d.7.3)
3 Ent. Sub division
Waltou & Brandhoek Areas.
Scale 1:40000. Secret

Appendix IV

SECRET.

COPY NO:- 14

61st DIVISION R.A.M.C., Order No: 37

(1) A. The O.C., 2/3rd Field Amb., (less one Tent Sub-Division and 2 Medical Officers) will take over the forward area and Medical Posts on the night 17/18 August from O.C., 109 Field Amb.,

B. One Tent Sub-Division (2/3 Field Amb.,) with 2 Medical Officers will be held in readiness to proceed to a C.C.S.,

C. Details of taking over will be arranged between the Os.C. Field Ambulance concerned.

(2) The O.C., 2/1 Field Amb., will detail 50 bearers to report to O.C., 2/3rd Field Amb., by 12 noon 17th instant for duty.

(3) The O.C., 2/2nd Field Amb., will hold his Bearer Division in reserve for work in the forward area.

(4) MOTOR AMBULANCES.
The O.C., 2/1 Field Amb., will detail four large Motor Ambulances to be at the Corps Main Dressing Station (RED FARM) by 4 p.m. 17th instant for use in forward area.

The O.C., 2/3rd Field Amb., will utilise his motor Ambulances to evacuate from the forward posts to Corps Main Dressing Station.

(5) HORSE AMBULANCES.
Horse Ambulances belonging to the three Field Ambulances will be held in readiness to proceed under orders to be issued separately.

(6) The A.D.M.S., will be notified when relief of forward area is complete.

(7) ACKNOWLEDGE.

Issued at 5 p.m. August 16th 1917.

C. Hawkins

Colonel A.M.S.
A.D.M.S., 61st Division.

Copies to :-
1-3. 2/1, 2/2, 2/3 Fd Ambs.,
4. 109 Fd Amb.,
5. D.D.M.S. XIX Corps. For information.
6. 61 Div "G" -do-
7. 61 Div "Q" -do-
8. 61 Div Train.
9-11. 182,183,184 Inf Bdes: -do-
12. C.R.E.
13. C.R.A.
14-15. War Diary.
16. File.
17. A.D.M.S.,36 Div.

SECRET.

Appendix V

Copy No..

MEDICAL ARRANGEMENTS 61st Division.

Map Reference - Shoets 27 & 28 Scale 1/40.000

The following Medical Arrangements will be carried out for the resumption of an offensive at a date to be notified later.

(1) Medical Posts.

(a) Regimental Aid Posts.

Regimental Aid Posts will be formed by each Medical Officer in consultation with the Officer Commanding the Battalion.
The O.C. Admanced Dressing Station is to be immediately informed of any change of locality.

(b) Bearer Relay Posts.

Bearer Relay Posts will be formed in front of WIELTJE under instructions of the O.C.Advanced Dressing Station.

(c) Advanced Dressing Stations.

1. The Advanced Dressing Station will be in the Mined Dugout, WIELTJE C.28.a.9.5.
2. Reserve A.D.S.at Canal Bank, I.1.b.7.7. for collection of local Casualties, and staffed by small number of R.A.M.C.personnel.
3. Collecting Post, I.3.a.3.7. (near St JEAN) for local and walking wounded.

(2) EVACUATION Lying and Sitting Cases.

(a) From front line to R.A.P.by Regimental Stretcher Bearers,assisted by any extra Stretcher Bearers which may be provided under Regimental arrangements.
(b) From Regimental Aid Posts through Relay Posts, and to A.D.S. by R.A.M.C.bearers and Auxiliary Regimental Stretcher Bearers. The tramway between Bank Farm and WIELTJE may be utilised if completed and serviceable.
(c) From Advanced Dressing Station to Corps M.D.S. by Divisional Motor Ambulances.
(d) Walking Wounded will be directed by directing signs via WIELTJE, St JEAN,POTIJZE Cross Roads, MENIN Road Corner,I.8.b.6.4., where lorries will call at regular intervals to convoy them to the Corps W.W.D.S.
If it is not advisable to use the St JEAN-POTIJZE Road, lorries will return direct from St JEAN.
(e) Use may be made of empty returning Road Construction lorries etc
(f) Returning empty trucks of Light Railway from C.27.d.1.3.(St JEAN and from I.3.b.6.3.(POTIJZE) back to H.4.c.1.9. where O.C. 2/1 S.M.Field Ambulance will arrange Horse Transport to convoy to C.W.W.D.S.(H.8.a.9.9.)VLAMERTINGHE MILL, those who are unable to walk.
(g) Horse Ambulances of the Division will be parked at VLAMERTINGHE MILL on Y/Z night with rations. Further instructions will be issued for Motor Ambulances.
(h) A Motor Ambulance rendezvous will be made at near Canal End I.2.c.2.5. These will be sent up when required by O.C. A.D.S. on his instructions

(3) ROUTE OF MOTOR AMBULANCES.
With reference to page 4,para3, (1),XIX Corps Medical Arrangements No 3.the direct route to WIELTJE is for 'up' traffic. If, however, it is finally decided that it is a two way road, cars can proceed as usual.

(4) TRANSPORT.

(a) Motor Ambulance Cars.
The 15 large Motor Ambulances of the Division will be parked at the Corps M.D.S.(G.5.d.2.5. RED FARM) by Zero on Z day.
(b) Horse Ambulances and G.S.Wagons of the Field Ambulances will be parked and under O.C.2/1 S.M.F.Ambulance by Zero on Z day.
(c)

(over)

TRANSPORT (contd).

(c) Wheeled Stretcher Carriages of the Division will be distributed as follows:-

20 under O.C., A.D.S. at WIELTJE.
5 under O.C., 2/1 S.M.F.Ambulance.

(d) Pack Animals - Applications for these will be sent to A.D.M.S., loads to be sent up stated, and destination.

Pack Saddles and Animals will be pooled for use in forward area and parked at ~~HILL FARM~~ VLAMERTINGHE MILL on Z/Z night. Rations to be taken.

(5) STRETCHER & BLANKET DUMP.

Stretcher and Blanket Dump will be arranged at the A.D.S. WIELTJE, Bearer Assembly Posts, and Regimental Aid Posts.

Forward dumps will be arranged by O.C., A.D.S.

(6) RATION DUMP.

A R.A.M.C. Ration Dump will be made of 500 Rations at I.3.a.6.7.(near St.JEAN).

(7) WATER DUMP.

A R.A.M.C. Drinking Water Dump will be made at A.D.S. WIELTJE, and sent forward when necessary for use of Regimental Medical Officers. Motor Ambulance cars conveying water in petrol cans to A.D.S.

(8) SALVAGE DUMP AT A.D.S.

Every care must be taken to salve Stretchers and Shell Haversacks and other Medical equipment.

(9) ARRANGEMENTS IN AN ADVANCE.

(a) An Advanced Dressing Station will be formed in front of WIELTJE and lying and sitting cases conveyed back by hand carriage, wheeled stretchers or motor transport.

The route from the new R.A.P's and the new A.D.S. and back will be marked by directing signs.

(b) Analysis of Water.

This will be done under instructions which have been issued separately to each Medical Officer.

The O.C., A.D.S. will have labels placed on all Water supplies tested. Records of all reports are to be kept and copy sent immediately to this office.

(10) STRAGGLERS POSTS.

Men who are not sick or wounded will be handed over to the posts at

I.1.b.8.5.
I.1.c.3.3.
H.12.a.2.3.

(11) RECORDING.

The 2/1 S.M.F.Ambulance is selected for recording purposes.

(12) MAPS.

No map of our own lines will be taken by any Officer, N.C.O. or man in front of Battalion Headquarters.

(13) GUIDES & R.A.M.C. SQUADS.

Guides and R.A.M.C. Squads will be attached to Regimental

Medical Officers. Guides for Walking Wounded will be arranged by O.C. 2/3 S.M.F.Ambulance.

(14) AUXILIARY STRETCHER BEARERS.

Two hundred (200) will be available on Y/Z night and will be at the following assembly posts:-

WIELTJE.
A.D.S. Canal Bank.
Collecting Post (I.3.a.6.7. near St.JEAN).
Corps M.D.S. (Red Farm, G.3.d.2.5.).

Stretcher Dumps will be placed there.

(15) URGENT SURGICAL CASES.

Abdominal, Chest, and Compound Fractures of Thighs will be sent direct to C.C.S., BRANDHOEK, and C.M.D.S. notified by A.F.W. 3210.

for Colonel, AMS.
A.D.M.S. 61st Division.

August 20th, 1917.

Copies to:-

1-3. 2/1,2/2,2/3 Field Ambulances.
4. 61st Division, "G". (For information).
5. 61st Division, "Q". "
6. D.D.M.S. XIX Corps. "
7. A.D.M.S. 48th Division. "
8. A.D.M.S. 15th Division. "
9. O.C. 1/1 S.M.F.Ambulance. "
10. O.C. 45 Field Ambulance. "
11. 182 Infantry Brigade. "
12. 183 Infantry Brigade. "
13. 184 Infantry Brigade. "
14. 61 Divl. Supply Col. ".

B.E.F.

SUMMARY OF MEDICAL WAR DIARIES OF 61st Div. 8th Corps.

5th ARMY. from 26.7.17.

19th Corps from August 15th.

5th Corps from Sept. 7th.

17th Corps III. ARMY from 18th Sept.

Western Front Operations - July - November 1917.

A.D.M.S. Col. C. Howkins.

D.A.D.M.S. - Capt. W.V. Corbett.

Summarised under the following headings:-

Phase "D" 1. Passchendaele Operations,"July- Nov.1917".

(a). Operations commencing 1/7/17.

(b). Operations commencing 1/10/17.
Canadians attacked Passchendaele, Oct.30th.
Canadians took Passchendaele, Nov 6th.

August 1st. Weather. Extremely bad.

Military Situation. Division in back area.

15th. Moves.) Division transferred to 19th Corps and
Transfer.)
moved to POPERINGHE.

61st Div. 19th Corps. 5th ARMY. WESTERN FRONT.
Aug. 1917.

A.D.M.S. Col. C. Howkins.

PHASE "D" 1. Passchendaele Operations, July - Nov. 1917.

(a). Operations commencing 1/7/1917.

H.Q. Poperinghe.

August 15th. Transfer. Division transferred to 19th Corps.

Medical Arrangements. (App. 2. attached paras. 1.,2.,3.) (Put back into Diary)

16th. T.D. of 2/1st S.M.F.A. proceeded to Moated Farm instead of T.D. of 2/3rd S.M.F.A.

17th-18th. Military Situation. 183rd Infantry Brigade moved into line.

Medical Arrangements. (App. 4. paras 1-5 attached.) (Put back into Diary) 2/3rd S.M.F.A. Headquarters established at G.11.a.central (Sheet 28).

18th. Moves. To Mersey Camp H.1.a.5.6. (Sheet 28).

Moves. F.A. 2/1st S.M.F.A. to G.11.a. central (Sheet 28).

19th. Medical Arrangements. 2/3rd S.M.F.A. took over A.D.S. Canal Bank I.1.b.7.7.

20th. Medical Arrangements. 2/1st S.M.F.A. took over 19th C.W.W.C.P. at VLAMERTINGHE MILL H.8.a.9.9. (Sheet 28) and Moated Farm (H.2.d.7.3).

21st. Casualties R.A.M.C. Capt. J.E. Wilson attached 2/1st Bucks wounded.

Military Situation. 184th Brigade relieved 183rd Brigade in line.

22nd. Operations. Zero 4.45 a.m.

61st Div. 19th Corps. 5th ARMY. WESTERN FRONT.
Aug. 1917.

A.D.M.S. Col. C. Howkins.

PHASE "D" 1. Passchendaele Operations, July-Nov. 1917.

(a). Operations commencing 1/7/1917.

Aug. 22nd. contd. Medical Arrangements.(App.V. paras 1.,2.,4.,7.,9.,10., 14.,15. attached). (Put back into Diary)

Casualties.) Evacuation.) Wounded were evacuated from all posts without trouble or congestion. All cleared by evening of 23rd.

Casualties R.A.M.C. Capt. W. Stobie wounded slightly.

23rd. 0 & 13 wounded 2/2nd S.M.F.A. while on way to A.D.S. as reliefs.

24th. Military Situation. 183rd Brigade relieved 184th Brigade in line.

26th. Casualties R.A.M.C. Capt. A. Coleman wounded.

Locations F.A. H.Q. 2/1st S.M.F.A. C.W.W.C.P. H.8.a.9.9. (Sheet 28).

" 2/2nd " C.R.S. L.20.b.6.4. (Sheet 27).

" 2/3rd " Forward Area C.28.a.9.2. (Sheet 28).

Weather. Very wet.

27th. Operations. Zero 2 p.m.

Casualties.) Evacuation.) Terrain. Evacuation of wounded progressed satisfactorily although slow, on account of muddy state of ground due to heavy rain. No congestion.

Casualties R.A.M.C. Capt. W.H. CORNELIUS wounded slightly .

29th. Lt.Col. Scott Williamson,Officer Commanding 2/3rd S.M.F.A. and 14 Other Ranks reported missing.

61st Div. 19th Corps. 5th ARMY. WESTERN FRONT. Aug.-- Sept.1917.

A.D.M.S. Col. C. Howkins.

5th Corps from Sept. 7th.

PHASE "D" 1. Passchendaele Operations,"July- Nov. 1917."

(a) - Operations commencing 1/7/1917.

Aug. 31st. Military Situation. 182nd Infantry Brigade relieved 183rd Infantry Brigade in line.

Casualties R.A.M.C. Capt. A.L. Anthony wounded.

Appendices.

II. R.A.M.C. Order 36.d. 13/8/1917.

IV. " " 37.d. 16/8/1917.

V. Med. Arr. 61st Div. d. 20/8/1917.

August 1st. <u>Weather</u>. Extremely bad.

<u>Military Situation</u>. Division in back area.

15th. <u>Moves</u>.) Division transferred to 19th Corps and
<u>Transfer</u>.)
moved to POPERINGHE.

61st Div. 19th Corps. 5th ARMY. WESTERN FRONT.
A.D.M.S. Col. C. Howkins. July - Aug.. 1917.

PHASE "D" 1. Passchendaele Operations, July - Nov. 1917.

(a). Operations commencing 1/7/1917.

H.Q. Poperinghe.

August 15th. Transfer. Division transferred to 19th Corps.

Medical Arrangements. (App. 2. attached paras. 1.,2.,3.)

16th. T.D. of 2/1st S.M.F.A. proceeded to Moated Farm instead of T.D. of 2/3rd S.M.F.A.

17th-18th. Military Situation. 183rd Infantry Brigade moved into line.

Medical Arrangements. (App. 4. paras 1-5 attached.)

2/3rd S.M.F.A. Headquarters established at G.11.a.central (Sheet 28).

18th. Moves. To Mersey Camp H.1.a.5.6. (Sheet 28).

Moves. F.A. 2/1st S.M.F.A. to G.11.a. central (Sheet 28).

19th. Medical Arrangements. 2/3rd S.M.F.A. took over A.D.S. Canal Bank I.1.b.7.7.

20th. Medical Arrangements. 2/1st S.M.F.A. took over 19th C.W.W.C.P. at VLAMERTINGHE MILL H.8.a.9.9. (Sheet 28) and Moated Farm (H.2.d.7.3).

21st. Casualties R.A.M.C. Capt. J.E. Wilson attached 2/1st Bucks wounded.

Military Situation. 184th Brigade relieved 183rd Brigade in line.

22nd. Operations. Zero 4.45 a.m.

61st Div. 19th Corps. 5th ARMY. WESTERN FRONT.
Aug. 1917.

A.D.M.S. Col. C. Howkins.

PHASE "D" 1. Passchendaele Operations, July-Nov. 1917.

(a). Operations commencing 1/7/1917.

Aug. 22nd. contd. Medical Arrangements. (App.V. paras 1.,2.,4.,7.,9.,10., 14.,15. attached).

Casualties.) Evacuation.) Wounded were evacuated from all posts without trouble or congestion. All cleared by evening of 23rd.

Casualties R.A.M.C. Capt. W. Stobie wounded slightly.

23rd. 0 & 13 wounded 2/2nd S.M.F.A. while on way to A.D.S. as reliefs.

24th. Military Situation. 183rd Brigade relieved 184th Brigade in line.

26th. Casualties R.A.M.C. Capt. A. Coleman wounded.

Locations F.A. H.Q. 2/1st S.M.F.A. C.W.W.C.P. H.8.a.9.9. (Sheet 28).

" 2/2nd " C.R.S. L.20.b.6.4. (Sheet 27).

" 2/3rd " Forward Area C.28.a.9.2. (Sheet 28).

Weather. Very wet.

27th. Operations. Zero 2 p.m.

Casualties.) Evacuation.) Terrain. Evacuation of wounded progressed satisfactorily although slow, on account of muddy state of ground due to heavy rain. No congestion.

Casualties R.A.M.C. Capt. W.H. CORNELIUS wounded slightly.

29th. Lt.Col. Scott Williamson, Officer Commanding 2/3rd S.M.F.A. and 14 Other Ranks reported missing.

B.E.F.

61st Div. 19th Corps. 5th ARMY.

A.D.M.S. Col. C. Howkins.

WESTERN FRONT.
Aug. - Sept.1917.

5th Corps from Sept. 7th.

PHASE "D" 1. Passchendaele Operations, "July- Nov. 1917."

(a) - Operations commencing 1/7/1917.

Aug. 31st. Military Situation. 182nd Infantry Brigade relieved 183rd Infantry Brigade in line.

Casualties R.A.M.C. Capt. A.L. Anthony wounded.

Appendices.

II. R.A.M.C. Order 36.d. 13/8/1917.

IV. " " 37.d. 16/8/1917.

V. Med. Arr. 61st Div. d. 20/8/1917.

CONFIDENTIAL

MEDICAL

9

140/2426

Vol 17

Sept 1917

WAR DIARIES

of

MEDICAL UNITS 61st DIVISION

FROM:- September 1st

TO:- September 30th 1917.

VOLUME 17

Diaries enclosed :- A.D.M.S., 61 Div.
2/1 Field Ambulance.
2/2 Field Ambulance.
2/3 Field Ambulance.

September 30th 1917.

C Hawkins

Colonel.
A. D. M. S., 61st, Div.

Sept. 6th. Operations. Z- day.

Casualties.) Evacuation of wounded progressed without
Evacuation.)
trouble-No congestion. Cases passed through C.W.W.C.P. were few.

7th. Appointment. Capt. C.L. Lander to Officer Commanding 2/3rd S.M.F.A. vice Lt.Col. G. Scott-Williamson, missing.

Transfer. To 5th Corps.

Sept. 6th. Operations. Z day.

Casualties.) Evacuation of wounded progressed without
Evacuation.)
trouble-no congestion. Cases passed through C.W.W.C.P.
were few.

7th. Appointment. Capt. C.L. Lander to Officer Commanding 2/3rd S.M.F.A. vice Lt.Col. G. Scott-Williamson, missing.

Transfer. To 5th Corps.

61st Div. 5th Corps. 5th ARMY.

A.D.M.S. Col. C. Howkins.

To 17th Corps III. ARMY. from 18th Sept.

WESTERN FRONT.
July - Sept. 1917.

PHASE "D" 1. Passchendaele Operations, "July-Nov.1917."

(a) - Operations commencing 1/7/1917.

H.Q. Mersey Camp H.1.a.5.6. (Sheet 28)

Sept. 7th. Transfer. To 5th Corps.

13th. Casualties. R.A.M.C. Capt. W.J. Evans attached 2/6th Glosters died of wounds.

15th. Military Situation. 61st Division relieved by 55th Div. in line.

Medical Arrangements. (App. 1. attached). (Put back into Diary)

Moves. To Wattou.

Locations F.A. 2/1st S.M.F.A. at K.17.b.2.2.
2/2nd S.M.F.A. at L.10.c.9.2.
2/3rd S.M.F.A. at L.19.b.3.6.
Sheet 27.

18th. Transfer.) Moves.) To 17th Corps III. ARMY and moved to Duisans. (Sheet 51c).

Appendices. I. R.A.M.C. Adm. Order 38 d.12/9/1917. and Appendix d 13/9/1917.

61st Div. 5th Corps. 5th ARMY.

A.D.M.S. Col. C. Howkins.

To 17th Corps III. ARMY. from 18th Sept.

WESTERN FRONT.
July - Sept. 1917.

PHASE "D" 1. Passchendaele Operations, "July-Nov.1917."

(a) - Operations commencing 1/7/1917.

H.Q. Mersey Camp, H.1.2.5.6. (Sheet 28).

Sept. 7th. Transfer. To 5th Corps.

13th. Casualties. R.A.M.C. Capt. W.J. Evans attached 2/6th Glosters died of wounds.

15th. Military Situation. 61st Division relieved by 55th Div. in line.

Medical Arrangements. (App. 1. attached).

Moves. To Wattou.

Locations F.A. 2/1st S.M.F.A. at K.17.b.2.2.
2/2nd S.M.F.A. at L.10.c.9.2. Sheet 27.
2/3rd S.M.F.A. at L.19.b.3.6.

18th. Transfer.) To 17th Corps III. ARMY and moved
Moves.) to Duisans. (Sheet 51c).

Appendices. I. R.A.M.C. Adm. Order 38 d.12/9/1917.
and Appendix d 13/9/1917.

Note:- All appendices attached to 1st copy.

CONFIDENTIAL

MEDICAL.

WAR DIARY

OF

A. D. M. S., 61st DIVISION

VOLUME - 17.

PERIOD :- SEPTEMBER 1st to SEPTEMBER 30th 1917.

Instructions regarding War Diaries and Intelligence Summaries are contained in F. S. Regs., Part II. and the Staff Manual respectively. Title pages will be prepared in manuscript.

Army Form C. 2118.

WAR DIARY
or
INTELLIGENCE SUMMARY.
(Erase heading not required.)

Place	Date	Hour	Summary of Events and Information	Remarks and references to Appendices
MERSEY CAMP. [H.1.a56. Sheet 28N.W]	Sept 1st		A.D.M.S inspected Red Rose Camp, also visited Reserve. D.S. (Canal Bank) + C.W.W.D.S. Capt. A.L. ANTHONY. RAMC. evacuated to C.C.S. A.D.M.S 59th Division called today. Routine duties. W.L.	
	2nd		Capt. W.V. WOOD. RAMC. (Temp'y O.C. 2/3 S.M. Fd Amb) called to see A.D.M.S. A.D.M.S. visited neighbouring camps. D.A.D.M.S inspected Sanitary condition of H.Q. 184 Brigade at "Goldfish Chateau" + camp of 2/1 Bucks at YPRES NORTH. H11C47. W.L.	
"	3rd		A.D.M.S. visited D.D.M.S. XIX Corps + Query Camp. D.A.D.M.S. visited A.D.S. Reserve A.D.S. (Canal Bank) + C.W.W.D.S The following officers reported for duty + were posted to the 2/1 (S.M.) Fd Amb. Captain W.D. DUNLOP. RAMC (T.C.) from ETAPLES. Captain J.N. GRIFFITHS " " " 1st A.D. R.F.C. Captain B. WALLACE " " " ENGLAND. W.L.	
	4th		D.A.D.M.S. visited Red Farm (Car Pool) + Corps Rest Station. A.D.M.S. held conference of Quartermasters at C.W.W.D.S. at 2.30 PM. Captain H.B. GOULDING. RAMC returned to duty from C.R.S. Captain T.S. STAFFORD. RAMC called on A.D.M.S.	
	5th		A.D.M.S. visited A.D.S. D.A.D.M.S. visited C.W.W.D.S. H.Q. 42nd Div. + Car pool (Red Farm). Lieut. F.M. BISHOP. R.A.M.C. reported for duty + was posted for temp'y duty with 2/1 (S.M.) Fd Amb. W.L.	

Instructions regarding War Diaries and Intelligence Summaries are contained in F. S. Regs., Part II. and the Staff Manual respectively. Title pages will be prepared in manuscript.

WAR DIARY
or
INTELLIGENCE SUMMARY.
(Erase heading not required.)

Army Form C. 2118.

Place	Date	Hour	Summary of Events and Information	Remarks and references to Appendices
	Sept			
MERSEY CAMP	6.		Z day. Capt. W. SPEEDY. R.A.M.C. reported for duty from 51 General Hospital & was posted for temp. duty with the 2/1 (S.M.) Fd Amb. D.A.D.M.S visited forward area. Evacuation of wounded progressing without trouble, no congestion. Not many cases passing through C.W.W.D.S. Capt. RIDGEWAY W.C. (R.A.M.C.) sent down from forward area to C.R.S. (Exhaustion). A.D.M.S visited O.C. C.M.D.S. & S.S.O. W.H.	
..	7th		Captain C. L. LANDER. R.A.M.C. att. 2/5th Glosters appointed O.C. 2/3rd (S.M.) Fd Amb. vice Lieut. Col. G. SCOTT-WILLIAMSON. R.A.M.C. (missing). A.D.M.S. visited A.D.S. & C.W.W.D.S. Capt. MANUEL. Capt. STAFFORD. Capt. WILKINSON proceeded on leave terminating on 21 9/17. 17 9/17. 17 9/17. respectively. D.A.D.M.S visited C.W.W.D.S & C.R.S. W.H.	
..	8th		Conference of O's Commanding Fd Ambs. D.A.A.G. & D.A.D.M.S. re replacing A.S.C. batmen with P.B. men. D.D.M.S & D.A.D.M.S. of V. Corps visited A.D.M.S. Captain A. RADFORD. R.A.M.C. called on A.D.M.S. A.D.M.S. examined Capt. B. WALLACE. R.A.M.C. re-sending him to the Base for a Medical Board. Captain LANDER. R.A.M.C. called to see A.D.M.S. 61st Division came under the administration of the V Corps Noon yesterday. W.H.	
..	9th		Captain C. L. LANDER. R.A.M.C. assumed command of the 2/3 (S.M.) Fd Amb. today. A.D.M.S. visited Transport lines. D.A.D.M.S. visited D.D.M.S. V Corps & 2/1 (S.M.) Fd Amb. The following	

2353 Wt. W2544/1454 700,000 5/15 D. D. & L. A.D.S.S./Forms/C. 2118.

Instructions regarding War Diaries and Intelligence Summaries are contained in F. S. Regs., Part II. and the Staff Manual respectively. Title pages will be prepared in manuscript.

WAR DIARY
or
INTELLIGENCE SUMMARY.
(Erase heading not required.)

Army Form C. 2118.

Place	Date	Hour	Summary of Events and Information	Remarks and references to Appendices
MERSEY CAMP.	Sept 9.		Medical Officers of the U.S. Army reported for duty & were posted to the 2/1 (S.M.) Fd Amb for duty pending disposal. They are to replace three M.O.'s who are to report to the Depot, Blackpool forthwith, for service in India. The officers reporting are 1st Lieutenants: F. T. WILLIAMS: E. V. WHITAKER: & R. E. THORNHILL. W.H.	
"	10.		A.D.M.S. visited C.R.S.: A.D.S: C.W.W.D.S. D.A.D.M.S. visited C.W.W.D.S. The following officers left today to report to the R.A.M.C. Depot, Blackpool viz. Capt: V.C.W. VICKERS (T.C.) Capt. J.L. WHATLEY (T.C.) Capt. H.S. PEMBERTON (S.R.). W.H.C.	
"	11.		D.A.D.M.S. inspected Camp of the D.C.L.I.: 2/5 Warwicks 2/7 Warwicks. Capt LANDER visited A.D.M.S. Capt. FAIRFAX proceeded on 10 days (special) leave. A.D.M.S & D.A.D.M.S. 55th Div: called. "Warning Administrative Instructions for Relief by 55 Division" received. W.H.	
"	12.		A.D.M.S. attended conference at D.D.M.S. 10.30 AM A.D.M.S. visited A.D.M.S. 59th Division re relief. D.A.D.M.S visited A.D.M.S. 55th Div. re-relief. Administrative Order No 38* issued. W.H.	* App: I
"	13.		A.D.M.S. visited A.D.S. D.A.D.M.S visited C.R.S. & C.W.W.D.S. Captain W. J. EVANS R.A.M.C. wounded & died of wounds. W.H.	
"	14.		Capt A. RADFORD proceeded on 10 days leave (in France). Division commencing to move out of the line. D.A.D.M.S visited 182nd & 183rd Brigade in Walon Area. Capt A.P. THOMSON R.A.M.C. rejoined his unit the 2/1 (S.M.) Fd Amb. W.H.	

Instructions regarding War Diaries and Intelligence Summaries are contained in F. S. Regs., Part II. and the Staff Manual respectively. Title pages will be prepared in manuscript.

WAR DIARY
or
INTELLIGENCE SUMMARY.
(Erase heading not required.)

Army Form C. 2118.

Place	Date	Hour	Summary of Events and Information	Remarks and references to Appendices
	Sept.			
WAT(T)OU (Sheet 27.)	15.		The Division moved from the line today. Forward area handed over to the 55th Division, Hosital farm handed over to the same Division. C.W.W.D.S. handed over to the 59th Division. C.R.S. all the moves & handing over completed by Noon. The Division moved into the WATTOU No 1.2.3. areas. Locations. A.D.M.S. WAT(T)OU. 2/1 (S.M.) Fd Amb. K 17 b 2 2. 2/2 (S.M.) Fd Amb. L 10 c 9 2. 2/3 (S.M.) Fd Amb. L 19. b 3 6. (Sheet 27) Capt. J. N. GRIFFITHS (T.C.) reported to 62 H.A.G. Capt. W. A. BERRY (T.C) left to report to D.D.M.S. XIX Corps. Lieut. Qm Brooks. E.S. returned from leave. W.H.	
"	16.		A.D.M.S. visited Fd Ambulances & 64 C.C.S. Capt. GOMPERTZ. R.A.M.C. will not sign on for further service. Preparations for further move. Administrative order No 39* issued. W.H.	* App. II.
"	17.		Field Ambulances moved to the following locations prior to entraining: 2/1st C.5 d 9.3. 2/2nd Q 19 c 3.6. 2/3rd G 11. a 9.8. [Sheet 27] Capt. GOMPERTZ. reported from 64 C.C.S. with 19 O.R. R.A.M.C. sent to their unit the 2/3rd (S.M.) Fd Amb. W.H.	
DUISANS (Sheet 51c)	18.		A.D.M.S. office closed 9 A.M. at WATOU & opened at DUISANS 2 P.M. A.D.M.S. & D.A.D.M.S. visited A.D.M.S. of 17th Division of 15th Division also D.D.M.S. XVII Corps under whose administration the Division now is. Location of Fd Ambs unchanged. Division on the move to new area. W.H.	
"	19.		A.D.M.S. visited 17th Div: forward area. D.A.D.M.S. visited detraining stations (ARRAS 1 & 2 & AUBIGNY). D.A.D.M.S. visited D.A.D.M.S. 17th Div re taking over. A.D.M.S. & D.A.D.M.S. visited H.Q. of 51st 52nd 53rd Fd Ambs.	

Instructions regarding War Diaries and Intelligence Summaries are contained in F. S. Regs., Part II. and the Staff Manual respectively. Title pages will be prepared in manuscript.

WAR DIARY
or
INTELLIGENCE SUMMARY.
(Erase heading not required.)

Army Form C. 2118.

Place	Date	Hour	Summary of Events and Information	Remarks and references to Appendices
	Sept.			
DUISANS.	19.		Field Ambulances moving to new area. R.A.M.C. order No 40* issued 10 P.M. W.L.	* App. No III.
" (Sheet 51.C.)	20.		Conference of O's C. Fd Amb. A.D.M.S. office 10 A.M. Move of Division complete. Locations of Fd Amb as follows 2/1 Fd Amb. DUISANS. 2/2 F.A. BERNEVILLE. 2/3 F.A. SIMENCOURT. *Addendum to R.A.M.C. order No 40 issued. Captain GOMPERTZ. R.A.M.C. reported to XVII Corps Musketry + Reinforcement Camp for duty (temp). Lieutenant D.H. CROOM R.A.M.C. (T.C.) reported from 14 Stationary Hospital + posted to 2/3rd F.A. Captain WILKINSON G.L. returned from leave. D.A.D.M.S. visited 2/1st F.A. W.L.	* App. No IV.
"	21.		Captain WILKINSON posted to No 19 C.C.S. for temy duty. Lieut. CROOM posted to 17th Corps Rest Station for temy duty. A.D.M.S. visited F.A's. Captains COATSWORTH + STOBIE visited A.D.M.S. W.L.	
"	22		2/3 F.A. taken over from 52nd Amb (17th Divn), the Main Dressing Station (Hospice des Vieillards). Routine. W.L.	
"	23.		Captain MANUEL reported back from leave + rejoined unit. Lieut. CROOM sick. Capt. DALE WOOD evacuated to C.C.S. D.A.D.M.S. visited 2/1 Fd Amb. Capt. ROBSON called on A.D.M.S. + also Capt. GREEN. a/O.C. 2/1 Fd Amb. 2/2 Fd Amb. taken over left subsector (GREENLAND HILL) from 51st F.A. W.L.	
"	24.		A.D.M.S. visited M.D.S. (ARRAS) + D.D.M.S. XVII Corps. D.H.Q. moving to forward area tomorrow. Division taking over the line. 2/3 F.A. taking over right subsector. Routine duties.	
ST NICHOLAS CAMP. G.17.a Sheet 51 B.	25		DADMS proceeded on leave. CAPT STOBIE RAMC T att 2/4 OBLI reported for temporary duty. DW HDQRS established at ST NICHOLAS (G17 A / 51 B). ADMS visited ADS's and Field Ambulances which moved to new area	W.S.

2353 Wt. W2544/1454 700,000 5/15 D. D. & L. A.D.S.S./Forms/C. 2118.

Army Form C. 2118.

WAR DIARY
or
INTELLIGENCE SUMMARY.
(Erase heading not required.)

Instructions regarding War Diaries and Intelligence Summaries are contained in F. S. Regs., Part II. and the Staff Manual respectively. Title pages will be prepared in manuscript.

Place	Date	Hour	Summary of Events and Information	Remarks and references to Appendices
ST NICHOLAS CAMP. Sheet 51 B G 17 A	Sept 26		ADMS visited right sector of forward area. Routine duties	W.S
	27		ADMS visited DDMS 17th Corps: main dressing stations and headquarters of field ambulances. Routine duties	W.S.
	28		ADMS inspected Bde transport lines: report to "Q" concerning throwing of rubbish into old trenches. The a/DADMS visited RAP's and bearer posts of right brigade sector. Routine duties	W.S
	29		ADMS visited ADS and RAP's in left sector: the a/DADMS visited camps of 184 Bde.	W.S
	30		ADMS visited the F As and the Reinforcement camp at SAVY. Capt STONE and CAPT HENER MORC U.S army reported for temporary duty with 2/3 Fd Amb. a DADMS visited reserve, support & front lines in connection with the water supply of left sector & also the RAP's in that sector. Capt JOYCE, TOWN MAJOR, ST NICHOLAS examined on instructions from 17th Corps & classified B1.	W.S

C Hinkins
Colonel AMS
ADMS. 61 Divn

2353 Wt. W2544/1454 700,000 5/15 D. D. & L. A.D.S.S./Forms/C. 2118.

Appendix I.

SECRET COPY NO: 19

61 DIVISION R.A.M.C., ADMINISTRATIVE ORDER No: 58

1. (a) The Advanced Medical Posts will be relieved by the 55th Division. Relief to be completed by daylight on 15th inst.
(b) The 2/3rd Field Ambulance will be attached to the 183rd Brigade Group on arrival in WATOU AREA.

2. (a) The Vth Corps Walking Wounded Dressing Station will be relieved by the 9th Division by 11 a.m. on the 15th instant. MOATED FARM will be relieved by the 55th Division by 11 a.m. on the 15th instant.
(b) The 2/1 Field Ambulance will be attached to the 184 Brigade Group on arrival in WATOU AREA.

3. (a) The 2/2 Field Ambulance will be relieved by the 59th Division on the 15th instant.
(b) The 2/2 Field Ambulance will be attached to the 182 Brigade Group on arrival in WATOU AREA.

4. Rear parties will be left behind where necessary and will rejoin their units under arrangements to be made by Os.C. concerned.

5. All Equipment over and above that authorised by Mobilization Table and G.R.Os. will be left behind. This will be checked before being handed over, and a receipt obtained from the incoming unit.

6. The R.A.M.C., detachments will rejoin their respective Units before the latter leave the Army Area.

7. Motor Ambulances will rejoin their units on relief.

8. Regimental Medical Officers will be present at the embussing and debussing of their battalions.
The O.C. 2/1 Field Amb., will detail a Motor Ambulance to be at the embussing of the 1/5 Duke Cornwall's Light Infantry at 4 p.m. on the 14th instant at VLAMERTINGHE. He will also detail a Motor Ambulance to be present at the embussing of the 184 Infantry Brigade at VLAMERTINGHE at 11 a.m. on the 15th inst. O.C. 2/1 Field Ambulance to arrange for a motor Ambulance to be at the debussing point of the 1/5 D.C.L.I., and the 184 Infantry Brigade.

9. Horse Ambulances will be detailed by Os.C. Field Ambulances to follow their associated Brigade Groups marching to WATOU AREA.

10. Os.C. Field Ambulances will detail a Medical Officer, a small detachment of R.A.M.C. personnel, and a motor Ambulance to arrive in the Stageing Area at the same time as their associated Brigade, and arrange for the disposal of any sick of the Brigade.

11. Patients can be disposed of by the following means in the Stageing area :-
(a) Detained by the Field Ambulance and discharged to duty.
(b) Transferred to the C.R.S., HILLHOEK. LUNA PARK. L.9.b.2.5. HOSPICE. WATOU. or, if serious, to 63 C.C.S.,

12. The A.D.M.S., Office will close at 10 a.m. on September 15th and reopen at the same hour at WATOU.

Issued at 9 p.m. September 12th 1917.

ACKNOWLEDGE

C Houken

Colonel A.M.S.
A.D.M.S., 61 Division.

Copies to :-

1.	O.C.	2/1 Field Ambulance.	
2.		2/2 Field Ambulance.	
3.		2/3 Field Ambulance.	
4.		D.D.M.S., Vth Corps for information.	
5.		61 Division "A"	-do-
6.		61 Division "G"	-do-
7.		C.R.A.,	-do-
8.		C.R.E.,	-do-
9.		182 Infantry Brigade.	-do-
10.		183 Infantry Brigade.	-do-
11.		184 Infantry Brigade.	-do-
12.		1/5 D.C.L.I.,	-do-
13.		61 Divisional Train.	-do-
14.		A.D.M.S., 9 Division.	-do-
15.		A.D.M.S., 55 Division.	-do-
16.		A.D.M.S., 59 Division.	-do-
17-18.		War Diary.	
19-20.		File.	

SECRET

app I

APPENDIX TO 61 DIVISION R.A.M.C., ORDER NO: 38.

(1) The O.C., 2/2 Field Ambulance will commence to hand ~~xxxxx~~ over the Corps Rest Station to an Advance Party from the 59th Division arriving on the 14th instant. The handing over will be completed on the 15th instant.

(2) The O.C., 2/1 Field Ambulance will hand over the MOATED FARM to the 1/3 West Lancs Field Ambulance on the morning of the 15th instant. The 1/3 West Lancs Field Ambulance will arrive by 7 p.m. 14th instant.

(3) The O.C. 2/3 Field Ambulance will proceed to hand over the Forward Medical Posts and lines of evacuation to the 2/1 West Lancs Field Ambulance commencing at 10 a.m. on the 14th instant.

(4) Details of above to be arranged by Os.C. concerned.

(5) Petrol Tins,&Yukon Packs in the forward area will be handed over to relieving units, the remainder of Yukon Packs will be handed over to the O.C. Divisional Bomb Store at H.8.a.4.9. Sheet 28 N.W., and receipt obtained.
List of above articles handed over to be sent to this office.

13/9/17.

Colonel A.M.S.
A.D.M.S., 61 Division.

Copies to :-
2/1 Field Ambulance.
2/2 Field Ambulance.
2/3 Field Ambulance.
61 Division "G" for information.
61 Division "Q" for information.
War Diary.
File.

MOVE TABLE ISSUED WITH A.D.M.S., 61 DIVISION ORDER NO: 38.

Date.	Unit or Detachment.	FROM	TO	ROUTE	REMARKS
September. Night 14/15.	2/3rd Field Ambulance (less 1 Tent Sub-Div:) Bearer Divisions of 2/1st & 2/2nd Field Ambulances.	LINE & Advanced Dressing Station.	VLAMERTINGHE No: 2.		On relief by bearers of 55th Division.
Sept: 15.	Headquarters and Tent Sub-DivisionSof 2/2nd Field Ambulance.	C.R.S., HILLHOEK.	WATOU No: 1.		On relief by 59 Division. To rejoin 182 Infantry Brigade.
Sept 15 .	2/1 Field Ambulance.	H.7.b.	WATOU No: 3.	By Bus at 11 a.m.	On relief by 9th Division & 55th Division. To rejoin 184 Infantry Brigade.
Sept: 15.	2/3 Field Ambulance (less 1 Tent Sub-Div:) with bearer Division of 2/2 Field Ambulance.	H.7.b.	WATOU No: 2.	By Bus at 11 a.m.	To rejoin 183rd Infantry Brigade.
Sept: 15.	Horse Transport of 2/1 & 2/3 Field Ambs.,	H.7.b.	WATOU AREA.		To follow transport of 184 Infantry Brigade and R.Engineers. Not to reach G.4.d.3.3. before 10 a.m. To join Brigade Groups on arrival in WATOU area.
	1 Tent Sub-Division of 2/3rd Field Amb.,	64 C.C.S.,	WATOU No: 2.		Under orders from O.C., 64 C.C.S.,

Colonel A.M.S.,
A.D.M.S., 61st Division.

Septe,ber 12th 1917.

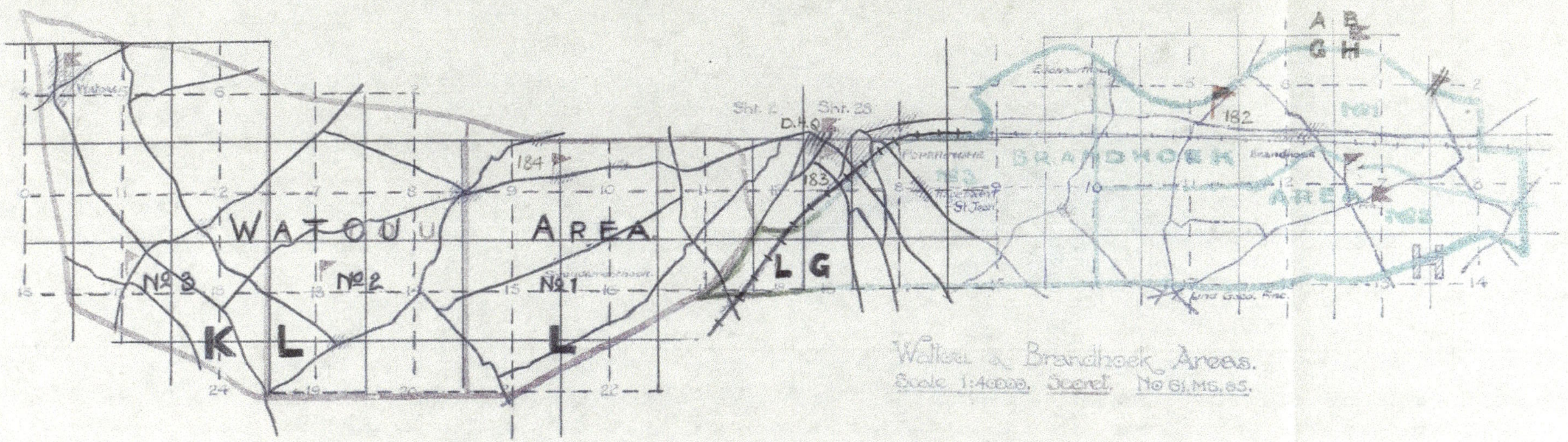
WATOU AREA
No 1
No 2
No 3
K
L
L
L G
184
183
182
D.H.Q.
Sht. 27
Sht. 28
Watou
BRANDHOEK AREA
No 1
No 2
No 3
Brandhoek
St. Jean
A B
G H
H
Watou & Brandhoek Areas.
Scale 1:40000. Secret. No 61.MS.65.

Appendix II.

SECRET | Copy No: *25*

61st DIVISION R.A.M.C. ADMINISTRATIVE ORDER NO:39

1. The Field Ambulances will be associated with their usual Brigade Groups.

2. During the move each O.C., Field Ambulance will detail 1 Motor Ambulance and a Medical Officer to be at the entraining and also at the detraining stations of their associated Brigades.

3. Upon arrival in new area the Os.C., Field Ambulances will arrange for the collection, treatment and, if necessary, transfer of sick and wounded of their Brigade Group.

4. Arrangements will be made when in the new area by each O.C. Field Ambulance to provide temporary accomodation for cases of sick and wounded.

5. Medical Officers with units which arrive in the new area before their associated Field Ambulances will apply to the Officer i/c Motor Ambulance at detraining stations in the event of their requiring any assistance to evacuate a case of sickness. The Officer i/c Motor Ambulance will do his best to assist them.

6. ACKNOWLEDGE.

Issued at 10.15 p.m. September 16th 1917.

W. Victor Corbett

Captain.
for A.D.M.S., 61 Div.

Copies:-

1. O.C. 2/1 Fd Amb.,
2. O.C. 2/2 Fd Amb.,
3. O.C. 2/3 Fd Amb.,
4-6. 182, 183, 184 Inf.Bdes.
7. 61 Div "G" for information.
8. 61 Div "Q" -do-
9. C.R.E., -do-
10. O.C. 61 Div.Train.
11. M.O. 2/5 Warwicks.
12. 2/6 Warwicks.
13. 2/7 Warwicks.
14. 2/8 Warwicks.
15. 2/4 Glosters.
16. 2/6 Glosters.
17. 2/7 Worcesters.
18. 2/8 Worcesters.
19. 2/4 Berks.
20. 2/4 Ox & Bucks.L.I.
21. 2/5 Glosters.
22. 2/1 Bucks.
23. 1/5 D.C.L.I.,
24. *War Diary*
25. *do*
26. *File.*

SECRET   Appendix III   Copy No: 19

61st DIVISION R.A.M.C., ORDER No: 40.

Ref: Map.
Sheet 51.B. N.W. 1/20,000.

(1) The Field Ambulances of the 61st Division will relieve those of the 17th Division. The reliefs will be completed by arrangement between the Os.C. Field Ambulances concerned.

(2) The completion of each relief will be reported by wire to this office.

(3) (a) The 2/3 Field Amb., will take over the Main Dressing Station - Hospice des VIEILLARDS, ARRAS (G.32.b.0.3.) from the 52nd Field Ambulance on the 21st instant. The relief to be completed by midnight 21/22nd instant. A party will be sent on in advance on the 20th instant.

(b) The 2/2 Field Ambulance will take over from the 51st Field Ambulance the forward A.D.S., (GREENLAND HILL Sub-sector) at TANK DUMP. (H.11.a.7.5.) and the lines of evacuation for this sub-sector. The relief will be completed by 10 p.m. on the 23rd instant.
The A.D.S. at L'ABBAYETTE (H.14.b.5.2.) will be taken over from the 53rd Field Ambulance. This relief will be completed by 10 a.m. on the 24th instant.

(c) 2/1 Field Ambulance will take over the collection and evacuation of sick and wounded in the "CHEMICAL Works Sub-sector" from the 53rd Field Ambulance. This relief will be completed by 10 a.m. on the 24th instant.

(4) The O.C. 2/3 Field Ambulance will detail four other ranks R.A.M.C. to report to the O.C. 51 Sanitary Section (Billet No: 1 ST NICHOLAS) on the 21st instant, to relieve four other ranks R.A.M.C. of the 52 Field Ambulance.

(5) The following medical personnel will be required in relief of similar personnel of the 17 Division :-
(a) One Medical Officer.
One Clerk.
These will be detailed by the O.C. 2/3 Field Ambulance to proceed to XVII Corps Rest Station at WARLUS on the 21st inst.

(b) One Medical officer. Will be detailed by the O.C. 2/2 Field Ambulance to proceed to No: 19 C.C.S., on the 21st instant.

(c) One Tent Sub-Division (less Medical officers) will be detailed by the O.C. 2/3 Field Ambulance to proceed to No: 19 C.C.S. on the 21st instant.

(6) Inventories of Stores taken over will be forwarded to this office in duplicate.

(7) ACKNOWLEDGE.

Issued at 10.30 p.m. September 19th 1917.

[signature]
Captain.
for A.D.M.S., 61 Division.

Copies to:-
1-3 2/1, 2/2, 2/3 Field Ambs.,
4-6 182, 183, 184 Inf.Bdes. For information.
7. D.D.M.S., XVII Corps. -do-
8. A.D.M.S., 17 Division. -do-
9-11 51, 52, 53 Field Ambs., -do-
12 61 Division "G" -do-
13 61 Division "Q" -do-
14 51 Sanitary Section.
15 C.R.A., -do-
16 C.R.E., -do-
17 61 Div Train. -do-
18. 1/5 D.C.L.I., -do-
19-20 War Diary.
21-22 File.

Appendix IV

SECRET

Copy No: 20

ADDENDUM TO 61 DIVISION R.A.M.C., ORDER No: 40.

A.D.M.S., Office will close at DUISANS at 10 a.m. 25th September 1917, and reopen at G.17.a. (Sheet 51.B.) at the same hour.

ACKNOWLEDGE.

Captain.
D.A.D.M.S., 61 Div.

Distribution:-
As for R.A.M.C., Order No: 40.

May 1917

~~Detached App. A and placed with first copy of summary~~

140/2158

S

A.D.M.S., 2nd Division.

11

Medical

Oct. 1917

Vol 18

CONFIDENTIAL

WAR DIARY

OF

A.D.M.S., 61st DIVISION.

From :- October 1st. To:- October 31st 1917.

- - - -VOLUME 18.- - - -

C. Hawkes

Colonel A.M.S.
A.D.M.S., 61 Division.

October 31st 1917.

Instructions regarding War Diaries and Intelligence Summaries are contained in F. S. Regs., Part II. and the Staff Manual respectively. Title pages will be prepared in manuscript.

WAR DIARY
or
INTELLIGENCE SUMMARY.
(Erase heading not required.)

Army Form C. 2118.

Place	Date Oct	Hour	Summary of Events and Information	Remarks and references to Appendices
ST NICHOLAS CAMP G17 A. (51B)	1		ADMS. inspected camps of Bucks + Berks in 184 Bde. Attended conference of DDMS XVII Corps. Examined several men re P.B. a/DADMS visited Div T.M.B. in connection with a case of diphtheria and two positive contacts and saw Sanitary Officer of district in this connection. Routine duties	WS
	2		ADMS. visited forward area in right sector. a/DADMS saw Lieut WHITTAKER U.S.A. at 61 Div Reinforcement camp at SAVY. Routine duties	WS
	3		ADMS visited the field ambulances. The a/DADMS visited the RAP of right battalion on left sector, + the 2 RAP'S + posts on Right. Routine duties	WS
	4		A.D.M.S. visited front line trenches. Capt LANDER O.C. 2/3 SM Fd Ambulance called to see the A.D.M.S. The a/DADMS. inspected area in CAM valley occupied by 47F Coy RE + suggested some improvements	WS
	5		ADMS visited 61st D.A.C. Experiment with food container carried out to see if contents remained good after opening a ambulances. ADMS 15th Div called. The a/DADMS called to see OC 51st Div San Section and S.S.O re boxes	WS

2353 Wt. W2544/1454 700,000 5/15 D. D. & L. A.D.S.S./Forms/C. 2118.

Instructions regarding War Diaries and Intelligence Summaries are contained in F. S. Regs., Part II. and the Staff Manual respectively. Title pages will be prepared in manuscript.

WAR DIARY
or
INTELLIGENCE SUMMARY.
(Erase heading not required.)

Army Form C. 2118.

Place	Date	Hour	Summary of Events and Information	Remarks and references to Appendices
	Oct			
St NICHOLAS G17A(51B)	6		ADMS visited Transport lines of Field ambulances. A/DADMS the RAP's in left sector. Routine duties	WS
"	7.		ADMS visited ADS at TANK DUMP. D.A.D.M.S returned from 10 days leave. Routine duties	WS
"	8.		A.D.M.S proceeded on 10 days leave. Lt Col. MACKIE (O.C. 2/1 (SM) Fd Amb) acting A.D.M.S. A.D.M.S. Div. visited A.D.M.S. today. Routine duties.	WH.
"	9.		a/A.D.M.S. visited medical posts of the right subsector. D.A.D.M.S. inspected M.D.S. (2/3 (SM) F.A.) also visited H.Q 2/1 & 2/2 Fd Amb. Routine duties.	WH
"	10		D.A.D.M.S. visited 2/2 (S.M) F.A. Routine duties.	WH,
	11		DADMS visited forward area with DAQMG with reference to the establishment of gum boot stores in forward area. Camps of 183 LTMB & 183 MGC inspected. R.D's	WS
	12		Routine duties. inspection of areas occupied by DAC & Div Artillery	WS
	13		a/ADMS & DADMS visited DDMS XVII Corps re prevention of Trench feet; also O.C Railway construction re conversion of wagons for evacuation of wounded. Routine duties. Acting ADMS visited forward area	WS

Army Form C. 2118.

WAR DIARY
or
INTELLIGENCE SUMMARY.
(Erase heading not required.)

Instructions regarding War Diaries and Intelligence Summaries are contained in F. S. Regs., Part II. and the Staff Manual respectively. Title pages will be prepared in manuscript.

Place	Date	Hour	Summary of Events and Information	Remarks and references to Appendices
ARRAS.	Oct. 14		D.A.D.M.S., visited 2/1st, 2/2nd, and 2/3rd Field Ambulances re establishing Trench Foot. Stations.	
ST NICHOLAS CAMP. G.17.a. Sheet 51B.			Captain W.STOBIE. reported to 306 Brigade R.F.A., for temporary duty. Routine duties	
	15th		Acting A.D.M.S., visited forward area. He also examined men recommended by Battalion Commanders as unfit for service. Also attended a Conference at D.D.M.S., XVII Corps. Routine duties	
	16th		Acting A.D.M.S., saw Railway Construction officer re conversion of waggons. Routine duties.	
	17th		Acting A.D.M.S., visited Rt Sub-sector Forward Area. D.A.D.M.S., visited A.D.S. L'Abbeyette and 2/2 S.M.Field Ambulance. Captain Robson returned from leave.	
	18th		D.M.S., Third Army inspected 2/1,2/2, and 2/3 Field Ambulances and A.D.S.,L'ABBEYETTE, D.D.M.S.,XVIIth Corps, a/A.D.M.S., and D.A.D.M.S., accompanied D.M.S. at this inspection. a/A.D.M.S. visited Forward Area.	
	19th.		O.C. 2/2nd Field Ambulance called. Routine Duties. Capt. HIRST relieved Capt. STOBIE at 306 Bde. R.F.A.	
	20th.		R.A.Ps. visited. 8 Medical Officers reported for duty, and posted as follows. To 2/1st Field Ambulance. Capt. NESBIT, H.F.. Capt. SHIELDS. To 2/2nd Field Ambulance. Capt. BOLSTER, L.E.. Capt. WATSON, R.N.. Lieut. DAY, W.L.M. To 2/3rd Field Ambulance. Lieut. CHAPPLE, H.. Lieut. LISTON, P.. Lieut. ARNOTT, G. D.A.D.M.S. visited 3 Field Ambulances.	

T2134. Wt. W708–776. 500000. 4/15. Sir J. C. & S.

Instructions regarding War Diaries and Intelligence Summaries are contained in F. S. Regs., Part II. and the Staff Manual respectively. Title pages will be prepared in manuscript.

WAR DIARY
or
INTELLIGENCE SUMMARY.
(Erase heading not required.)

Army Form C. 2118.

Place	Date	Hour	Summary of Events and Information	Remarks and references to Appendices
	October.			
ST.NICHOLAS CAMP. Sheet 51. B. G.17.a.cent.	21st.		A.D.M.S. returned from Leave. D.A.D.M.S. visited R.A.Ps. & A.D.Ss. Captain GREEN and Lieut. BISHOP proceeded on 10 days Leave, and Capt. RENNIE on 14 days Contract Leave. Lt. Col. LANDER returned from Leave.	
	22nd.		A.D.M.S. visited Forward Area re new Aid Posts in Left and Right Sectors. D.A.D.M.S., visited 2/2nd S.M.F.Ambulance.	
	23rd.		A.D.M.S. visited H.Qs. of the three Field Ambulances. D.A.D.M.S. visited XVII Corps Musketry & Reinforcement Camp, and 61 Div. Supply Column. Lt.Col. BURROUGHES proceeded on 10 days leave.	
	24th.		A.D.M.S. visited M.D.S. and the "Prison" Barracks.(2/5 & 2/7 R.Warwicks). D.A.D.M.S. visited A.D.S., L'ABBEYETTE. A/O.C. 2/2nd Field Ambulance visited A.D.M.S.	
	25th.		A.D.M.S. visited Forward Area and M.D.S.(ARRAS). Also A.D.S. TANK DUMP. Routine Duties.	
	26th.		A.D.M.S. accompanied O.C., 2/1st S.M.F.Ambulance and D.A.Q.M.G.61 Div. to Baths ATHIES. D.A.D.M.S. inspected Corps Reinforcement and Musketry Camp at SAVY. Routine Duties.	
	27th.		A.D.M.S. inspected "Barge" evacuation of wounded. Visited A.D.S., TRIPLE ARCH, R.A.P. right sector. D.A.D.M.S. inspected Transport Lines of 182 & 184 Inf. Brigades. Os.C. 2/1 & 2/2 F.Ambs. called on A.D.M.S. Routine duties.	
	28th.		A.D.M.S. visited 2/3rd F.Amb., FAMPOUX and BORDER LANE to A.D.S. D.A.D.M.S. visited LEVIS Barracks and proposed D.H.Q., ARRAS.	
ARRAS. G.27.b.8.4.	29th.		A.D.M.S. visited 17th Divn A.D.M.S.- 17th C.R.S. Attended D.D.M.S. conference 3 p.m. D.A.D.M.S. visited 2/1st Field Ambulance. D.H.Q. closed ST. NICHOLAS CAMP 10 a.m. and opened ARRAS (G.27.b.8.4.)	
	30th.		A.D.M.S., visited forward area (TANK DUMP) D.A.D.M.S., inspected forward baths (ATHIES) and visited 2/2 Fd.Amb. Routine duties.	

A5834 Wt. W4973/M687 750,000 8/16 D. D. & L. Ltd. Forms/C.2118/13.

Army Form C. 2118.

WAR DIARY
or
INTELLIGENCE SUMMARY.
(Erase heading not required.)

Instructions regarding War Diaries and Intelligence Summaries are contained in F. S. Regs., Part II. and the Staff Manual respectively. Title pages will be prepared in manuscript.

Place	Date	Hour	Summary of Events and Information	Remarks and references to Appendices
ARRAS. G.27.b.8.4.	Oct 31		A.D.M.S. inspected Brigade Schools at ARRAS and visited 2/2 Field Ambulance. Lieut Thornhill.U.S.M.Service. called on A.D.M.S. Routine duties.	

C. Hunter
Colonel AMS
ADMS. 61 Division

D. D. & L., London, E.C.
(A7883) Wt W809/M1672 350,000 4/17 Sch. 52a Forms/C/2118/14

17

Medical

Vol 19

CONFIDENTIAL

Nov. 1917

WAR DIARY

OF

A.D.M.S., 61st Division.

Period :- November 1st - 30th 1917.

VOLUME :- 19.

* * * * *

C. Howkins

Colonel A.M.S.
A.D.M.S., 61 Div.

1/12/17.

Instr[...]s regarding War Diaries and Intelligence Summaries are contained in F. S. Regs., Part II. and the Staff Manual respectively. Title pages will be prepared in manuscript.

WAR DIARY
or
INTELLIGENCE SUMMARY.
(Erase heading not required.)

Army Form C. 2118.

Place	Date	Hour	Summary of Events and Information	Remarks and references to Appendices
ARRAS.	Nov. 1.		A.D.M.S., visited Horse lines of 2/3rd S.Mid.Field Amb., and Mobile Veterinary Section. Administrative Medical Officers of the U.S.A., shown round the forward area, including A.D.Ss. and R.A.Ps. Routine duties.	WS
	2.		A.D.M.S., visited 2/3rd S.Mid.Field Amb., He also inspected the Prison and Levis Barracks.	WS
	3.		A.D.M.S., visited Aid Posts and Gumboot stores of RIGHT SECTOR. Lieut THORNHILL at C.R.S., and Lieut WHITAKER at 61 Div Reinforcement Camp. visited. Acting O.C. 2/3 Field Ambulance called on A.D.M.S., Routine duties.	WS
	4.		A.D.M.S., visited 3rd Field Ambulance and Divisional Baths., and inspected Brigade Schools. Routine duties.	WS
	5.		A.D.M.S., visited 2/3 Field Amb., with Inspector of Catering Third Army, who also visited 2/5 Gloucesters and 2/4 Berks. Routine duties.	WS
	6.		A.D.M.S., inspected M.D.S. (ARRAS) and visited forward area. Lieut Col SHAW, Major Mac DONALD and Lieut WILLIAMS, U.S.Med Service called on A.D.M.S. Captain STAFFORD, R.A.M.C. visited A.D.M.S.	WS
	7.		D.A.D.M.S., proceeded on 48 hours leave to BOULOGNE. A.D.M.S., visited Baths and Divisional Depot battalion. A/D.A.D.M.S., accompanied Commandant. Third Army Cookery School to 306, 307 Brigades R.F.A., and 61 D.A.C., and also to Field Ambulances, Divisional Train and Reserve Field Co R.E. Routine duties.	CA
	8.		A.D.M.S., visited 2/3 Fd.Amb., and 61 Div.Baths. A/D.A.D.M.S., inspected Prison and Brigade Schools. Captain Cahill and Lt.Thornhill called on A.D.M.S., Routine duties.	WS

2353 Wt. W2544/1454 700,000 5/15 D. D. & L. A.D.S.S./Forms/C. 2118.

Instructions regarding War Diaries and Intelligence Summaries are contained in F. S. Regs., Part II. and the Staff Manual respectively. Title pages will be prepared in manuscript.

WAR DIARY
or
INTELLIGENCE SUMMARY.
(Erase heading not required.)

Army Form C. 2118.

Place	Date	Hour	Summary of Events and Information	Remarks and references to Appendices
ARRAS	Nov 9.		D.A.D.M.S., returned from 48 hours leave. A.D.M.S., visited forward area of LEFT Sector. A/D.A.D.M.S., visited 2/2 and 2/3 Field Ambulances, and O.C. 61 Sanitary Section.	
	10.		A.D.M.S., inspected Brigade Schools and 61 Div.Depot Battalion. Routine duties.	
	11.		A.D.M.S., inspected Brigade Transport Lines. D.A.D.M.S., visited 2/1st and 2/2 Field Ambs. Routine duties.	
	12.		A.D.M.S., visited Medical officers of Brigade in Rest viz:- 2/4 & 2/6 Gloucesters and 2/7 & 2/8 Worcesters. A.D.M.S., attended D.D.M.S., Con-ference. D.A.D.M.S., visited R.A.Ps and A.D.Ss (TANK DUMP and L'ABBAYETTE) Routine duties.	
	13.		Captain E.F.O'Connor R.A.M.C.,(T.C.) reported from D.D.M.S., HAVRE. and posted to 2/1 F.Amb. Routine duties.	
	14.		A.D.M.S., inspected Main Dressing Station and visited the forward area. Captain Goulding R.A.M.C., called.	
	15.		Lieut.Col. REASON, Captain JONES, R.A.M.C., and Captain RADFORD called. Routine Duties.	
	16.		A.D.M.S., visited Transport Lines. Lieut Col.G.Mackie. and Lieut Whitaker (M.O.R.C.) called. Routine duties.	
	17.		A.D.M.S., inspected Town sewers and RONVILLE CAVES with O.C. 5a Sanitary Section. A.D.M.S., and D.A.D.M.S., attended Clinical Meeting at No: 8 C.C.S.,	
	18.		A.D.M.S., visited Div.Workshops. Examined Major N.R.L.Chance. 307 Bde R.F.A., and Capt.J.A.Young 2/6 Bn. Gloucestershire Regt, and recommended them for ?P.B. Routine duties.	
	19.		A.D.M.S., inspected Main Dressing Station (2/3 Fd.Amb.) Conference of Os.C.Field Ambs. 2.30 p.m. Routine duties.	

Instructions regarding War Diaries and Intelligence Summaries are contained in F. S. Regs., Part II. and the Staff Manual respectively. Title pages will be prepared in manuscript.

WAR DIARY
or
INTELLIGENCE SUMMARY.
(Erase heading not required.)

Army Form C. 2118.

Place	Date	Hour	Summary of Events and Information	Remarks and references to Appendices
ARRAS.	Nov. 20.		A.D.M.S., visited Forward area. D.A.D.M.S., visited No: 19 C.C.S., Routine duties.	
	21.		A.D.M.S., visited ~~CUBA trench and TRIPLE ARCH~~. [Forward area.] Routine duties.	
	22.		Captains Craig and Fairfax called on A.D.M.S., after tour in the line. Routine duties.	
	23.		A.D.M.S., visited Main Dressing Station (2/3 Field Amb.,) 2/2 Field Ambulance and Div.Sanitary Workshop. Captain Dunlop called after tour in the line. Routine duties.	
	24.		A.D.M.S., inspected Transport Lines. D.A.D.M.S., visited 2/2 Field Ambulance. Routine duties.	
	25.		A.D.M.S., inspected ~~LEWIS barracks~~. [Brigade Schools] D.A.D.M.S., visited XVII Corps. The undermentioned medical officers of the United States Army reported for duty from ENGLAND and were posted as shown :- 1st Lieut.J.R.SANFORD. U.S., M.O.R.C. 2/1 Field Amb., 1st Lieut.E.D.PETERSON. U.S., M.O.R.C. -do- 1st Lieut.W.S.GARRISON. U.S., M.O.R.C. -do- 1st Lieut.B.J.GALLAGHER. U.X., M.O.R.C. 2/2 Field Amb., 1st Lieut.R.J.ERICKSON. U.S., M.O.R.C. -do-	
	26.		A.D.M.S., attended D.D.M.S., Conference at 2.30 p.m. D.A.D.M.S., inspected 61 Div. Supply Column and Main Dressing Station (2/3 Field Ambulance) also visited Headquarters 2/1 abd 2/2 Field Ambulances.	

Army Form C. 2118.

WAR DIARY
or
INTELLIGENCE SUMMARY.
(Erase heading not required.)

Instructions regarding War Diaries and Intelligence Summaries are contained in F. S. Regs., Part II. and the Staff Manual respectively. Title pages will be prepared in manuscript.

Place	Date	Hour	Summary of Events and Information	Remarks and references to Appendices
ARRAS.	Nov 27.		A.D.M.S., inspected the LEVIS and PRISON Barracks. Warning to move received. R.A.M.C., order No: 41 issued at 11 p.m. Routine duties.	App.1.
	28.		A.D.M.S., visited Baths etc. D.A.D.M.S., visited XVII Corps. ROUTINE duties.	
	29.		A.D.M.S. visited new area and V Corps. Captain Speedy called, and Captain Stafford. D.A.D.M.S., visited 2/1, 2/2and 2/3 F.Ambs. 2/2 Field Amb., moved to WANQUETIN. Brigades coming out of the line. Relief of medical posts completed.	
	30.		Division moving to new area. A.D.M.S., office closed at ARRAS at 12 noon, and re-opened at LITTLEWOOD Camp YTRES:- Locations as follows :- Sheet 57.C. A.D.M.S., LITTLEWOOD CAMP. YTRES. P.26.b.1.1. 2/1 Fd.Amb., BERTINCOURT. 2/2 Fd.Amb., Q.15.a.6.6. 2/3 Fd.Amb., Q.15.a.7.5.	
	1/12/17.		C. Hr[illegible] Colonel A.M.S. A.D.M.S., 61 Division.	

D. D. & L., London, E.C.
(A7883) Wt W809/M1672 350,000 4/17 Sch. 52a Forms/C/2118/14

Appendix I

SECRET. COPY NO: 20

R.A.M.C. ORDER NO: 41
by
Colonel C.H.Howkins. D.S.O., A.M.S.,

November 27th 1917.

1. The 61st Division (less Artillery) will be relieved by the 15th Division. Relief will be completed by night of 29/30th November.

2. The Field Ambulances will be associated with the following Infantry Bdes during the move :-

2/1 Field Ambulance with the 184 Infantry Brigade.
2/2 Field Ambulance -do- 182 Infantry Brigade.
2/3 Field Ambulance -do- 183 Infantry Brigade.

3. The O.C. 2/2 Field Amb., will arrange that a detachment accompanies the 182 Infantry Brigade to DAINVILLE on the 28th instant.

4. RELIEF OF FORWARD MEDICAL POSTS. The relief of medical posts in the forward area will be arranged by the Os.C. 2/1 and 2/2 Field Ambulances with the O.C. 46 Field Ambulance. Relief to be completed by night of 29/30th.

5. MAIN DRESSING STATION. The O.C. 2/3 Field Ambulance will dispose of the cases now at the M.D.S., as follows :-
(a) Those fit for duty - to their units.
(b) Those who will be fit in a short time - under arrangements to be issued.
(c) The remainder to the C.C.S.

6. On arrival in new area, the Field Ambulances will collect sick etc from their associated Infantry Brigades.

7. ENTRAINING AND DETRAINING ARRANGEMENTS. Os.C. Field Ambulances will arrange for a Medical officer and motor ambulance to be detailed for duty during the entraining and detraining of the units of their associated Bde.

8. BRIGADE TRANSPORT. Os.C. Field Ambulances will detail a medical officer and motor ambulance to be attached to each Brigade transport column.

9. TRENCH STORES. All Trench stores, Maps, Medical and Surgical equipment etc over and above Mobilization Scale or held under G.R.Os. will be handed over to the relieving unit.

10. COMPLETION OF RELIEF. Os.C. Field Ambulances will notify this office completion of all reliefs.

11. ACKNOWLEDGE.

D. Victor Corbett
Captain,
for A.D.M.S., 61 Div.

Issued at 11 p.m.

Copies:-
1-3. 2/1,2/2,2/3 Field Ambs.
4-6. 182,183,184 Inf.Bdes. for information.
7. 61 Div "G" "
8. 61 Div "Q" "
9. D.D.M.S.,XVII Corps. "
10. A.D.M.S., 15 Division. "
11. O.C.46 Field Ambulance. "
12. 1/5 D.C.L.I. "
13. C.R.A., "
14. C.R.E., "
15. 61 Div Train. "
16. 61 Div.Supply Col. "
17. 5a Sanitary Secn. "
18. 51 Sanitary Secn. "
19. War Diary.
20. File.

MEDICAL

C O N F I D E N T I A L

W A R   D I A R Y

OF

A.D.M.S., 61st DIVISION.

PERIOD. December 1st to December 31st 1917.

VOLUME :- 20.

C Hawkins

Colonel A.M.S.
A.D.M.S., 61 Div.

31/12/17.

ons regarding War Diaries and Intelligence
maries are contained in F. S. Regs., Part II.
the Staff Manual respectively. Title pages
will be prepared in manuscript.

WAR DIARY
or
INTELLIGENCE SUMMARY.
(Erase heading not required.)

Army Form C. 2118.

Place	Date	Hour	Summary of Events and Information	Remarks and references to Appendices
ETRICOURT	Dec.			
Map Ref. 57 C. V.14.a.8.8.	1.		Divisional Headquarters moved from LITTLEWOOD Camp. YTRES. to-day. 183 Brigade going into line to-night to relieve a Brigade of the 20th Division. Positions of Field Ambulances :- 2/1 Field Amb., BERTINCOURT. 2/2 Field Amb., Q.15.a.6.6. 2/3 Field Amb., Q.15.a.7.5. A.D.M.S., visited forward area and Field Ambulances	
	2.		182 Brigade moving into the line. 184 Brigade in reserve. 2/3 Field Amb., taking over Medical posts and lines of evacuation from 20th Division. R.A.M.C., Order No: 42 (App.1) Administrative Order (App.ii) Medical Arrangements (App iii) issued at 6.30 p.m. Positions of Field Ambulances :- 2/1 Fd.Amb. BERTINCOURT. 2/2 Fd.Amb. Q.15.a.6.6. 2/3 Fd.Amb. Q.20.a.0.1. Captain C.H.ROBSON. R.A.M.C., T.C., 2/2 Fd.Amb., temporarily attached as Regimental Medical officer to the 2/4 Glosters reported killed in action. A.D.M.S., visited A.D.M.S., 20th Division.	
	3.		183 Infantry Brigade in the line. Taking over of medical posts etc in forward area completed. 182 and 183 Infantry Brigades heavily engaged. Locations :- 2/1 Fd.Amb. BERTINCOURT. 2/2 Fd.Amb. V.10.a.8.8. 2/3 Fd.Amb. V.12.c.9.8. A.D.M.S., visited forward area. D.A.D.M.S., visited O.C. 21 M.A.C. and obtained use of motor lorries for evacuating walking wounded to the C.M.D.S., Captain J.MANUEL. R.A.M.C. reported wounded. Captain H.H.FAIRFAX missing - believed wounded. Captain RENNIE called.	
	4.		~~Captain~~ 2/1 Field Amb., took over C.M.D.S., from 61st Field Amb., relief completed at 2 p.m. A.D.M.S., visited O.C. Central Control 3rd Army Light Railway. Captain H.B.Goulding reported prisoner of war. Locations :- 2/2 and 2/3 Field Ambs unchanged. 2/1 Fd.Amb., Headquarters and Transport lines also C.M.D.S., V.18.c. Captain J.K.RENNIE.R.A.M.C., called. Casualties have been heavy - evacuation of wounded proceeding satisfactorily.	

Instructions regarding War Diaries and Intelligence Summaries are contained in F. S. Regs., Part II. and the Staff Manual respectively. Title pages will be prepared in manuscript.

WAR DIARY
or
INTELLIGENCE SUMMARY.
(Erase heading not required.)

Army Form C. 2118.

Place	Date	Hour	Summary of Events and Information	Remarks and references to Appendices
ETRICOURT	Dec. 5		Auxilliary Stretcher Bearers (80) obtained fmrom "Q" Evacuation proceeding satisfactory. Advanced Bearer Post established at R.8.c.3.7. (Sheet 57C) 36th Division taking over portion of our line on the left. A.D.M.S., visited the A.D.S., Routine duties.	
	6		Captain W,Stobie. returned from leave. Adaanced Bearer Post handed over to 36th Division. A.D.S., being used jointly by 36th and 61st Divisions. Evacuation progressing satisfactorily nearly all R.A.Ps cleared. A.D.M.S., attended D.D.M.S., 111 Corps Conference. D.A.D.M.S., visited 2/3 Fd.Amb.2/2Fd.Amb.2/4Glosters & 2/6Warwicks. 2/3 H.Q. moved to V.11.b.4.4. owing to being shelled badly yesterday. 30 Auxiliary Stretcher bearers obtained. Routine duties.	
	7.		O.C. 2/2 Field Amb., called. A.D.M.S., visited forward area. Routinenduties.	
	8.		A.D.M.S., called on D.A.D.M.S., 111 Corps re railway. D.A.D.M.S., Visited 21 and 48 C.C.Ss. and 2/2 Field Ambulance.	
	9.		A.D.M.S., investigated the Decauville Railway from TRESCAULT and visited the Advanced Dressing Station. 2/1 and 2/2 Field Amb., O.C. 2/1 Fd.Amb., called. A.D.M.S., and D.A.D.M.S., 19 Division and D.A.D.M.S., 6 Div called. Routine duties.	
	10.		O.C.2/2 Field Amb., called to see A.D.M.S., D.A.D.M.S., sick in billet. Acting D.A.D.M.S., visited 2/2 Field Amb., C.M.D.S., and American Engineering Coy Headquarters at FINS with reference to Decauville Railway. Routine Duties.	
	11.		A.D.M.S., called on A.D.M.S., 36th Division and visited C.M.D.S. acting D.A.D.M.S., visited A.D.S., and W.W.C.P., at TRESCAULT.	

A5834 Wt. W4973/M687 750,000 8/16 D. D. & L. Ltd. Forms/C.2118/13.

Army Form C. 2118.

Instructions regarding War Diaries and Intelligence Summaries are contained in F. S. Regs., Part II. and the Staff Manual respectively. Title pages will be prepared in manuscript.

WAR DIARY
or
INTELLIGENCE SUMMARY.
(Erase heading not required.)

Place	Date	Hour	Summary of Events and Information	Remarks and references to Appendices
ETRICOURT	Dec 12.		A.D.M.S., visited O.C. No: 9 Light Railway Operating Co at YTRES. A.D.A.D.M.S., visited battalions of reserve Brigade in HAVRINCOURT WOOD and 2/2 Fd.Amb., Routine duties.	W.S
	13.		A.D.M.S. visited Forward Area. D.A.D.M.S. returned to duty. Routine duties.	WL
	14.		A.D.M.S. visited HAVRINCOURT WOOD site, and billets occupied by Reserve Brigade. Routine duties.	WL
	15.		A.D.M.S., attended D.D.M.S., 111rd Corps Conference at 2.15 p.m. Os.C. Field Amb., attended A.D.M.S., conference at 2.30 p.m. 61 Division passed from under the administration of 111rd Corps at 12 noon. Routine duties. Medical arrangements No 1 issued dated 15.12.17.*	* Appendix IV. WL
	16.		D.A.D.M.S., visited Rest Station at BUS. Os.C. 2/1 & 2/2 Field Ambs., called. M.O.i/c 81 Batty.R.F.A., called. Battery is rejoining 20th Division. 182 and 183 Brigades coming out of the line. 184 Brigade going into the line. 2/1 Field Ambulance moved to LECHELLE. Routine duties. Further medical arrangements issued dated 16.12.17. (x)	(x) Appendix V. WL
	17.		A.D.M.S., visited A.D.M.S., 63rd Division and 2/1 Field Ambulance. Routine duties.	WL
	18.		A.D.M.S., attended D.D.M.S., Conference at 10.30 a.m. D.A.D.M.S., visited Headquarters 2/3 Field Ambulance. 182 Brigade less one battalion moved to MANANCOURT. O.C. 2/3 Field Ambulance called re handing over A.D.S., to 63rd Division. 61 Division Warning Order received. R.A.M.C., Order No: 43 issued. (x)	WL (x) App.VI.
	19.		A.D.M.S. visited Forward area. ADVANCED DRESSING STATION handed over to 63rd Division. D.A.D.M.S. visited camp of 2/6, 2/7, 2/8 Warwicks MANANCOURT. Routine duties.	WL

A5834 Wt. W4973/M687 750,000 8/16 D. D. & L. Ltd. Forms/C.2118/13.

Instructions regarding War Diaries and Intelligence Summaries are contained in F. S. Regs., Part II. and the Staff Manual respectively. Title pages will be prepared in manuscript.

WAR DIARY
or
INTELLIGENCE SUMMARY.
(Erase heading not required.)

Army Form C. 2118.

Place	Date	Hour	Summary of Events and Information	Remarks and references to Appendices
ETRI COURT	Dec 20.		A.D.M.S., visited new area. Routine duties.	W.L.
	21 .		Conference of Os.C. Field Ambulances at 9.15 a.m. re move. R.A.M.C., Order No: 44 issued. Routine duties.	App.VII W.L.
	22.		A.D.M.S., visited new area. Lt Col Hockee & Lt Col [illegible] called. Routine duties.	W.L.
MERICOURT.	23.		Division moving to new area. A.D.M.S., office closed at ETRICOURT at 10 a.m. and opened 12 Noon at MERIECOURT. 182 Infantry Brigade moved to new area accompanied by 2/2 Field Ambulance Weather conditions ~~xxxxxx~~ severe. Road conditions bad. Locations 2/2 Field Ambulance SAILLY-LE-SEC.	W.L.
Map Ref. Sheet No: AMIENS .17..	24.		183 and 184 Brigades moving to new area accompanied by 2/3 and 2/1 Field Ambulancesrespectively. Locations :- 2/1 Fd.Amb., CAPPY. 2/3 Field Amb., BRAY. A.D.M.S., and D.A.D.M.S., visited 2/2 Field Amb., and 2/6 and 2/7 Batts.R.Warwick Regt.	W.L.
	25.		Move completed. A.D.M.S., and D.A.D.M.S., visited 2/7 Worcesters. D.A.D.M.S., visited 2/3Field Ambulance. 2nd LIEUT. C. Q. NORTH. M.O.R.C. reported for duty from England & was posted to 2/3 Fd Amb.	W.L.
	26.		O.C. 2/1 Fd.Amb., called. A.D.M.S., visited 2/1 and 2/3 Field Ambs. Routine duties.	W.L.
	27.		D.A.D.M.S., visited 2/2 and 2/3 Field Ambs., Warning Order to move received. Routine duties.	W.L.
	28.		O.C. 2/3 Field Amb., called. A.D.M.S., visited 2/2 and 2/1 Field Ambs., D.A.D.M.S., visited 2/1 Field Amb., Routine duties.	W.L.
	29.		R.A.M.C., Order No: 45 issued. Routine duties.	App.VIII W.L.

A5834 Wt. W4973/M687 750,000 8/16 D. D. & L. Ltd. Forms/C.2118/13.

Army Form C. 2118.

Instructions regarding War Diaries and Intelligence Summaries are contained in F. S. Regs., Part II. and the Staff Manual respectively. Title pages will be prepared in manuscript.

WAR DIARY
or
INTELLIGENCE SUMMARY.
(Erase heading not required.)

Place	Date	Hour	Summary of Events and Information	Remarks and references to Appendices
MERICOURT SUR-SOMME	Dec 30		182 Brigade moved to new area. Routine duties.	
HARBONNIERES Map ref AMIENS 17.	31.		183 and 184 Brigade Groups moved to new area. LOCATIONS :- A.D.M.S., HARBONNIERES. 2/1 Field Amb., Ecole des Filles. ROSIERES. 2/2 Field Amb., LE QUESNIL. 2/3 Field Amb., MARCELCAVE.) Sheet AMIENS 17. 1/100,000.	

C Howkins

Colonel A.M.S.
A.D.M.S., 61 Division.

T2134. Wt. W708—776. 500000. 4/15. Sir J. C. & S.

Appendix I

SECRET

COPY No: 17.

R.A.M.C., ORDER No: 42
by
Colonel C.H.Howkins. D.S.O., A.M.S.,

Ref.Map. Sheet 57C.

December 2/17

(1) The 61st Division will relieve the 20th Division on the 2nd instant, and night of 2nd/3rd instant.

(2) The 2/3rd South Midland Field Ambulance will take over the forward Medical posts and lines of evacuation from the 60th Field Ambulance. Details regarding relief to be arranged by Os.C. Field Ambulances concerned.

(3) The headquarters of the 2/3rd South Midland Field Ambulance will be temporarily at METZ (Q.20.a.0.1.)

(4) The Os.C. 2/1, 2/2, 2/3 Field Ambulances will detail medical officers and other ranks, and motor ambulances as laid down in Administrative order dated December 2nd 1917.

(5) The 2/1st South Midland Field Ambulance will collect the sick from the Transport lines, and Brigade in reserve, and transfer them to the Corps Sick Station on the FINS - NURLU Road (V.18.c...

(6) The Transport lines situated in W.13. at present occupied by the 20th Division, are being taken over on the 3rd instant by units of this Division. Os.C. Field Ambulances will therefore get into touch with the Transport Officer of their associated Brigade as soon as possible, and ascertain the situation of their Transport lines. They will take over on the date stated.

(7) ACKNOWLEDGE.

W. Victor Corbett
Captain.
for A.D.M.S., 61 Div.

Issued at 6.30 p.m.

Copies:-
1-3. 2/1, 2/2, 2/3 Field Ambs.,
4. 61 Div "G" for information.
5. 61 Div "Q" -do-
6. D.D.M.S., 111 Corps -do-
7-9. 182, 183, 184 Inf.Bdes. -do-
10. A.D.M.S., 20 Div. for information.
12. 1/5 D.C.L.I.,
13. C.R.E., for information.
14. 61 Div. Train.
15. S.S.O.
16. File.
17-18. War Diary.

AMENDMENT TO R.A.M.C. Order No: 42

Para. 6. For "The Transport lines situated in W.13. at present occupied by the 20th Division, are being taken over on the 3rd inst by units of this Division "
SUBSTITUTE:-
"Brigade Group Transport lines, Quartermasters Stores and 61 Divisional Train will move to EQUANCOURT to-morrow morning "

W. Victor Corbett
Captain.
for A.D.M.S. 61 Div.

2/12/17.

Distribution as for R.A.M.C. order No: 42.

Appendix II

No. 11

SECRET.

ADMINISTRATIVE ORDER.

The following will be supplied by the Units named below:-

2/1 Field Ambulance.

(1) 2 Medical Officers to report to O.C. 2/3 Field Ambulance at METZ (map reference Q.20.a.0.1.) for temporary duty.

(2) N.C.Os and men of one Bearer sub-division to O.C. 2/3 Field Ambulance at METZ, for temporary duty.

(3) 2 Daimler Motor Ambulances to O.C. 2/3 Field Ambulance, to rendesvouz at Headquarters 60th Field Ambulance at FINS. (57.C. V.12.central).

(4) 2 other ranks (clerks) to report to O.C. No.21 C.C.S. at YTRES.
2 other clerks to report to O.C. No. 48 C.C.S. at YTRES.

2/2 Field Ambulance.

(1) 1 Medical Officer to report to O.C. 2/3 Field Ambulance METZ (map reference Q.20.a.0.1) for temporary duty.

(2) N.C.Os and men of Bearer Division to report to O.C. 2/3 Field Ambulance at METZ.

(3) 2 Daimler Motor Ambulances to report to O.C. 2/3 Field Ambulance, to rendesvouz at Headquarters 60th Field Ambulance at FINS. (57.C. V.12.central).

(4) 3 other ranks (clerks) to report to O.C. III Corps M.D.S. on the FINS - NURLU Road.

2/3 Field Ambulance.

(1) 1 N.C.O. (clerk) and 3 other ranks (clerks) to O.C. III Corps M.D.S. on the FINS - NURLU Road.

The above instructions must be carried out forthwith and the completion of moves reported to this officeby each Unit concerned.

W. Victor Corbett
for Capt.
Colonel, A.M.S.
A.D.M.S., 61st Division.

2/12/17.

Copies to:-
1-3. 2/1, 2/2, 2/3 Field Ambulances.
4. 61st Division, "G". (for information)
5. 61st Division, "Q". "
6-8. 182, 183, 184 Infantry Brigades.
9. D.D.M.S., III Corps.
10-11. Warw Diary.
12. File.

Appendix III

SECRET.

Ref. Map Sheet 57C. MEDICAL ARRANGEMENTS.

1. The collection and evacuation of sick and wounded from the forward area will be carried out by the 2/3rd South Midland Field Ambulance -Headquarters at METZ.

2. The collection and evacuation of the sick of the Brigade in reserve and from the Transport lines will be carried out by the 2/1 South Midland Field Ambulance. - Headquarters at the foot of BUCKSHEE LANE. BERTINCOURT.

3. EVACUATION ARRANGEMENTS.

(a) Each Regimental Medical officer will have 2 squads of R.A.M.C. bearers attached to him - these will be relieved periodically. Lying cases are hand-carried or conveyed by wheeled stretchers from Regimental Aid Posts to Advanced Dressing Station.

(b) ADVANCED DRESSING STATIONS.

1. FARM RAVINE R.20.a.2.8. (300 yards S.E. of VILLERS PLOUICH)
2. GOUZEAUCOURT (closed at present) Q.36.d.5.9.

The evacuation of cases from the Advanced Dressing Station in use is via VILLERS PLOUICH and BEAUCAMP to eastern side of CHARING CROSS CRATER (Q.17.b.0.8.) where a Bearer Post in charg of a Medical officer is situated. Lying cases are hand-carrie or conveyed by wheeled stretcher from the A.D.S., to the wagon rendesvouz at the west side of CHARING CROSS CRATER.

(c) At the Wagon rendesvouz a Horse Ambulance wagon is stationed and loaded. This conveys patients to E. side of TRESCAULT CRATER (Q.17.b.0.7.)

(d) A Motor Ambulance rendezvous is situated on the west side of TRESCAULT CRATER. At this point cases are shifted from the "horse" to the "motor" ambulance and proceed via METZ or FINS to either a C.C.S. (lying cases) or to the Corps Main Dressing Station (FINS-NURLU Road. V.18.cent.) (slightly wounded)

NOTE. When the A.D.S., at GOUZEAUCOURT is again in use it will be probably possible to evacuate patients as before, by motor Ambulanc from the A.D.S., straight down the GOUZEAUCOURT-FINS Road to their destination. Further a Decauville railway also links up the A.D.S., with the C.C.Ss at YTRES.

W. Victor Corbett
Captain.
for A.D.M.S., 61 Div.

2/12/17.

Distribution :-
2/1, 2/2, 2/3 Field Ambs.,
61 Division "G" for information.
61 Division "Q" -do-
182, 183, 184 Inf.Bdes. -do-
All Regimental M.Os.

Appendix IV

SECRET. A.D.M.S. No: 913M/17.

61st DIVISION MEDICAL ARRANGEMENTS. No: 1

1. The 61st Division passes to the V Corps from 12 noon December 15th 1917.

2. The 2/1st South Midland Field Ambulance will proceed to LECHELLE on being relieved at the IIIrd Corps Main Dressing Station.

3. The collection of sick and wounded from the following areas will be arranged to take place on December 15th and until further notice –

2/1 Field Amb.,	-	HAVRINCOURT WOOD area and the MEDICAL Post at Q.15.a.5.7.
2/2 Field Amb.,	-	EQUANCOURT and Brigade Transport Lines.
2/3 Field Amb.,	-	Forward area.

Os.C. Field Ambulances concerned will make all necessary arrangements.

4. The arrangements for evacuation will be as follows :-

Sick & Walking wounded (slight cases)	- REST STATION. BUS.
Walking wounded	- V Corps Main Dressing Station RUYAULCOURT
Lying Wounded	- V Corps Main Dressing Station RUYAULCOURT or, if very urgent, direct to C.C.S. Full particulars of each case to be sent to C.M.D.S., for entry in "A & D" Book. O.C., A.D.S., will be responsible for seeing that this is done.

5. Evacuation will be carried out by the following means :-

(a) Decauville Railway.
(b) Motor Ambulance cars.
(c) Horse Ambulance wagons.

6. The Decauville Railway trains will be under the supervision of the A.D.M.S., 59th Division. Further details will be issued later.

7. The Medical post at railhead at TRESCAULT will be administered by the A.D.M.S., 63rd Division.

8. ACKNOWLEDGE.

W. Victor Corbett
Captain.
for A.D.M.S. 61 Div.

15/12/17.

Distribution:-
Os.C.Fd.Amb.,
182,183,184 Inf.Bdes.for information.
61 Division "G" & "Q" -do-
D.D.M.S. V Corps -do-
A.D.M.S., 59th & 63rd Divs -do-
27 M.A.C., -do-
1/5 D.C.L.I. -do-
61 Div Train. -do-
C.R.E., -do-
Os.C. V C.M.D.S., V C.R.S. -do-
O.C. No: 9 Lt.Rly.Op.Co. -do-

War Diary

SECRET

Appendix V.

MEDICAL ARRANGEMENTS FOR THE EVACUATION OF WOUNDED
61st DIVISION. (No: 7)

Ref.Map Sheet 57C.

FORWARD AREA

Wounded are sent from the Regimental Aid Posts of the Divisional Front at R.8.c.0.9., R.15.d.7.7., R.20.a.7.8. to the Advanced Dressing Station (R.13.a.8.8.) by :-

Hand carriage.
They can then be conveyed by wheeled Stretcher carriages, and Ford Ambulance cars.
along CAMBRAI-VILLERS PLOUICH-BEAUCAMP road from S.W. of R.8.c.7.8.

From the Advanced Dressing Station lying and sitting cases are evacuated either by :-

Ford Ambulance car or
Wheeled stretcher carriage.
to large car loading post at CHARING CROSS CRATER (Q.17.b.2.8.), and from thence to the Vth C.M.D.S.,

URGENT LYING CASES are sent from the A.D.S., direct to C.C.Ss. at YTRES (Nos: 21 & 48)

WALKING WOUNDED are directed to the Walking Wounded Collecting Post situated at Q.10.a.4.4.(where hot tea etc is giben) and then sent to the Corps Main Dressing Station either by :-

Decauville Railway.
Motor Ambulance (large)
Horse Transport.
The Decauville trains run at stated intervals and go direct to the C.M.D.S

PERSONNEL.

Advanced Dressing Station. Three Medical officers and a few Nursing Orderlies at the A.D.S., (R.13.a.8.8.)
The number of bearers depends on tactical circumstances. Usually a complete Bearer Division is utilised , but when there is activity this number is augmented by reserve Bearer Divisions and Auxilliary Stretcher Bearers,

LOADING POST. (Large cars)
A small number of Nursing orderlies are kept at the Loading Post (Q.17.b.2.8.) and also a small Bearer detachment. In times of active hostilities 2 Medical officers are attached to the Post.

TRANSPORT.
Motor Transport. The large Divisional Ambulances and Ford cars - with 4 M.A.C. cars are pooled in active hostilities, and utilised by the Field Ambulances evacuating from the forward area.

BACK AREA

(1) The sick and wounded from the Brigade in reserve (HAVRINCOURT WOOD) are collected and evacuated by the 2/1 S.Mid.Field Amb. LECHELLE. A Medical Post is at Q.15.a.5.7. where a motor ambulance is kept to evacuate any urgent case. There is sufficient accomodation provided to detain cases pending evacuation.
(2) The sick and wounded from the Transport lines at EQUANCOURT are collected and evacuated by the 2/2 S.Mid.Field Amb., EQUANCOURT.

ACKNOWLEDGE.

W. Victor Corbett Captain
for Colonel A.M.S.
A.D.M.S., 61 Div.

16/12/17.

Appendix VI

SECRET. COPY NO: 15

R.A.M.C., Order No: 43
by
Colonel C.H.Howkins D.S.O., A.M.S.,
A.D.M.S., 61 Div.

1. The 63rd Division will take over the A.D.S., at R.13.a.1.8. from the 61st Division on 19/12/17.

2. The O.C. 2/3rd South Midland Field Ambulance will leave 1 Medical Officer, 30 other ranks, 2 Ford Cars and 3 Large cars at the A.D.S., for the treatment and evacuation of the sick and wounded of the 61st Division.

3. Details of relief will be arranged between the Os.C. Field Ambulances concerned.

4. The detachment mentioned in para. 2 will find its own reliefs.

5. All Stretchers, blankets etc in excess of Mobilization Equipment or held under G.R.Os. will be handed over to the relieving unit.
Receipts are to be obtained - copies of which will be sent to this office.

6. The evacuation of sick and wounded from the 61st Division front will be supervised by the O.C. 2/3 South Midland Field Ambulance.

7. Sick and Wounded of the 61st Division will be evacuated by the Divisional Motor Ambulances.

8. Completion of the relief will be notified to this office.

9. ACKNOWLEDGE.

Issued at 7 p.m. 18/12/17.

W. Victor Corbett
Captain.
for A.D.M.S., 61 Div.

Copies to :-
1. 2/3 Field Ambulance.
2-3. 2/1, 2/2 Field Ambs for information.
4. 61 Division "G" -do-
5. 61 Division "Q" -do-
6-8. 182, 183, 184 Bdes. -do-
9. D.D.M.S., V Corps -do-
10. A.D.M.S., 63 Div. -do-
11. C.R.E., -do-
12. Div Train. -do-
13. 1/5 D.C.L.I., -do-
14. File.
15. War Diary
16. -do-

Appendix VII

SECRET. Copy No: 19

R.A.M.C., Order No: 44
by
Colonel C.H.Howkins. D.S.O., A.M.S.,
A.D.M.S., 61 Division.

December 21st 191

1. The 61st Division (less Artillery) will be relieved by the 63rd (R.N.) Division. Relief will be completed by the morning of the 23rd instan

2. On completion of the relief the Division (less Artillery) will commence to concentrate in the ETRICOURT Area.

3. The Field Ambulances will be prepared to move to the New area with their Brigade Group as follows :-

182 Brigade Group.	2/2 S.Mid.Field Amb.,
183 Brigade Group.	2/3 S.Mid.Field Amb.,
184 Brigade Group.	2/1 S.Mid.Field Amb.,

4. Each Field Ambulance will be responsible for the collection and disposal of the sick and wounded of its associated Brigade Group from the time of its assembly until further orders.

5. The 2/1st and 2/2 S.Mid.Field Ambs., will not vacate their present sites until they move with their Brigade Group to the New area. The 2/3 S.Mid.Field Amb., (less Transport)will move on 23rd to HAVANCOURT, leaving a detachment to attend sick of Transport Lines.

6. The O.C. 2/3 S.Mid. Field Amb., will withdraw all the remaining personnel from the forward area and lines of evacuation on the relief of the 183 Brigade. He will also return Motor Ambulances from other on completion of above relief.

7. The O.C. 2/1 S.Mid.Field Amb., will arrange to collect the sick and wounded from HAVRINCOURT WOOD and will withdraw the Medical Post when this Area is vacated by the 61st Division.

8. The present arrangements for the collection and evacuation of sick from the Brigade Transport lines (EQUANCOURT) will be carried out until the 2/2 S.Mid.Field Amb., moves to the "New area" after which time the 2/3 S.Mid.Field Amb., will be responsible.

9. All stores etc over and above Mobilization equipment, or held under G.R.Os. will be handed over and receipts obtained. A copy of these receipts will be sent to this office.

10. A.D.M.S., office will close December 23rd - details to be issued later.

11. Movement Table attached (for Field Ambs., only)

12. Field Ambulances ACKNOWLEDGE.

William Stobie
Captain.
for A.D.M.S., 61 Div.

Issued at 4,15 p.m.

Distribution:-
- 1-3. Os.C. 2/1,2/2,2/3 S.Mid.Field Ambs.
- 4. 61 Div. "G" for information.
- 5. 61 Div "Q" -do-
- 6-8. 182, 183, 184 Inf.Bdes. for information.
- 9. D.D.M.S., V.Corps for information.
- 10. D.D.M.S., XVIIICorps -do-
- 11. A.D.M.S., 63rd Div. -do-
- 12. 61 Divisional Train. -do-
- 13. C.R.E., -do-
- 14. 1/5 D.C.L.I. -do-
- 15. 37 Sanitary Sec. YTRES. -do-
- 16. V Corps Main Dressing Stn -do-
- 17. V Corps Rest Stn. for information.
- 18-19. War Diary.
- 20. File.

M A R C H   T A B L E.

Date.	Brigade etc.	From.	To.
ec. 23rd.	184 Brigade Group.	HAVRINCOURT WOOD.	MANANCOURT AREA.
ec. 22/23rd. ec. 23rd.	183 -do-	LINE. HAVRINCOURT WOOD.	HAVRINCOURT WOOD. MANANCOURT AREA.
ec. 23rd.	182 -do-	MANANCOURT.	NEW AREA.
ec. 23rd.	REAR D.H.Q.	ETRICOURT.	NEW AREA.
ec. 24th.	184 Brigade Group.	MANANCOURT AREA.	NEW AREA.
ec. 24th.	183 -do-	MANANCOURT AREA.	NEW AREA.
ec. 24th.	Advanced H.Q.	Advanced D.H.Q.	NEW AREA.

Appendix VIII

SECRET.

COPY No: 15

R.A.M.C., ORDER NO: 45
by
Colonel O.H.Howkins. D.S.O., A.M.S.,
A.D.M.S., 61 Div.

Ref Map.
AMIENS 17. 1/100,000

December 29th 1917.

1. Reference 61 Division Order No: 147 dated 29/12/17, the 61 Division (less Artillery) accompanied by the Divisional Supply Column, and one Cable Section, will march to the PROYART area on December 30th and 31st.

2. The Field Ambulances will remain in their present Brigade Groups, viz :-
2/1 Field Amb., - 184 Inf.Brigade Group.
2/2 Field Amb., - 182 Inf.Brigade Group.
2/3 Field Amb., - 183 Inf.Brigade Group.

3. Each Field Ambulance will be responsible for the collection and evacuation of the sick and wounded of its Brigade Group until further orders.

4. Each O.C. Field Ambulance will detail one Medical Officer to accompany the transport of their associated Brigade during the move.

5. Each O.C. Field Ambulance will detail an Ambulance wagon to follow in rear of their associated Brigade during the move. At the conclusion of the move the Ambulance wagons will rejoin their respective units.

6. The O.C. 2/1 Field Amb., will note that at 6 p.m. on December 30th the 1/5 Bn. D.C.L.I., (Pioneers) will be transferred to 184 Brigade Group.

7. The A.D.M.S., office will close at MERICOURT-SUR-SOMME at 9 a.m. on 31st instant, and re-open at HARBONNIERES on arrival.

8. Field Ambulances acknowledge.

Issued at 6 p.m. Dec.29th.

W. Victor Corbett
Captain.
for A.D.M.S., 61 Div.

Distribution :-

1-3. Os.C. Field Ambs.
4-6. 182,183,184 Inf.Brigades for information.
7. 61 Div "G" -do-
8. 61 Div "Q" -do-
9. D.D.M.S., XVIII Corps. -do-
10. 1/5 D.C.L.I., -do-
11. 61 Div Train. A.S.C. -do-
12. C.R.E., -do-
13. 61 Div Supply Column. -do-
14-15. War Diary.
16. File.
17-18. Spare.

9

Medical

CONFIDENTIAL

Jan. 1918

V.R. 21

WAR DIARY

OF

A.D.M.S., 61 DIVISION.

VOLUME No: 21.

From :- January 1st to 31st 1918.

C. Hawkins

Colonel A.M.S.
A.D.M.S., 61 Division.

31/1/18.

Army Form C. 2118.

Instructions regarding War Diaries and Intelligence Summaries are contained in F. S. Regs., Part II. and the Staff Manual respectively. Title pages will be prepared in manuscript.

WAR DIARY
or
INTELLIGENCE SUMMARY.
(Erase heading not required.)

Place	Date	Hour	Summary of Events and Information	Remarks and references to Appendices
HARBONNIERES Map Ref: AMIENS 17.	Jan 1. 1918.		D.A.D.M.S., proceeded on 48 hours special leave to BOULOGNE. A.D.M.S., visited 2/1 Field Amb., at ROSIERES. 2/2 Field Amb., at LE QUESNIL. 2/3 Field Amb., at MARCELCAVE. Warning Order for relief of 5th French Division received. Catain Radford. M.O.i/c 307 Bde R.F.A., called.	WS
	2		A.D.M.S., held conference of Os.C. 2/1, 2/2, and 2/3 Field Ambs., A/D.A.D.M.S., visited 2/5 and 2/8 Warwicks. Routine duties.	WS
	3		A.D.M.S., inspected 2/3 Field Ambulance. Captain W.N.H.Bell. M.O. 306 Bde R.F.A., Captain W.V.Wood and Lieut G.Arnott called. D.A.D.M.S., returned from 48 hours leave of absence to BOULOGNE. Routine Duties.	WL
	4		A.D.M.S., inspected 2/3 Field Ambulance and saw them on the march. Routine duties.	WL
	5.		A.D.M.S., visited 2/3 Field Amb., G.O.C., inspected 2/3 Field Ambulance at 3 p.m. D.A.D.M.S., visited new billeting area. Routine duties.	WL
	6.		R.A.M.C., Order No: 46 issued. Routine duties.	APP.1. WL
NESLE. Map Ref. Amiens 17.	7.		Division moving to NESLE Area prior to relieving the 5th French Division. Locations :- A.D.M.S., Headquarters NESLE. 2/1 Field Ambulance. BETHENCOURT. 2/2 Field Ambulance. NESLE. 2/3 Field Ambulance. ROYE. A.D.M.S., visited Chief Medical Officer 5th French Division. D.A.D.M.S., visited S.M.O. American Hospital NESLE, re infectious diseases in the neighbourhood	WL

D. D. & L., London, E.C.
(A7883) Wt W809/M1672 350,000 4/17 Sch. 52a Forms/C/2118/14

Army Form C. 2118.

Instructions regarding War Diaries and Intelligence Summaries are contained in F. S. Regs., Part II, and the Staff Manual respectively. Title pages will be prepared in manuscript.

WAR DIARY
or
INTELLIGENCE SUMMARY.
(Erase heading not required.)

Place	Date	Hour	Summary of Events and Information	Remarks and references to Appendices
NESLE. Map Ref. AMIENS SHeet 17.	Jan 8.		D.A.D.M.S., visited ETALON re reported cases of Dysentery among the French Troops. Os.C. 2/1 and 2/2 Field Ambulances called. R.A.M.C., Order No: 47 issued Routine duties.	App.ii.
	9.		Division moving into the GERMAINE Area. Locations. Map Ref. Sheet 66.D. 2/1 Fd.Amb., LANCHY. 2/2 Fd.Amb., GERMAINE. 2/3 Fd.Amb., GERMAINE. Routine duties.	
	10.		D.A.D.M.S., visited 2/1,2/2,2/3 Fd.Ambs, Routine duties.	
	11.		2/1 Field Ambulance completed taking over the LEFT Sector from the French. 184 Brigade in the left sector of the line. Routine duties.	
AUROIR. Map.Ref. Sheet 66D.	12.		A.D.M.S., visited the Medicin Chief of the outgoing 5th French Division. D.H.Q., moved to AUROIR at 10 a.m. 2/2 Field Amb., completed taking over the RIGHT sector from the French. 182 Brigade in the Right Sector of the line. Routine duties.	
	13.		Os.C. 2/1 and 2/2 Field Ambs called. A.D.M.S., visited proposed new site for Headquarters 2/2 Field Amb., at VAUX. Routine duties.	
	14.		D.A.D.M.S. visited Medical Posts and Left Battalion R.A.P. of the Right Sector, also M.D.S. and Headquarters 2/2nd F.Ambulance. Routine Duties.	

D. D. & L., London, E.C.
(A7883) Wt W809/M1672 350,000 4/17 Sch. 52a Forms/C/2118/14

Instructions regarding War Diaries and Intelligence Summaries are contained in F. S. Regs., Part II. and the Staff Manual respectively. Title pages will be prepared in manuscript.

WAR DIARY
or
INTELLIGENCE SUMMARY.
(Erase heading not required.)

Army Form C. 2118

Place	Date	Hour	Summary of Events and Information	Remarks and references to Appendices
AUROIR, Map Ref. Sheet 66D.	15.		Medical Board on Major T.M. DUNCAN, 306 Bde. R.F.A. Captain STAFFORD and Captain W.V. WOOD, R.A.M.C. called. A.D.M.S. visited A.D.S. at MAISSEMY. Routine Duties.	WS
	16.		Routine Duties.	WS
	17.		D.A.D.M.S. visited Transport Lines 184 Inf.Brigade & 307 Bde. R.F.A. Routine Duties.	WS
	18.		D.A.D.M.S., visited D.D.M.S., XVIII Corps. A.D.M.S., visited D.M.S. Fifth Army. Routine duties.	WS
	19.		A.D.M.S., visited 2/1,2/2,2/3 Field Ambs. D.A.D.M.S., inspected Transport lines 182 Brigade 2/3 and 2/1 Field Ambs. O.C. 267 Machine Gun Company called re medical attention for Coy. O.C. 2/1 Field Amb., called. Lieut F.T.Williams. M.O.R.C., USA., transferred to Home Service at the expiration of his leave on January 13th and struck off the strength. Routine duties.	WS
	20.		O.C. 23 sanitary Section called. Conference of Os.C. Field Ambulances at 2.30 p.m. Routine duties.	WS
	21.		A.D.M.S., attended Conference of D.D.M.S., XVIII Corps. A.D.M.S., examined men considered by R.M.Os. to be unfit for further service in forward area. D.A.D.M.S., proceeded on 14 days leave to ENGLAND. Capt.Stafford. R.A.M.C., att 61 D.A.C., called. O.C. 23 San.Sec. called. Routine duties.	WS
	22.		A.D.M.S., visited A.D.S., at MAISSEMY and baths at ETREILLERS. A/D.A.D.M.S., visited Headquarters 2/1 and 2/2 Field Ambs. Routine duties. Presentation of ribbons of Immediate Awards to R.A.M.C. recipients.	WS

D. D. & L., London, E.C.
(A7883) Wt W809/M1672 350,000 4/17 Sch. 52a Forms/C/2118/14

Instructions regarding War Diaries and Intelligence Summaries are contained in F. S. Regs., Part II, and the Staff Manual respectively. Title pages will be prepared in manuscript.

WAR DIARY
or
INTELLIGENCE SUMMARY.
(*Erase heading not required.*)

Army Form C. 2118.

Place	Date	Hour	Summary of Events and Information	Remarks and references to Appendices
AURCIR.	Jan. 23.		A.D.M.S., visited Baths GERMAINE. MARTEVILLE. 184 & 183 Bde H.Q. Gum Boot Stores MARTEVILLE A.D.S., at HOLNON. One of the Bn.R.A.Ps. in Right Sector. Dressing Station BOIS de SAVY. A/D.A.D.M.S., inspected Water cart of 267 M.G.C., Visited springs between DOUILLY and TOULLE to obtain samples of water, and Headquarters 2/1 Field Amb., Col.Brown and Capt Stafford. O.C. and M.O., 61 D.A.C., and Capt Coatsworth M.O. 1/5 D.C.L.I. called.	WS
	24.		A.D.M.S., visited 61 C.C.S., HAM. A/D.A.D.M.S., visited A.D.S., and Bombing Posts left sector. Routine duties.	WS
	25.		D.D.M.S., XVIII Corps inspected M.D.S., H.Q. 2/1 Fd.Amb., & 2/2 Fd.Amb. and Medical Post at SAVY. 2 Medical Officers reinforcements reported for duty. Capt.Dobson to 2/2 Fd.Amb., Capt.McCombie to 2/3 Fd.Amb., Routine duties.	WS
	26.		A.D.M.S., and A/D.A.D.M.S., visited baths at GERMAINE. Officers Rest House at FORESTE. A.D.S., at BOIS DE SAVY and HOLNON and R.A.Ps. of Right Sector. Routine duties. Captain A.P.Thomson called. A.D.M.S., examined Capt.H.B.DONE. 61 D.A.C., 2 Medical officer reinforcements reported for duty. Capt Clancy G.S., R.A.M.C. T.C., to 2/3 Field Amb., 1st Lieut L.N.OSSMAN. M.O.R.C., U.S.A., t 2/3 Fd.Amb.,	WS
	27.		A.D.M.S., visited Main Dressing Station and Baths at GERMAINE. A/D.A.D.M.S., visited baths at MARTEVILLE. A.D.S., at MAISSEMY. R.A.Ps and Relay Post of Left Sector. Routine duties.	WS
	28.		A.D.M.S. held his weekly examination of men for re-classification. A/D.A.D.M.S. visited 2/3 Field Ambulance, 2/5 Glosters, and 1/5 D.C.L.I.: also water supplies at HOLNON WOOD. Captain WALLIS, R.A.M.C. reported for duty and was posted to 2/3 Field Ambulance. O.C. 2/1 Field Amb., called. Routine duties.	WS

D. D. & L., London, E.C.
(A7883) Wt. W809/M1672 350,000 4/17 Sch. 52a Forms/C/2118/14

Army Form C. 2118.

Instructions regarding War Diaries and Intelligence Summaries are contained in F. S. Regs., Part II. and the Staff Manual respectively. Title pages will be prepared in manuscript.

WAR DIARY
or
INTELLIGENCE SUMMARY.

(Erase heading not required.)

Place	Date	Hour	Summary of Events and Information	Remarks and references to Appendices
AUROIR.	Jan. 29.		A.D.M.S., visited Main Dressing Station. A/D.A.D.M.S., visited 2/3 and 2/1 Field Ambulances. O.C. 2/1 Field Amb., called. Routine duties.	WS
	30.		A.D.M.S., and A/D.A.D.M.S., visited A.D.S., at MAISSEMY and R.A.P.'s, and Relay Posts of left Sector. Routine duties.	WS
	31.		A.D.M.S., presided at a Medical Board at XVIII Corps Headquarters. He also held a Conference of Quartermasters at the M.D.S., at which the D.A.Q.M.G. was present. The A/D.A.D.M.S., accompanied the A.A.Q.M.G., to the water supply between TOULLE & DOUILLY with reference to proposed Divisional Soda Water factory. Captain J.Manuel M.C., R.A.M.C., M.O. i/c 2/7 Bn.Worcester Regt called.	WS

C Hawkins
Colonel A.M.S.
A.D.M.S., 61 Division.

A5834 Wt. W4973/M687 750,000 8/16 D. D. & L. Ltd. Forms/C.2118/13.

Appendix I

SECRET. Copy No: 17

61 Division R.A.M.C. Order No: 46
by
Colonel C.H.Hawkins, D.S.O., A.M.S.,
A.D.M.S., 61 Division.

Ref.Map.
AMIENS 17. 1/100,000. January 6th 1918.

1. Reference 61 Division Order No: 148 dated January 5th the 61 Division (less Artillery and Ammunition Sub Park) accompanied by the Divisional Supply Column, and one Cable Section, will move to the NESLE Area on January 7th 1918.

2. The Field Ambulances will remain "grouped" as at present.

3. The collection and evacuation of sick will be carried out under the present arrangements, i.e. each Field Ambulance will be responsible for its own Brigade Group.

4. Os.C. Field Ambulances will make the usual arrangements regarding Medical Officers accompanying the Brigade Transport; and Ambulance wagons following the troops.

5. A Motor Ambulance will be attached to the S.M.O. 61st Division R.F.A., under orders issued seperately.

6. The A.D.M.S., office will close at HARBONNIERES at 10 a.m. on January 7th and reopen at NESLE on arrival.

7. Field Ambulances ACKNOWLEDGE.

W. Victor Corbett

Issued at 5 p.m.

Captain.
for A.D.M.S., 61 Div.

Distribution :-

1-3. Os.C. Field Ambulances.
4-6. 182,183,184 Inf.Bdes. for information.
7. 61 Division "G" -do-
8. 61 Division "Q" -do-
9. D.D.M.S., XVIII Corps -do-
10. 1/5 D.C.L.I., -do-
11. 61 Div. Train A.S.C., -do-
12. C.R.E., -do-
13. C.R.A., -do-
14. 61 Div.Supply Column. -do-
15. M.O.i/c 61 D.A.C., -do-
16-17. War Diary.
18. File.
19-20. Spare.

Appendix II

SECRET.

Copy No: 29

61 Division R.A.M.C., Order No: 47
by
Colonel C.H.Hawkins. D.S.O., A.M.S.,
A.D.M.S., 61 Division.

Reference Maps.
AMIENS 17. 1/100,000.
Sheet 62C. S.E., 1/20,000
62B. S.W., "
66C. N.W. "
66D. N.E. "

January 8th 1918.

1. Reference 61st Division Order No: 149 dated 5th January 1918, the 61st Division will relieve the 5th French Div. in the line N.W. of ST QUENTIN commencing on January 10th 1918.
   (a) The relief of the 5th French Division (less Artillery) will be completed during the night 11/12th January.
   (b) The relief of the 5th French Division Artillery will commence on January 12th and will be completed by 6 a.m. January 14th.

2. Field Ambulances will remain "grouped" as at present, and will be responsible for the collection and evacuation of the sick and wounded of their Brigade Groups until the 61st Division takes over the line.

3. Os.C. Field Ambulances will make the usual arrangements regarding Medical Officers accompanying the Brigade Transport, and Ambulance wagons following the troops during the move.

4. On arrival in the GERMAINE Area the Field Ambulances will come under the orders of the A.D.M.S.,

5. (a) The 2/1 Field Ambulance will take over the French Medical Posts and lines of evacuation in the LEFT Sector. Relief to be completed by midnight January 10/11th.
   (b) The 2/2 Field Ambulance will take over the French Medical Posts and lines of evacuation in the RIGHT Sector. Relief to be completed by midnight January 11/12th.

6. The 2/3 Field Ambulance will take over the French Ambulance site at GERMAINE (Sheet 66D. E.17.a.2.8.) and establish a Divisional Main Dressing Station which will be ready to receive patients by midnight January 10/11th.

7. Details of reliefs to be arranged by Os.C. Field Ambulances concerned. Completion of reliefs will be notified to this office.

8. Os.C. Field Ambulances will send advance parties to reconnoitre the ground and act as guides.

9. The 2/1 Field Ambulance will undertake the evacuation of sick and wounded from the LEFT Sector.
The 2/2 Field Ambulance will undertake the evacuation of sick and wounded from the RIGHT Sector.
The 2/3 Field Ambulance will undertake the collection and evacuation of sick and wounded of the Reserve Brigade.

Continued. P.T.O.

Continued.

10. The 2/3 Field Ambulance will undertake the collection and evacuation of the sick and wounded of the 1/5 Bn. D.C.L.I. (Pioneers) during the time that the battalion is in the FORESTE Area.

11. The A.D.M.S., office will close at NESLE at 10 a.m. on January 12th and reopen at AUROIR at the same hour.

12. Field Ambulances ACKNOWLEDGE.

Issued at 11 p.m.

Victor Corbett.
Captain.
for A.D.M.S., 61 Division.

Distribution :-

1-3-Os.C. Field Ambulances.
4-6-182,183,184 Inf.Bdes. for information.
7-8.61 Division "G" and "Q" -do-
9.D.D.M.S., XVIII Corps. -do-
10.1/5. D.C.L.I., -do-
11.61 Div Train A.S.C., -do-
12.C.R.E., -do-
13.C.R.A., -do-
14.61 Div Supply Column. -do-
15.M.O. 2/5 Warwicks. -do-
16.M.O. 2/6 Warwicks. -do-
17.M.O. 2/7 Warwicks. -do-
18.M.O. 2/8 Warwicks. -do-
19-22.M.Os.Battalions 183 Bde. -do-
23-26.M.Os.Battalions 184 Bde. -do-
27.M.O. 61 Div. R.E. -do-
28-29.War Diary.
30.File.
31-38.Spare.

CONFIDENTIAL

Medical

Feb. 1918. 14 14 d2782 Vol 22

WAR DIARY

OF

A. D. M. S. 61 DIVISION

FROM :- FEBRUARY 1st 1918.

TO :- FEBRUARY 28th 1918.

VOLUME - 22

J. Hunter

Colonel A.M.S.
A.D.M.S., 61 Division.

Army Form C. 2118.

WAR DIARY
or
INTELLIGENCE SUMMARY.
(Erase heading not required.)

Instructions regarding War Diaries and Intelligence Summaries are contained in F. S. Regs., Part II. and the Staff Manual respectively. Title pages will be prepared in manuscript.

Place	Date	Hour	Summary of Events and Information	Remarks and references to Appendices
AUROIR. 66.D.	Feb. 1st.		A.D.M.S., held a Conference of Medical officers of the Division at the 2/3rd South Midland Field Ambulance. O.C. 2/1 Field Ambulance called. Routine duties.	
	2nd.		A.D.M.S., visited Baths at GERMAINE and ETREILLERS. Also 2/1 Field Amb., and M.O. 1/5 Gordon Highlanders (on arrival in the Division) A/D.A.D.M.S., visited A.D.S., Left Sector. Headquarters and wagon lines of 306 Bde R.F.A., Headquarters 184 L.T.M.B., M.O. 2/4 Berks. O.C. 23 Sanitary Section and 2/3 Field Amb., re cases of Diphtheria. Routine duties.	
	3rd.		A.D.M.S., with O.C. 2/1 Field Amb., visited TIRLANCOURT (V.22.a.2.8. Sheet 66.D.) re Corps Rest Station. O.C. 2/2 Field Amb., and O.C. 23 Sanitary Section called. Routine duties.	
	4th.		A.D.M.S., held his usual weekly examination of men considered by Medical officers as unfit for service in the forward area. Lieut E.V.WHITAKER. reported from hospital and was sent to 2/2 Field Ambulance. A/D.A.D.M.S., visited MESNIL ST NICAISE with reference to a case of Infectious disease there,last month and the question of the billet being again used by troops. Routine duties.	
	5th.		A.D.M.S., visited M.O. 1/5 Gordon Highlanders and inspected water cart and equipment and saw the Stretcher Bearers drilling. He also inspected the officers and mens Rest Huts. A/D.A.D.M.S., saw the M.O. 306 Bde R.F.A., and 2/7 Worcesters and O.C. 267 M.G.C., also a billet at BEAUVOIS where a case of Diphtheria had occurred. He also visited Headquarters 2/1 Fd.Amb., Routine duties.	
	6th.		A.D.M.S., with Os.C. 2/1 and 2/2 Fd.Ambs., attended D.D.M.S., XVIII Corps Conference. A/D.A.D.M.S., visited 1/5 Gordons and 2/7 Worcesters. D.A.D.M.S., returned from leave. Routine duties.	
	7th.		A.D.M.S., visited officers and mens Rest Huts at FORESTE, Bombing Posts and proposed Dressing Station at MARTEVILLE. O.C. 2/3 Field Amb., and Captain Bell. called. Conference of Os.C. Field Ambs., at 2.30 p.m. Routine duties.	

A5834 Wt. W4973/M687 750,000 8/16 D. D. & L. Ltd. Forms/C.2118/13.

Army Form C. 2118.

Instructions regarding War Diaries and Intelligence Summaries are contained in F. S. Regs., Part II. and the Staff Manual respectively. Title pages will be prepared in manuscript.

WAR DIARY
or
INTELLIGENCE SUMMARY.
(Erase heading not required.)

Place	Date	Hour	Summary of Events and Information	Remarks and references to Appendices
AUROIR.	Feb 8th.		A.D.M.S., proceeded on leave. O.C. 2/1 Field Ambulance acting A.D.M.S., D.A.D.M.S., visited 2/1 Field Ambulance. Routine duties.	W.H.
	9th.		D.A.D.M.S., visited 2/3 Field Ambulance. Routine duties.	W.H.
	10th.		A/A.D.M.S., visited D.D.M.S., XVIII Corps. O.C. 2/2 Field Amb., called. Acting O.C. 2/3 Field Amb., called. Lieut SHANNON.MORC.USA. Medical Officer 1/9th Bn.Royal Scots called. Routine duties.	W.H.
	11th		Routine duties.	W.H.
	12th		A/A.D.M.S., and D.A.D.M.S., visited 2/3 Field Amb., Routine duties.	W.H.
	13th		D.D.M.S., XVIII Corps accompanied by D.A.D.M.S., 61 Div. visited 2/3, 2/2, 2/1 Field Ambs. Lieut Thornhill.M.O.R.C., USA, called. Routine duties.	W.H.
	14th		D.A.D.M.S., lectured at the XVIII Corps School. Acting O.C. 2/2 Field Amb., called, and Captain Walmsley R.A.M.C.,. Routine duties.	W.H.
	15th		D.D.M.S., Conference attended by A/A.D.M.S., D.A.D.M.S., A/OS.C. 2/2 and 2/3 Field Ambs., Captain Stafford. R.A.M.C., called. Captain McCombie reported prior to departure. Routine duties.	W.H.
	16th		A/A.D.M.S., visited the forward area. D.A.D.M.S., visited Main Dressing Stn (2/3 Field Amb.,) Routine duties.	W.H.

Instructions regarding War Diaries and Intelligence Summaries are contained in F. S. Regs., Part II. and the Staff Manual respectively. Title pages will be prepared in manuscript.

Army Form C. 2118.

WAR DIARY
or
INTELLIGENCE SUMMARY.
(*Erase heading not required.*)

Place	Date	Hour	Summary of Events and Information	Remarks and references to Appendices
AUROIR.	Feb 17.		D.A.D.M.S., visited 2/1 Field Ambulance and 2/3 Field Ambulance. Routine duties.	W.K.
	18.		D.D.M.S., accompanied by A/A.D.M.S., visited Dressing Stations under construction at MARTEVILLE and ETREILLERS. D.A.D.M.S., visited Baths at GERMAINE. Captain WOOD and Major WATERHOUSE called. Routine duties.	W.K.
	19.		61 Division Warning Order received. Portion of Northern front line is being handed over to Dismounted Divisions, and a portion of the Southern front line to 30th Division. D.A.D.M.S., visited A.D.M.S., Dismounted Divisions re handing over A.D.S., MAISSEMY and Medical Posts. A.D.M.S., 30 Division called and visited Headquarters 2/2 S.Mid.Field Amb., and Medical Posts at SAVY and BOIS DE SAVY, re taking them over by the 98th Field Amb., D.A.D.M.S., called on 2/1 Field Amb., re above. Routine duties.	W.K.
	20.		A.D.M.S., Dismounted Divisions called re line of evacuation. D.D.M.S., and D.A.D.M.S., XVIII Corps called and, accompanied by D.A.D.M.S., 61 Div. inspected the Advanced Gas Centre at the Main Dressing Station (2/3 Field Amb.,) D.A.D.M.S., called on 2/2 and 2/3 Field Ambs., re handing over to 30th Division. Captain STAFFORD. RAMC, and acting O.C. 2/2 Field Amb., called. R.A.M.C. Order No 48 issued. Appendix I. Routine duties.	W.K. App I.
	21.		A/A.D.M.S., visited the forward ares, Left Sector. Canadian Cavalry Field Ambulance took over A.D.S., at MAISSEMY and Medical Posts in this area. D.A.D.M.S., visited 2/2 and 2/3 Field Ambulances, also, in company with acting O.C. 2/2 Field Amb. visited proposed site for Right Sector Dressing Station. O.C. 31 M.A.C., called, and acting O.C. 2/2 Field Amb., called. Routine duties.	W.K.
	22.		D.D.M.S., Conference. A/A.D.M.S., visited forward area. 2/2 Field Amb., began to hand over to 30th Division. D.A.D.M.S., visited 2/3 and 2/2 Field Ambulances. Routine duties.	W.K.

A5834 Wt. W4973/M687 750,000 8/16 D. D. & L. Ltd. Forms/C.2118/13.

Army Form C. 2118.

Instructions regarding War Diaries and Intelligence Summaries are contained in F. S. Regs., Part II, and the Staff Manual respectively. Title pages will be prepared in manuscript.

WAR DIARY
or
INTELLIGENCE SUMMARY.
(Erase heading not required.)

Place	Date	Hour	Summary of Events and Information	Remarks and references to Appendices
AUROIR.	Feb. 23.		A/A.D.M.S., and D.A.D.M.S., visited Dressing Station at MARTEVILLE and proposed Dressing Station at F.2.a.3.8. 30th Division completed taking over Medical Posts from 2/2 Field Ambulance. A/O.C. ~~and~~ 2/3rd and A/O.C. 2/2 Field Ambulances called. Lieut SHANNON. MORC. called. Routine duties.	
	24.		A/A.D.M.S., visited forward area. D.A.D.M.S., met D.D.M.S., Cavalry Corps and A.D.M.S., Dismounted Divisions at VERMAND Dressing Station (No: 3 Cavalry Field Amb.,) re handing over Medical Posts. D.A.D.M.S., visited Dressing Station at MARTEVILLE (construction progressing well) and M.D.S., Captain THOMSON. M.O. i/c 2/6 Bn.R.Warwick Regt called. A.D.M.S., returned from leave. Routine duties.	
	25.		A.D.M.S., and O.C. 2/1 Field Ambulance visited proposed site of Right Sector Dressing Station F.2.a.3.8. O.C. 2/1 and 2/2 Field Ambs. called. A.D.M.S., visited D.D.M.S., XVIII Corps. Routine duties.	
	26.		A.D.M.S., and D.D.M.S., XVIII Corps ~~A.D.A.D.M.S.~~ visited proposed Dressing Station Right Sector D.A.D.M.S., called on O.C. 23 Sanitary Section and visited MARTEVILLE and 2/1 Field Amb., A/O.C. 2/2 and A/O.C. 2/3 Field Ambs called. D.A.D.M.S., called at XVIII Corps. Routine duties.	
	27.		A.D.M.S., called on D.D.M.S., A.D.M.S., visited Left Sector. D.A.D.M.S., in company with O.C. 23 Sanitary Section inspected Sanitary conditions of MARTEVILLE and VILLEVEQUE. D.A.D.M.S., inspected progress of work at Dressing Station MARTEVILLE. O.C. 2/3 Fd.Amb., and A/O.C. 2/2 Fd.Amb., called. Routine duties.	

D. D. & L., London, E.C.
(A7883) Wt. W809/M1672 350,000 4/17 Sch. 52a Forms/C/2118/14

Army Form C. 2118.

Instructions regarding War Diaries and Intelligence Summaries are contained in F. S. Regs., Part II. and the Staff Manual respectively. Title pages will be prepared in manuscript.

WAR DIARY
or
INTELLIGENCE SUMMARY.
(Erase heading not required.)

Place	Date	Hour	Summary of Events and Information	Remarks and references to Appendices
AUROIR.	Feb. 28.		A.D.M.S., visited 2/1 and 2/3 Field Ambulances, and also inspected equipment of the 1/9 Bn. R.Scots. "Stand to" order received. D.A.D.M.S., visited 2/1, 2/2, and 2/3 Field Ambulances re preparations for an attack. A.D.M.S., visited D.D.M.S., XVIII Corps. Routine duties. A/O.C. 2/1 Field Amb., called.	
28/2/18.			Colonel A.M.S. A.D.M.S., 61 Division.	

A5834 Wt. W4973/M687 750,000 8/16 D. D. & L. Ltd. Forms/C.2118/13.

SECRET

Appendix I

COPY NO: 21

61 DIVISION R.A.M.C., ORDER NO: 48
by
Lieut-Colonel G.Mackie. D.S.O., R.A.M.C.(T)
acting A.D.M.S. 61 Division

Reference 61 Division Orders Nos: 155 and 157. February 20th '18

Maps Sheet 62C. S.E.)
62B. S.W.)
66C. N.W.) 1/20,000.
66D. N.E.)

1. (a) The XVIII Corps front will be held by three Divisions in the line, 36th Division on the right, 30th Division in the centre, and 61 Division on the left. The boundaries of the Division will run as follows.

(b) Southern boundary. (with 30th Division)
S.11.d.6.2. - S.10.d.5.8. - S.9.c.8.4. - S.8.d.7.0. - X.23.b.6.2. X.15.c.Central - thence to VAUX and GERMAINE (both inclusive to 61 Division, but allowing accomodation for one battalion 30th Division in VAUX)

(c) Northern boundary. (with Dismounted Divisions)
M.16.c.90.15. - M.21.b.75.80 - M.15.c.50.10 - M.20.b.60.65 - (ESSLING TRENCH exclusive to 61st Division) - R.24.c.2.4. (trench M.20.b.60.65. - R.24.c.10.15 - inclusive to 61 Division) direct to R.27.c.35.40, and thence along river OMIGNON as at present.

2. The Divisional front will be held with three Brigades in the line, and consequent upon the alteration in the Divisional area and the Divisional front, the following alterations in the Medical arrangements will take place.

3. LEFT SECTOR
(a) The portion of line handed over to the Dismounted Divisions will come under the administrative control of the A.D.M.S., Dismounted Divisions at 6 a.m. February 21st.

(b) The 2/1 South Mid. Field Amb., will prepare to hand over the A.D.S., at MAISSEMY EAST and Medical Posts in this area, to the 7th Canadian Cavalry Field Ambulance.

(c) The Railway post, systems of evacuation, and the MAISSEMY - VILLECHOLLES Road will be used mutually for the present, by both units.

(d) The Evacuation route - FRESNOY - MAISON DE GARDE - MARTEVILLE will be developed as an alternative route.

4. RIGHT SECTOR.
(a) The relief of part of the Divisional front on the right, will be completed by 10 a.m. February 23rd.

(b) The 2/2 South Mid. Field Amb., will vacate their present headquarters at VAUX by 12 noon on the 22nd instant, and will be accomodated with the 2/3 South Mid. Field Amb., at E.17.a.2.8 until further orders.

(c) The 2/2 South Mid. Field Amb., will hand over their headquarters and Medical Posts at ETREILLERS - SAVY and BOIS DE SAVY to the 98th Field Ambulance on the night 22/23rd February. Details of relief to be arranged between the Os.C. concerned.

(d) The Evacuation Route from the A.D.S., (HOLNON WOOD) will remain as before.

5. Completion of reliefs will be notified to this office.

continued.

Continued.

6. Receipts will be obtained for all Stores etc handed over, and a copy sent to this office.

7. The following please acknowledge :-

2/1, 2/2, 2/3 Field Ambulances.
A.D.M.S., 30 Division.
A.D.M.S., Dismounted Divisions.

Issued at 10.30 p.m.

Captain
D.A.D.M.S., for A.D.M.S.
61 Division.

Distribution:-

1-3. Os.C. 2/1, 2/2, 2/3 Field Ambulances.
4-6. 182,183,184 Infantry Bdes for information.
7. 61 Division "G" -do-
8. 61 Division "Q" -do-
9. D.D.M.S., Cavalry Corps. -do-
10. D.D.M.S., XVIII Corps. -do-
11. A.D.M.S., Dismounted Division -do-
12. A.D.M.S., 30th Division. -do-
13. D.M.S., Fifth Army. -do-
14. O.C. 1/5 D.C.L.I., -do-
15. C.R.A., -do-
16. C.R.E., -do-
17. 61 Division Train. -do-
18. 31 M.A.C., -do-
19. A.P.M., -do-
20. Area Commandant. VAUX. -do-
21-22. War Diary.
23-24. Spare.
25. File.

CONFIDENTIAL

26

Medical

Vol 23

WAR DIARY

OF

A. D. M. S. 61 DIVISION

From :- March 1st To March 31st 1918

140/2845

VOLUME - 23

March
1918

Army Form C. 2118.

Instructions regarding War Diaries and Intelligence Summaries are contained in F. S. Regs., Part II. and the Staff Manual respectively. Title pages will be prepared in manuscript.

WAR DIARY
or
INTELLIGENCE SUMMARY.
(Erase heading not required.)

Place	Date	Hour	Summary of Events and Information	Remarks and references to Appendices
AUROIR. Sheet 66D.	March 1st		A.D.M.S., visited Advanced Dressing Station MARTEVILLE, and proposed site for A.D.S., at VAUX D.A.D.M.S., visited 2/3rd Field Ambulance. A/O.C. 2/2 and A/O.C. 2/1 Field Ambulances called. O.C. 31 M.A.C., called. Positions of Field Ambulances :- 2/1 Field Amb., LANCHY. 2/2 Field Amb., FORESTE. 2/3 Field Amb., GERMAINE. Routine duties.	
	2nd		D.A.D.M.S., visited R.A.Ps. at FRESNOY and the QUARRY, A.D.S.,(HOLNON WOOD) W.W.C.P., and A.D.S., MARTEVILLE. A.D.M.S., inspected progress of work at A.D.S., at VAUX. A/O.C. 2/1 Field Ambulance called. Routine duties.	
	3rd		A.D.M.S., visited A.D.S., (HOLNON WOOD) and R.A.P., (SELENCY) Captain RENNIE. Major WATERHOUSE. and O.C. 2/3 Field Ambulance called. Captain A.L.E.F.COLEMAN. R.A.M.C., T.C., reported for duty from 19th Division and was posted to 2/3 Field Ambulance. Routine duties.	
	4th.		D.A.D.M.S., visited Baths at UGNY. A.D.M.S., 20th Division called and visited forward area, accompanied by A.D.M.S., 61 Division. Major WATERHOUSE and Captain WOOD called. Routine duties.	
	5th		D.A.D.M.S., inspected progress of work at A.D.Ss (MARTEVILLE and VAUX) also visited Divisional Theatre at BEAUVOIS re its use as a Walking Wounded Dressing Station. A.D.M.S., visited 2/3 Field Ambulance; No: 41 C.C.S., and Advanced Gas Centre 36th Division. Routine duties.	
	6th		A.D.M.S., visited A.D.M.S., 30th Division. D.A.D.M.S., visited 2/2, 2/1 and 2/3 Field Ambs., also 1/8 Argyll & Sutherland Highlanders. A.D.M.S., visited forward posts. Captain J.T.BOYLE. R.A.M.C., T.C., reported from the Base and posted to 2/1 Fd.Amb., Routine duties.	

A5834 Wt. W4973/M687 750,000 8/16 D. D. & L. Ltd. Forms/C.2118/13.

Army Form C. 2118.

Instructions regarding War Diaries and Intelligence Summaries are contained in F. S. Regs., Part II. and the Staff Manual respectively. Title pages will be prepared in manuscript.

WAR DIARY
or
INTELLIGENCE SUMMARY.

(Erase heading not required.)

Place	Date	Hour	Summary of Events and Information	Remarks and references to Appendices
AUROIR.	Mar. 7.		A.D.M.S., visited Headquarters. Brigades. also 2/3 and 2/1 Field Ambulances. Routine duties.	
	8.		A.D.M.S., inspected Baths at UGNY. D.A.D.M.S., visited BEAUVOIS and UGNY, also inspected A.D.Ss under construction at MARTEVILLE and VAUX. Routine duties.	
	9.		D.A.D.M.S., inspected progress of work at A.D.Ss. Inspected Sanitation of MARTEVILLE and visited Baths at UGNY. Routine duties.	
	10.		A.D.M.S., visited forward area. A.D.M.S., 20th Division called. D.A.D.M.S., inspected billets of battalion at BEAUVOIS and visited 2/1 Field Amb., Routine duties.	
	11.		A.D.M.S., attended D.D.M.S., Conference. D.D.M.S., accompanied by A.D.M.S., inspected progress of A.D.Ss and forward area. Routine duties.	
	12		D.A.D.M.S., accompanied by D.A.D.M.S., 20th Division visited all Medical Posts in the forward area. Routine duties.	
	13.		D.A.D.M.S., visited 2/1, 2/2, & 2/3 Field Ambulances. A.D.M.S., attended Quartermaster's Conference. Routine duties.	
	14.		D.D.M.S. XVIII Corps accompanied by A.D.M.S., visited forward area. A.D.M.S., visited 2/1 Field Amb., Routine duties.	
	15.		D.A.D.M.S., visited 2/1 and 2/3 Field Ambs., Inspected sanitation of battalion at GERMAINE. Captain BISHOP. AND CAPTAIN RENNIE. R.A.M.C., called. Routine duties.	

A5834 Wt. W4973/M687 750,000 8/16 D. D. & L. Ltd. Forms/C.2118/13.

Army Form C. 2118.

Instructions regarding War Diaries and Intelligence Summaries are contained in F. S. Regs., Part II. and the Staff Manual respectively. Title pages will be prepared in manuscript.

WAR DIARY
or
INTELLIGENCE SUMMARY.
(Erase heading not required.)

Place	Date	Hour	Summary of Events and Information	Remarks and references to Appendices
AURIOR.	Mar 16.		Routine duties.	Int.
	17.		D.A.D.M.S., inspected Sanitary conditions of Battalion at GERMAINE. Routine duties.	Int.
	18.		D.M.S., Fifth Army called. A.D.M.S., attended G.O.Cs., conference. D.A.D.M.S., visited 55 C.C.S., re recent gassed cases. Routine duties.	Int.
	19.		Os.C., Field Ambulances, also D.G.O., and O.C., Baths attended A.D.M.S., conference re Gas attack. D.A.D.M.S., visited Quartermasters Stores of 182 Infantry Brigade re Blankets. Routine duties.	Int.
	20.		A.D.M.S., visited R.A.Ps. Os.C., Field Ambulances attended A.D.M.S., conference. The Consulting Physician Fifth Army (Colonel NIXON) called and, accompanied by the D.A.D.M.S., visited the Advanced Gas Centre (GERMAINE) and the Gas treatment centres established in connection with the Baths. Routine duties.	Int.
	21.	4-20am	Order to Man Battle Stations received 4-20a.m. Os.C., Field Ambulances notified. Heavy barrage put down by both sides. Some Mustard Gas shelling by the enemy. D.A.D.M.S., visited:- (1) A.D.S., MARTEVILLE, working well - a few casualties coming through, evacuation proceeding easily. (2) H.Q., 2/1 Field Ambulance (LANCHY) local casualties being treated and evacuated to Divisional Rest Station GERMAINE (2/3 Field Ambulance. (3) Visited Walking Wounded Dressing station VAUX (THE THEATRE) - few walking wounded passing through - evacuation satisfactory. (4) VAUX A.D.S., not completed and so not working. (5) Divisional Rest Station GERMAINE acting as A.D.S., for Right Sector and Advanced Gas Centre - not many casualties, evacuation satisfactory.	Int.

A5834 Wt. W4973/M687 750,000 8/16 D. D. & L. Ltd. Forms/C.2118/13.

Army Form C. 2118.

Instructions regarding War Diaries and Intelligence Summaries are contained in F. S. Regs., Part II. and the Staff Manual respectively. Title pages will be prepared in manuscript.

WAR DIARY
or
INTELLIGENCE SUMMARY.
(Erase heading not required.)

Place	Date	Hour	Summary of Events and Information	Remarks and references to Appendices
AURIOR	Mar 21.	(Continued)		
			(6) A.D.S., FORESTE 2/2 Field Ambulance ready for cases, will now act in place of Divisional Rest Station at GERMAINE. M.A.C., Cars arrived and in circuit, ditto Motor Lorries. Railway Train circuits for Walking wounded working satisfactorily.	
		Noon	Walking Wounded Collecting Post (Near MAISON DE GARDE) abandoned owing to heavy shell fire. Os.C., 2/1., 2/2., 2/3., Field Ambulances called. Captain G.S.CLANCY R.A.M.C., reported "Missing". A.D.M.S., visited H.Q., 2/1., 2/2., and 2/3., Field Ambulances.	
		10pm.	D.A.D.M.S., again visited Field Ambulance H.Q., A.D.Ss., and Medical Posts and found them clear.	
	Mar 22.		Fighting very severe.A.D.S.,MARTEVILLE evacuated and also W.W.C.P.,VAUX. A.D.S.,FORESTE now dealing with Walking Wounded. A.D.S. formed at LANCHY by 2/1 F.Ambce - H.QM of which has moved to "Y" and Transport to BETHENCOURT. D.H.Q. moved to RETHONVILLERS and Advanced D.H.Q. to MATIGNY. 2/3 F.Ambce ordered to close and move to RETHONVILLERS. Total Casualties evacuated up to 6 am this morning 23 Officers 557 Other Ranks. Captain G.S.CLANCY R.A.M.C., now reported as wounded and evacuated, not missing.	

Locations.	Headqrs.	A.D.S.,	Horse Transport.	ADS falling back on:
2/1 Fd Amb.	"Y"	LANCHY.	BETHENCOURT.	"Y"
2/2 Fd Amb.	MATIGNY.	FORESTE.	VOYENNES.	MATIGNY.
2/3 Fd Amb.	MARCHE ALLOUARDS.	-	MARCHE ALLOUARDS.	-
A.D.M.S.,	Advance: MATIGNY.			
	Rear. RETHONVILLERS.			

(Map references for all above is- Sheet 66D. 1/40,000.)

XVIII Corps H.Q moved from HAM to NESLE.

Army Form C. 2118.

Instructions regarding War Diaries and Intelligence Summaries are contained in F. S. Regs., Part II, and the Staff Manual respectively. Title pages will be prepared in manuscript.

WAR DIARY
or
INTELLIGENCE SUMMARY.
(Erase heading not required.)

Place	Date	Hour	Summary of Events and Information	Remarks and references to Appendices
RETHONVILLERS Map Sheet AMIENS 17.	Mar 23.		The Division has continued to withdraw. Locations of Headquarters Field Ambulances :- 2/1 Field Ambulance - CREMERY. 2/2 Field Ambulance - GRUNY 2/3 Field Ambulance - Unchanged. A.D.M.S., - Unchanged. Advanced Divisional Headquarters returned to RETHONVILLERS. O.C. 2/1 Field Amb., called at 10.15 a.m. EXTRACT of arrangements issued to Field Ambulances with regard to the collection and evacuation of sick and wounded :- 2/1 Field Ambulance - 183 Infantry Brigade in MANINCOURT Area. 2/2 Field Ambulance - 184 Infantry Brigade in HERLY Area. 2/3 Field Ambulance - 182 Infantry Brigade in HOMBLEUX Area. In case the 182 Brigade is called upon for work in the line, the 2/3 Field Ambulance will do the forward work. All cases of sick and wounded will be sent to ROYE.	
		Noon	Forward A.D.Ss. withdrawn and established at :- CREMERY 2/1 Field Ambulance. GRUNY. 2/2 Field Ambulance. HOMBLEUX. 2/3 Field Ambulance.	
		6p.m.	D.A.D.M.S. visited all the three Field Ambulances.	
		11p.m.	D.A.D.M.S. Visited A.D.S. HOMBLEUX - evacuation proceeding well, not many casualties coming through.	
	24		A.D.S. HOMBLEUX (2/3 Fd.Amb.) evacuated during the night and established at CRESSY. D.A.D.M.S. visited M.O. i/c French troops at BIARRE and made arrangements for their sick and wounded to be evacuated through the 2/3 Field Ambulance.	
		6 pm	2/1 Field Ambulance moving to ROUVROY (leaving a Medical Post at CREMERY) 2/2 Field Ambulance moving to LE QUESNOY (leaving a Medical Post at GRUNY) 2/3 Field Ambulance no change, but sending transportto FRANSART. Divisional Headquarters moving to PARVILLERS. Evacuation of casualties progressing satisfactorily.	
PARVILLERS Map Sheet AMIENS 17	25		Remains of Division retiring on RETHONVILLERS - CRESSY line. 2/1 Field Ambulance moving to BEAUFORT. 2/2 Field Ambulance moving to QUESNEL 2/3 Field Ambulance moving to WARVILLERS (Transport only)	

Army Form C. 2118.

Instructions regarding War Diaries and Intelligence Summaries are contained in F. S. Regs., Part II. and the Staff Manual respectively. Title pages will be prepared in manuscript.

WAR DIARY
or
INTELLIGENCE SUMMARY.
(Erase heading not required.)

Place	Date	Hour	Summary of Events and Information	Remarks and references to Appendices
PARVILLERS	Mar 25 contd		Medical Post at CREMERY handed over to the French. D.A.D.M.S. visited D.D.M.S., XVIII Corps A.D.M.S., 20 Division 2/3 Field Ambulance and 2/1 Field Ambulance. D.D.M.S. called. Divisional Headquarters closed at 10 p.m. and moved to BEAUCOURT.	
BEAUCOURT Map Sheet AMIENS 17	26		2/1 Field Ambulance moved to MEZIERES (Parked) 2/2 Field Ambulance moved to VILLERS aux ERABLES (Parked) 2/3 Field Ambulance moved to FRESNOY-en-CHAUSSEE. All forward posts closed.	
	27		2/2 Field Ambulance establishing an A.D.S. at VILLERS-aux-ERABLES for evacuation of 61 Division casualties, and also 133 French Division casualties. 61st Division is being relieved by 133 French Division. 2/1 Field Ambulance moving to COTTENCHY (Parked) 2/2 Field Ambulance moving to MOREUIL (Main Dressing Station) 2/3 Field Ambulance moving to MORISEL. (Parked)	
VILLERS BRETONNEUX Map Sheet AMIENS 17.	28		The Division embussed at midnight 27/28th for MARCELCAVE. Divisional Headquarters closed at BEAUCOURT-en-SANTERRE and opened at VILLERS BRETONNEUX.	
		2 am	A.D.M.S., and D.A.D.M.S., visited A.D.S., 134 Field Ambulance at VILLERS-BRETONNEUX and arranged for the evacuation of our sick and wounded pending the arrival of the 2/3 Field Ambulance. D.A.D.M.S., visited MARCELCAVE and made medical arrangements for casualties in the event of the Division attacking LA MOTTE.	
		Noon	2/3 Field Amb., sent up party to establish A.D.Ss at VILLERS BRETONNEUX and MARCELCAVE. Wounded being evacuated.	
		5.30 pm	Orders to evacuate VILLERS BRETONNEUX A.D.Ss cleared and A.D.S. established at GENTELLES Division Headquarters moved to BOVES. 2/1 Field Ambulance moved to HAILLES. 2/2 Field Ambulance closed M.D.S. at MOREUIL and moved to DURY (Parked) Transport to CLAIRY. 2/3 Field Ambulance established Headquarters and A.D.S. at GENTELLES and sent transport to BOVES.	
BOVES. Map Sheet AMIENS 17	29		2/1 Field Ambulance establishing a Main Dressing Station at BOVES, and transport sent to ST FUSCIEN. A.D.M.S., visited GENTELLES (A.D.S.) wounded being evacuated well.	
		11pm	D.A.D.M.S. visited A.D.S., everything clear. Locations of Ambulances unchanged. D.D.M.S., called.	

A5834 Wt. W4973/M687 750,000 8/16 D. D. & L. Ltd. Forms/C.2118/13.

Army Form C. 2118.

Instructions regarding War Diaries and Intelligence Summaries are contained in F. S. Regs., Part II. and the Staff Manual respectively. Title pages will be prepared in manuscript.

WAR DIARY
or
INTELLIGENCE SUMMARY.
(Erase heading not required.)

Place	Date	Hour	Summary of Events and Information	Remarks and references to Appendices
BOVES.	Mar 30.		Locations no change. D.D.M.S., called, also A.D.M.S. 2 Cavalry Division and A.D.M.S., 20th Div. A.D.M.S., visited forward posts.	
	31.		Locations no change. D.D.M.S., called and, accompanied by A.D.M.S. 61 Div. and A.D.M.S., 20th Div visited AMIENS re sites for Medical establishments. A.D.M.S. 18 Division called. This Division is without Field Ambulances; arranged to leave 2/1 Field Ambulance to run his Main Dressing Station at BOVES. A.D.M.S. 18th Division is arranging to relieve forward posts and A.D.S. at GENTELLES. Evacation proceeding smoothly.	

31/3/18.

C. H[illegible]
Colonel A.M.S.
A.D.M.S., 61 Division.

A5834 Wt. W4973/M687 750,000 8/16 D. D. & L. Ltd. Forms/C.2118/13.

CONFIDENTIAL

Medical

April 1918

Vol 24

140/2973

WAR DIARY

OF

A.D.M.S., 61 DIVISION

FROM:- April 1st 1918

TO:- April 30th 1918.

- - - - - -

VOLUME - 24.

Colonel A.M.S.
A.D.M.S., 61 Division.

Instructions regarding War Diaries and Intelligence Summaries are contained in F. S. Regs., Part II, and the Staff Manual respectively. Title pages will be prepared in manuscript.

WAR DIARY
or
INTELLIGENCE SUMMARY.
(Erase heading not required.)

Army Form C. 2118.

Place	Date	Hour	Summary of Events and Information	Remarks and references to Appendices
BOVES. Sheets AMIENS & DIEPPE 1/100,000.	April 1.		A.D.M.S., visited A.D.S., D.D.M.S. XVIII COrps and D.D.M.S. XIX Corps called. A.Ds.M.S. 14th and 18th Divisions called. Routine duties.	
PISSY. Sheet AMIENS 17.	2.		Infantry Brigades and associated Field Ambulances assembling at LONGEAU. Divisional Headquarters moved to PISSY. Routine duties.	
	3.		Brigades moving to new area. Locations :- A.D.M.S. PISSY. 2/1 Field Amb., AVELESGES. 2/2 Field Amb., FLOXICOURT. 2/3 Field Amb., St MAULVIS. Routine duties.	
	4.		A.D.M.S., sick in quarters. Lt.THORNHILL. MORC.USA. called. Routine duties.	
	5.		D.A.D.M.S., visited 2/2 Field Ambulance. Routine duties.	
	6.		D.A.D.M.S., visited 2/1 and 2/3 Field Ambulances. O.C. 2/1 Fd.Amb., called. Routine duties.	
	7.		Passed from the administration of the XVIII Corps to XIX Corps. Routine duties.	
	8.		Warning order to move on the 10th received. Routine duties.	
	9.		A.D.M.S., returned to duty. O.C. 2/1 Field Amb., called. A.D.M.S., visited 2/2 Field Amb. R.A.M.C., order No: 50 issued.	App. 1.

D. D. & L., London, E.C.
(B8S1) Wt. W809/M1672 350,000 4/17 Sch. 52a Forms/C/2118/14

Army Form C. 2118.

Instructions regarding War Diaries and Intelligence Summaries are contained in F. S. Regs., Part II, and the Staff Manual respectively. Title pages will be prepared in manuscript.

WAR DIARY
or
INTELLIGENCE SUMMARY.
(Erase heading not required.)

Place	Date	Hour	Summary of Events and Information	Remarks and references to Appendices
PISSY.	Apl 10		Division moving North, entraining at HANGEST and St ROCH (AMIENS). A.D.M.S. proceeded to new destination. D.A.D.M.S. remained and visited entraining centres.	WD
AIRE. (Ref Sheet HAZEBROUCK 5a)	11th		Division continuing to entrain. Field Ambulances entraining today. D.A.D.M.S. visited entraining stations and then proceeded to join Division at AIRE. Division proceeding into the line opposite St VENANT under administration of XIth Corps. (1st Army)	WD
AIRE.	12th		Heavy fighting. Fld Ambulances clearing wounded of their associated Brigades. (2/1 F.Amb- 184 Bde, 2/2 F.Amb-182 Bde, 2/3 F.Amb - 183 Bde). A.D.M.S. visited forward area. O.C.25 M.A.C. called. D.D.M.S. XIth Corps called.	WD
AIRE.	13th		Locations. A.D.M.S. AIRE. 2/1 F.Amb. H.Q., Transport Lines, and M.D.S. BERGUETTE. 2/2 F.Amb. H.Q., O.11.d.8.3. Transport Lines, BERGUETTE. W.W.D.S. GUARBECQUE. 2/3 F.Amb. H.Q., O.11.c.8.8. Transport Lines. BERGUETTE. A.D.S., P.5.c.1.8. (Canal Bank St VENANT.) O.C., 2/1 Field Ambulance called. A.D.M.S., visited Forward Posts and H.Q. XIth.Corps. D.D.M.S., XIth.Corps called and also O.C., 25 M.A.C.	
		6-0pm	2/2 Field Ambulance established H.Q., and W.W.D.S., at MOLINGHEM. GUARBECQUE is now a W.W.C.P. Evacuation progressing without any hitch.	WD
	14th		Evacuation of wounded quite satisfactory. A.D.M.S. visited A.D.Ss. and W.W.C.P.. Routine duties. Lieut J.C.THOMPSON. MORC. reported for duty from the Base and posted to 2/2 Field Amb., Capt. F.B.MACDONALD. RAMC. TC. -do- " " 2/1 Field Amb., Captain G.SCOTT WILLIAMSON. RAMC. TF. -do- " " 2/3 Field Amb., Captain S.R.GLEED. RAMC. TC. -do- " " 2/3 Field Amb.,	
	15.		A.D.M.S. visited 2/1, 2/2, 2/3 Field Ambs., Routine duties. Captain C.T.NEVE. RAMC. TC. reported for duty from Base, and posted to 2/1 Field Amb.,	WD
	16.		D.A.D.M.S., visited forward area. Evacuation of wounded satisfactory. Routine duties.	WD

D. D. & L., London, E.C. (A7883) Wt W809/M1672 350,000 4/17 Sch 52a Forms/C/2118/14

Instructions re[illegible] War Diaries and Intelligence Summaries are contained in F. S. Regs., Part II. and the Staff Manual respectively. Title pages will be prepared in manuscript.

WAR DIARY
or
INTELLIGENCE SUMMARY.
(Erase heading not required.)

Army Form C. 2118.

Place	Date	Hour	Summary of Events and Information	Remarks and references to Appendices
AIRE	April 17.		A.D.M.S. visited the forward area. Medical Posts clear. Routine duties.	
	18.		A.D.M.S. visited A.D.Ss. and D.A.D.M.S. accompanied A.A.Q.M.G. 61 Div. on tour of inspection (re food for patients) at W.W.C.P. and A.D.Ss. Very few casualties from the line. Routine duties. Captain J.R.RICHMOND RITCHIE. RAMC. TC. absorbed from 24 Entrenching Battalion and posted to 2/2 Field Amb.,	
	19.		A.D.M.S. visited A.D.Ss and W.W.C.P. and also attended D.D.M.S. XI Corps Conference. .Lieut A.S.BUGBEE. MORC. USA. reported for duty from the Base and posted to 2/3 Field Amb.,	
	20.		D.A.D.M.S. visited Transport Lines 182 and 184 Brigades (re Sanitation). A.D.M.S. visited 2/1, 2/2, 2/3 Field Ambs., Routine duties.	
	21.		Line quiet. Routine duties.	
	22.		D.A.D.M.S. visited Transport lines 183 Brigade re sanitation. Very few casualties from the line. Routine duties.	
	23.		Attack by the 2/5 Glosters - few casualties. A.D.M.S. visited A.D.Ss. evacuations progressing smoothly. D.A.D.M.S., visited D.D.M.S. XI Corps at 11 p.m. re salvage.	
	24.		Enemy counter attack this morning. D.A.D.M.S. visited A.D.Ss and W.W.C.P. and Headquarters 2/1,2/2,2/3 Field Ambs., Very few casualties to be cleared - all evacuations performed smoothly. Captain M.DALE WOOD. RAMC. TF. and Lieut BUTLER. RAMC.TC. reported for duty from Base and posted to 2/3 Field Amb.,	
	25.		D.D.M.S. XI Corps and D.M.S. First Army called. D.A.D.M.S. visited R.A.Ps - all were clear. A.D.M.S. visited 2/1, 2/2, 2/3 Field Ambulances. Lieut G.K.STONE. RAMC. SR. reported for duty from Base and was posted to 2/3 Field Amb., Routine duties.	

D. D. & L., London, E.C.
(A7883) Wt. W809/M1672 350,000 4/17 Sch. 52a Forms/C/2118/14

Army Form C. 2118.

Instructions regarding War Diaries and Intelligence Summaries are contained in F. S. Regs., Part II. and the Staff Manual respectively. Title pages will be prepared in manuscript.

WAR DIARY
or
INTELLIGENCE SUMMARY.
(Erase heading not required.)

Place	Date	Hour	Summary of Events and Information	Remarks and references to Appendices
AIRE.	Apl. 26.		D.A.D.M.S. inspected Transport Lines of 182 Brigade. Routine duties.	
	27.		D.A.D.M.S. visited R.A.Ps & Loading post centre sector. No cases coming through. Also visited 2/1 A.D.S. and W.W.D.S., very few cases. Routine duties.	
	28.		A.D.M.S. VISITED FORWARD AREA. D.A.D.M.S., inspected D.H.Q., and ST VENANT Asylum. Routine duties.	
	29.		D.A.D.M.S. inspected Transport Lines 184 Brigade, also visited A.D.Ss. M.D.S., and W.W.D.S., Captain R.L.RITCHIE. RAMC. reported for duty from 26 Amb.Train. and was posted to the 2/2 Fd. Ambulance. Captain J.E.J.ROCHE-KELLY RAMC. reported for duty from 2 Amb.Train. and was posted to 2/3 Fd. Ambulance. D.A.D.M.S., visited Headquarters 2/1 and 2/2 Field Ambulance. Routine duties.	
	30.		A.D.M.S., visited Advanced Gas Centre (2/1 Field Amb.,) D.A.D.M.S., visited A.D.S., M.D.S., and W.W.D.S., and Advanced Gas Centre. Routine duties.	
			30/4/18 Colonel A.M.S. A.D.M.S., 61 Division.	

D. D. & L., London, E.C.
(A7883) Wt W809/M1672 350,000 4/17 Sch. 52a Forms/C/2118/14

MEDICAL

C O N F I D E N T I A L

14

Vol 25

May 1918.

140/2943

WAR DIARY

OF

A.D.M.S., 61 DIVISION.

From:- MAY 1st 1918

To:- MAY 31st 1918.

- - - - - - - - - - -

VOLUME 25

C Hoskins

Colonel A.M.S.
A.D.M.S., 61 Division.

Army Form C. 2118.

Instructions regarding War Diaries and Intelligence Summaries are contained in F. S. Regs., Part II. and the Staff Manual respectively. Title pages will be prepared in manuscript.

WAR DIARY
or
INTELLIGENCE SUMMARY.
(Erase heading not required.)

Place	Date	Hour	Summary of Events and Information	Remarks and references to Appendices
AIRE. Map Sheet HAZEBROUCK 5a.	May. 1st.		DMDMS visited A.D.Ss, M.D.S., and W.W.D.S., and Car Loading Posts - the latter have been moved owing to heavy shelling. A.D.M.S., visited 183 Brigade Headquarters. Routine duties.	WdL
	2nd.		D.A.D.M.S., visited A.D.S., 2/1 Field Ambulance and inspected Transport lines of the 183 Bde. Routine duties.	WdL
	3rd.		D.A.D.M.S., inspected billets, Transport Lines etc of ~~DxMxQx~~ D.A.C., 306 and 307 Bdes R.F.A., Routine duties.	WdL
	4th.		D.A.D.M.S., visited A.D.S., of 2/3 Field Ambulance and R.A.P., Left and Centre Sub-sectors, also inspected Transport lines of 183 Brigade. Routine duties.	WdL
	5th		D.A.D.M.S., Sanitary inspection of D.H.Q., ~~A.D.M.S., visited Right sub-sector.~~ Routine duties.	WdL
	6th		A.D.M.S., accompanied by O.C. 2/3 Field Ambulance visited Left sub-sector of Line. D.A.D.M.S., visited M.D.S., and W.W.D.S., Routine duties.	WdL
	7th.		A.D.M.S., held Conference of Os.C . Field Ambulances. D.D.M.S., XI Corps called. D.A.D.M.S., began inspection of Water Carts. Routine duties.	WdL
	8th.		A.D.M.S., and A.A.&.Q.M.G., visited XI Corps. D.A.D.M.S., continued inspection of Water Carts; also inspected 184 Brigade School. Routine duties.	WdL

D. D. & L., London, E.C.
(A7883) Wt W809/M1672 350,000 4/17 Sch. 52a Forms/C/2118/14

Army Form C. 2118.

Instructions regarding War Diaries and Intelligence Summaries are contained in F. S. Regs., Part II. and the Staff Manual respectively. Title pages will be prepared in manuscript.

WAR DIARY
or
INTELLIGENCE SUMMARY.
(Erase heading not required.)

Place	Date	Hour	Summary of Events and Information	Remarks and references to Appendices
AIRE.	May. 9th.		D.A.D.M.S., continued inspection of Water Carts. A.D.M.S., held conference of Os.C., Field Ambulances. Routine Duties.	WH
	10th		D.A.D.M.S., continued inspection of water carts, and inspected Sanitation of A.D.S., (2/1 Fd. Amb.,) Routine duties.	WL
	11th		D.A.D.M.S., continued inspection of Water Carts. A.D.M.S., visited D.R.S., O.C. 52 Sanitary Section called. Routine duties.	WL
	12th.		A.D.M.S., visited Forward Area. D.A.D.M.S., Sanitary inspected D.H.Q., and visited MAZINGHEM re outbreak of Measles among civilian population. Routine Duties.	WL
	13th.		D.M.S., First Army., and D.D.M.S., XIth.Corps., accompanied by A.D.M.S., visited A.D.Ss - M.D.S., - W.W.D.S., - and D.R.S. Routine Duties.	WL
	14th.		A.D.M.S., visited XIth.Corps Rest Station. Routine Duties.	WL
	15th.		D.A.D.M.S., inspected sanitation of portion of Asylum (ST VENANT) occupied by battalions of 183 Brigade., also visited M.D.S., and inspected water carts of Divisional Train. Routine Duties.	WL
	16th.		A.D.M.S., visited the three Field Ambulances. Routine Duties.	WL
	17th.		A.D.M.S., attended XIth.Corps Conference. Severe bombing raid last night - no casualties to D.H.Q. O.C., 2/1., 2/2., and 2/3 Field Ambulances called. Routine Duties.	WL

D. D. & L., London, E.C.
(A7883) Wt. W809/M1672 350,000 4/17 Sch. 52a Forms/C/2118/14

Army Form C. 2118.

Instructions regarding War Diaries and Intelligence Summaries are contained in F. S. Regs., Part II. and the Staff Manual respectively. Title pages will be prepared in manuscript.

WAR DIARY
or
INTELLIGENCE SUMMARY.
(Erase heading not required.)

Place	Date	Hour	Summary of Events and Information	Remarks and references to Appendices
LAMBRES. Sheet 36A	May 18.		D.H.Q., closed at AIRE at 4 p.m. and reopened at LAMBRES at the same hour. A.D.M.S., accompanied by O.C. 2/3 Field Amb., visited 183 Brigade Sector and inspected cookhouses at the Asylum ST VENANT. Routine duties.	WH
	19.		A.D.M.S., and D.A.D.M.S., accompanied by Staff Captains 183 and 184. Brigades inspected ASYLUM D.A.D.M.S., visited D.D.M.S., XI Corps. Routine duties.	WH
	20.		D.A.D.M.S., visited O.C. 66 Sanitary Section. Sanitary Inspection of Divisional Train. Visited 184 (Adv) Bde.H.Q., The A.D.M.S., had a sanitary inspection of the 184 Bde.Transport lines. Routine duties.	WH
	21.		D.A.D.M.S., and Staff Captain 183 Bde. visited ASYLUM. ST VENANT. A.D.S., (2/3 Fd.Amb.) 183 Bde Transport lines and R.A.P. (Carvin Farm) Routine duties.	WH
	22.		Sanitary Inspection of LA HERRIERE and HAMET Billet. A.D.M.S., visited 183 Bde.Sector. Routine duties.	WH
	23.		D.D.M.S., XI Corps accompanied by A.D.M.S., and D.A.D.M.S., inspected LA MIQUELLERIE. Routine duties.	WH
	24		A.D.M.S., visited forward area. D.A.D.M.S., inspected 61 Mob.Vet.Sec. Routine duties.	WH
	25.		A.D.M.S., inspected 2/3 Fd.Amb., and 61 M.G.C., D.A.D.M.S., inspected cookhouses 183 Bde. Transport lines. Routine duties. D.A.D.M.S., visited O.C. 66 San.Sec. and 182 and 184 Bdes.	WH
	26.		A.D.M.S., visited 183 Bde.H.Q., and inspected transport lines of 1/5 D.C.L.I., Visited detraining centre for new battalions arriving to join the Division. D.A.D.M.S., inspected Transport lines and Headquarters of 306 Bde R.F.A., Routine duties.	WH

D. D. & L., London, E.C. Sch. 52a. Forms/C/2118/14

Instructions regarding War Diaries and Intelligence Summaries are contained in F. S. Regs., Part II, and the Staff Manual respectively. Title pages will be prepared in manuscript.

WAR DIARY
or
INTELLIGENCE SUMMARY.
(*Erase heading not required.*)

Army Form C. 2118.

Place	Date	Hour	Summary of Events and Information	Remarks and references to Appendices
	May. 27.		A.D.M.S., visited Medical officers of new battalions, also LA MIQUELLERIE and LA PIERRIERE. D.A.D.M.S., inspected 61 D.A.C., Routine duties.	WHL
	28.		A.D.M.S., attended XI Corps conference. D.A.D.M.S., inspected 307 Bde R.F.A., Routine duties.	WHL
	29.		A.D.M.S., visited 182 Brigade Sector of the line. D.A.D.M.S., inspected the sanitary condition of the ASYLUM. ST VENANT, visited reserve A.D.S., BUSNES; inspected the sanitation of 282 Army Bde Field Artillery and called on O.C. 66 Sanitary Section. Routine duties.	WHL
	30.		A.D.M.S., visited D.R.S., D.A.D.M.S., proceeded on 14 days special leave of absence to ENGLAND. Routine duties. Captain E.F.O'CONNOR. RAMC. reported to A.D.M.S., office for temporary duty as acting D.A.D.M.S.,	EFOC
	31.		A.D.M.S., and A/D.A.D.M.S., visited 251 Employment Company at CRECQUES AND CLETY and held a Medical Board. Also reconnoitred FAUQUEMBERGUES Area with a view to selecting alternative sites for Dressing Stations etc. Routine duties.	EFOC

[signature]
Colonel A.M.S.
A.D.M.S., 61 Division.

D. D. & L., London, E.C.
(A7883) Wt. W809/M1672 350,000 4/17 Sch. 52a Forms/C/2118/14

CONFIDENTIAL

MEDICAL

16

I

Vol 26

140/3092.

June 1918.

W A R   D I A R Y

OF

A.D.M.S., 61 DIVISION.

FROM:- June 1st 1918

TO:- June 30th 1918.

V O L U M E 27.

[signature]

Colonel A.M.S.,
A.D.M.S., 61 Division.

Army Form C. 2118.

Instructions regarding War Diaries and Intelligence Summaries are contained in F. S. Regs., Part II. and the Staff Manual respectively. Title pages will be prepared in manuscript.

WAR DIARY
or
INTELLIGENCE SUMMARY.
(Erase heading not required.)

Place	Date	Hour	Summary of Events and Information	Remarks and references to Appendices
LAMBRES. Sheet 36A.	June 1st.		A.D.M.S., visited Field Ambulance commanders and proceeded to ABBEVILLE to hold a Medical Board on details of the 251 Employment Company. A/D.A.D.M.S., inspected sanitation of D.H.Q., troops. Routine duties.	
	2nd.		A.D.M.S., visited A.D.S., Left Sector and made a sanitary inspection of the Asylum St VENANT. Routine duties.	
	3rd		A.D.M.S., inspected the quarters of the 1/9 Northumberland Fusiliers at HAM EN ARTOIS and visited Sanitary Section. Routine duties.	
	4th.		O.C. 76 Sanitary Section called. A.D.M.S., visited Divisional Skin Depot. Routine duties.	
	5th.		A.D.M.S., visited Main Dressing Station and Advanced Dressing Stations and Walking Wounded Dressing Station. Routine duties.	
	6th.		A.D.M.S., visited LINGHEM, CRECQUES and MARTHES in search of a new site for the Div.Rest Stn. Routine duties.	
	7th.		A.D.M.S., visited battalions billeted in GUARBECQUE and LA MICQUELLERIE. Routine duties.	
	8th.		A.D.M.S., attended Conference held by the D.G.M.S., at No: 6 Canddian C.C.S., and visited 9th Inniskilling Fusiliers and 5th R.Irish Fusiliers. Routine duties.	
	9th.		A.D.M.S., reconnoitred back areas. A.D.M.S., went for an aeroplane flight in order to see Red Crosses on Hospitals; Ammunition Dumps etc. Routine duties. A/D.A.D.M.S.. INSPECTED sanitaion of D.H.Q., troops.	
	10th.		A.D.M.S., visited R.A.Ps. ROBECQ Sector and A.D.S., and M.D.S., Routine duties.	

D. D. & L., London, E.C.
(A7883) Wt. W809/M1672 350,000 4/17 Sch. 52a Forms/C/2118/14

Army Form C. 2118.

Instructions regarding War Diaries and Intelligence Summaries are contained in F. S. Regs., Part II. and the Staff Manual respectively. Title pages will be prepared in manuscript.

WAR DIARY
or
INTELLIGENCE SUMMARY.
(Erase heading not required.)

Place	Date	Hour	Summary of Events and Information	Remarks and references to Appendices
	JUNE ~~May.~~			
LAMBRES.	11th		A.D.M.S., visited forward area, ST FLORIS Sector and A.D.S., A.D.M.S., proceeded to ABBEVILLE to hold Medical examination on details of 251 Employment Coy. Routine duties.	[initials]
	12th.		A.D.M.S., visited D.A.C., and 184 Inf.Bde.Transport lines. Routine duties.	[initials]
	13th.		A.D.M.S., inspected Machine Gun Battalion and 2/6 Bn.R.Warwick Regt. He also visited the 251 Employment Coy at CLETY. Routine duties.	[initials]
	14th.		A.D.M.S., visited Main Dressing Station and Advanced Dressing Station; and called to see O.C. 66 Sanitary Section. A.D.M.S., also visited 2/4 Bn. Oxford & Bucks Light Inf. to investigate an outbreak of P.U.O. in that battalion. Also visited MARTHES to inspect Field Ambulance site. Captain E.F.O'CONNOR proceeded to rejoin the 2/1 S.Mid.Fd.Amb., Routine duties.	[initials]
	15th.		Instructions received that the 2/1 South Midland Field Ambulance would take over the Corps Rest Station, and Officers Rest Station from a Field Ambulance of the 5th Division on the 16th instant. The A.D.M.S., visited 2/1 S.M.F.Amb., at BERGUETTE in this connection. A.D.M.S., held a Conference of Os.C. Field Ambulances in the afternoon at which it was arranged that the 2/2 Field Ambulance should take over the LEFT Sector of the Divisional front, and the 2/3 S.M.F.Amb., the RIGHT Sector of the Divisional front. The 2/3rd S.M.F.A., would move their headquarters to the site previously occupied by the 2/1 S.M.F.Amb at BERGUETTE. All Medical Posts and Dressing Stations would remain unaltered. Arrangements were also made for the 2/2nd and 2/3rd S.M.F.Amb., to take over the medical and sanitary charge of all units previously attended by the 2/1 S.M.F.Amb., Captain McRAE. RAMC. att 9 Northumberland Fusiliers admitted to C.C.S., and Lieut. ~~Captain~~ J.C. THOMPSON. MORC. proceeded to the 9 North.Fus. for temporary duty. Routine duties.	[initials]
	16th		A.D.M.S. visited the A.D.S., of Right Divisional Sector and 2/2 Field Amb., Notification received that Major W.V.CORBETT. had been appointed DADMS XVIII Corps and that Major H.E.A.BOLDERO. is appointed D.A.D.M.S., 61 Division. Capt.A.F.L.SHIELDS reported from Hospital Routine duties.	[initials]

D. D. & L., London, E.C.
(A7883) Wt W809/M1672 350,000 4/17 Sch. 52a Forms/C/2118/14

Army Form C. 2118.

WAR DIARY
or
INTELLIGENCE SUMMARY.

(Erase heading not required.)

Instructions regarding War Diaries and Intelligence Summaries are contained in F. S. Regs., Part II. and the Staff Manual respectively. Title pages will be prepared in manuscript.

Place	Date	Hour	Summary of Events and Information	Remarks and references to Appendices
LAMBRES	June 17.		A.D.M.S., visited Divisional Reception Camp. Lieutenant (Temporary Major) H.E.A.BOLDERO. RAMC. reported from 10th Field Ambulance, 4th Division for duty as D.A.D.M.S., 61 Division. Routine duties. HB	
	18.		A.D.M.S., showed D.A.D.M.S., round all the forward medical posts, visiting R.A.Ps at P.24.d.8.8., P.17.b.2.3., P.11.a.8.1., P.5.c.8.5., and found all were in good order. These Posts now have a satisfactory amount of protective covering, and are as good as any in this district Routine duties. HB	1st sheet 36A 1/20,000
	19.		A.D.M.S., visited various units during the morning, and also saw Os.C. 2/2 and 2/3 Field Ambulances, about increased accommodation for retention of sick at their headquarters as there is a considerable amount of P.U.O. in the Division. HB	
	20.		Lieut H.C.THOMSON. MORC. USA. M.O.i/c 9 Northumberland Fusiliers admitted to hospital sick (P.U.O.) As the Division is extremely short of Medical officers namely:- Sick-6. Detached-6. Deficient-4. Captain BLAKELEY. 10th Canadian Field Amb., is borrowed from A.D.M.S., 3rd Division(Canadian) for temporary duty with the 2/2 Field Amb., HB	
	21.		A.D.M.S., saw the G.O.C. 61 Division about the P.U.O. cases and it was decided to keep some of these cases regimentally in cases where no detriment to the man would follow his retention. This form of P.U.O. should be given a name, for it is a definite and clear disease. All figures are therefore misleading as P.U.O. is used to diagnose more than one disease. I suggest a good name would be "T.D.FEVER" - the letters would represent three day fever. As far as the experience of this Division goes, the first cases were on June 6th. The cases are very similar and on these lines - Patient complains of pains in the back and limbs generally, frontal headaches, and many complain of a ticklish cough. On examination - the tongue is coated. The tonsils and pharynx are hyperaemic but there is no true Tonsillitis. In the early stages no signs in the chest and no expectoration. Herpes Labialis is not uncommon. Slight photophobia. The onset is very sudden. A patient can sometimes say the hour at which it started. Temperature rises rapidly 101°-104° and falls to normal on 3rd or 4th days. Malaise continues for a day or two and patient makes uninterrupted recovery and is usually fit for duty on 8th to 9th day. so far no sequelae and very few relapses.	

D. D. & L., London, E.C. (A8004) Wt. W1771/M2031 750,000 5/17 Sch. 52 Forms/C2118/14

Instructions regarding War Diaries and Intelligence Summaries are contained in F. S. Regs., Part II. and the Staff Manual respectively. Title pages will be prepared in manuscript.

WAR DIARY
or
INTELLIGENCE SUMMARY.
(Erase heading not required.)

Army Form C. 2118.

Place	Date	Hour	Summary of Events and Information	Remarks and references to Appendices
LAMBRES.	June 21.		CONTINUED. There are a few relapses reported, but it is quite possible that such patients are really Trench Fever cases. Incubation period, I think, will be proved to be 3 or 4 days. I am convinced it is not due to Lice and is a naso - pharyngeal infection. It is extremely infectious and I believe it will be proved that an immunity is developed after an attack. How long that immunity lasts I have no idea. We are keeping some cases in the Divisional area as there is a lot of this disease in the First Army area and men evacuated are lost; and cases do as well in comfortable billets.	JHB
	22.		To-day there are 883 P.U.O. cases being treated regimentally. The biggest figures are :- 2/7 Warwicks 380. 2/6 Warwicks.140. 306 Bde R.F.A., 120. 307 Bde R.F.A., 100. The first two regiments are in billets. It is noticed that the disease does not spread so quickly in Units in the line. Only 82 cases in the Division had to be sent to Field Ambs.,	JHB
	23.		712 P.U.O. cases regimentally detained. 2/7 Warwicks 310 and 2/6 Warwicks 130. Admissions to Field Ambulances - 85, so that a large number of cases are being saved to the Division. New Medical arrangements were produced to keep posts up to date.* No big changes. The front is very quiet.	JHB *A
	24.		Brigades are relieving to-day. The cases of P.U.O. that have been detained regimentally will remain in the resting Brigade area as shewn in orders in Appendix "B"	JHB B
	25.		It has been decided to collect together these regimentally detained P.U.O. cases, and a suitable place has been found just East of AIRE. Appendix "C" shows the arrangements that have been made.	JHB C
	26.		To-day the P.U.O. cases which are being detained in Infantry Units have been moved by lorries and Ambulance cars to the new P.U.O. Detention Camp (P.D.C.) - approximately 400 cases.	JHB

D. D. & L., London, E.C.
(A8001) Wt. W1771/M2031 750,000 5/17 Sch. 52 Forms/C2118/14

Instructions regarding War Diaries and Intelligence Summaries are contained in F. S. Regs., Part II. and the Staff Manual respectively. Title pages will be prepared in manuscript.

WAR DIARY
or
INTELLIGENCE SUMMARY.
(Erase heading not required.)

Army Form C. 2118.

Place	Date	Hour	Summary of Events and Information	Remarks and references to Appendices
LAMBRES.	June 27.		Total number of all ranks under treatment for P.U.O. in the Division is 1102. Distribution :- 1. In Medical Units - 165. 2. In P.D.C. 418. 3. In Units, mainly R.F.A., M.G.Bn. Pioneers etc 519.	
	28.		P.U.O. cases - 1. In Medical Units - 202. 2. In P.D.C., - 401. 3. In Units. - 555. Total 1158. The numbers on paper are increasing, but I do not believe the disease is spreading. The apparent increase is due to the facts - We now get correct returns and send very few cases to C.C.S., - only 13 to-day. Those sent to C.C.S., seldom return as the C.C.Ss are very full at present.	
	29.		P.U.O. cases - (1) In Medical Units 204 (2) In P.D.C. 372 (3) In units. 466 Total. 1042. to-day we have only evacuated 13 to C.C.S., The average time these cases are off duty is 7 days.	
	30.		P.U.O. Cases - (1) In Medical Units 198. (2) In P.D.C., 355 (3) In Units. 426 Total 979 Evacuated to C.C.S.- 15. So the month closes with a definite diminution of fresh cases and unless any hitherto unaffected units become ~~affected infective~~ infected, the numbers out of action will steadily decrease. All is being done that is possible to check the spread, but there is one link of the chain missing and that is that the civilians, who are ubiquitous are infected and I fear they are the means of keeping the infection present amongst the troops. The difficulty lies in the fact that they do not report sick. Colonel A.M.S. A.D.M.S., 61 Div.	

D. D. & L., London, E.C.
(A8004) Wt. W1771/M2031 750,000 5/17 Sch. 52 Forms/C2118/14

17

17

SECRET.

A.D.M.S. No: 913.

MEDICAL ARRANGEMENTS

The following are the Field Ambulance Posts for the evacuation of sick and wounded :-

Map Reference - Sheet 36A.

1. CAR LOADING POSTS.

	RIGHT SECTOR.	LEFT SECTOR.
	P.24.b.3.3.	P.5.c.1.9.
	P.17.c.0.2.	
	P.26.b.6.0.	

2. R.A.M.C. BEARER POSTS

	P.31.b.8.7.	
	P.17.c.0.5.	
	P.27.b.1.3.	P.5.c.1.9.
	P.15.a.0.5.	

3. ADVANCED DRESSING STATIONS.

	O.18.b.1.4.	P.2.c.6.1.

4. MAIN DRESSING STATION.

O.16.c.6.7. (BERGUETTE)

5. WALKING WOUNDED COLLECTING POST.

O.17.b.5.5. (GUARBECQUE)

6. WALKING WOUNDED DRESSING STATION.

O.13.b.9.6. (MOLINGHEM)

- -

H Boldero

Major.
for A.D.M.S., 61 Div.

D.H.Q.,
23/6/18.

SECRET. B A.D.M.S., No: 913. B

TEMPORARY MEDICAL ARRANGEMENTS ON RELIEF OF 184 Infantry Brigade by 182 Infantry Brigade.

1. (a) The 184 Infantry Brigade will be relieved by the 182 Infantry Brigade on the night 24th/25th June.
The 2/4 R.Berks. and 2/5 Gloucesters will be billeted on the 25th in LINGHEM.
The 2/4 Bn. Oxford & Bucks L.I. will be billeted in LA PIERRIERE.

(b) The 2/6 R.WarwicksRegt and 2/7 Bn R.Warwick Regt. will take over the RIGHT Divisional Sector and the 2/8 Bn. Worcester Regt will remain at LA MIQUELLERRIE.

2. Sick of 2/6 Bn.R.Warwick Regt and 2/7 Bn.R.Warwick Regt - P.U.O. cases of the 2/6 Bn.R.Warwick Regt and 2/7 Bn. R.Warwick Regt. will be dealt with as follows :-

2/6 Bn.R.Warwick Regt. The O.C. 2/3rd South Midland Field Ambulance will detail a detachment of R.A.M.C. to attend to the sick left behind and will also provide Medical Comforts and generally supervise. The sick will be attended by the Medical officer from the Advanced Dressing Station, GUARBECQUE.

2/7 R.Warwick Regt. The O.C. 2/2nd South Midland Field Ambulance will detail a detachment of R.A.M.C., under a Medical officer to be detailed by the A.D.M.S. He will live temporarily in HAM and attend the sick. The O.C. 2/2nd South Midland Field Ambulance will generally supervise, and provide Medical Comforts etc.

3. Rations will be arranged by the Battalions concerned.

4. Disposal of sick. When fit for light duty they will be sent to the Transport lines of their units.

5. Cases of P.U.O. occuring in the line from the 2/6 Bn. R.Warwick Regt and the 2/7 Bn.R.Warwick Regt will be sent to GUARBECQUE and HAM-on-ARTOIS, unless seriously ill.

[signature]

Colonel, A.M.S.
A.D.M.S. 61 Division.

24/6/18.

Distribution:-
O.C. 2/2 Field Amb.
O.C. 2/3 Field Amb.
182 Inf. Bde. (for information)
184 Inf. Bde. -do-
61st Division "Q" -do-
O.C. 2/1 Field Amb. -do-
M.O. i/c 2/6 Bn.R.Warwicks. -do-
M.O. i/c 2/7 Bn.R.Warwicks. -do-
M.O. i/c 2/8 Bn.Worcesters. -do-

SECRET. A.D.M.S., No: 913/A.

Reference this office No: 913 of the 24th instant. Please amend para. 1 (b) to read as follows :-

"The 2/8 Bn. Worcester Regt and 2/7 Bn.R.Warwick Regt "will take over the RIGHT Divisional sector, and the "2/6 Bn.R.Warwick Regt will be at LA MIQUELLERIE."

The Medical Arrangements will therefore be amended to the following:-

Any sick of the 2/8 Bn. Worcester Regt. left in LA MIQUELLERIE, will be looked after by the Medical officer i/c 2/6 Bn.R.Warwickshire Regt.

Suitable sick of the 2/8 Bn.Worcester Regt, while in the line will go to HAM-EN-ARTOIS and will be looked after under the arrangements laid down in the last part of para 2 of the above quoted letter.

H Bolders
Major.
for A.D.M.S. 61 Div.

24/6/18.

Copies to all recipients of No: 913.

C

A.D.M.S., No: 913

C

TEMPORARY MEDICAL ARRANGEMENTS IN CONNECTION WITH 61 DIVISION LETTER No: A.135

1. Cases of P.U.O. (Three day fever) in Infantry Units will be accommodated in the Aerodrome hangars near TREIZENNE after 2 p.m. on the 26th instant.

2. The O.C. 2/2nd South Midland Field Ambulance will detail a Medical officer and a detachment of R.A.M.C. to attend to the patients, and also provide Medical comforts.

3. The blanket dump at FERGUETTE will be moved to the hangars on the morning of the 26th instant, by the O.C. 2/3rd South Midland Field Ambulance.

4. Cases of "Three day fever" will be transferred with kits and blankets, to the hangars on the afternoon of the 26th instant. The Medical officer i/c of P.U.O. patients in HAM-EN-ARTOIS and GUARBECQUE will notify the A.D.M.S. by 3 p.m. 25th instant the probable number requiring removal -

(a) in lorries.
(b) in Motor Ambulances.

Medical officers i/c Infantry Units detaining any cases, will also inform the A.D.M.S., of probable numbers by the same time, together with their location.

5. A temporary "Admission & Discharge" book will be kept for Divisional reference.

6. Suitable cases of P.U.O. occurring after 2 p.m. on the 26th instant, will be sent to the P.U.O Detention Camp direct. Cases which are not suitable for the camp - from a high temperature etc - will be marked "Field Ambulance" and admitted into a Medical Unit.

7. Field Ambulances will collect and convey cases to the Camp.

8. Cases when fit for discharge will be returned to their Transport lines or units.

H Boldero.

Major.

June 24th 1918. for A.D.M.S. 61 Div.

Distribution :-

Os.C. Field Ambulances.
All Regimental Medical officers.
M.O. 330 Bde. R.F.A.,
M.O. 331 Bde. R.F.A.,
M.O. 66 D.A.C.,
61 Division "Q" for information.
182,183,184 Inf.Bdes. -do-
C.R.A., 61 Division. -do-
C.R.A., 66 Division. -do-
C.R.E., 61 Division. -do-
61 Division Train. -do-

MEDICAL

Vol 27

CONFIDENTIAL

July 1918.

140/3123.

W A R   D I A R Y

OF

A. D. M. S., 61 st D I V I S I O N

From :- July 1st 1918

To :- July 31st 1918.

VOLUME - 27

H Baldero Major
Colonel A.M.S.
A.D.M.S., 61 Division.

Instructions regarding War Diaries and Intelligence Summaries are contained in F. S. Regs., Part II. and the Staff Manual respectively. Title pages will be prepared in manuscript.

WAR DIARY
or
INTELLIGENCE SUMMARY.
(Erase heading not required.)

Army Form C. 2118.

Place	Date	Hour	Summary of Events and Information	Remarks and references to Appendices
LAMBRES. Sheet 36.A.	July 1st.		All the forward Regimental Aid Posts were visited and found to be in good working order. An endeavour is being made to make a new R.A.P. for the battalion holding the Left sub-sector. The present site is at P.5.c.7.5. and proposed one at P.5.d.3.3. (Sheet 36.A.) The advantages are that the latter is a cellar and a great deal stronger; also it would afford increased accommodation - there are no disadvantages. The A.D.M.S. is adopting incineration for the disposal of faeces in suitable places. This morning we came under the administration of the Fifth Army who have taken over two Corps (XIth and XIIIth) from the First Army - this brings the Fifth Army into line again; on this occasion between the First Army on their right and the Second Army on their left.	HB
	2nd.		P.U.O. is very slowly decreasing, but no marked alteration in figures.	HB
	3rd.		Four American Medical officers reported for duty :- Lieut J.A.McSWEENEY. MORC.USA. posted to 2/3rd South Mid. Field Amb., Lieut P.THOMPSON. MORC. USA. -do- -do- Lieut J.P.STOUT. MORC. USA. posted to 2/2nd South Mid. Field Amb., Lieut R.M.MacGUFFIE. MORC. USA. -do- -do-	HB
	4th.		Orders have been received for Lieut P.E.THORNHILL. MORC. USA. to report to Casual Officers Depot S.O.S., when his relief comes up.	HB
	5th.		The epidemic of P.U.O., is steadily decreasing.	HB
	6th.		Routine work.	
	7th.		Routine work.	HB
	8th.		The Division is to be relieved by the 74th Division. The latter is now in Corps reserve.	HB
	9th.		P.U.O. figures are most satisfactory :- "A" 1. No: detained in Medical units - 160. 2. -do- in P.U.O. Camp. - 174. 3. -do- in Units. - 82 416 "B" No: admitted in last 24 hours - 83. No: evacuated to C.C.S. -do- - 26.	HB
	10th		Medical arrangements for relief of Division produced (App."A") and arrangements for collection of sick after relief (App. "B")	A. B

Wt W1771/M2031 750,000 5/17 Sch. 52 Forms/C2118/14

Instructions regarding War Diaries and Intelligence Summaries are contained in F. S. Regs., Part II. and the Staff Manual respectively. Title pages will be prepared in manuscript.

WAR DIARY
or
INTELLIGENCE SUMMARY.
(Erase heading not required.)

Army Form C. 2118.

Place	Date	Hour	Summary of Events and Information	Remarks and references to Appendices
LAMBRES.	July 11th		Arrangements for Special cases produced (App. "C") Routine duties. JHB	C
	12th		The Division is in process of being relieved. The area into which our units are moving is not equipped with Sanitary appliances - this causes a large ~~supply~~ demand on existing supplies. At the same time we are given to understand that we may not occupy this area very long and so it is inadvisable to erect standing camps. Would it not be a great saving in time, labour and material if areas were administered by area staffs to a greater extent than they are at present. JHB	
	13th		Routine work. JHB	
NORRENT-FONTS. Sheet 36.A.	14th		61 Division Headquarters moves to NORRENT FONTES. The 2/1st Field Ambulance are still doing the XI Corps Rest Station. Application has been made for their return as we are in 24 hours notice, in G.H.Q. Reserve. 2/2nd Field Ambulance is at FONTES and 2/3rd Field Amb., at BOURECQ. Sheet 36.A. For Medical arrangements see appendix "B" JHB	
	15th 16th 17th		As the Division is in G.H.Q. Reserve a great deal of time is being spent in reconnoitring the areas which may be occupied by the Division. JHB	
	18th 19th 20th		Routine work. Nothing of importance is occurring on this front. JHB	
	21st		2/1 Field Amb., is relieved from XI Corps Rest Station, so the Brigade grouping of Ambulances is complete. See appendix "D" JHB	D
WARDRECQUES Sheet 36A.	22nd		The whole Division moves in one day to XV Corps Second Army with headquarters WARDRECQUES. JHB	
	23rd		This area is very compact. The A.D.M.S. reconnoitred the ground round CAESTRE which is one of the tasks the Division may have to fulfil. Conference of Os.C. Field Ambs. at A.D.M.S., office. Provisional Defence Scheme arranged verbally. It is quite uncertain what the Div will be asked to do. JHB	

D. D. & L., London, E.C.
(A5304) Wt W1771/M2031 750,000 5/17 Sch. 52 Forms/C2118/14

Instructions regarding War Diaries and Intelligence Summaries are contained in F. S. Regs., Part II. and the Staff Manual respectively. Title pages will be prepared in manuscript.

WAR DIARY
or
INTELLIGENCE SUMMARY.
(Erase heading not required.)

Army Form C. 2118.

Place	Date	Hour	Summary of Events and Information	Remarks and references to Appendices
WARDRECQUES	July 24.		A.D.M.S., went round all the forward area of the 9th Division with the D.A.D.M.S. 9th Div. HB	
	25.		D.A.D.M.S., reconnoitred the forward area of the 31 Div. HB	
	26.		The XV Corps front line has now been thoroughly reconnoitred, and is held from North to South by 9th Division, 1st Australian, and 31st Divisions, with 40th Division in reserve; and 61st Division is in G.H.Q. Reserve at 24 hours notice. HB	
	27.		Medical arrangements in connection with 61 Division Defence Instructions with Map reference of medical posts circulated. HB	AppE and E(a)
	28.		A.D.M.S. visited the 182 Brigade Units during the afternoon. The supply of sanitary appliances in this Corps (XV) is on a sound basis, i.e. Units indent on Area, or sub-area Commandants who obtain the articles from the O.C. Sanitary Section concerned. They are strictly Area stores and no wood or material is issued to Divisions for the construction of Sanitary appliances. HB	
	29.		Routine work. The Corps front is quiet. HB	
	30.		The A.D.M.S., is organizing a Stretcher bearers competition the preliminary arrangements of which form appendix "F"	F
	31.		The Division is to move to-night and Divisional Headquarters to-morrow, back to the XI Corps area. We shall be in reserve. For provisional arrangements for collection of sick in new area see appendix "G" The Units will be in same sites as when we left XI Corps. The Ambulances are now with their normally associated Brigades, namely :- HB	G
			2/1 Field Amba, with 184 Inf. Bde.group2/2 Field Amb., with 182 Inf. Bde.group. 2/3 Field Amb., with 183 Inf. Bde.group. HB	

H B[illegible] major
Lt Colonel A.M.S.
A.D.M.S. 61 Division.

D. D. & L., London, E.C.
(A7883) Wt. W809/M1672 350,000 4/17 Sch. 52a Forms/C/2118/14

SECRET   A.D.M.S., No: 913/955

17

MEDICAL ARRANGEMENTS - 61 DIVISION
ON RELIEF BY 74th DIVISION

1. The 61st Division in the line will be relieved by the 74th Division as follows :-

183 Inf. Bde. on night of 10th/11th July.
182 Inf. Bde. on night of 11th/12th July.
61 Div. Artillery on nights 12th/13th and 13th/14th July.

2. The O.C. 2/3rd South Midland Field Ambulance will detail one section to proceed to the billeting area of the 183rd Inf. Bde. on the night 10th/11th July; and arrange that an Ambulance Wagon follows each Infantry battalion of the 183rd Inf. Bde.

The 2/3rd South Midland Field Ambulance will be relieved on the night 11th/12th July by the 230th Field Ambulance who will take over the Main Dressing Station, Medical Posts, and lines of evacuation from the RIGHT Divisional Sector.

The O.C. 2/2nd South Midland Field Ambulance will hand over the Walking Wounded Dressing Station, and the Medical Posts and lines of evacuation from the LEFT Divisional Sector, to the O.C. 231 Field Ambulance on night of 10th/11th July; and proceed to the area of the 182nd Inf. Bde. on night 11th/12th July.
O.C. 2/2nd South Midland Field Ambulance will arrange that an Ambulance wagon follows each Infantry battalion of the 182 Inf. Bde.

3. Details of the above reliefs will be arranged by Os.C. Field Ambulances concerned.

4. The 61 Division Field Ambulances will take away only such Equipment as is authorised by the Mobilization Store Table, and that held und r G.R.Os.
All Trench and Area Stores will be carefully checked and handed over and receipts in duplicate obtained from relieving Field Ambulances. A copy of these receipts will be forwarded to this office for transmission to Division "Q"

5. Os.C. 2/2nd and 2/3rd Field Ambulances will leave behind a Senior Medical officer and small detachment of R.A.M.C., personnel. These will remain behind for such period as their services are required.

6. 61 Division P.U.O. Detention Camp. The Medical staff at the 61 Div. P.U.O., Detention Camp will remain and receive cases until further orders.

7. The O.C. 2/3rd South Midland Field Ambulance will arrange for an Ambulance to follow the 61 Div. R.F.A., Units during their route march on nights 12th/13th and 13th/14th July.

8. Collection of sick in new area. Details regarding the collection of sick in the new area will be issued later.

9. Os.C. 61 Div. Field Ambs., will hand over to relieving Field Ambulances a list of sick parades of Corps Troops etc which they have been attending.

C. Howkins

Colonel A.M.S.
A.D.M.S., 61 Div.

July 9th 1918.

For distribution see over.

Distribution :-

Os.C. Field Ambulances.	
All Regimental Medical Officers.	
61 Division "G" for information.	
61 Division "Q"	-do-
182,183,184 Inf.Bdes.	-do-
C.R.A.,	-do-
C.R.E.,	-do-
61 Bn. M.G.C.,	-do-
1/5 D.C.L.I.,	-do-
61 Div. Train A.S.C.,	-do-
D.A.D.V.S.,	-do-
A.P.M.,	-do-
D.D.M.S., XI Corps	-do-
A.D.M.S., 74th Div.	-do-
A.D.M.S., 5th Div.	-do-
25 M.A.C.,	-do-

SECRET A.D.M.S., No: 913.

B

COLLECTION OF SICK ETC ON COMPLETION OF RELIEF

The following arrangements will be carried out until further orders :-

1. The O.C. 2/3rd South Midland Field Ambulance will collect Sick and wounded from the 183rd Infantry Brigade, 61 Div. Royal Field Artillery and 61 Divisional Headquarters.

2. The O.C. 2/2nd South Midland Field Ambulance will collect Sick and wounded from the 182nd and 184th Infantry Brigades, Royal Engineers, 61 Batt. Machine Gun Corps and 1/5 D.C.L.I. (Pioneers)

3. The O.C. 2/3rd South Midland Field Ambulance will hand over 2 large cars to the O.C. 2/2nd South Midland Field Ambulance.

4. The 61st Division Train A.S.C., and 61 Mobile Veterinary Section will be attended as follows :-

No: 521 Company Train	-	O.C. 2/3rd Field Amb.,
522 -do-	-	O.C. 2/2nd Field Amb.,
523 -do-	-	O.C. 2/3rd Field Amb.,
524 -do-	-	O.C. 2/2nd Field Amb.,
61 Mobile Vet Sec	-	O.C. 2/2nd Field Amb.,

C Howkins

Colonel A.M.S.
A.D.M.S. 61 Div.

9/7/18.

Distribution:-
Os.C. Field Ambs.,
All R.M.Os.
61 Division "Q" for information.
182,183,184 Inf.Bdes. -do-
C.R.A., -do-
C.R.E., -do-
O.C. Train. -do-
61 Bn. M.G.C., -do-
1/5 D.C.L.I., -do-
Camp Commandant -do-
D.A.D.V.S., -do-
A.P.M., -do-
61 Mob.Vet.Sec. -do-
Senior Chaplain. -do-

A.D.M.S., No: 913

MEDICAL ARRANGEMENTS - 61 DIVISION.

C

DENTAL CASES.

The Dental Surgeon is at No: 51 Casualty Clearing Station.
The following is the allottment of places :-

2/2 Field Amb., - 20 cases to arrive at No: 51 C.C.S., by 9 a.m. on Mondays, Wednesdays, and Fridays.

2/3 Field Amb., - 10 cases to arrive at No: 51 C.C.S., by 11 a.m. on Mondays Wednesdays, and Fridays.

Special appointments must be made for officers, and any case requiring urgent treatment.

Dental cases will be sent in Divisional cars.

EAR, NOSE & THROAT CASES.

The Ear, Nose & Throat centre is at No: 12 Stationary Hospital ST POL.
The following is the allottment of cases :-

2/2 Field Amb., - 4 cases.) To arrive at No: 12
2/3 Field Amb., - 2 cases.) Staty Hos. by 9 a.m.

All cases will be collected at the Headquarters 2/2nd Field Ambulance early on the morning of the allotted day (Wednesday)
Os.C. Field Ambs., will arrange to wire this office by 4 p.m. on Tuesdays, the number of cases for the Centre; in order that M.A.C. cars can be arranged.
Officers will be seen on Sundays.

OPHTHALMIC CASES.

The Ophthalmic Centre is at No: 22 C.C.S., PERNES.
The following is the allottment of cases :-

2/2 Field Amb., - 8 cases.) To arrive at No: 22
2/3 Field Amb., - 4 cases.) C.C.S., by 9 a.m.

All cases will be collected at the Headquarters 2/2nd Field Amb., early on the morning of the allotted day (Tuesday)
Os.C. Field Ambs., will wire this office by 4 p.m. on Mondays, the number of cases for the Centre so that M.A.C. car can be arranged.
Officers will be seen on Sundays.

SCABIES. Cases of Scabies will continue to be treated by O.C. 2/2nd Field Amb., until further orders.

H Boldero

Major.
for A.D.M.S. 61 Div.

10/7/18.

D

SECRET.

ARRANGEMENTS FOR THE COLLECTION OF SICK.

1. The following arrangements will take place with effect from midnight July 20th/21st.

2. Field Ambulances will collect sick from their present associated Brigade Groups, namely :-

2/1 Field Ambulance.,	-	183 Infantry Brigade.
2/2 Field Ambulance.,	-	182 Infantry Brigade.
2/3 Field Ambulance.,	-	184 Infantry Brigade.

3. Until the formation of Brigade Groups, or other arrangements are made, the following will take effect :-

The 2/1 Field Ambulance will collect sick from :-

1/5 Bn. D.C.L.I., (Pioneers)
61st.Division R.Es.
61st.Mobile Veterinary Section.

The 2/2 Field Ambulance will collect sick from :-

61st.Div.Artillery.
61st.Bn Machine Gun Corps.

4. Sick of the Divisional Train A.S.C., will be collected under arrangements to be made with Field Ambulances by Medical Officers attending the Train Companies.

Hawkins
Colonel.,
A.D.M.S., 61st.Division.

21/7/18.

Distribution :-

2/1., 2/2., 2/3 Field Ambs.
182., 183., 184 Inf.Brigades.
61st.Bn M.G.C.
61st.Bn D.C.L.I.
O.C., 61st.Div Train.
C.R.A.
C.R.E.
D.A.D.V.S.

S E C R E T.   A.D.M.S.No 913/1094.

MEDICAL ARRANGEMENTS IN CONNECTION WITH 61 DIVISIONAL DEFENCE INSTRUCTIONS NO 1.APPENDIX "A" para 8.
(61 Div. No:G.C.45/1/1 dated 26/7/18.

E

1. On the order "Man Battle Stations" being issued, each Field Ambce will detail a Bearer Division to proceed to the concentration area of its associated Brigade.

Wheeled Stretcher Carriages will be taken.

The officer i/c bearers will report to the Staff Captain on arrival.

2. A Tent Sub-Division with sufficient transport to form an Advanced Dressing Station will accompany the Bearer Division.

3. Officers Commanding Field Ambulances will arrange that motor Ambulances will be available to evacuate patients as required.

4. The closest touch must be maintained between the Regimental Medical Officers, and the officer i/c bearers, and the Field Ambce headquarters.
Runners will be attached to each Regimental Medical Officer for this purpose.

5. The route of evacuation of casualties, and locations of Advanced Dressing Stations etc, depends on the line which will be held.

6. Each Field Ambulance Commander will ensure that all Ambulance officers are familiar with the routes leading to the Concentration area, and with the Medical Arrangements of the Divisions in the XVth Corps.

7. On the formation of a Main Dressing Station the A.D.M.S. will be notified immediately, in order that arrangements can be made for evacuation by M.A.C.Cars.

8. The headquarters of Field Ambulances will not move until further orders are issued.

9. The Divisional Rest Station will take in Sick and slightly wounded cases who will be likely to be fit within 48 hours.

10. Officers Commanding Field Ambulances will render Situation reports to be at the A.D.M.S., Office daily by 8.a.m.
Any unusual occurrence will be notified at once.

11. Medical Arrangements of Divisions in the Corps attached.

12. The following maps in connection with the above arrangements are enclosed (Field Ambulances only)
T.S.194 Sheets "A","B", and "C".
T.S.223 (Routes to concentration area.)

C Howkins

Colonel.,

27-7-18.   A.D.M.S., 61st Division.

Distribution :

182,183,184 Inf Bdes.
O.C.1/5 D.C.L.I.
O.C.61 M.G.Bn.
D.D.M.S.XV Corps.
61 Divn "G".
C.R.A.,
C.R.E.,
O.C.61 Div Train.
All R.M.Os.
14 M.A.C.

SECRET

E A.

The following Medical Arrangements are forwarded for your information and guidance with reference to this office No: 913/1094 dated July 26th 1918 :-

DISPOSITIONS OF MEDICAL UNITS, XV CORPS FRONT

9th Division.

Divisional Collecting Post ....27/W.6.d.9.9.
Advanced Dressing Station...................27/W.3.a.
(CHATEAU CAESTRE)
Walking Wounded Post........................27/Q.31.a.
Main Dressing Station.......................27/V.4.c.
(near HONDEGHEM)

1 Australian Division.

Advanced Dressing Station.....BORRE,.........27/W.19.c.
Main Dressing Station.......................27/V.9.b.1.5.
Divisional Rest Station.....................27/U.5.a.9.3.

31 Division.

Advanced Dressing Station...................36A/D.18.a.6.4.
Main Dressing Station.......................36A/C.5.a.7.8.

Divisional Rest Station.....................27/T.18.d.7.8.

Corps Walking Wounded Collecting Post.

EBBLINGHEM. 27/U.19.a.5.0.

40 Division.

Advanced Dressing Station.....(135 Fd.Amb.)36A/C.16.c.8.8.
Advanced Dressing Station.....(137 Fd.Amb.)27/U.20.b.9.4.
Advanced Dressing Station.....(136 Fd.Amb.)27/V.1.d.9.5.

Main Dressing Station.........(136 Fd.Amb.)27/T.18.c.8.7.
Main Dressing Station.........(135 Fd.Amb.)36A/B.18.c.0.6.

- - - - - - - - - - - - - - - - - - - -

A.D.M.S. No: 833

F.

STRETCHER BEARERS COMPETITION

1. This Competition will take place next week at a time and place to be notified later.

2. Bandages, Dressings, Blankets, Stretchers, Ground sheets, Splints etc, will be provided.

3. "Patients" will be labelled with a tally on which will be written the assumed signs, symptoms, or disability, and any necessary directions.
Stretcher bearers will render first aid, and, if necessary, carry the patient a short distance.

4. Stretcher bearers are also expected to be familiar with the -

(a) Diagrams on pages 21, 22, 23, 24 & 25 of "Manual of Injuries and Diseases of the War"

(b) Application of Thomas' Splint (any recognised method)

(c) Prophylactic treatment against Trench feet.

5. Transport arrangements to the competition will be notified later.

6. Splints etc may be borrowed from any Field Ambulance of the Division for purposes of practice.

7. Tea will be provided for the competitors.

8. Arrangements will be made so that Regimental Medical officers of the Division can attend.

8. The Judges of the events will be arranged from Field Ambulances.

10. Marks will be given for efficiency, speed, neatness and initiative.

H Boliaro Maj.
for Colonel A.M.S.
A.D.M.S. 61 Div.

30/7/18.

Distribution:-
All Os.C. Units.
All Regimental M.Os.
Os.C. Field Ambulances.
182, 183, 184 Inf.Bdes.
C.R.A.,
C.R.E.,
61 Div "Q" and "G"

SECRET   A.D.M.S. No: 913

G.

PROVISIONAL ARRANGEMENTS FOR COLLECTION OF SICK COMMENCING AUGUST 1st 1918

1. Field Ambulances will collect from, and arrange attendance for units without a medical officer in, their associated Brigade.

2/1 Field Amb., - 184 Inf. Bde.
2/2 Field Amb., - 182 Inf. Bde.
2/3 Field Amb., - 183 Inf. Bde.

2. Probable locations of Field Ambulances are :-

2/1 Field Amb., - BOURECQ.
2/2 Field Amb., - LAMBRES.
2/3 Field Amb., - FONTES.

3. All Scabies cases will be treated by 2/1 Field Amb.,

4. Dental, Ear Nose & Throat, and Ophthalmic cases will be collected at 2/3 Field Amb.,

5. The 2/3 Field Amb., will collect sick from the Division Field Artillery Group in ESTREE BLANCHE Area. Sick of the Trench Mortar Batteries and No: 1 Coy. Train will be attended by the nearest medical officer of the Artillery Group.

6. The 2/2 Field Amb., will collect sick from the Machine Gun Bn. at WITTERNESSE. 1/5 D.C.L.I., at BLESSY and the 61 Division R.Es. at HAM (near BLESSY)

7. Sick of the 61 Mobile Veterinary Section will be attended to by 2/2 Field Ambulance.

A.B. Owen
Major.
for Colonel A.M.S.
A.D.M.S. 61 Div.

31/7/18.
Distribution :-
Os.C. Field Ambulances.
All Regimental M.Os.
C.R.A.,
182, 183, 184 Inf.Bdes.
C.R.E.,
1/5 D.C.L.I.,
61 Bn. M.G.C.,
D.A.D.V.S.,
61 Div. Train.

CONFIDENTIAL

MEDICAL

9

Vol 28

140/3201

WAR DIARY

OF

A. D. M. S., 61 st DIVISION

Aug 1918

From :- August 1st 1918.

To :- August 31st 1918.

- - - - - - - - - - - - -

VOLUME - 28.

C Hunter

Colonel A.M.S.,
A.D.M.S., 61 Division.

Army Form C. 2118.

Instructions regarding War Diaries and Intelligence Summaries are contained in F. S. Regs., Part II. and the Staff Manual respectively. Title pages will be prepared in manuscript.

WAR DIARY
or
INTELLIGENCE SUMMARY.

(Erase heading not required.)

Place	Date	Hour	Summary of Events and Information	Remarks and references to Appendices
WARDRECQUES & NORRENT FONTES Sheet 36A. 1/40,000.	Aug. 1. 1918.		Divisional Headquarters moved from WARDRECQUES to NORRENT FONTES. The Division is now in the XIth Corps and is still in G.H.Q. reserve at 24 hours notice. HB	
	2.		No one Ambulance having more accommodation than another, and all being reasonably well off, each Field Ambulance will detain its own sick of its associated Brigade Group. HB	
	3.		Medical Arrangements produced (Appendix "A") also Medical Arrangements in connection with 61st Division Defence Instructions (Appendix "B") HB	App "A" App "B"
	4.		The Division is to relieve the 5th Division and take over the Left Sector of the XI Corps front. The A.D.M.S., visited A.D.M.S., 5th Division and went to all the forward posts. R.A.M.C. Order No: 65 in connection with the relief issued (Appendix "C") Appendix "C.1" gives the Medical Arrangements and locations of Posts; and Appendix "C.2" deals with the evacuation of special cases. HB	App "C" App "C.1" App "C.2"
	5.		Various units of the Division are moving to-day. When in the new area they come under G.O.C., 5th Division - so Medical Units will send their returns in to the A.D.M.S., 5th Division until G.O.C. 61 Division takes over. HB	
	6.		It would be a great advantage and convenience if a location table of all Medical Units in France - less Divisional and Mobile units - was compiled and issued. It might be worth while to include the name of the C.O. and nature of work done at the Hospital, together with, possibly, the names of the Surgical or other Specialist. In other words a volume produced at intervals - say monthly, on the lines of the Yellow book, with addition of the location which is the essential point, as a certain amount of time and wiring is at present spent on this work. HB	
I.19.d.1.9. Sheet 36A.	7.		Divisional Headquarters moved to a collection of houses between THIENNES and AIRE - Map reference I.19.d.1.9. Sheet 36A. G.O.C. 61 Division took over command of the line at 10 a.m. There are two points about Medical Arrangements in this area :- (i) There is only one line of evacuation, and that by 20 lbs Railway through the Forest of NIEPPE. (ii) From Main Dressing Station, the Canal is used as well as M.A.C., Both are liable to cause delay in replenishing stretchers, blankets, splints etc to the forward	

D. D. & L., London, E.C. (A7883) Wt. W809/M1672 350,000 4/17 Sch. 52a Forms/C/2118/14

Instructions regarding War Diaries and Intelligence Summaries are contained in F. S. Regs., Part II. and the Staff Manual respectively. Title pages will be prepared in manuscript.

WAR DIARY
or
INTELLIGENCE SUMMARY.
(Erase heading not required.)

Army Form C. 2118.

Place	Date	Hour	Summary of Events and Information	Remarks and references to Appendices
	Aug. 7.		Contd: Area, as the same train or barge does not necessarily return direct to the front; so an extra large forward dump will have to be made. The close proximity of the Wood to the front line renders this sector a very excellent target for enemy gas shells. We are providing a gas picket of 1 N.C.O., and 12 men whose duties are - (i) To warn troops of gassed areas. (ii) To fill in gas shell holes with Lime, and then earth. Lieut-Colonel H.N.Burroughes. O.C. 2/2nd (South Midland) Field Ambulance proceeds on a month's special leave to the United Kingdom. HB	
	8.		There is evidence that the Germans will retire on this front - we do not know to what extent. If an advance takes place, it would be a long and tedious way to bring all the wounded via the Wood (the only present existing route) so a Southern line of evacuation is being opened to-day along the main road MERVILLE - CROIX MARRAISE - TANNEY - THIENNES Road. For Medical Arrangements see Appendix "D" HB	App "D"
	9.		The Germans are retiring, and using Gas very freely indeed. Total battle casualties for 24 hours ending 6 a.m. 9th is :- Officers 9. Other Ranks 234. of these - 7 officers and 170 other ranks are Gassed. HB	
	10.		The Germans have gone back on the average 1,000 yards - in some places 1,500 yards. It is decided to attack him to establish a river crossing. It is anticipated that a considerable number of casualties will be received. Special R.A.M.C., order appended (Appendix "E")	App."E"
	11.		We attacked at 4.15 a.m. - fewer wounded than was anticipated though the operation was not a success. The Germans were in force. Total Casualties for 24 hours ending 6 a.m. 11th - Officers 6. Other Ranks 84. 22 of the Other Ranks were Gassed. HB	
	12.		Almost all our Gas casualties are being evacuated by the C.C.S., as they have many patients, so a Divisional Gas Centre is going to be formed at BOESEGHEM with the idea of retaining more	

Instructions regarding War Diaries and Intelligence Summaries are contained in F. S. Regs., Part II. and the Staff Manual respectively. Title pages will be prepared in manuscript.

WAR DIARY
or
INTELLIGENCE SUMMARY.
(*Erase heading not required.*)

Army Form C. 2118.

Place	Date	Hour	Summary of Events and Information	Remarks and references to Appendices
	Aug. 12.		Contd. of the lightly gassed cases in the Division. Major W.V.WOOD. MC. RAMC.TF. is in charge. It is hoped that knowledge may be obtained from his records both of how cases became casualties and the best method of treatment. Since we have been in the line our total gas casualties have been Officers - 8. Other Ranks 337. HB	
	13.		Under Orders from the Fifth Army a Divisional Diarrhoea Centre is being opened at STEENBECQUE under the care of O.C. 2/2nd (South Midland) Field Ambulance. Appendix "F" gives orders that have been issued to all concerned. HB	App "F"
	14.		As there are a certain number of very light Gassed cases, arrangements - Appendix "G" - have been made whereby men can wash at any Medical Post. Soda-Bicarb is not kept at these Posts as soap and water are equally efficient, and soda-bicarb is wasted. HB	App "G"
	15.		The Diarrhoea Centre has caused yet another Return to be rendered by Regimental Medical Officers. They have to wire us every Saturday the number of men who have reported sick to them during the week ending noon Saturday, with Diarrhoea. There is sure to be a difficulty in getting this return in , as it is not always easy to render returns when one is working in a shell and one has no clerks. It is desirable to reduce the number of returns from Regimental Medical Officers as much as possible, and in this case they have orders only to keep a man for 24 hours and then admit him to an Ambulance. HB	
	16.		The front is quiet - very few wounded. The great majority of our cases is due to Gas. The enemy is using a very great deal of gas - more so than on other fronts, and it is suggested that he is using up large dumps which he had accumulated to use against the Forest of NIEPPE - an ideal target; but now he cannot comfortably reach the Forest, so the front line, and more so the Support line is suffering. HB	
	17.		Our first consolidated return of Diarrhoea and Dysentery goes in to-day. In the whole of the 61 Division only 38 men reported sick with Diarrhoea to Medical Officers and 22 have been admitted to the Diarrhoea Centre (2/3 Field Amb., STEENBECQUE) This is a very small figure. HB	

D. D. & L., London, E.C.
(A7883) Wt W809/M1672 350,000 4/17 Sch. 52a Forms/C/2118/14

Instructions regarding War Diaries and Intelligence Summaries are contained in F. S. Regs., Part II. and the Staff Manual respectively. Title pages will be prepared in manuscript.

WAR DIARY
or
INTELLIGENCE SUMMARY.
(*Erase heading not required.*)

Army Form C. 2118.

Place	Date	Hour	Summary of Events and Information	Remarks and references to Appendices
	Aug. 18		I cannot help thinking that next week will show an increase in the number reporting sick with Diarrhoea, for the weather is hot and dry, and the green apple season is in full swing. Another point is the possibility of a man who has been slightly gassed and not reported, developing intestinal symptoms with diarrhoea later. I think it more than likely. JHB	
	19.		Lieut-Colonel G.Mackie. DSO. O.C. 2/1 (South Midland) Field Ambulance goes on a month's special leave; and Major G.Scott Williamson will act as O.C. in his absence. JHB	
	20.		News received that enemy is retiring again. For Medical Arrangements see Appendix "H" 61 Division "G" are using a Brigade as an Advance Guard, so a portion of the 2/3rd Field Amb., is being sent with it, as there is no certainty as to how far the enemy means to withdraw. JHB	App "H"
	21.		Casualties slight. Enemy has withdrawn from MERVILLE but not very far yet. Medical Posts all pushed up. JHB	
	22.		A very large number of Gassed cases - Officers 5 and Other Ranks 240 - The heaviest casualties were sustained in the 11th Suffolks. The enemy obtained many direct hits on bits of trenches held by this battalion. A large number of cases show no respiratory signs but have large extensive body burns - almost all severe burns. A large proportion of these cases had to be evacuated to C.C.S., JHB	
	23.		The slighter cases from yesterday's bombardment are now reporting - Officers 17 and Other Ranks 140. A large proportion of these have gone to the Divisional Gas Centre. JHB	
	24.		Diarrhoea Return - the numbers reporting sick to Medical officers during the week = 110. Number admitted to Field Ambulances - 76. This is not an alarming figure as nearly all the cases are slight. No positive rectal swabs have been reported up to date. I understand many Divisions and Formations at present have a good many cases of Diarrhoea. JHB	
	25.		Gas Casualties from 10 a.m. August 7th to noon to-day - Officers - 29. Other Ranks - 1008. JHB	

D. D. & L., London, E.C.
(A7883) Wt W809/M1672 350,000 4/17 Sch. 52a Forms/C/2118/14

Army Form C. 2118.

Instructions regarding War Diaries and Intelligence Summaries are contained in F. S. Regs., Part II, and the Staff Manual respectively. Title pages will be prepared in manuscript.

WAR DIARY
or
INTELLIGENCE SUMMARY.
(Erase heading not required.)

Place	Date	Hour	Summary of Events and Information	Remarks and references to Appendices
	Aug. 26.		The D.M.S., Fifth Army visited the Divisional Diarrhoea Centre at STEENBECQUE and Divisional Gas Centre at BOESEGHEM. Very few gassed cases admitted to-day - Officers 1. Other Ranks 10.	HB
	27.		It was decided to alter the duties of Ambulances on account of the numerous small forward moves and the increasing amount of work to be done at the Divisional Gas and Diarrhoea Centres; so orders were issued (Appendix "I") that 2/3rd Field Amb., would do all forward work. 2/1 Field Ambulance the Main Dressing Station, and 2/2 Field Amb., withdrawn from the line to do all sick at BOESEGHEM and STEENBECQUE, with their Headquarters at STEENBECQUE. This defines their duty more clearly and gives O.C. 2/3rd Field Ambulance a freer hand in the forward area, which is now very important work as the Medical Posts alter fairly often. Major W.V.WOOD. MC. (Gas Specialist) is remaining behind to run the Gas Centre under the administration of the 2/2nd Field Amb., A portion of the Divisional Reception Camp at WITTES is being taken over to be run as a Divisional Rest Station and will be part of the 2/2nd Field Ambulance. It is a beautiful place - no signs of war in their wooded park. Men should quickly get fit and improve their morale. I believe the importance of surroundings in raising morale is often overlooked - nice quiet surroundings with no war sights and noises are of great importance. The place is being fitted up now.	App "I" HB
	28.		The D.M.S., Fifth Army, with the A.D.M.S., 61 Division is going round the Dressing Stations.	HB
	29.		D.A.D.M.S., during the early morning, went round all the Advance Brigade (184 Inf. Bde.) RAPs. The Car Posts are well advanced, and evacuation easy. ESTAIRES is burning and many fires reported behind enemy line. A.D.M.S., visited WITTES where the Divisional Reception Camp is situated, and has started forming a Divisional Rest Station in a portion of their compound. There are now 150 patients there - mostly slightly gassed sent from the Divisional Gas Centre. Very few gas casualties to-day. Colonel MILLER. A.M.S., Consulting Physician Fifth Army visited us, and was satisfied with the Diarrhoea centre, and told us that other formations had quite as much diarrhoea and there is nothing of serious import in our numbers and cases.	HB
	30.		The Germans are retiring slowly. Medical Posts are being pushed up.	HB

D. D. & L., London, E.C.
(A7883) Wt. W809/M1672 350,000 4/17 Sch. 52a Forms/C/2118/14

Army Form C. 2118.

Instructions regarding War Diaries and Intelligence Summaries are contained in F. S. Regs., Part II. and the Staff Manual respectively. Title pages will be prepared in manuscript.

WAR DIARY
or
INTELLIGENCE SUMMARY.

(Erase heading not required.)

Place	Date	Hour	Summary of Events and Information	Remarks and references to Appendices
	31.		R.A.M.C., Order No: 68 produced after Conference of Field Ambulance commanders. (see Appendix "I") "G" go as Advanced Divisional Headquarters to CROIX MARRAISE to-day. The monthly sick wastage for the Division shows nothing unusual. No large number of Gassed cases since August 25th. Our total Gas casualties from 10 a.m. August 7th to noon August 31st are :- Officers 33. Other Ranks 1,057. There is nothing of importance in the monthly Sanitary Report.	App. "I"

Colonel A.M.S.
A.D.M.S., 61 Div.

D. D. & L., London, E.C.
(A7883) Wt W809/M1672 350,000 4/17 Sch. 52a Forms/C/2118/14

SECRET A.D.M.S., No: 913

A

MEDICAL ARRANGEMENTS 31 DIVISION

The evacuation of cases is as follows :-

LYING SICK -	54 Casualty Clearing station.
LYING WOUNDED -	Advanced Operating Centre. FORT GASSION
OTHER SICK & WOUNDED -	1 & 2 C.C.S., BLENDECQUES. 11 C.C.S., MOULLE. 18 C.C.S., MALASSISE. 58 C.C.S., LONGUENESSE.
N.Y.D.N.; S.I.W.; INFECTIOUS CASES less Dysentery and suspect dysentery	51 C.C.S., COYECQUES.
DYSENTERY & SUSPECT DYSENTERY	8 C.C.S., ELNES.
INDIAN DRIVERS	6 C.C.S., PERNES.
PORTUGUESE	8 Portuguese Ambulance. HERBELLE.
CHINESE	11 C.C.S., MOULLE.
SCABIES	2/1 Field Ambulance.

- - - - - - - - - - * - - - - - - - - -

SPECIAL CASES

DENTAL CASES.

The Dental Surgeon attached No: 54 Casualty Clearing station will attend at the 2/3rd South Midland Field Ambulance at 9 a.m. on TUESDAYS and THURSDAYS.
Each Field Ambulance has an allotment of 10 cases to arrive at 8.30 a.m. on Tuesdays and Thursdays.
Special appointments must be made for officers and urgent cases.

EAR, NOSE & THROAT CASES.

The Centre is at 51 Casualty Clearing station at COYECQUES. Cases will be seen there at 9 a.m. every WEDNESDAY.
Each Field Ambulance has an allotment of three cases which will be collected at 2/3rd South Midland Field Amb., on Tuesday evenings.
Cs.C. Field Ambulances will wire this office by 4 p.m. Tuesdays, the number of cases for the centre, in order that M.A.C. cars can be arranged.
Officers will be seen on Sundays.

P.T.O.

OPHTHALMIC CASES.

The Ophthalmic Centre is at No: 22 Casualty Clearing station PERNES, and cases are seen there on Tuesdays at 9 a.m.
Each Field Ambulance has an allottment of 4 cases.
Cases will be collected at 2/3rd South Midland Field Ambulances on Monday evenings.
Os.C. Field Ambulances will wire this office by 4 p.m. on MONDAYS, the number of cases for the Centre in order that M.A.C. cars can be arranged.
Officers will be seen on Sundays.

H. Bolton
Major.
for A.D.M.S. 61 Div.

3/8/18.

A.D.M.S. No: 913/1094

SECRET

B

MEDICAL ARRANGEMENTS IN CONNECTION WITH 61 DIVISION DEFENCE INSTRUCTION NO: 3 (G.C.45/1/3 dated 1/8/18)

1. BEARERS WITH BRIGADES IN CONCENTRATION AREAS.

On receipt of the order "MAN BATTLE STATIONS" each Officer Commanding Field Ambulance will arrange that a Bearer Division with one Tent sub-division, is sent to the concentration area of its associated Brigade.

2. MOTOR & HORSE AMBULANCE WAGONS.

Motor & Horse Ambulance wagons will be available immediately to convoy cases from Car Loading Posts to the Advanced Dressing station, and Main Dressing Station.

3. R.A.M.C., BEARERS.

When in the concentration area, Officers Commanding Field Ambs., will arrange to send to each Regimental Medical Officer of their associated Brigade, two squads of R.A.M.C., bearers, and one runner, to ensure communication with the Advanced Dressing Station.

- -

4. IN THE EVENT OF AN ATTACK ON THE CORPS ON THE IMMEDIATE RIGHT OF XI CORPS.

(i & iii) An Advanced Dressing Station can be established, in the vicinity of U.11.a.3.3. (N.E. of LILLERS) with the Main Dressing station at the Brewery, BOURECQ (U.1.c.3.6.); or an alternative scheme can be adopted in which case casualties will pass through the Dressing Stations of the 74th Division, which will be augmented by R.A.M.C., personnel and cars of the 61st Division Field Ambs.,

(ii) An Advanced Dressing Station at BOURECQ, with a Car Relay Post at U.11.a.3.3. (N.E. of LILLERS), and a Main Dressing Station at the School NORRENT FONTES or FONTES.

5. IN THE EVENT OF AN ATTACK AGAINST CENTRE OF XI CORPS FRONT.

Casualties North of Canal DE LA LYS.
These will pass through the Walking Wounded Dressing Station of the 5th Division at I.30.c.8.3. and then to the 5th Division Main Dressing Station at I.17.c.5.1. (West edge of NIEPPE FOREST); or to a Main Dressing Station which will be opened up at BOESEGHEM or FORT GASSION and, possibly later on, at RINCQ.

Casualties South of the Canal DE LA LYS.
These will go through the [illegible] Dressing Stations of the 74th Div.

In either of the above cases, the 5th and 74th Divisions will have their Dressing Stations augmented by personnel and cars of the 61st Division.

P.T.O.

6. IN THE EVENT OF AN ATTACK ON THE CORPS ON THE IMMEDIATE LEFT OF XI CORPS.

(i, ii, & iii) A Field Ambulance of the 61st Division will form a Dressing Station at STEENBECQUE with Advanced Posts at MORBECQUE and D.28.b.8.8.
Cases can then be sent to the Main Dressing Station of the 5th Division or 31st Division at C.5.a.6.8. (S.E. of WALLON CAPPEL) or, if the latter has moved, to the reserve site at EBBLINGHEM.

7. CLERICAL WORK.

Clerks are to be sent to the Dressing Stations of other Divisions which receive cases of 61st Division.

8. A.Ds.M.S., OFFICES.

A.D.M.S., 5th Division - I.19.c.8.9. (Sheet 36A.1/40,000)
A.D.M.S. 31st Division - WALLON CAPPEL (U.28.b. Sheet 27 1/40,000)
A.D.M.S., 74th Division - MOLINGHEM.

9. Field Ambulances ACKNOWLEDGE.

H Boldero Maj
for Colonel A.M.S.
A.D.M.S., 61 Division

August 3rd 1918,

Distribution:-
Os.C. Field Ambulances.
Regimental Medical Officers.
61 Division "G" for information.
61 Division "Q" -do-
182,183,184 Inf.Bdes. -do-
C.R.A., -do-
C.R.E., -do-
1/5 D.C.L.I., (P) -do-
61 Bn. M.G.C., -do-
A.D.M.S., 5th Division -do-
A.D.M.S., 31st Division-do-
A.D.M.S., 74th Division-do-
D.D.M.S., XI Corps -do-
25 M.A.C., -do-
A.D.M.S. 4th Division -do-

S E C R E T

R.A.M.C. ORDER NO: 65
BY
Colonel C.H.Howkins. D.S.O., A.M.S.
A.D.M.S., 61 Division

August 4th 1918.

Ref.Map.Sheet 36A.1/40,000.

1. The 61st Division will relieve the 5th Division in the Left Sector of XIth Corps front, commencing on the 4th August. Relief to be completed by 8th August.

2. The 2/1st South Midland Field Ambulance will take over the Main Dressing Station at I.17.c.5.1., and Walking Wounded Collecting Post at I.30.c.8.3. from the 13th Field Ambulance. Advance parties to be sent to-day (August 4th) Relief to be completed by noon August 5th.

3. The 2/2nd South Midland Field Ambulance will take over all forward posts from the 15th Field Ambulance, with headquarters at STEENBECQUE, and Advanced Dressing Station at J.16.d.7.2., and be responsible for clearing the line. Advance parties will be sent to-day (August 4th) Relief to be completed by noon August 5th.

4. The 2/3rd South Midland Field Ambulance will take over from the 14th Field Ambulance at BOESEGHEM. Advance parties to be sent on August 5th. Relief to be completed by noon August 6th.

5. The A.D.M.S., 5th Division is arranging to leave Rear parties for twenty-four hours.

6. All equipment and stores, less Mobilization equipment and that held under G.R.Os. will be taken over from Field Ambulances of the 5th Division.

7. Details of reliefs will be arranged between Os.C. concerned.

8. Completion of reliefs to be reported to this office.

9. Field Ambulances ACKNOWLEDGE.

H Baldwin
Major
for Colonel A.M.S.
A.D.M.S., 61 Division.

Issued at 4.15 p.m.

Distribution:-
Os.C. Field Ambulances.
182,183,184 Inf.Bdes. for information.
C.R.A., -do-
C.R.E., -do-
1/5 D.C.L.I. (P) -do-
61 Bn. Machine Gun Corps -do-
61 Division "G" -do-
61 Division "Q" -do-
A.D.M.S., 5 Div. -do-
A.D.M.S., 74 Div. -do-
D.D.M.S., XI Corps. -do-
61 Div. Train. -do-
D.A.D.V.S., -do-
A.P.M., -do-
Senior Chaplain. -do-
25 M.A.C., -do-
War Diary
File.

S E C R E T   [illegible]

PROVISIONAL MEDICAL ARRANGEMENTS FOR LEFT SECTOR OF XIth CORPS FRONT

Ref. Map. 36A. 1/40,000.

1. REGIMENTAL AID POSTS.

	Left Sector.	Right Sector.
Left Battalion -	K.3.d.5.3.	K.13.b.9.1.
Right Battalion -	K.14.a.5.9.	K.25.a.1.9.
Support Battalion-	K.9.a.0.2.	K.13.a.3.1.

2. R.A.M.C. POSTS FOR LOCAL CASUALTIES.

(i) J.10.b.2.3.
(ii) J.21.d.9.5.
(iii) I.30.c.8.3.
(iv) J.18.c.4.5.

3. CAR POSTS.

(i) K.14.a.9.5.
(ii) K.23.a.0.5.

4. ADVANCED DRESSING STATION.

J.16.d.7.2.

5. MAIN DRESSING STATION.

I.17.c.5.1.

6. LOCATIONS OF FIELD AMBULANCES HEADQUARTERS.

2/1 Field Ambulance.(M.D.S.)	I.17.c.5.1.
2/2 Field Ambulance.	STEENBECQUE.
2/3 Field Ambulance.	BOESEGHEM.

7. ROUTE OF EVACUATION.

Cases are cleared from Regimental Aid Posts by hand, and push trucks, and also by cars via ROMA to the Advanced Dressing Station, thence by light railway to Main Dressing Station. From Main Dressing Station by barges and M.A.C. cars to Casualty Clearing Stations.

8. R.A.M.C. BEARERS FOR REGIMENTAL MEDICAL OFFICERS.

The O.C. 2/2 Field Ambulance will arrange that, during the Divisional relief, each incoming Medical officer has one squad of bearers and a runner attached to him who knows the ground to ensure communicating the routes of evacuation.

H Botorro major
for Colonel A.M.S.
A.D.M.S. 61 Div.

August 4th 1918.
Copies to:-

Os.C. Field Ambs., (4 copies)
All Regimental M.Os.
182,183,184 Inf.Bdes.for information.
61 Div "Q" for information.
61 Division Train -do-

SECRET. A.D.M.S., No: 913. C2

"Medical Arrangements 61st Division" issued under this office No: 913 dated August 3rd, are cancelled, and the following substituted :-

The evacuation of cases is as follows :-

LYING SICK	54 Casualty Clearing Stn.
LYING WOUNDED	Advanced Operating Centre FORT GASSION
OTHER SICK & WOUNDED	1 & 2 C.C.S. BLENDECQUES. 11 C.C.S. MOULLE. 18 C.C.S. MALASSISE. 58 C.C.S. LONGUENESSE.
N.Y.D.N., S.I.W., INFECTIOUS (except Dysentery and suspect dysentery) ...	51 C.C.S. OOYECQUES.
DYSENTERY & SUSPECT DYSENTERY	8 C.C.S. ELNES.
INDIAN DRIVERS	6 C.C.S. PERNES.
PORTUGUESE	8 Portuguese Amb., HERBELLE.
CHINESE	11 C.C.S. MOULLE.
SCABIES	2/3 Field Amb.,

- - - - - - - - - * - - - - - - - - -

DENTAL CASES.

The Dental Surgeon attached 54 Casualty Clearing Station will attend at the 2/3rd South Midland Field Ambulance at 9 a.m. on MONDAYS, WEDNESDAYS, and FRIDAYS.
Not more than 30 cases (including officers) can be seen on any one day.
Applications for vacancies will be sent to the O.C. 2/3rd Field Ambulance who is responsible that the allotted number is not exceeded.
Special appointments must be made for urgent cases.

EAR, NOSE & THROAT CASES.

The Centre is at 51 Casualty Clearing Station at OOYECQUES.
Cases will be seen there at 9 a.m. every Wednesday.
Not more than 6 cases will be sent on the allotted day.
Applications for vacancies will be made direct to the O.C. 2/3rd Field Ambulance, who is responsible that the allotted number is not exceeded.
Cases will be collected at the 2/3 Field Amb., on Tuesday evenings.
O.C. 2/3 Field Amb., will wire this office by 12 noon on Tuesdays the number of cases for the Centre so that M.A.C. cars can be arranged.
Officers will be seen on Sundays.

P.T.O.

OPHTHALMIC CASES.

The Ophthalmic Centre is at No: 22 C.C.S., PERNES.
Cases are seen there on TUESDAYS at 9 a.m.
Not more than 12 cases will be sent on the allotted day.
Applications for vacancies will be made to the O.C. 2/3rd Field Amb., who is responsible that the allotted number is not exceeded.
Cases will be collected at 2/3rd Field Ambulance on Monday evenings.
O.C. 2/3 Field Amb., will arrange to wire this office by 12 noon on Monday the number of cases for the centre so that M.A.C. cars can be arranged.
Officers will be seen on Sundays.

H Boldero

4/8/18.

Major.
for A.D.M.S. 61 Div.

S E C R E T   A.D.M.S., No: 913/1094

D

MEDICAL ARRANGEMENTS IN CASE OF AN ADVANCE - 61 DIVISION.

1. Ref.Map Sheet 36A.1/40,000.

1. In case of an advance by the 183rd Inf.Bde. 61st Div., the following Medical arrangements will be carried out :-

2. One squad of R.A.M.C. Bearers, and 2 runners, will be attached to each Regimental Medical officer at once.
These bearers will join with stretchers and wheeled stretcher carriages, and proceed with the Regimental Medical Officer to the R.A.P., and evacuate cases to a Relay Post.

3. Relay Posts will be :-

For N. Sector - The Halte (E. end of VIA ROMA)
For S. Sector - On the HAVERSKERQUE Road(under arrangements made by officer i/c evacuation S. Sector.)

4. Car Loading Posts will be arranged by the officer i/c evacuation of each Sector.

5. Evacuation will be arranged as follows :-

From the forward area to the Main Dressing station by :-
N. Sector - O.C. 2/2nd South Midland Field Ambulance.
S. Sector - O.C. 2/3rd South Midland Field Ambulance.

6. Advanced Dressing Stations :-

J.16.d.7.2. (EDITH Station) This will take in cases from N.Sector.
J.29.d. - This will take in cases from the S.Sector, and will be formed on orders being received from A.D.M.S.;

7. There will be two Main Dressing stations under the O.C. 2/1 South Midland Field Ambulance :-

The CANAL M.D.S., (I.17.c.5.1.)
The BARN M.D.S., (I.30.c.7.4.) THIENNES-HAVERSKERQUE Road.

8. Walking Wounded.
These will be conveyed by horse Ambulance wagons from the Walking Wounded Collecting Post at [illegible].28.b.2.0. to the BARN M.D.S.,
Horse Ambulance will be held in readiness to form there by Os.C. 2/1 and 2/3rd Field Ambulances on orders being received from A.D.M.S.

9. The M.A.C. will collect from Main Dressing Stations.

10. Stretcher Dumps.
Extra stretchers will be at each Advanced Dressing Station.

11. Recording Centre. The 2/1st South Mid. Field Amb., will be the Recording Centre.

12. Os.C. 2/2 and 2/3rd Field Ambulances will be prepared to push forward the Advanced Dressing Stations and Car Loading Posts.

C Hoskins

Colonel A.M.S.
A.D.M.S., 61 Division.

August 7th 1918.

S E C R E T

A.D.M.S., No: 913

D1

Map.Ref. Sheet 36A.1/40,000

An Advanced Dressing Station has been established at the Forge (Smithy) J.28.d.4.7. on the CROIX-MARRAISSE - MERVILLE Road; with a Car Loading Post at J.30.d.5.1. and R.A.M.C., Relay Post at K.25.d.9.4.

This should render evacuation from the Right Brigade sector (except its extreme left) easier, and will avoid the wood and railway.

This route of evacuation - as far as the BARN M.D.S., (I.30.c.7.4.) - is supervised by the C.O. 2/3rd South Midland Field Ambulance.

The road is marked by flags W. of LE SART.

The former route of evacuation is still available, i.e., through the Wood by the VIA ROMA - Advanced Dressing Station at EDITH Station (J.16.d.7.2.) and Main Dressing Station on the Canal (I.17.c.5.1.)

Hawkins

Colonel A.M.S.,
A.D.M.S., 61 Div.

Aug. 9th 1918.

Distribution :-
All Regimental M.Os.
Os.C. Field Ambs., for information.
61 Division "G" & "Q" -do-
182,183,184 Inf. Bdes. -do-
C.R.A., -do-
C.R.E., -do-
1/5 D.C.L.I., -do-
61 Bn. M.G.C., -do-
85 M.A.C., -do-
D.D.M.S., XI Corps. -do-
A.D.M.S., 74 Div. -do-

SECRET

E

LIGHT RAILWAY ARRANGEMENTS FOR EVACUATION OF WOUNDED

Issued with 61 Division R.A.M.C., Order No: 66.

"A" TRAIN. 10 Ration trucks, 5 Ambulance trucks at MEREDITH SIDING for A.D.S., at ZERO plus 0.30.
This to run between MEREDITH and EDITH till evacuation of wounded is completed.

"B" TRAIN. 10 Ration trucks, 5 Ambulance trucks to be at EDITH Station at ZERO plus 1 hour.
This to run between EDITH and CANAL Dressing Station till evacuation of wounded is completed.

"C" TRAIN. 10 Ration trucks, 5 Ambulance trucks to be at CROWE at ZERO plus 1 hour.
This to proceed to EDITH as soon as "B" Ambulance Train has passed CROWE on the way to CANAL Dressing Station.
This will also run between EDITH and CANAL Dressing Station till the evacuation of the wounded is completed.

H Boldero
Major
for Colonel A.M.S.
A.D.M.S. 61 Div.

August 10th 1918.

SECRET   COPY No: ______

R.A.M.C., ORDER No: 66
by
Colonel C.H.HOWKINS. D.S.O., A.M.S.,
A.D.M.S., 61 Division

E

August 10th 1918

1. On 11th August, at an hour to be notified later, the 184 Inf. Bde. will cross the PLATE BECQUE and establish a Bridge-head on the general line K.22.b.7.7. (LES PURESBECQUES incl.) - Houses at K.17.a.6.6. (incl.) - PLATE BECQUE at approx. K.11.c.7.2.

2. The 182nd Inf. Bde, conforming to the above, will push forward its left in close touch with the 184th Inf. Bde., and establish itself on the general line K.22.d.0.5. - K.22.b.7.7.

3. Objectives when reached will be at once consolidated. 184th Inf. Bde. will pay particular attention to their left flank from which counter-attacks are likely to come.

4. Extra R.A.M.C. Squads. The O.C. 2/2nd Field Amb., will attach two R.A.M.C., Squads and a runner to the medical officers of the 184th Inf. Bde.

5. The O.C. 2/3 Field Amb., will attach 6 R.A.M.C. Squads with stretchers and three wheeled stretcher carriages, to the 2/2 Field Amb., for temporary duty.
These squads will report as follows :-

4 Squads to EDITH Advanced Dressing Station.
2 Squads to FORGE Advanced Dressing Station (J.28.d.4.7.)

The squads to report by 6 p.m. to-night.

6. Horse Ambulances. Walking wounded will be evacuated from FOREST CORNER (J.23.a.0.5.) to the BARN M.D.S., if any congestion occurs at EDITH A.D.S.,
Each Field Ambulance will detail two horsed Ambulances for this purpose.
Further orders regarding those will be issued separately.
This line of evacuation will be supervised by O.C. 2/3rd Field Amb.,

7. Motor Ambulances. The O.C. 2/1 Field Amb., will attach two motor Ambulances to O.C. 2/2 Field Amb., These cars to report to FOREST CORNER by ZERO plus 1 hour.
The O.C. 2/3 Field Amb., will detail one motor Ambulance to report to FORGE A.D.S., by ZERO plus 1 hour, to assist in evacuation on application from EDITH A.D.S.,

8. Railway. A train will be at MEREDITH Station at ZERO plus ½ hour, and a train will be at EDITH at ZERO plus 1 hour.
One train will run between MEREDITH and EDITH Stations.
Two trains will ply between EDITH and CANAL M.D.S., as long as necessary.

9. Extra assistance. If extra Medical assistance is required at EDITH A.D.S., application can be made to the FORGE A.D.S.,

10. Evacuation of urgent cases. A M.A.C., Car will be at each M.D.S. to evacuate urgent cases.
Those cars will be replaced at once by the M.A.C.,

11. Stretchers. Each Main Dressing Station will see that stretchers are sent back promptly.
A dump of 25 stretchers will be at the FORGE A.D.S.,

12. 184th Inf. Bde. will establish Battle H.Q. at STATION INN (K.14.a.5.9.)
182nd Inf. Bde. will remain in their present position.

P.T.O.

13. Field Ambulances ACKNOWLEDGE.

C. Hawkins

Colonel A.M.S.,
A.D.M.S., 61 Division.

Distribution :-

1-3.	Os.C. Field Ambs.,	
4-6.	182,183,184 Inf.Bdes. for information.	
7.	61 Div "G"	-do-
8.	61 Div "Q"	-do-
9.	C.R.A.,	-do-
10.	C.R.E.,	-do-
11.	61 Bn. M.G.C.,	-do-
12.	1/5 D.C.L.I.,	-do-
13.	A.P.M.,	-do-
14.	D.D.M.S., XI Corps.	-do-
15.	25 M.A.C.,	-do-
16.	A.D.M.S., 74 Div.	-do-
17-31.	Regimental M.Os.	-do-
32-33.	War Diary.	
34-37.	Spare.	

A.D.M.S.,No. 232.

F

DYSENTERY AND DIARRHOEA.

The following arrangements for dealing with Dysentery and Diarrhoea will be adopted in this Division.

1. Any man passing blood and mucus will be sent at once to a Field Ambulance, and considered as suffering from Dysentery.

2. The Divisional Diarrhoea Centre will be at the 2/2nd South Midland Field Ambulance STEENBECQUE.

3. Cases of diarrhoea may be held for observation in Units for not more than 24 hours, if the following conditions can be fulfilled ;-

(i) The faeces can be incinerated.
(ii) The accommodation is good and patients can be segregated.
(iii) The Medical Officer can keep the patients under observation for that period.

Medical Officers i/c Units will inform the A.D.M.S., if this is possible, giving map references, so that the place may be inspected by him.

4. Os.C. Field Ambulances and Medical Officers i/c Infantry battalions, 1/5 D.C.L.I., 61 Bn. M.G.C., R.E., 306 and 307 Bdes R.F.A., 61 D.A.C., R.F.A., will wire the A.D.M.S., to reach this Office by 5 p.m. every Saturday, the numbers by Units, of men reporting sick to him with diarrhoea and dysentery during the week ending Saturday 12 noon. This return is very important, and NIL returns will be rendered.

5. Medical Officers i/c Units must see that every sanitary precaution is taken. It must be remembered that intestinal diseases are very prevalent at this time of year, and any lack of sanitary precaution, neglect in cookhouses, or contamination of food by flies or dust, may cause any outbreak.

6. COOKHOUSE ORDERS. XIth.Corps Cookhouse Orders must be placed in each cookhouse, and M.Os., i/c Units will pay particular attention to them.

7. Fifth Army Routine Order No.8 (this Office No.913 dated August 8th) is cancelled.

C Hawkins

Colonel A.M.S.,
13/8/18. A.D.M.S., 61st.Division.

G

A.D.M.S., No: 62.

Reference 61 Division No: G.C.17/3 dated August 9th "Instructions for Defence against Gas" para. 7 (c)

1. Field Ambulances concerned will arrange that the undermentioned posts are equipped with -

(a) Washing Basins - 2
(b) Towels - 4
(c) Soap.

These should be kept constantly ready for use at :-

K.25.d.9.4.
J.30.d.5.1.
J.28.d.4.7. (SMITHY ADS)
J.21.d.9.6. (DRUMMOND POST)
K.13.b.7.8. (nr MEREDITH STN)
J.18.c.4.4. (SAW MILLS)
J.16.d.7.2. (EDITH A.D.S.)
J.10.b.2.2. (GUNNERS POST A)
J.4.b.6.2. (GUNNERS POST B)
D.28.b.8.6. (New GUNNERS POST)

and at all R.A.Ps.

PRESENT POSITIONS

	LEFT SECTOR.	RIGHT SECTOR.
LEFT	K.3.d.5.3.	K.13.b.9.1.
RIGHT	K.14.a.5.9.	K.25.a.1.9.
SUPPORT	K.9.a.0.2.	K.13.a.3.1.

2. Articles mentioned in para. 1 will be treated as Trench Stores.

H B [signature]
Major.
for A.D.M.S. 61 Div.

13/8/18.

Distribution :-

Os.C. Field Ambulances.
61 Division "G" for information.
61 Division "Q" -do-

Secret

H.

A.D.M.S.
61st DIVISION.
913/1097

MEDICAL ARRANGEMENTS.

61st Division.

1. Information.

The enemy is withdrawing but it is uncertain to what points he has decided to retire.

The Advance guard of the Division is composed as follows:-

G.O.C.183 Infantry Brigade.
2 Batteries R.F.A.
2 Sections F.Co RE.
1 Machine Gun Coy. - 183 Inf.Bde.
Portion of a Field Ambulance.

These will push forward boldly and endeavour to establish itself on the general line LOUNGE House (L.32.b.8.8.) CHAPELLE DUVELLE TROMPE BRIDGE RUE MONTIGNY today.

If enemy is not encountered the Advance Guard will continue the forward movement within boundaries allotted to the Division till touch with enemy is established.

Boundaries

Southern Boundary - Lys Canal.
Northern Boundary - VIERHOUCK. - COCHIN CORNER (excluded) L.15.a.0.0. thence along Grid Line due east.

2. The A.D.S. at EDITH Station will move forward forthwith and establish an A.D.S. at MEREDITH STATION (K.13.b.7.7.) A small detachment of R.A.M.C. will establish a Relay Post at EDITH STATION. The Car loading post at FOREST Corner will move to MEREDITH Station A.D.S.

3. The FORGE A.D.S. (J.28 d.4.7.) will move East along the TANNAY-MERVILLE Road and establish an A.D.S. near LONETREE (K.26.c.) A small party of R.A.M.C. will be left and establish a Relay Post at the FORGE J.28.d.4.7.

4. The O.C.2/3 S.M.Field Ambulance will detail one section with 2 Medical Officers to proceed forthwith and report to the Advanced H.Q.183 Infantry Brigade for duty.

5. Evacuation of Wounded and Sick.- These will be evacuated from the Advanced Guard through the A.D.S. at MEREDITH STATION and LONETREE.

6. Car Loading Posts and Relay Posts will be formed as the tactical situation develops.

H Boldero
Major for
Colonel.,
A.D.M.S.,61st Division.

7.30 pm.
29-8-18.

Distribution:-

Os.C.Field Ambulances.
182,183,184 Inf Bdes.
All R.M.Os.
O.C.1/5 D.C.L.I.
O.C.61 Bn M.G.Co.
C.R.A.,
C.R.E.,
Div Train.
61st Div "G"
61st Div "Q"
D.D.M.S.,XIth Corps.
25 M.A.C.
A.D.M.S.74 Division.
A.D.M.S.31 Division.

SECRET.

COPY NO: 25

R.A.M.C., ORDER NO: 68
BY
Colonel C.H.HOWKINS. D.S.O., A.M.S.,
A.D.M.S., 61st Division.

August 27th 1918.

Ref.Map.Sheet.36A. 1/40,000.

1. The O.C.2/2nd (South Midland) Field Ambulance will take over the Ambulances premises at BORRECHEN from the O.C.2/3rd (South Midland) Field Ambulance.
Relief to be completed by 6 pm 29th inst. Details to be arranged by O.C.F.Ambulances concerned.

2. The O.C. 2/3rd (South Midland) Field Ambulance will establish his Headquarters at the FORGE (J.28.d.4.7.) and be responsible for the Advanced Dressing Stations and evacuation from the forward area.

3. Divisional Gas Centre.
Major W.V.WOOD. RAMC. and a detachment of the 2/3rd (South Midland) Field Ambulance, now employed in the Divisional Gas Centre, will be attached to the 2/2nd (South Midland) Field Ambulance, and carry out their former duties.

4. Divisional Rest Station.
The accommodation set apart in the 61st Division Reception Camp will form the Divisional Rest Station. This will be under the administration of the 2/2nd (South Midland) Field Ambulance. Very slight convalescent Gassed and other cases will be transferred there.

5. ACKNOWLEDGE. (Field Ambulances only)

Issued at 3.pm.

H.P.Balaine
Major
for Colonel, A.M.S.
A.D.M.S., 61st Division.

Distribution:-

1-3.	Os.C.Field Ambulances.	
4.	61 Division "G" for information.	
5.	61 Division "Q"	-do-
6-8.	182,183,184 Inf Bdes	-do-
9.	C.R.A.	-do-
10.	C.R.E.	-do-
11.	1/5 D.C.L.I.	-do-
12.	61 Bn M.G.C.,	-do-
13.	61 Div Train.	-do-
14.	D.A.D.V.S.	-do-
15.	Senior Chaplain.	-do-
17.	D.D.M.S., XI Corps.	-do-
18.	A.D.M.S., 59 Div.	-do-
19.	A.D.M.S., 40 Div.	-do-
20.	Div Gas Officer.	-do-
21.	C.O.Div Reception Camp	-do-
22.	25 M.A.C.	-do-
23-24.	War Diary.	
25-28.	Spare.	

S E C R E T   COPY NO: 32

J

61st DIVISION R.A.M.C. ORDER NO: 68
BY
Colonel C.H.HOWKINS. D.S.O., A.M.S.,
A.D.M.S., 61st Division.

Ref. Map Sheet 36A. 1/40,000.   August 31st 1918.

1. The O.C. 2/1 (South Midland) Field Ambulance will move the Main Dressing Station from present site at CANAL (I.17.c.5.1.) to MEREDITH (K.13.b.7.7.)
A Medical officer and a small party will remain at I.17.c.5.1. which will act as a Divisional Sick Collecting Post.

2. The Headquarters 2/1st (South Midland) Field Ambulance will move to the Brewery, HAVERSKERQUE.

3. The BARN Main Dressing Station at TANNAY will be vacated.

4. The O.C. 2/3rd (South Midland) Field Ambulance will form an Advanced Dressing Station at K.29.a.8.5., and push forward his Car Posts to keep in close touch with the Regimental Aid Posts.

5. Evacuation of casualties :-

All wounded and sick by hand and car through the Advanced Dressing Station to the Main Dressing Station at MEREDITH.

From Main Dressing Station :-

(a) Wounded and sick for Casualty Clearing Stations by M.A.C. cars.
(b) Sick for transfer to Divisional Units, by rail to the Divisional Sick Collecting Post - thence by horse Ambulance wagons.

6. Moves, which will be completed by 2 p.m. September 1st, will be reported tothis office.

7. A.D.M.S., office will close at I.19.d.1.9. at 9 a.m. on September 1st and reopen at I.22.d.1.1. (Billet No: 20 TANNAY) at the same hour.

8. Field Ambulances ACKNOWLEDGE.

Issued at 6 p.m.

H B Boldero
Major
for Colonel A.M.S.
A.D.M.S., 61 Div.

Distribution:-
1-3. 2/1,2/2,2/3 Field Ambs.
4-18. Regimental Medical Officers.
19. 61 Div. "G" for information.
20. 61 Div. "Q" -do-
21-23. 182,183,184 Inf.Bdes-do-
24. 61 Div. Train. -do-
25. D.A.P.M., -do-
26. D.A.D.V.S., -do-
27. D.D.M.S., XI Corps -do-
28. 25 M.A.C., -do-
29. A.D.M.S., 59 Div. -do-
30. A.D.M.S., 40 Div. -do-
31-32. War Diary.
33. File.
34-40. Spare.
41. C.R.A -do-
42. C.R.E -do-
43. Foreways -do-

CONFIDENTIAL 21

Medical

WD 29

September 1918

140/3262.

W A R   D I A R Y

OF

A.D.M.S., 61st DIVISION.

From:- September 1st 1918.

To:- September 30th 1918.

VOLUME 29.

Instructions regarding War Diaries and Intelligence Summaries are contained in F. S. Regs., Part II. and the Staff Manual respectively. Title pages will be prepared in manuscript.

WAR DIARY
or
INTELLIGENCE SUMMARY.
(*Erase heading not required.*)

Army Form C. 2118.

Place	Date	Hour	Summary of Events and Information	Remarks and references to Appendices
ANNAY. heet 36.A. /40,000	Sept 1st.		The Medical Posts are moved forward in accordance with the German retirement. Advanced Dressing Station established at MERVILLE. Main Dressing Station at MEREDITH (K.8.c.2.2.) Reference Appendix "A" HB	App."A"
	2nd.		Germans have evacuated ESTAIRES. Very few casualties. HB	
	3rd.		Advanced Dressing Station now established at L.22.c.2.8. on NEUF BERQUIN - ESTAIRES Road. Main Dressing Station at L.27.d.cent. The evacuation of casualties is very easy owing to the fact that the roads are in good condition, and in all cases cars can reach the R.A.Ps. The Divisional Rest Station moves to LA LACQUE Camp with the Divisional Reception Camp. HB	
	4th.		A party of the 2/2nd (South Midland) Field Ambulance commenced cleaning up the Brewery at HAVERSKERQUE as it is intended to move the 2/2nd Field Ambulance from STEENBECQUE to HAVERSKERQUE. The 2/3rd Field Ambulance ceased to take in Gassed cases at BOESEGHEM. HB	
	5th.		Advanced Dressing Station established at G.27.c.4.3. NOUVEAU MONDE. HB	
	6th.		The 2/2 Field Amb., open a Divisional Rest Station at HAVERSKERQUE for the reception and treatment of all sick. The Main Dressing Station has had to move back a thousand yards as they were shelled last night - probably due to the proximity of R.E. Dump, Light Railway, and Canal. See Appendix "C" New Medical Arrangements (Appendix "B") produced. The principle that is being pursued during this advance is that collections of sick, for example, D.R.S., Gas Centre at BOESEGHEM, and Diarrhoea Centre at STEENBECQUE, are being left until they are free of patients. Fresh admissions being kept further forward. This causes a considerable splitting up of the Ambulances, but this is preferable to the alternatives of either evacuating, or transferring forward, the sick. The Hospital at the Brewery. HAVERSKERQUE is being rapidly cleaned up and improved. HB	App "B" App "C"
	7th.		The Rest Station at LA LACQUE Camp is now closed. The number of gassed cases at BOESEGHEM is now reduced to 43. HB	
	8th.		BOESEGHEM closes down - their few remaining patients being transferred to HAVERSKERQUE. This allows the whole of the 2/3rd Field Ambulance to be used for clearing the forward area. HB	

A5834 Wt. W4973/M687 750,000 8/16 D. D. & L. Ltd. Forms/C.2118/13.

Army Form C. 2118.

Instructions regarding War Diaries and Intelligence Summaries are contained in F. S. Regs., Part II. and the Staff Manual respectively. Title pages will be prepared in manuscript.

WAR DIARY
or
INTELLIGENCE SUMMARY.
(Erase heading not required.)

Place	Date	Hour	Summary of Events and Information	Remarks and references to Appendices
CROIX-MARRAISE. J.21.c. Sheet 36A. 1/40,000.	9th		Routine duties.	
	10th.		The number of Diarrhoea cases occurring in the Division is slowly diminishing. There are now 65 cases under treatment at STEENBECQUE. The great majority of these cases are simple diarrhoea which readily yield to treatment. Only a few are being evacuated and no positive Dysentery has yet been reported. The cases are occurring in all Units of the Division, no one unit having any appreciable number.	
	11th.		Discussion concerning what preventative measures to be taken against Trench Feet is in progress in this Division.	
	12th.		The 2/1 (South Midland) Field Ambulance are doing very good constructional work at the Main Dressing Station, and are making out of a small house, a very good Main Dressing Station. They have painted a large Red cross on the tiles of their roof.	
	13th.		It has been decided in this Division to adopt the Camphor Prophylactic treatment against Trench Feet. The following are the principles :- 1. <u>When in rest.</u> Men should be taught how to rub the feet and toes. This should be carried out periodically under the supervision of an officer. Foot inspections should also take place, with the Company chiropodist and, if possible, the Medical officer in attendance. Care should be taken that the boots and socks are examined and defects remedied. 2. <u>Before starting for the trenches.</u> Foot bath houses must be erected at convenient places, Each man must - (a) Wash his feet with ordinary soap & water. (b) Wash them with Camphor soap. (c) Draw clean socks, dust them sparingly with Camphor powder, and put them on. (d) Take with him a supply of Camphor powder for use in the trenches. 3. <u>In the trenches.</u> Men must remove their boots and socks as often as possible; dust their feet with Camphor powder, and put on dry socks. 4. <u>On return from the trenches.</u> The feet must be washed and examined when dry and clean socks put on.	

A5834 Wt. W4973/M687 750,000 8/16 D. D. & L. Ltd. Forms/C.2118/13.

Instructions regarding War Diaries and Intelligence Summaries are contained in F. S. Regs., Part II. and the Staff Manual respectively. Title pages will be prepared in manuscript.

WAR DIARY
or
INTELLIGENCE SUMMARY.
(Erase heading not required.)

Army Form C. 2118.

Place	Date	Hour	Summary of Events and Information	Remarks and references to Appendices
	13th.		Trench feet continued. The constituents of the soap and powder are :- (a) The Soap. Soft Potash soap 1,000 parts. Powdered Camphor 25 parts Powdered Sodium Borate 100 parts. (b) The Powder. Powdered Talc 1,000 parts. Powdered camphor 25 parts. Each man requires a teaspoonful of Powder and a ¼ ounce of Soap. A Division for one week requires - Soft Potash Soap - 300 lbs. Camphor - 22 lbs. Sodium Borate - 35 lbs. Talc Powder - 500 lbs.	HB
	14th		Orders are issued to 2/3rd Field Ambulance to be prepared to make up these ingredients for Trench Feet.	HB
	15th		The last few days a good many houses, cross roads, and shelters have been blowingup, due to delayed action shells and mines that the enemy left behind. This causes difficulties in accommodation, for example - the cellar at the Advanced Dressing Station has been reported by the R.Es. to be suspected mined and so is not being used. Fortunately there is a large Ferro-concrete stable near, which is now being used.	HB
	16th		The 2/2nd Field Ambulance closed down their Hospital at STEENBECQUE and moved to Brewery HAVERSKERQUE. The Ambulances are now no longer split up. The 2/3rd being only used for evacuating the forward area. The 2/1st Field Amb., for Main Dressing Station work; and 2/2nd Field Ambulance at HAVERSKERQUE for all classes of sick.	HB
	17th		The A.D.M.S., lectured to Regimental Medical Officers on the precautions to be adopted against Trench feet.	HB
	18th.		Routine duties. HB	

A5834 Wt. W4973/M687 750,000 8/16 D. D. & L. Ltd. Forms/C.2118/13.

Army Form C. 2118.

Instructions regarding War Diaries and Intelligence Summaries are contained in F. S. Regs., Part II. and the Staff Manual respectively. Title pages will be prepared in manuscript.

WAR DIARY
or
INTELLIGENCE SUMMARY.
(Erase heading not required.)

Place	Date	Hour	Summary of Events and Information	Remarks and references to Appendices
	19th.		The old difficulty has arisen of the gunners requiring our Advanced Dressing Station site for Gun positions, and on this occasion we have decide-d to move the Advanced Dressing Station back about 300 yards, to a burnt out house, which has good cellars intact, and which are not now expected have been mined. Map reference of new site is - G.26.d.3.0. Lieut-Colonel G.MACKIE. DSO. Comdg. 2/1 Field Amb., returned from his month's leave, and Colonel C.H.HOWKINS. DSO. A.D.M.S., proceeds on leave. Lieut Colonel G.MACKIE. took over duties of A.D.M.S.,	HB
	20th		Considerable difficulty has been experienced in getting the Sterilizing Water motor lorries moved forward. The Fifth Army has laid down that they shall not be nearer the front line than 10,000 yards. This considerably detracts from their utility, as all Unit transport lines are considerably in advance of this distance. Two lorries are now working 2,000 yards W. of ESTAIRES on the Canal Bank.	HB
	21st.		Lieut-Colonel H.N.BURROUGHES. Comdg. 2/2 Field Ambulance returned from six weeks leave yesterday.	HB
	22nd.		Routine duties.	HB
	23rd.		Routine duties.	HB
	24th.		Preparations are being made for further enemy withdrawal. The point which is giving rise to most consideration is the water supply for drinking purposes. On the previous retirement, the principle adopted was this - The R.Es. working independently discovered wells and reported on their possibilities as a source of supply. Orders were then issued for R.A.M.C., personnel to test and label them. This process was laborious, but successful to a certain degree; the failure being that they are mostly shallow wells and rapidly run dry. A water cart often having to go to three wells to complete its complement of 110 gallons. As the line went forward fixed water points were established - (a) at MERVILLE (old town water supply) (b) A chlorinating and clarifying apparatus was installed on the Canal Bank at the LYS BRIDGE (N. of LA GORGUE) (c) At NOUVEAU MONDE - the civilian water supply to a sugar refinery. (d) 2 Motor Sterilizing lorries on Canal Bank 500 yards W. of LYS BRIDGE.	HB

Instructions regarding War Diaries and Intelligence Summaries are contained in F. S. Regs., Part II. and the Staff Manual respectively. Title pages will be prepared in manuscript.

WAR DIARY
or
INTELLIGENCE SUMMARY.
(Erase heading not required.)

Army Form C. 2118.

Place	Date	Hour	Summary of Events and Information	Remarks and references to Appendices
	25th		The following arrangements have been made to provide drinking water in the event of a further enemy withdrawal:- A Special water exploiting party consisting of R.Es. and R.A.M.C., will work forward immediately behind the advancing infantry to repair, test, label, and report on all possible water supplies. This should provide ~~xxxx~~ water for the forward troops until fixed points can be established, which may be done in one of the following ways :- 1. The Division has the use of 2 small water tank motor lorries which will convey water from established sources forward, to storage tanks. 2. Chlorinating and Clarifying Apparatus' will be moved forward as soon as possible. 3. It is hoped still to have the use of 2 Motor Chlorinating lorries, but it is doubtful whether the country will offer a sufficient volume of water, because the canal leaves the Divisional area.	
	26th.		Routine duties.	
	27th.		Lieut-Colonel C.L.LANDER. MC. Comdg. 2/3rd Field Ambulance proceeded on leave to the United Kingdom.	
	28th.		Lieut-Colonel GRAY. Consulting Dermatologist for the Army Areas called and inspected our arrangements for the treatment of Skin diseases at HAVERSKERQUE, and he expressed his satisfaction with what he saw. During the advance it has been impossible to establish fixed Bath houses, so the mobile units have been supplied with Lander Spray baths; and clean clothes have been drawn by units. Thus Units have been made responsible for their own bathing arrangements. A whole battalion can be bathed in one day with three Lander Spray Baths. They are extremely portable, easy to erect, and economical with the amount of water used. There has been no increase of skin affections.	
	29th.		R.A.M.C., Order No: 69 published (see Appendix "D") Medical Arrangements have had to be revised, and are appended marked "E". As the Infantry are to attck an enemy strong point to-morrow morning Appendix "F" was published.	App "D" App "E" App "F"
	30th.		The Infantry attacked and captured JUNCTION POST. The evacuation of wounded was rapid as the majority of them arrived at the M.D.S., one and a half hours after being wounded. It was thought that this operation might be the commencement of an enemy withdrawal, but up to-date there are no signs of any such movement occurring.	

G.E. Mackie
Lieut-Colonel.

A5834 Wt. W4973/M687 750,000 8/16 D. D. & L. Ltd. Forms/C.2118/13.

SECRET. **A.D.M.S. No: 913.**

B

MEDICAL ARRANGEMENTS 61 DIVISION

Medical Arrangements 61 Division issued under this office No: 913 dated August 4th, are cancelled, and the following substituted :-

1. **EVACUATION OF CASES.** All sick and wounded and gassed cases, and all cases of Suspected Primary Syphilis to No: 39 Stationary Hospital (FORT GASSION)

All sick and wounded and gassed cases from XI Corps to 54 Casualty Clearing Station. (AIRE)

THE ABOVE MEDICAL UNITS WILL RECEIVE ON ALTERNATE DAYS

N.Y.D.N., Cases. Self Inflicted Wounds. Infectious cases (except Dysentery and Enteric Fever)	51 C.C.S., COYECQUES.
Army Dysentery Centre. Cases of Enteric Group.	8 C.C.S., ELNES.
INDIAN Drivers.	6 C.C.S., PERNES.
PORTUGUESE.	8 Portuguese Field Amb., HERNELLES.
CHINESE.	11 C.C.S., MOULLE.
VENEREAL (Other than Syphilis)	To Receiving C.C.S.,
SCABIES.	2/3 Field Ambulance.

\- - - - - - - - - - 0 - - - - - - - -

2. **DENTAL CASES.** The Dental Surgeon attached 54 C.C.S., will attend at the 2/2nd (South Midland) Field Ambulance. HAVERSKERQUE. at 9 a.m. on MONDAYS, WEDNESDAYS, and FRIDAYS.
Not more than 30 cases (including officers) can be seen on any one day.
Applications for vacancies will be sent to the O.C. 2/2nd Field Ambulance who is responsible that the allotted number is not exceeded.
Special appointments must be made for urgent cases.

3. **EAR, NOSE & THROAT CASES.** The Ear, Nose & Throat Centre is at No: 51 C.C.S., COYECQUES.
Cases will be seen there at 9 a.m. every WEDNESDAY.
Not more than 6 cases will be sent on the allotted day.
Applications for vacancies will be made direct to O.C. 2/2nd Field Ambulance who is responsible that the allotted number is not exceeded.
Cases will be collected at the 2/2nd (South Midland) Field Ambulance at HAVERSKERQUE on TUESDAYS.
O.C. 2/2nd Field Ambulance will wire this office by 12 noon on TUESDAYS the number of cases for the Centre, so that M.A.C. cars can be arranged.
Officers will be seen on SUNDAYS.
Duplicate sick reports must be sent with all cases.

4. OPHTHALMIC CASES. The Fifth Army Ophthalmic Centre is at No: 51 C.C.S., COYECQUES.

(a) Cases of defective vision due to errors of refraction.

These will be sent on MONDAYS and THURSDAYS.
Not more than 6 cases will be sent on the allotted days.
Applications for vacancies will be made direct to O.C. 2/2nd Field Ambulance who is responsible that the allotted number is not exceeded.
All cases will be collected at 2/2nd Field Amb., HAVERSKERQUE.
The O.C. 2/2nd Field Ambulance will wire this office by 12 noon on SUNDAYS AND WEDNESDAYS the number of cases for the Centre, so that M.A.C. cars can be arranged.

(b) Surgical diseases of the eye.

1. Cases requiring examination and treatment by an eye specialist will be sent daily by all units when necessary, to reach the Ophthalmic Centre by 9.30 a.m. The transport will remain to take back any cases that require to be returned to their Unit the same day.

2. Urgent Injuries, wounds, and acute diseases of the eye will be admitted at any time.

(c) Officers.

Defective vision due to errors of refraction will be seen every Sunday morning by appointment made with the Ophthalmic Specialist by the A.D.M.S.,

O.C. 2/2nd Field Ambulance will arrange that the general instructions contained in D.M.S., Fifth Army Circular Memorandum No: 5 dated August 28th, forwarded under this office No: 913/48 of the 30th ult. are strictly complied with.

5. ADVANCED DEPOT OF MEDICAL STORES. The Advanced Depot of Medical Stores for the XI Corps is No: 31 at FORT GASSION.
Indents for Medical Stores will be submitted by Os.C. Field Ambulances to reach this office by 6 p.m. on MONDAYS.
Stores will be drawn from Advanced Depot on THURSDAY.
Urgent demands will be met at any time. In such cases the indent will be submitted direct to the Adv. Depot Medical Stores and a copy sent in duplicate to this office for countersignature by the A.D.M.S., and D.D.M.S.,

6. MOBILE LABORATORIES. No: 9 Mobile (Hygiene) Laboratory - THEROUANNE.
Sheet 36D. L.28.

No: 39 Mobile (Bacteriological) Laboratory - FORT GASSION.

H Bolton Major
for Colonel A.M.S.
A.D.M.S. 61 Div.

61 D.H.Q.,
6/9/18.

Distribution:-

Os.C. Field Ambs.,	All Regimental M.Os.
61 Division "Q"	Dental Surgeon 54 C.C.S.,
Ear,Nose&Throat Centre)	Ophthalmic Surgeon)
51 C.C.S.,)	51 C.C.S.,)
25 M.A.C.,	31 Adv. Depot.Medical Stores.
61 Div.Gas.Centre.	3 Australian Light Rly.Coy.
DHQ Med.Inspec.Room.	61 Div. Train.
D.D.M.S. XI CORPS	

A.

S E C R E T

A.D.M.S., 913.

AMENDMENT TO 61 Division R.A.M.C., ORDER No: 68. 31/8/18

Delete para. 2, and substitute :-

"The Headquarters 2/1st (South Midland) Field Ambulance are at "MEREDITH (K.13.b.7.7.) and Transport Lines and Quartermaster's "Stores at the Brewery. HAVERSKERQUE "

H Baldwin

Major.
for Colonel A.M.S.
A.D.M.S., 61 Div.

1/9/18.

To all recipients of R.A.M.C., Order No: 68.

SECRET. **A.D.M.S., NO: 915/1**

Map.Ref. Sheets 36 & 36A.
1/40,000

1. The Advanced Dressing Station, under command of O.C. 3/3rd (South Midland) Field Ambulance is situated at G.27.c.4.2.

2. The Main Dressing Station, under command of O.C., 2/1st (South Midland) Field Ambulance, is situated at L.27.c.2.6.

3. The Divisional Sick Collecting Post, under command of O.C. 2/2nd (South Midland) Field Ambulance, is situated at J.27.d.6.6. (The Brewery HAVERSKERQUE)

Major for
Colonel A.M.S.
A.D.M.S., 61 Div.

September 6th 1918.
2 p.m.

Distribution:-

Os.C. Field Ambulances.
61 Division "Q"
182, 183, 184 Inf. Bdes.
C.R.E.,
1/5 D.C.L.I.,
25 M.A.C.,
All Regimental M.Os.
D.D.M.S., XI Corps.
C.R.A.,
61 Bn. M.G.C.,
61 Div Train.
3 Australian Light Rly.Coy.

SECRET

COPY NO: 37. D

R.A.M.C., ORDER NO: 69
By
Lieut-Colonel Geo. MACKIE. D.S.O., RAMC.TF.
Acting A.D.M.S. 61 Div

Ref.Map.Sheet
36 N.W.1/20,000

Information. 1. It is possible that the 61st Division may be called upon to advance suddenly on its present front, and the following R.A.M.C., arrangements will be carried out directly the order to advance is issued.

Objectives. 2. 1st objective - CROIX BLANCHE - FLEURBAIX - ERQUINGHEM.

2nd objective - LA BOUTILLERIE (exclusive) BOIS GRENIER - RUE MARLE (exclusive)

Dispositions 3. The Division will advance on a two Brigade front, each Brigade having two battalions in the line. Inter-brigade boundary will be the grid line running E & W. through H.19. central.

Medical Arrangements 4. The 2/2nd (South Midland) Field Ambulance will stand fast, but O.C. 2/2nd (S.M)Field Ambulance will prepare to send forward 60 Bearers with N.C.Os, and, if necessary, Officers, as reinforcements.

5. The O.C. 2/1st (South Midland) Field Ambulance will continue to administer the Main Dressing Station on its present site, and will arrange to follow and clear the Right Brigade front as detailed.

6. The O.C. 2/3rd (South Midland) Field Ambulance will continue to administer the Advanced Dressing Station on its present site, and will arrange to follow and clear the Left Brigade front as detailed. He will be ready to move the Advanced Dressing Station forward on receipt of orders from this office.

Advance Party details. 7. Os.C. 2/1st and 2/3rd (South Midland) Field Ambulances will attach at least 4 bearers to each battalion of their Brigade. These may act as bearers, but will be chiefly used as connecting files and guides working between battalion Medical Officers and Ambulance forward parties.

Ambulance forward party 8. This should consist of one officer with Nursing and Bearer personnel at discretion of O.C., Light transport with stores and 2 tents, 1 Water cart and, if possible, 1 Ford Ambulance car and 1 motor cyclist. Ambulance signs must be carried, and this party will be responsible for keeping contact between battalions and the present Advanced Dressing Station. Temporary Field Dressing Stations will be organized as found necessary.

Stretcher bearers. 9. Bearer reinforcements will be sent to the Main Dressing Station by the A.D.M.S., and be moved forward in empty cars at the discretion of Os.C. concerned.

Motor Ambulance Cars. 10. Arrangements for extra Ambulance transport will be made by A.D.M.S.,

Regimental Medical Officers. 11. The R.M.Os of the battalions in the line will follow their advancing troops as closely as possible, and may leave their wounded, dressed and sheltered, in charge of attached R.A.M.C. guides, to be picked up by the forward Ambulance parties.

Water parties. 12. Trained Water Duty men from No: 57 Sanitary Section will be attached to the Special R.E., Water parties, to test, label, and report immediately upon all wells in the new area.

13. ACKNOWLEDGE (Field Ambulances only)

Lieut-Colonel.
A/A.D.M.S., 61 Div.

Issued at 4.30 p.m. 28-9-18

Distribution :-

Copy No: 1. 2/1 Field Amb.,
2. 2/2 Field Amb.,
3. 2/3 Field Amb.,
4 -18. Regimental M.Os.
19. 61 Div "G" for information.
20. 61 Div "Q" -do-
21-23. 182,183,184 InfBdes-do-
24. C.R.A., -do-
25. C.R.E., -do-
26. 1/5 D.C.L.I.(P) -do-
27. 61 Bn. M.G.C., -do-
28. 61 Div. Train -do-
29. D.A.P.M., -do-
30. Senior Chaplain -do-
31. D.A.D.V.S., -do-
32. Div Gas Officer -do-
33. D.D.M.S.,XI Corps -do-
34. A.D.M.S.,40 Div. -do-
35. A.D.M.S.,59 Div. -do-
36-37. War Diary.
38-42. Spare.
43. 57 Sanitary Section.-do-
44. 25. M.A.C.

SECRET   A.D.M.S., No: 913.

E

MEDICAL ARRANGEMENTS 61 DIVISION

Medical Arrangements, 61 Division, issued under this office No: 913 dated September 6th 1918, are cancelled, and the following substituted :-

1. EVACUATION OF CASES. All Lying Wounded to 1st AUSTRALIAN C.C.S., ST VENANT.
All Sick and Other Wounded, including gassed cases, to 1st AUSTRALIAN C.C.S., and to No: 39 STATIONARY HOSPITAL, FORT GASSION, AIRE, on alternate days.
ST VENANT to receive from noon 26th to 9 a.m. 27th: FORT GASSION, AIRE, to receive from 9 a.m. 27th to 9 a.m. 28th, and so on alternately.

N.Y.D.N., cases. Self Inflicted Wounds. Infectious Diseases (except Dysentery and Enteric Fever)	To 51 C.C.S., COYECQUES.
Enteric & Dysentery. All cases and suspected cases to be sent to -	39 Stationary Hospital. FORT GASSION.
INDIAN DRIVERS All casualties occurring amongst Natives of India to -	No: 6 C.C.S., RUITZ.
PORTUGUESE troops.	8 Portuguese Fd. Amb. HERBELLE.
CHINESE Troops.	11 C.C.S. MOULLE.
VENEREAL cases (other than Primary Syphilis)	To Receiving C.C.S..
PRIMARY SYPHILIS.	39 STATIONARY Hospital.

- -

2. DENTAL CASES. The Dental Surgeon attached 54 C.C.S., will attend at the 2/2nd (South Midland) Field Ambulance. HAVERSKERQUE. at 9 a.m. on MONDAYS, WEDNESDAYS, & FRIDAYS.
Not more than 30 cases (including officers) can be seen on any one day.
Applications for vacancies will be sent to the O.C. 2/2nd (South Midland) Field Ambulance who is responsible that the allotted number is not exceeded.
Special appointments must be made for urgent cases.

3. EAR, NOSE & THROAT CASES. The Ear, Nose & Throat Centre is at No: 51 C.C.S., COYECQUES.
Cases will be seen there at 9 a.m. every WEDNESDAY. Not more than 6 cases will be sent on the allotted day.
Applications for vacancies will be made direct to O.C. 2/2 (South Midland) Field Ambulance who is responsible that the allotted number is not exceeded.
Cases will be collected at the 2/2 S.M.Field Amb., at HAVERSKERQUE on TUESDAYS.
O.C. 2/2 Field Amb., will wire this office by 12 noon on TUESDAYS the number of cases for the Centre, so that MAC cars can be arranged.
Officers will be seen on SUNDAYS.
Duplicate sick reports must be sent with all cases.

P.T.O

4. OPHTHALMIC CASES. The Fifth Army Ophthalmic Centre is at No: 51 C.C.S., COYECQUES.

(a) Cases of defective vision due to errors of refraction

These will be sent on MONDAYS and THURSDAYS.
Not more than 3 cases will be sent on the allotted days.
Applications for vacancies will be made direct to O.C. 2/2 (South Midland) Field Amb., who is responsible that the allotted number is not exceeded.
All cases will be collected at 2/2 Field Amb., HAVERSKERQUE
The O.C. 2/2 Field Amb., will wire this office by 12 noon on SUNDAYS and WEDNESDAYS the number of cases for the Centre, so that M.A.C., cars can be arranged.

(b) Surgical diseases of the eye.

1. Cases requiring examination and treatment by an Eye Specialist will be sent daily by all units when necessary, to reach the Ophthalmic Centre by 9.30 a.m. The transport will remain to take back any cases that require to be returned to their unit the same day.

2. Urgent injuries, wounds, and acute diseases of the Eye will be admitted at any time.

(c) Officers.

Defective vision due to errors of refraction will be seen every SUNDAY morning by appointment made with the Ophthalmic Specialist by the A.D.M.S.,

O.C. 2/2nd Field Ambulance will arrange that the general instructions contained in D.M.S., Fifth Army Circular Memorandum No: 5 dated August 28th, forwarded under this office No: 913/48 of the 30th August, are strictly complied with.

5. ADVANCED DEPOTS OF MEDICAL STORES. The Advanced Depot of Medical Stores for the XIth Corps is No: 31 at FORT GASSION, AIRE.
Indents for Medical Stores will be submitted by Os.C, Field Ambulances, in duplicate, to reach this office by 6 p.m. on MONDAYS.
Stores will be drawn from Advanced Depot on THURSDAY.
Urgent demands will be met at any time. In such cases the indent will be submitted direct to the Advanced Depot of Medical Stores and a copy sent in duplicate to this office for countersignature by the A.D.M.S., and D.D.M.S.,

6. MOBILE LABORATORIES. No: 9 Mobile (Hygiene) Laboratory. THEROUANNE. Sheet 36D. - L.28.

No: 39 Mobile (Bacteriolgical) Laboratory. FORT GASSION, AIRE.

7. SCABIES CASES. All cases of Scabies will be sent to the 2/2nd (South Midland) Field Ambulance. HAVERSKERQUE.

H Bolton major
for Lieut-Colonel.
A/A.D.M.S., 61 Div.

September 28th 1918.

Distribution :-

Os.C. Field Ambs.,	Regimental M.Os.	61 Division "Q"
Dental Surgeon.	Ophthalmic Surgeon	Ear Nose & Throat Centre
25 M.A.C.,	31 Adv.Dep.Med.Strs.	61 Div.Gas Centre.
61 Div Train.	D.D.M.S. XI Corps.	3 Aus.Lt.Rly.Coy.
D.H.Q., Med.Ins.Room.		

SECRET A.D.M.S., No: 913/1094

F F

Map.Sheet. 36 NW. 1/20,000

Reference R.A.M.C., Order No: 69

1. As the Divisional front is now held by two Brigades in the line, the arrangements detailed in case of an advance, will come into force as soon as preliminary operations begin.

2. The extra bearers will therefore join their respective Battalions before dusk to-day.

3. The O.C. 2/1st (South Midland) Field Ambulance will be responsible for clearing the Right Brigade front from mid-night September 29th/30th.

4. Any necessary alterations of Ambulance Car Posts will be made by Os.C. Field Ambulances concerned, in consultation.

Lieut-Colonel.
A/A.D.M.S. 61 Div.

Sept. 29th 1918.

Distribution:- To all recipients of R.A.M.C., Order No: 69.

CONFIDENTIAL 16

MEDICAL

Vol 30

Oct 1918

140/3723

WAR DIARY

OF

A. D. M. S., 61 DIVISION

From:- October 1st 1918.
To:- October 31st 1918.

Volume - 30.

* * *

WAR DIARY
or
INTELLIGENCE SUMMARY.
(Erase heading not required.)

Army Form C. 2118.

Instructions regarding War Diaries and Intelligence Summaries are contained in F. S. Regs., Part II. and the Staff Manual respectively. Title pages will be prepared in manuscript.

Place	Date	Hour	Summary of Events and Information	Remarks and references to Appendices
CROIX MARRAISSE	Oct. 1st.		R.A.M.C. Order No: 70 issued as we have just heard that the Division is to be relieved quickly by the 59th Division.	App "A"
	2nd.		Further details of the relief fixed up (Appendices "B" and "C") Field Ambulances have been Brigaded for the purposes of the move. The Division will entrain on October 5th and 6th. The enemy is again retiring in this sector to-day. We reached Southern outskirts of ARMENTIERES at 1700 hours to-day.	App "B" & "C"
	3rd.		Two Field Ambulances move to-day into their associated Brigade areas, namely - 2/3rd Field Amb., to STEENBECQUE to join the 183 Infantry Brigade, and the 2/2nd Field Ambulance to MOLINGHEM with the 182 Infantry Brigade.	App "D"
	4th.		The 2/1 Field Amb., moves out to-day and joins the 184 Infantry Brigade at THIENNES. The three Field Ambulances are now all Brigaded. Appendix "D" issued to cover any accidents whilst entraining and detraining.	
	5th.		Lieut-Colonel G.Mackie. DSO. Acting A.D.M.S., proceeded by road to the new area to visit the D.D.M.S., XVII Corps and also to see the early detraining.	
DOULLENS.	6th.		The Division is detraining in the DOULLENS Area. Each Field Ambulance is looking after its associated Brigade. The 2/2nd Field Ambulance are, in addition, looking after the Divisional Artillery; and the 2/1st the 61 Bn. M.G.C., and Reception Camp etc.	
	7th.		The Division is to be prepared to move.	
	8th.		All Transport goes by road. Horse Ambulance wagons follow in rear of Brigades.	
LAGNICOURT	9th.		Personnel of Division moves by train to HERMIES Station and bivouac the night between CAMBRAI and BAPAUME. Divisional Headquarters established at LAGNICOURT.	
	10th		Appendix "E" shows the re-arrangement of Field Ambulances that is necessitated by the D.D.M.S., XVII Corps, Third Army, using the 2/3rd Field Ambulance to run the Corps Rest Station; also by the fact that the 2/1st Field Amb., are to clear the line when the Division goes in; and the 2/2 Field Amb., will be used to supply the various details required by the Corps. Contd.	App "E"

A5834 Wt. W4973/M687 750,000 8/16 D. D. & L. Ltd. Forms/C.2118/13.

Instructions regarding War Diaries and Intelligence Summaries are contained in F. S. Regs., Part II. and the Staff Manual respectively. Title pages will be prepared in manuscript.

WAR DIARY
or
INTELLIGENCE SUMMARY.
(Erase heading not required.)

Army Form C. 2118.

Place	Date	Hour	Summary of Events and Information	Remarks and references to Appendices
	Oct.		Continued.	
LAGNICOURT	10th		The Corps front is only about 3,000 yards broad; and there are three Divisions in the XVII Corps- 24th Division in line; 19th Division in support; and we are in reserve. The enemy is retiring under pressure, so the Division moves Eastward to conform - now lying 3 or 4 miles S.W. of CAMBRAI.	
	11th		Eye,Ear Nose & Throat arrangements produced - see Appendix "F"	App "F"
	12th		Colonel C.H.HOWKINS. DSO. AMS. A.D.M.S., returned from leave to the United Kingdom.	
NOYELLES.	13th		A.D.M.S., visited the whole of the Divisional area. The Division stands fast. Divisional Headquarters moves to NOYELLES.	
	14th		Routine duties.	
	15th.		D.A.D.M.S., proceeded on fourteen days leave to the United Kingdom. Major A.RADFORD. MC. RAMC 2/3rd Field Ambulance assumed duties of acting D.A.D.M.S., A.D.M.S., attended Conference of D.D.M.S., XVII Corps at Corps Main Dressing Station, and afterwards visited the forward area.	
	16th.		Routine duties. 2/3rd Field Amb., (Corps Rest Station) moved to day to College Notre Dame de Grace. CAMBRAI.	
	17th.		Orders received that the 61st Division would become the Supporting Group of the XVII Corps. The 19th Division is in the Forward Group. The 61st Division the Supporting Group. and the 24th Division the Reserve Group. Infantry Brigade Groups are moving into new areas to-day. On arrival the 2/1st South Midland Field Ambulance will be responsible for the collection and evacuation of sick and wounded of the Advanced Guard Group (183 Inf. Bde.) and the Support Group (182 Inf. Bde.) The 2/2 Field Amb., will be responsible for the Reserve Group (184 Inf. Bde.) Divisional Headquarters remains at NOYELLES. A.D.M.S., visited the 9th Bn. Northumberland Fusiliers, 2/2 Field Amb., and Corps Rest Station. Routine duties. The newareas are as follows :- 183 Inf. Bde. - Area about A.22 - A.23.a & c. 182 Inf. Bde. - Area about A.21 - A.16.c & d. 184 Inf. Bde. - CANTAING Area.	

Instructions regarding War Diaries and Intelligence Summaries are contained in F. S. Regs., Part II. and the Staff Manual respectively. Title pages will be prepared in manuscript.

WAR DIARY
or
INTELLIGENCE SUMMARY.
(Erase heading not required.)

Army Form C. 2118.

Place	Date	Hour	Summary of Events and Information	Remarks and references to Appendices
	Oct. 18th.		Orders received that the Division will move forward to-morrow, the 19th instant, and will become the Supporting Division of the XVII Corps. Field Ambulances Brigaded as follows :- 2/1 Field Amb., - 183 Inf. Bde. 2/2 Field Amb., - 182 and 184 Inf. Bdes. Routine duties.	
RIEUX.	19th		The Division moved to-day by march route. Divisional Headquarters closed at NOYELLES and re-opened at RIEUX. Field Ambulances are located as follows :- 2/1 Field Amb., - AVESNES lez AUBERT. 2/2 Field Amb., - B.4.b.6.8. Sheet 57B. 2/3 Field Amb., - Corps Rest Station. CAMBRAI. 2/1st Field Amb., is looking after the sick of the 183 Inf. Bde. (Advanced Guard Brigade Group) and 2/2nd Field Amb., the 182 and 184 Inf. Bde. Groups (the Support and Reserve Bdes respectively)	
	20th		Routine duties.	
	21st		A.D.M.S., visited 2/1 Field Amb., Routine duties.	
	22nd		61 Division Order No: 224 received stating that the Division will move forward on the 23rd inst. preparatory to operations to take place on the 24th instant. Field Ambulances of 61 Division are taking over from Field Ambulances of the 19th Division - see R.A.M.C., Order No: 73 (Appendix "G") Instructions also published to all concerned regarding Medical Arrangements in the event of active operations by this Division. (Appendix "H") The A.D.M.S., visited 2/1st Field Amb., A.D.M.S., 19th Division at St AUBERT, and the Advanced Dressing Station of 19th Division (57th Field Amb.,) in HAUSSY. Routine duties.	App "G" App "H"
	23rd.		2/1st South Midland Field Ambulance moved to-day from AVESNES LEZ AUBERT to ST AUBERT. Location of 2/2nd South Midland Field Ambulance also in ST AUBERT. Routine duties.	

2353 Wt. W2544/1454 700,000 5/15 D. D. & L. A.D.S.S./Forms/C. 2118.

Instructions regarding War Diaries and Intelligence Summaries are contained in F. S. Regs., Part II. and the Staff Manual respectively. Title pages will be prepared in manuscript.

WAR DIARY
or
INTELLIGENCE SUMMARY.
(Erase heading not required.)

Army Form C. 2118.

Place	Date	Hour	Summary of Events and Information	Remarks and references to Appendices
ST AUBERT	Oct. 24.		Divisional Headquarters closed at RIEUX and re-opened at ST AUBERT. Operations proceeding satisfactorily. Owing to strong enemy resistance in the region of VENDIGIES, the 184 Inf. Bde. (Reserve Brigade) went into action. All objectives were eventually taken. Routine duties. a.d.	
	25		Very few wounded have passed through. New A.D.S., at Q.20.a.1.7. opened for the reception of wounded at 3 p.m. to-day. There is a forward Collecting Post with a permanent staff and 2 cars at BERMERAIN (Q.22.a.2.1.) Everything is ready for a further forward move at any moment. a.d.	
VENDIGIES	26.		Divisional Headquarters closed at ST AUBERT and re-opened at VENDIGIES. Present locations of Field Ambulances areas follows :- A.D.M.S., office - VENDIGIES. Q.14.a.8.5. 2/1 Field Amb., (A.D.S.,) - Q.20.a.1.7. 2/2 Field Amb., - P.30.b. 2/3 Field Amb., (Corps Rest Station) CAMBRAI. A.16.a.7.8. a.d. There are a fair number of casualties passing through the A.D.S., but everything is working smoothly and evacuation is easy. Routine duties. a.d.	
	27.		D.D.M.S., XVII Corps visited the 2/1 Field Amb., A.D.S., Everything going well and evacuation is smooth and easy and so far there has been no congestion. The A.D.M.S., visited the A.D.S., and Regimental Aid Posts. The A.D.S., will be pushed further forward at the first possible chance. Routine duties. a.d.	
	28.		A.D.M.S., visited Advanced Dressing Station and Regimental Aid Posts. A new A.D.S., has been opened to-day at Q.22.a.5.9. This is also a Bearer Relay Post. Forward area has been quiet and there has not been a large number of casualties coming through. All arrangements continue to work smoothly. A.D.M.S., attended D.D.M.S., XVII Corps Conference this afternoon. Routine duties. Locations of Medical Units 61 Division published to all concerned, see Appendix "I" a.d.	App "I"

Instructions regarding War Diaries and Intelligence Summaries are contained in F. S. Regs., Part II. and the Staff Manual respectively. Title pages will be prepared in manuscript.

WAR DIARY
or
INTELLIGENCE SUMMARY.
(Erase heading not required.)

Army Form C. 2118.

Place	Date	Hour	Summary of Events and Information	Remarks and references to Appendices
	Oct. 29.		A.D.M.S., visited the forward area and the A.D.S., D.D.M.S., called. 61 Division Order No: 228 received with reference to impending operations. Medical Arrangements issued - Appendix "J" Routine duties.	App "J"
	30.		D.D.M.S., XVII Corps called and visited the forward area with the A.D.M.S., Revised medical arrangements in the event of the Division being called upon to take active part in operations, published. These cancel those issued yesterday. (Appendix "K") Routine duties.	App "K"
	31.		D.D.M.S., XVII Corps called. A.D.M.S., visited Field Ambulances and forward posts. All medical arrangements completed for the operations which commence in the early morning of the 1st November. Routine duties. November 1st 1918. Colonel A.M.S. A.D.M.S., 61 Division.	

A5834 Wt. W4973/M687 750,000 8/16 D. D. & L. Ltd. Forms/C.2118/13.

SECRET COPY NO: 24

R.A.M.C., ORDER NO: 70
BY
Lieut-Colonel Geo. Mackie. DSO. RAMC.
Acting A.D.M.S. 61 Div.

October 1st 1918

1. The 59th Division will relieve the 61st Division in the line October 2nd - October 5th.

2. The 2/3rd (South Midland) Field Ambulance will be relieved by the 2/1st (North Midland) Field Ambulance by 1000 October 3rd.

3. An advance party of 2/1st (North Midland) Field Ambulance will arrive at the LA GORGUE-ESTAIRES Bridge (L.29.d.9.1.) at 1600 hour to-morrow October 2nd, and will be met by a guide from the 2/3rd (South Midland) Field Ambulance, and escorted to the Advanced Dressing Station.

4. Os.C. 2/1st and 2/3rd (South Midland) Field Ambulances will post the relieving Ambulance bearers to all Regimental Aid Posts in the line, so that all bearers of the 2/3rd (South Midland) Field Ambulance can be withdrawn by 0600 October 3rd; and all Bearers of 2/1st (South Midland) Field Ambulance on night of October 3rd/4th.

5. Remainder of 2/1st (North Midland) Field Ambulance will arrive at Headquarters 2/3rd (South Midland) Field Ambulance on morning of October 3rd.
Relief to be completed by 1000.

6. On relief the 2/3rd (South Midland) Field Ambulance will join the 183rd Infantry Brigade in their new area.

7. The 2/3rd (North Midland) Field Ambulance will relieve the 2/1st (South Midland) Field Ambulance who will join the 184th Infantry Brigade on relief.
The 2/2nd (North Midland) Field Ambulance will relieve the 2/2nd (South Midland) Field Ambulance who will join the 182nd Infantry Brigade on relief.
Details of relief will be issued later.

8. All Trench and Area Stores, and equipment etc held surplus to Mobilization Store Table and G.R.Os will be handed over to relieving Field Ambulances, and receipts obtained.
Receipts to be forwarded to this office.

9. Completion of reliefs to be reported to this office.

10. ACKNOWLEDGE (Field Ambulances only)

Issued at 2100

H Baldwin major
for Lieut-Colonel.
A/A.D.M.S., 61 Div.

P.T.O.

Distribution:-

Copy No: 1-3.	2/1, 2/2, 2/3 Field Ambulances.	
4-6.	182, 183, 184 Infantry Bdes.	for information
7.	61 Division "G"	-do-
8.	C.R.A.,	-do-
9.	C.R.E.,	-do-
10.	1/5 D.C.L.I., (P)	-do-
11.	61 Bn. M.G.C.,	-do-
12.	61 Division Train.	-do-
13-14.	Senior Chaplains.	-do-
15.	D.A.P.M.,	-do-
16.	D.A.D.V.S.,	-do-
17.	61 Division "Q"	-do-
18.	D.D.M.S., XI Corps.	-do-
19.	25 M.A.C.,	-do-
20.	A.D.M.S., 59th Division.	-do-
21.	A.D.M.S., 40th Division.	-do-
22.	A.D.M.S., 74th Division.	-do-
23-24.	War Diary.	
25-30.	Spare.	
31.	57 Sanitary Section.	-do-
32.	A.D.M.S., 19th Division.	-do-

SECRET.   A.D.M.S., No: 913.

B

On completion of relief the Division will be in G.H.Q. reserve at 24 hours notice, and will be ready to entrain, if ordered, on or after October 5th.

Each Field Ambulance will, therefore, be administered by its associated Infantry Brigade, and will come under orders of G.O.C. Brigade for any subsequent move from the new area.

On arrival in the new area, Field Ambulances will be responsible for the collection and evacuation of sick and wounded of their associated Brigade, and will make necessary arrangements for the medical attention of units in their area who are without a Medical officer.

2/1 Fd.Amb. - 184 Inf.Bde.
2/2 Fd.Amb. - 182 Inf. Bde.
2/3 Fd.Amb. - 183 Inf. Bde.

H Baldwin Major
for Lieut-Colonel.
A/A.D.M.S., 61 Division.

Oct. 2nd 1918.

Distribution:-
Os.C. Field Ambulances.
182,183,184 Inf. Bdes.
61 Division "G" and "Q" for information.
61 Division Train.

SECRET

A.D.M.S., No: 913/1094

Reference para. 7 of R.A.M.C., Order No: 70 dated October 1st 1918 :-

The 2/2nd (South Midland) Field Ambulance will be relieved on October 3rd, by the 2/2nd (North Midland) Field Ambulance and will proceed to, and be billeted in the 182 Infantry Brigade Area.

The 2/1st (South Midland) Field Ambulance will be relieved on the morning of October 4th, by the 2/3rd (North Midland) Field Ambulance, and will proceed to, and be billeted in the 184 Infantry Brigade Area.

H Bowen
Major
for Lieut-Colonel.
A/A.D.M.S., 61 Division.

October 2nd 1918.

To all recipients of R.A.M.C., Order No: 70.

SECRET. COPY NO: 43

D

R.A.M.C., ORDER NO: 71
BY
Lieut-Colonel Geo.Mackie. DSO. RAMOT.
Acting A.D.M.S., 61 Div.

October 4th 1918.

The 61st Division will be transferred by rail from the XIth Corps, Fifth Army, to the XVII Corps, Third Army, on October 5th, 6th and 7th.

During the move of the Division to the new area, the following Medical arrangements will be made :-

ENTRAINING. 1. There are three Entraining Stations :-

182 Inf. Bde.	-	BERGUETTE.
183 Inf. Bde.	-	STEENBECQUE.
184 Inf. Bde.	-	THIENNES.

2. The O.C. 2/3rd (South Midland) Field Amb., will detail one Medical Officer for duty during the entraining of the Division.
He will detail one Nursing Orderly for duty at each station.

The Medical Officer will have two motor ambulance cars - one at BERGUETTE Station, and one to serve THIENNES and STEENBECQUE Stations.
The Medical officer will visit all stations frequently and inform entraining officers of his location and movements.

3. Entraining begins at 2130 hours on October 5th, and will be completed about 0510 hours on October 7th.

4. All casualties will be sent to No: 39 Stationary Hospital, AIRE as direct admissions, and a nominal roll sent to this office on completion of move.

DETRAINING. 5. There are two detraining stations :-

182 & 183 Inf. Bdes.	-	DOULLENS.
184 Inf. Bde.	-	ROSEL.

6. The O.C. 2/2nd (South Midland) Field Amb., will similarly detail 1 Medical Officer and 2 Nursing Orderlies, with 2 motor ambulance cars, to do duty at the Detraining Stations.

7. Detraining begins approximately at 0200 hours October 6th and ends about 1130 hours on October 7th.

8. Arrangements for the disposal of sick in the new area will be sent to the Detraining Medical officer as soon as possible.

9. Motor ambulance transport will move independently by road to the new area.

10. Attention is directed to the special orders being issued by Brigades regarding "Lorries" and "Surplus Kit"

11. ACKNOWLEDGE (Field Ambulances only)

ISSUED AT 1200.

Geo. Mackie
Lieut-Colonel.
A/A.D.M.S., 61 Div.

P.T.O.

Distribution:-

1-3.	2/1, 2/2, 2/3 Field Amb.,	
4-18.	Regimental M.Os.	
19-21.	182, 183, 183 Inf. Bdes.	for information.
22.	61 Division "G"	-do-
23.	61 Division "Q"	-do-
24.	C.R.A.,	-do-
25.	C.R.E.,	-do-
26.	61 Div. Train.	-do-
27.	1/5 D.C.L.I., (P)	-do-
28.	61 Bn. M.G.C.,	-do-
29-30.	Senior Chaplains.	-do-
31.	D.A.P.M.,	-do-
32.	D.A.D.V.S.,	-do-
33.	Camp Commandant.	-do-
34-35.	War Diary.	
36-40.	Spare.	
41.	File.	

SECRET.

COPY NO: 37

E

R.A.M.C., ORDER NO: 72
By
Lieut-Colonel Geo Mackie. DSO. RAMC.T
Acting A.D.M.S. 61 Div

Ref.Maps. Sheets -
57B. 57C. 51A. 1/40,000.

Oct. 10th 1918.

1. In order to conform to the rapid advance, the 61st Division will move to a new area to-day.

2. The following R.A.M.C. Arrangements will come into force to-day.

3. The 2/3rd (South Midland) Field Amb., will take over and administer the XVII Corps Rest Station at J.7.c. at once.

4. The O.C. 2/3rd (South Mid.) Field Amb., will hold his Bearer Division in readiness to move forward at short notice.

5. The 2/1st (South Mid.) Field Amb., will be transferred from 184th Inf. Bde. Group to 183rd Inf. Bde. Group (Advanced Guard Brigade) as from 1400 hrs to-day.

6. O.C. 2/1st (South Mid.) Field Amb., will come under orders of G.O.C. 183rd Inf. Bde. and move to new area forthwith.

7. The 2/2nd (South Mid.) Field Amb., will be transferred from 182 Inf. Bde. Group to 184 Inf. Bde. Group (Reserve Brigade) and will be responsible for the medical attention of both 182 and 184 Inf. Bdes Groups until further orders.

8. O.C. 2/2nd (South Mid.) Field Amb., will come under orders of G.O.C. 184 Inf. Bde. and will move with his Brigade Group when necessary.
He will hold his Bearer Division in readiness to go forward at short notice when required.

9. The XVII Corps BoundariesEast of CAMBRAI tend E. by N.E., towards MONTRECOURT inclusive (N) and HAUSSY inclusive (S)

10. ACKNOWLEDGE (Inf. Bdes. and Field Ambs., only)

Geo. Mackie
Lieut-Colonel.
A/A.D.M.S., 61 Div.

Issued at 1600 hours.

Distribution :-

1-3. 2/1,2/2,2/3 Field Ambs.,
4-6. 182,183,184 Inf. Bdes.
7-8. 61 Division "G" and "Q" for information.
9. C.R.A., -do-
10. C.R.E., -do-
11. 1/5 D.C.L.I.,(P) -do-
12. 61 Bn. M.G.Corps. -do-
13. 61 Division Train. -do-
14. D.A.P.M., -do-
15. D.A.D.V.S., -do-
16. D.D.M.S., XVII Corps. -do-
17. D.G.C., -do-
18-32. All Regimental M.Os. -do-
33-34. Senior Chaplains. -do-
35-36. War Diary.
37-40. Spare.
41. File.

F

SECRET. A.D.M.S.No.913/48.

MEDICAL ARRANGEMENTS - SPECIAL CASES.

1.OPHTHALMIC CASES.

Eye cases will be sent to reach the Corps Main Dressing Station on Wednesdays, to arrive during the morning. Officers are seen on Sundays at No 21 Casualty Clearing Station GEZAINCOURT. Appointments should be made for Officers through O.C.Corps Main Dressing Station.
Patients must be in possession of:-
(a) A.B.64.
(b) Full Kit and 2 days rations.

2.Ear,Nose,and Throat Cases.

Patients, with full kit and one days rations will be sent to the Corps Main Dressing Station on Tuesdays and Fridays to arrive during the morning.

3.DENTAL CASES.

Arrangements will be notified later.

J H Beldon
Major.,
for A.D.M.S., 61st Division.

11-10-18.

Distribution.
O.C.2/1 F.Amb.
O.C.2/2 F.Amb.
O.C.2/3 F.Amb.
O.C.,C.M.D.S.
All Regimental M.Os.

SECRET.   COPY NO: 23

G.

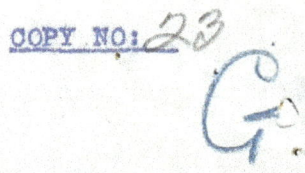

R.A.M.C., Order No: 73
by
Colonel C.H.Howkins. D.S.O., A.M.S.,
A.D.M.S. 61 Division

Ref.Map Sheet 51A.1/40,000.   October 22nd 1918.

In connection with 61 Division Administrative Instructions No: Q.57/7/3 dated October 21st, the following moves will take place :-

1. The 2/1st (South Midland) Field Amb., will take over from the 57th Field Amb., the sites occupied by them in ST AUBERT and HAUSSY. Details to be arranged by Os.C., concerned. Relief to be completed by 06.00 hours October 24th.

2. The O.C. 2/2nd (South Midland) Field Ambulance will take over the Ambulance site at ST AUBERT (U.24.a.6.9.) Move to be completed by 18.00 hours on October 23rd.

3. The O.C. 2/3rd (South Midland) Field Ambulance will detail the Bearer Division to report to O.C. 2/1st (South Midland) Field Amb., at AVESNES lez AUBERT (U.28.b.1.6.) by 16.00 hours on October 23rd.

4. The motor Ambulance cars of the 2/2nd and 2/3rd (South Midland) Field Ambulances (less 1 large car and 1 Ford car per Amb.,) will report to O.C. 2/1st (South Midland) Field Amb., at St AUBERT (U.18.d.7.7.) by 06.00 hours on October 24th.

5. Completion of reliefs to be reported to this office.

6. The numbers of D.D.M.S., Stretchers and Blankets taken over from outgoing units will be forwarded to this office as soon as possible after relief.

7. ACKNOWLEDGE (Field Ambs., only)

Issued at 18.00 hours.

C.Radford
Major.
Acting D.A.D.M.S.
61 Division.

Distribution :-

1-3.	2/1,2/2,2/3 Field Ambs.,	
4.	61 Division "G" for information.	
5.	61 Division "Q"	-do-
6-8.	182,183,184 Inf.Bdes.	-do-
9.	1/5 D.C.L.I.,(P)	-do-
10.	61 Bn. M.G.C.,	-do-
11.	C.R.A.,	-do-
12.	C.R.E.,	-do-
13.	D.A.P.M.,	-do-
14.	D.A.D.V.S.,	-do-
15-16.	Senior Chaplains.	-do-
17.	O.C. Train.	-do-
18.	D.D.M.S., XVII Corps	-do-
19.	A.D.M.S., 19 Division	-do-
20.	A.D.M.S., 24 Division	-do-
21.	XVII C.M.D.S.,	-do-
22-23.	War Diary.	
24.	File.	
25-30.	Spare.	

SECRET. A.D.M.S., No: 955/A. H.

Ref. Map.
Sheet 51A. 1/40,000.

In the event of active operations by the 61 Division, the following Medical Arrangements will be carried out :-

1. The O.C. 2/1st (South Midland) Field Ambulance will supervise the collection and evacuation of casualties.

2. The Bearer Division of the 2/3rd (South Midland) Field Ambulance will be attached to the 2/1st (South Midland) Field Ambulance for temporary duty.

   The 2/2nd (South Midland) Field Amb., (less 2 Tent Sub-Divisions) will be held in reserve.

3. The Advanced Dressing Station will be at HAUSSY (V.11.b.9.1.)

4. CIVILIANS. Arrangements will be made by O.C. 2/1st (South Midland) Field Ambulance to assist infirm and sick civilians as long as this does not interfere with military operations.

A Sanford
Major.
Acting D.A.D.M.S.
61 Division.

Oct. 22nd 1918.

Distribution :-

Cs.O. Field Ambulances.
61 Division "G" and "Q"
C.R.A.,
C R.E.,
182,183,184 Inf. Bdes.
1/5 D.C.L.I., (P)
61 Bn. M.G.C.,
O.C. Train.
D.A.P.M.,
D.A.D.V.S.,
Senior Chaplains.
All Regimental M.Os.
XVII C.M.D.S.,
D.D.M.S., XVII Corps.

SECRET A.D.M.S., No. 779.

MEDICAL LOCATIONS - 61 DIVISION.

Advanced Dressing Stations - Q.20.a.1.7.
Q.22.a.5.9.

Motor Ambulance Car routes - (i) From A.D.S., via LA JUSTION (Q.10.a.8.9.) to LE TAPAGE (K.24.a.0.8.)

(ii) LARBIN to Q.11.d.8.3.

(iii) LA FOLIE to Q.18.c. (BERMERAIN-RUESNES Road)

Horse Ambulances - BERMERAINE - LARBIN (Walking pas[illegible]

Field Ambulance Headquarters -

2/1 (South Mid.) Field Amb., - Q.20.a.1.7.
2/2 (South Mid.) Field Amb., - P.30.b.
73rd Field Amb., (24th Div.) - HAUSSY.

Map reference - Sheet 51A. 1/40,000.

Issued at 19.00 hours. 28/10/19.

C. H[illegible]

Colonel A.M.S.
A.D.M.S. 61 Div.

Distribution:-

61 Division "G"	O.C. Train.
61 Division "Q"	D.D.M.S., XVII Corps.
C.R.A.,	A.D.M.S., 2 Div.
C.R.E.,	A.D.M.S., 4 Div.
182 Inf. Bde.	A.D.M.S., 24 Div.
183 Inf. Bde.	A.D.M.S., 19 Div.
184 Inf. Bde.	Senior Chaplains.
1/5 D.C.L.I., (P)	D.A.P.M.
61 Bn. M.G.C.,	D.A.D.V.S.
	Town Major St MARTIN.
	-do- BERMERAIN.
	-do- VENDEGIES.
	-do- SOMMAING.

SECRET A.D.M.S., No: 913/1094.

J.

61 Division Medical arrangements.

Ref. Map. Sheet 51A. 1/40,000.

In the event of the Division being engaged in active operations the following Medical arrangements will be carried out :-

1. Walking cases. Walking cases will be conveyed or directed to the Advanced Dressing Station in BERMERAIN (Q.22.a.5.9.) and from there they will be conveyed by horse ambulance wagons etc, to the Corps Walking Wounded Collecting Station at B.29.b. (P.29.b.)

2. Lying & Sitting cases.

Lying and sitting cases will be conveyed to the Advanced Dressing Station at Q.30.a.1.7.

3. Sick & Gassed cases.

Sick and Gassed patients will be sent to the Advanced Dressing Station at Q.30.a.1.7.
INDIANS will be sent to the 2/2nd (South Midland) Field Ambulance.

4. Evacuation. The D.D.M.S., XVII Corps will arrange evacuation from the Advanced Dressing Station at Q.30.a.1.7. and from the Walking Wounded Collecting Station at P.29.b.

5. Recording. Field Medical Cards will be made out at the Advanced Dressing Stations; and the A.Fs.W.3210 at the Corps Main Dressing Station except in the case of Walking wounded sent to the Corps Walking Wounded Collecting Station. In these cases A.Fs.W.3210 will be made out at the Advanced Dressing Station and sent to the Corps Main Dressing Station.

6. A.T.S. Cases going to the Corps Walking Wounded Collecting Station will receive A.T.S., at the Advanced Dressing Station.

7. Reserves. The 2/2nd (South Midland) Field Amb., will be held in reserve.

8. Field Ambulances ACKNOWLEDGE.

Issued at 18.30 hours 29/10/18.

for A. Macfarlane
Colonel A.M.S.
A.D.M.S. 61 Div.

Distribution:-

Os.C. Field Ambulances.
61 Div "G" and "Q"
1/5 D.C.L.I. (P)
C.R.A., and C.R.E.,
D.G.O.,
D.A.P.M.,
D.D.M.S., XVII Corps.
A.D.M.S., 19 Division.
15 M.A.C.,
Regimental M.Os.
182,183,184 Inf. Bdes.
61 Bn. M.G.C.
O.C. Train.
D.A.D.V.S.,
Senior Chaplains.
XVII C.M.D.S.,
A.D.M.S. 24 Division.

SECRET. A.D.M.S.No 913/1094a.

K.

61st Division Medical Arrangements.

Ref Map Sheet 51A. 1/40,000.

The Medical Arrangements - A.D.M.S.No 913/1094 of 29-10-18 are cancelled.

In the event of the Division being engaged in active operations the following Medical arrangements will be carried out :-

1. Walking and Sick Cases.
Walking and Sick cases will be conveyed or directed to the Advanced Dressing Station in BERMERAIN (Q.22.a.5.9.) and from there they will be conveyed by horse ambulance wagons etc, to the Corps Walking Wounded Collecting Station at P.29.b.

2. Lying, Sitting and Gassed Cases.
Lying, Sitting and Gassed cases will be conveyed to the Advanced Dressing Station at Q.20.a.1.7.

3. Indian Troops.
Indians will be sent to the 2/2nd (South Midland) Field Ambulance.

4. Evacuation.
The D.D.M.S.,XVII Corps will arrange evacuation from the Advanced Dressing Station at Q.20.a.1.7. and from the Walking Wounded Collecting Station at P.29.b.

5. Recording.
Field Medical Cards will be made out at the Advanced Dressing Stations -except filling in Medical Unit : and the A.F.W.3210 for all cases at the Corps Main Dressing Station.

6. A.T.S. Cases going to the Corps Walking Wounded Collecting Station will receive A.T.S., at the Advanced Dressing Station if it can be arranged, if not, at the Corps Main Dressing Station.

7. Reserves. The 2/2nd (South Midland) Field Amb., will be held in reserve.

8. Field Ambulances ACKNOWLEDGE.

Colonel.,
A.D.M.S., 61st Division.

Issued at 18.00 hours 30-10-18.

Distribution.

Os.C.Field Ambces.
61 Div "G" and "Q"
1/5 D.C.L.I.(P)
C.R.A., and C.R.E.
D.G.O.
D.A.P.M.
D.D.M.S.,XVII Corps.
A.D.M.S., 19 Divn.
15 M.A.C.
Regimental M,Os.
182,183,184 Inf Bdes.
61 Bn M.G.Co.
O.C.Train.
D.A.D.V.S.
Senior Chaplains.
XVII C.M.D.S.
A.D.M.S., 24 Divn.

CONFIDENTIAL 17

MEDICAL

Nov 1918

98 31

W A R D I A R Y

O F

A. D. M. S., 61 DIVISION

140/3403

From :- November 1st 1918

To:- November 30th 1918

Diaries enclosed :-

A.D.M.S., 61 Division.
2/1 (South Mid) Field Amb.
2/2 (South Mid) Field Amb.,
2/3 (South Mid) Field Amb.,

VOLUME 31.

Colonel A.M.S.
A.D.M.S., 61 Division.

CONFIDENTIAL

MEDICAL

WAR DIARY

OF

A. D. M. S., 61 DIVISION

From :- November 1st 1918

To:- November 30th 1918

VOLUME 31.

C. Hunter

Colonel A.M.S.
A.D.M.S., 61 Division.

Instructions regarding War Diaries and Intelligence Summaries are contained in F. S. Regs., Part II. and the Staff Manual respectively. Title pages will be prepared in manuscript.

WAR DIARY
or
INTELLIGENCE SUMMARY.
(Erase heading not required.)

Army Form C. 2118.

Place	Date	Hour	Summary of Events and Information	Remarks and references to Appendices
VENDEGIES Sheet:- 51A. Scale - 1/40,000.	Nov. 1st.		The 61st.Division attacked this morning. All Medical arrangements and evacuation working smoothly. A.D.M.S., visited the Forw ard Area.	HEAB
			Orders received that the Division is being releived by the 19th and 24th.Divisions on the 3rd.November. Divisional Headquarters will move to ST AUBERT to-morrow. A.D.M.S., 19th.Div ision called with reference to the impending relief. R.A.M.C. Order No.75 issued (Appendix "A")	HEAB
ST AUBERT.	2nd.		Major H.E.A.BOLDERO., D.A.D.M.S., returned from leave last night; resumed his duties this morning. Major RADFORD returned to his Unit. Headquarters 61st.Division moved back to ST AUBERT.	HEAB
	3rd.		A.D.M.S., attended D.D.M.S., conference this morning concerning the proposed offensive to-morrow. During the afternoon information arrives that the enemy are withdrawing. Division is moving forward to-morrow, vide appendix "B" still in Corps Support with 19th and 24th Divisions in Front Line.	HEAB
	4th.		2/1 Field Ambulance with 182 Infantry Brigade moved to HAUSSY to-day. Routine duties.	HEAB
	5th Routine Duties			
	6th.		2/2 Field Ambulance with 184 Infantry Brigade moved to BERMERAIN. The Brigade Grouping has been altered as it is intended that the 2/2 Field Ambulance should be responsible for clearing the Forward Area on the next occasion that the Division goes into the Line.	HEAB HEAB
	7th.		The last two days have been very wet but there is no increase in the incidence of disease.	HEAB
	8th Routine Duties			
VENDEGIES.	9th.		Divisional Headquarters move to VENDEGIES.	HEAB HEAB
	10th.		Routine Duties.	HEAB
	11th.		Wire received at 0815 hours that hostilities will cease at 1100hours.	HEAB
	12th.		Routine Duties.	
	13th.		Routine Duties. Influenza at Divisional Headquarters has ceased. Appendix "C" produced.	HEAB
RIEUX.	14th.		Division moves by route march towards CAMBRAI. 182 Infantry Brigade and 2/1 Field Ambulance move to AVESNES lez AUBERT. 183 Infantry Brigade and 2/2 Field Ambulance move to AUBERT, and 184 Infantry Brigade to HAUSSY. The latter are being looked after by the 2/2 Field Ambulance.	HEAB
	15th.		The Division less Artillery moves to CAMBRAI by march route - see appendix "D".	HEAB
CAMBRAI.	16th.		The billets in CAMBRAI are good and Sanitary. Appliances in general are sufficient.	HEAB
	17th.		Routine Duties.	HEAB
	18th.		The 2/3 Field Ambulance is released from duty with D.D.M.S., XVIIth.Corps and comes under our orders again at 0600 to-day - see appendix "E".	HEAB

Instructions regarding War Diaries and Intelligence Summaries are contained in F. S. Regs., Part II. and the Staff Manual respectively. Title pages will be prepared in manuscript.

WAR DIARY
or
INTELLIGENCE SUMMARY.
(Erase heading not required.)

Army Form C. 2118.

Place	Date	Hour	Summary of Events and Information	Remarks and references to Appendices
CAMBRAI.	19th.		The 2/3 Field Ambulance who are remaining at the College Notre Dame de Grace CAMBRAI are treating the Scabies of the Division. and are prepared to take in Officers requiring simple treatment.	
	20th.		Routine Duties.	
	21st.		R.A.M.C..Order No. 79 produced. see appendix "F". The D.D.M.S.. requires a Field Ambulance to be left behind in CAMBRAI to deal with all local sick in the town - so again we shall have to move less one Field Ambulance. It was decided to leave the 2/3 Field Ambulance as they are the only Ambulance with a suitable site for retention of sick.	
	22nd.		Medical Arrangements in connection with 61st.Division move to BERNAVILLE Area produced appendix (G) they are rather ample because the transport is moving by road and will be travelling for 3 days using two staging camps - the personnel are going by train.	
	23rd.		The times of trains have been altered slightly necessitating ana amendment (appendix "H") to Medical Arrangements (Appendix) "G".	
	24th.		Entraining begins from CAMBRAI Ville Station.	
	25th.		Divisional Headquarters move by Road in lorries to BERNAVILLE.	
	26th.		All the trains are very late. There was an accident to the train conveying the 2/8 Worcesters The casualties were quickly cleared to C.C.S.. by the waiting cars.	
	27th.		There is difficulty in getting any Medical Arrangements produced for this Area as the Corps has not yet published any. but essentials have been notified to Field Ambulance Commanders.	
	29th.		Wire received that the 2/3 Field Ambulance who are employed forming Medical Posts at the four staging camps between CAMBRAI and DOULLENS will rejoin the Division on December 2nd.	
	30th.		There is very great difficulty in getting adequate accommodation in this Area. Application has been made for our Area to be enlarged as the billets are cold and not weather proof.	

C. J. [signature]
Colonel and
ADMS 61 Division

SECRET. COPY NO:

R.A.M.C., ORDER NO: 75
by
Colonel C.H.HOWKINS.D.S.O., A.M.S.,
A.D.M.S., 61 Division.

Ref.Map.Sheet 57A. 1/40,000. November 1st 1918

The following arrangements in connection with the relief of the 61st Division, by the 19th and 24th Divisions, will be carried out :-

1. The O.C. 2/1st (South Midland) Field Ambulance will hand over the premises utilised as Advanced Dressing Stations and Medical Posts, to the O.C. 57th Field Ambulance.
Relief to be completed by 10.00 hours on November 3rd.
Details of relief to be arranged between Os.C. concerned.

2. On relief, all personnel, ambulances etc, at present attached to the 2/1st (South Midland) Field Ambulance will be returned to their Units.

3. The numbers of D.D.M.S., Stretchers and blankets handed over to relieving unit, will be forwarded to this office as early as possible after completion of relief.
All stores held in excess of Mobilization Table and G.R.Os., will be handed over and receipts obtained and forwarded to this office.

4. O.C. 2/1st (South Midland) Field Ambulance will arrange that Ambulances follow the 182nd and 183rd Infantry Brigades, during the march

5. O.C. 2/2 d (South Midland) Field Ambulance will arrange that Ambulances follow the 184 Inf. Bde. during the march.

6. Collection of sick. On arrival in the new area the O.C. 2/1st South Midland Field Ambulance will arrange collection of sick from the AVESNES LEZ AUBERT area; and the O.C. 2/2nd South Midland Field Ambulance from the ST AUBERT area.

7. The A.D.M.S., office will close at VENDEGIES at 11.00 hours to-morrow the 2nd November, and re-open in ST AUBERT at the same hour.

8. Field Ambulances ACKNOWLEDGE.

C Howkins

Issued at 16.50 hours.

Colonel A.M.S.,
A.D.M.S., 61 Division.

Distribution :-

1-3.	2/1, 2/2, 2/3 Field Ambulances.	
4-5.	61 Div "G" and "Q" for information.	
6-8.	182, 183, 184 Inf.Bdes.	-do-
9.	C.R.A.,	-do-
10.	C.R.E.,	-do-
11.	1/5 D.C.L.I., (P)	-do-
12.	61 Bn. M.G.C.,	-do-
13.	D.A.D.V.S.,	-do-
14.	D.A.P.M.,	-do-
15.	C.C. Train.	-do-
16.	D.G.O.,	-do-
17-18.	Senior Chaplains.	-do-
19.	D.D.M.S., XVII Corps.	-do-
20.	A.D.M.S., 19th Division	-do-
21.	A.D.M.S., 24th Division	-do-
22.	XVII C.M.D.S.,	-do-
23.	File.	
24-30.	Spare.	
31-32.	War Diary.	

B

SECRET.

COPY NO:

R.A.M.C., ORDER NO: 76
By
Colonel C.H.HOWKINS. D.S.O., A.M.S.,
A.D.M.S., 61st Division.

November 3rd 1918.

The following arrangements will come into force for the next move of Infantry Brigades :-

1. 2/1st (South Midland) Field Ambulance will move and be billeted under the orders of G.O.C., 182nd Infantry Brigade.

2. 2/2bd (South Midland) Field Ambulance will move and be billeted under the orders of G.O.C. 184th Infantry Brigade.

3. The 2/1st (South Midland) Field Ambulance will continuo to collect sick from the 183rd Infantry Brigade.

Issued at 1900 hours.

H E R Baldwin
Major
for Colonel A.M.S.,
A.D. M.S., 61 Div.,

Distribution :-

1-3. 2/1,2/2,2/3 Fd.Ambs.
4-6. 182,183,184 Inf.Bdes.
7-8. 61 Division "G" "Q")
9. 1/5 D.C.L.I.,(P))
10. 61 Bn. M.G.C.,)For information.
11. C.R.E.,)
12. O.C. Train.)
13-27. All Regimental M.Os.)
28-29. War Diary.
30. File.
31-35. Spare.

SECRET. R.A.M.C., ORDER No: 76. Copy No. 30.

By

Colonel C.H.HOWKINS.D.S.O., A.M.S.,

A.D.M.S., 61st.Division.

C.

Reference Map Sheet 51.A. 1/40,000. November 13th. 1918.

1. The Division is moving to HAUSSY - ST AUBERT - AVESNES - lez - AUBERT Area on 14/11/18.

2. The 2/1 S.M.Field Ambulance will remain brigaded with 182nd Inf.Brigade.

3. The 2/2 S.M.Field Ambulance will move under orders of G.O.C., 184th.Inf.Brigade but on arrival will be billeted in ST AUBERT Area and come under orders of G.O.C., 183rd.Inf.Brigade.

4. The 2/3 S.M.Field Ambulance will remain under orders of D.D.M.S., XVIIth.Corps at CAMBRAI.

5. O.C., 2/1 S.M.Field Ambulance will arrange transport to follow 182nd.Inf.Brigade and O.C., 2/2 S.M.Field Ambulance will arrange transport to follow 183rd., and 184th.Inf.Brigades on the march.

6. On arrival in the new area O.C., 2/1 S.M.Field Ambulance will arrange medical attention for units without Medical Officers in 182nd.Inf.Brigade Group and collect sick from 182nd.Inf.Brigade Group and 1/5 Bn D.C.L.I.

7. On arrival in the new area O.C., 2/2 S.M.Field Ambulance will arrange medical attention for units without Medical Officers in the 183rd., and 184th.Inf.Brigade Groups and collect sick from the 183rd., and 184th.Inf.Brigade Groups and 61 Machine Gun Bn.

8. Field Ambulances and Infantry Brigades ACKNOWLEDGE.

H E A Baldwin

Major.,

Issued at 23.30 hours. for A.D.M.S., 61st.Division.

Distribution :-

1-3	2/1, 2/2, 2/3 Field Ambulances.	
4-5	61st.Division "G" and "Q" For information.	
6-8	182, 183, 184 Inf.Bdes.	-do-
9	C.R.A.	-do-
10	C.R.E.	-do-
11	1/5 D.C.L.I. (P)	-do-
12	61 Bn.M.G.C.	-do-
13	D.A.D.V.S.	-do-
14	D.A.P.M.	-do-
15	O.C., Train.	-do-
16	D.G.O.	-do-
17-18	Senior Chaplains.	-do-
19	D.D.M.S., XVIIth.Corps.	-do-
20	XVIIth.Corps Main Dressing Stn.	-do-
21	File.	
22-28	Spare.	
29-30	War Diary.	

SECRET.

R.A.M.C., Order No. 77.
By
Colonel G.H.HOWKINS.D.S.O., A.M.S.
A.D.M.S., 61st.Division.

Copy No........

Reference Map Sheet 51.A. 1/40,000.
51. 1/40,000.

November 14.1918.

1. The Division (less Artillery) will march to CAMBRAI Main Town on 15th, and 16th.instant.

2. The 2/1 S.M.Field Ambulance will march under orders of G.O.C., 182nd.Inf.Brigade to CAMBRAI "C" (S.W.) Area on 15th.instant.

3. The 2/2 S.M.Field Ambulance will march under orders of G.O.C., 183rd.Inf.Brigade to CAMBRAI "B" (N.E.) Area on 15th.instant.

4. The 2/3 S.M.Field Ambulance will remain under orders of D.D.M.S., XVIIth.Corps at CAMBRAI.

5. O.C., 2/1 S.M.Field Ambulance will arrange transport to follo w 182nd.Inf.Brigade and O.C., 2/2 S.M.Field Ambulance will arrange transport to follow 183rd., and 184th.Inf.Brigades on their marches, the latter on 15th.instant to CAGNONCLES and on 16th. instant to CAMBRAI.

6. On arrival in the new Area O.C., 2/1 S.M.Field Ambulance will arrange medical attention for units without Medical Officers in 182nd.Inf.Brigade Group and collect sick from 182nd.Inf. Brigade Group and 1/5 Bn.D.C.L.I.

7. On arrival in the new area O.C., 2/2 S.M.Field Ambulance will arrange medical attention for units without Medical Officers in the 183rd., and 184th.Inf.Brigades Groups and collect sick from the 183rd., and 184th.Inf.Brigade Groups and 61 Machine Gun Bn.

8. A.D.M.S., Office closes at RIBUX at 1100 hours 15th.instant and opens at CAMBRAI at the same hour.

9. Field Ambulances ACKNOWLEDGE.

H R A Baker

D.H.Q.
Issued at 1900 hours.

Major.,
for A.D.M.S., 61st.Division.

Distribution :-

1-3	2/1, 2/2, 2/3 Field Ambulances.	
4-5	61st.Division "G" and "Q" For information.	
6-8	182, 183, 184 Inf.Brigades.	-do-
9	C.R.A.	-do-
10	C.R.E.	-do-
11	1/5 D.C.L.I., (P)	-do-
12	61st.Bn M.G.C.	-do-
13	D.A.D.V.S.	-do-
14	D.A.P.M.	-do-
15	O.C., Train.	-do-
16	D.G.O.	-do-
17-18	Senior Chaplains.	-do-
19	D.D.M.S., XVIIth.Corps	-do-
20	XVIIth.Corps Main Dressing Stn.	-do-
21	File.	
22-28	Spare.	
29-30	War Diary.	

SECRET.

Copy No. 22

E

R.A.M.C., Order No 78.
by
Colonel C.H.HOWKINS D.S.O., A.M.S.
A.D.M.S., 61st Division.

Map Reference Sheet 57 B. 1/40,000

Novr 18th18.

1. The 2/3rd S.M.Field Ambulance came under orders of the 61st Division again at 0600 hours today.

2. The 2/3rd S.M.Field Ambulance will remain at the College, Notre Dame de Grace A.16.a.7.3.

3. From 0001 hours on 19th November O.C.2/3 S.M.Field Ambulance will take over from O.C.2/3 S.M.Field Ambulance the Medical attention of Units without Medical Officers in, and the collection of sick from, the 184th Infantry Brigade Group.

4. On and after the arrival of the Divisional Artillery in CAMBRAI, O.C.2/3rd S.M.Field Ambulance will collect their sick.

5. O.C.2/2nd S.M.Field Ambulance is providing Medical attention for the 61st Division Reception Camp.

H E A Bolton

D.H.Q.,
Issued at 1030 hours.

Major.,
for A.D.M.S., 61st Division.

Distribution:-

1-3	2/1, 2/2, 2/3 F.Ambces.	
4-5	61st Division "G" and "Q" for Information.	
6-8	182, 183, 184 Inf Bdes	-do-
9	C.R.A.	-do-
10	C.R.E.	-do-
11	1/5 D.C.L.I.(P)	-do-
12	61 Bn M.G.Co.	-do-
13	D.A.D.V.S.	-do-
14	D.A.P.M.	-do-
15	O.C., Div Train.	-do-
16	D.G.O.	-do-
17-18	Senior Chaplains.	-do-
19	D.D.M.S., XVII Corps.	-do-
20	61st Divisional Reception Camp	-do-
21	File.	
22-28	Spare.	
29-30	War Diary.	

S E C R E T.

Copy No....29...

F

R.A.M.C., Order No 79.
by
Colonel C.H.HOWKINS., DSO., AMS.
A.D.M.S., 61 Division.

November 21st. 1918.

1. The 2/1st S.M.Field Ambulance will remain in the 182nd Infantry Brigade Group and move und er orders of G.O.C. 182nd.Infantry Brigade.

2. The 2/2nd S.M.Field Ambulance will remain in the 183rd Infantry Brigade Group and move under orders of G.O.C.183rd Infantry Brigade.

3. The 2/3rd S.M.Field Ambulance will not move with the 184th Infantry Brigade but will remain in CAMBRAI at the COLLEGE NOTRE DAME de GRACE until further orders.
O.C., 2/3rd S.M.Field Ambulance will continue to clear the sick of the 184th Infantry Brigade Group until the latter leaves CAMBRAI.

4. FIELD AMBULANCES ACKNOWLEDGE.

H.E.A. Boldero.
Major,
for A.D.M.S., 61 Division.

D.H.Q.,
Issued at 1930 hours.

Distribution:-

1-3	2/1, 2/2, 2/3 Field Ambulances.	
4-5	61st.Division "G" & "Q"	For information.
6-8	182, 183, 184 Infantry Brigades.	-do-
9	C.R.A.	-do -
10	C.R.E.	-do-
11	1/5 D.C.L.I., (P)	-do-
12	61 Machine Gun Bn.	-do-
13	D.A.D.V.S.	-do-
14	D.A.P.M.	-do-
15	O.C., Div.Train.	-do-
16	D.G.O.	-do-
17-18	Senior Chaplains.	-do-
19	D.D.M.S., XVIIth.Corps	-do -
20	61st.Division Reception Camp.	-do-
21	File.	
22-28	Spare.	
29-30	War Diary.	

G

ADMS No 93

21

MEDICAL ARRANGEMENTS IN CONNECTION WITH 61st Divn MOVE TO BERNAVILLE AREA.

Ref Map sheet VALENCIENNES 12. 1/100,000
LENS 11. 1/100,000.

22-11-18.

1. The Division al Artillery are proceeding to new area by route march commencing 23rd inst, arriving 25th inst. O.C.3/3rd F.Ambce will detail a large motor Ambulance car to accompany the Artillery under orders of M.O.i/c D.A.C.

2. (a) The remainder of Divisional Transport (less that on tactical trains) is proceeding by route march commencing 23rd inst, arriving 25th inst and are staging:-
   i. first night HAVLINCOURT and BERTINCOURT area.
   ii. second night around ALBERT station.

(b) Two horse drawn Ambulance wagons of 3/1 F.Amb will be marching with 182 Brigade group, and two 3/3 S.M.Fld Ambce wagons with 183 Bde Group.

In addition O.C.3/1 and 3/3 F.Ambce will each provide one to march in the rear of the whole column (i.e. behind H.Q.Train)

(c) O.C.3/1st F.Amb will detail one Medical Officer to accompany the transport mentioned in 2 (a), and will arrange daily to clear him of sick.

(d) There is a C.C.S. at DELSAUX FARM (3½ miles E of BAPAUME), another at GREVILLERS (1½ miles W. of BAPAUME), and another at FILLIEVRES (6 miles N.of AUXI le CHATEAU).It is believed a C.C.S. will open at the CITADEL,DOULLENS on 24th inst.

3. O.C.3/3rd F.Amb will provide Medical personnel to be present during entraining at CAMBRAI VILLE Station. They will report to Entraining officer of each Brigade.
(The first troops arrive 0700 hours on 24th inst, last train leaves 1800 hours on 25th inst)

4. O.C.3/3 F.Ambce will provide Medical personnel and transport to report to Brigade Detraining officers at (a) AUXI le CHATEAU, and (b) CONTEVILLE.
Approximate hours of train arrivals :-
   Train No 1-3 at (a) first at 1800 hours on 24th and last at 0300 hours 25th.
   Train No 4-9 at (b) first at 0000 hours on 25th and last at 0300 hours on 26th.

5. O.C.3/1 F.Amb will detail an N.C.O.to travel with Train No 1, and O.C.3/3 F.Amb will detail N.C.Os to travel with trains 4 and 7. On arrival at Detraining Stations they will rejoin units.

6. In the new area O.C.3/1st F.Amb will collect sick from, and arrange medical attention for Units without M.Os in, 182 Brigade Group and Div Arty.
O.C.3/3 F.Ambce will make similar arrangements for 183 and 184 Brigade Groups.

7. ACKNOWLEDGE. Field Ambulances only.

H.E.A. Boldero
Major.,
for A.D.M.S., 61st Division.

D.H.Q.
Distribution:-

1-3 3/1,3/2,3/3 F.Amb.
4-5 61 Div "G" & "Q" for Infmn.
6-8 182,183,184 Inf Bdes for Infmn.
9 C.R.A. -do-
10 C.R.E. -do-
11 1/5 D.C.L.I.(P) -do-
12 61 Bn M.G.Co. -do-
13 D.A.D.V.S. -do-
14 D.A.P.M. -do-
15 O.C.Train for Inform.
16 D.G.O. -do-
17-18 Senior Chaplains -do-
19 D.D.M.S.XVII Corps"
20 File.
21-27 Spare.
28-29 War Diary.

27

A.D.M.S.No 913

H

AMENDMENTS TO MEDICAL ARRANGEMENTS IN CONNECTION WITH

61st DIVN MOVE TO BERNAVILLE AREA issued 23-11-18.

Para 4 "Approximate hours of train arrivals" is cancelled and the following substituted.

Train No 1-3 at (a) first at 20.40 hours on 24th and last at 04.40 hours 25th.

Train No 4-9 at (b) first at 09.00 hours on 25th and last at 05.00 hours on 26th.

H S A Baldero

Major.,
for A.D.M.S.,61st Divn.

23-11-18.

Distribution:-

1-3	2/1, 2/2, 2/3 Field Ambulances.	
4-5	61 Division "G" & "Q" For information.	
6-8	182, 183, 184 Inf.Bdes.	-do-
9	C.R.A.	-do-
10	C.R.E.	-do-
11	1/5 D.C.L.I. (P)	-do-
12	61 Bn.M.G.C.	-do-
13	D.A.D.V.S.	-do-
14	D.A.P.M.	-do-
15	O.C., Train.	-do-
16	D.G.O.	-do-
17-18	Senior Chaplains.	-do-
19	D.D.M.S., XVIIIth.Corps.	-do-
20	File.	
21-27	Spare.	
28-29	War Diary.	

CONFIDENTIAL

Medical

4

Dec 1918

/

VA 32

140/3489

WAR DIARY

OF

A. D. M. S., 61st DIVISION

From:- December 1st 1918.

To:- December 31st 1918.

VOLUME 32.

Army Form C. 2118.

Instructions regarding War Diaries and Intelligence Summaries are contained in F. S. Regs., Part II. and the Staff Manual respectively. Title pages will be prepared in manuscript.

WAR DIARY
or
INTELLIGENCE SUMMARY.

(Erase heading not required.)

Place	Date	Hour	Summary of Events and Information	Remarks and references to Appendices
BERNAVILLE	Dec. 1.		It is still uncertain whether the Divisional area is going to be altered.	HEAB
	2.		At present Field Ambulances have no accommodation or facilities for retention of sick.	HEAB
	3.		COULONVILLERS was prospected as a possible Hospital site, but nothing suitable was found.	HEAB
	4.		The greater part of the area has been searched for buildings that could be used as Hospital sites, w-ithout success, for t-he area is composed of small villages, labourers cottages and farms mostly. It is evident that Nissen huts will have to be used to form small Brigade Hospitals. The original idea of one large Divisional hospital has had to be abandoned.	HEAB
	5.		The work of the 2/3rd Field Ambulance now having ceased, i.e., no more units marching through the staging camps between CAMBRAI and DOULLENS; they have concentrated at PUCHEVILLERS.	HEAB
	6.		The Divisional area has been increased Westwards; this necessitated re-arrangement of Field Ambulances. For arrangements see Appendix "A"	HEAB App "A"
	7.		The 2/1st Field Ambulance move to BUIGNY L'ABBE and are now affiliated wit-h the 183 Infantry Brigade. The 2/3rd Field Ambulance marched to BERNAVILLE (staging for DOMART)	HEAB
ST RIQUIER	8.		The 2/2nd Field Ambulance move to AGENVILLE and are now affiliated with 182 Infantry Brigade. In addition they are responsible for the Artillery Brigade which is in the AUXI-LE-CHATEAU area, just North of 182 Brigade area. Divisional Headquarters move to ST RIQUIER to-day.	HEAB
	9.		The 2/3rd Field Ambulance move to DOMART to-day. They are now affiliated with the 184 Infantry Brigade. Under War Office orders, Major G,Scott Williamson RAMC. leaves for the United Kingdom. This is the beginning of our reduction in Medical officers. There is every reason to suppose that we shall not get any more reinforcements.	HEAB
	10.		Routine duties.	HEAB
	11.		The A.D.M.S. is continually going round the area which is getting into shape. Main lines of	HEAB

D. D. & L., London, E.C.
(A8304) Wt W1771/M2031 750,000 5/17 Sch. 52 Forms/C2118/14

Army Form C. 2118.

Instructions regarding War Diaries and Intelligence Summaries are contained in F. S. Regs., Part II. and the Staff Manual respectively. Title pages will be prepared in manuscript.

WAR DIARY
or
INTELLIGENCE SUMMARY.
(Erase heading not required.)

Place	Date	Hour	Summary of Events and Information	Remarks and references to Appendices
			improvement are repair of billets and construction of sanitary appliances. There is now no overcrowding and extraordinarily little sick wastage.	HHB
	12.		The 2/3rd Field Ambulance have found a house suitable for use as a Hospital, It is not large but will prove adequate as a Brigade hospital. The 2/1st and 2/2nd Field Ambulances will have to rely on huts which have been on demand some time.	HHB
	13.		The Division is doing nothing in particular. Drills, parades, etc with recreational training and the Educational scheme fill in the time.	HHB
	14.		It is feared that Venereal disease might become very prevalent, but so far this is not the case. One woman in DOMART has been identified and certified by the French doctor as infectious, but she is not yet removed.	HHB
	15.		Routine duties.	HHB
	16.		All offices and orderly rooms are busy with inumerable papers and forms in connection with Demobilization.	HHB
	17.		A.D.M.S., visited the 183 Infantry Brigade area.	HHB
	18.		The Huts for Field Ambulances are arriving and will be ready for erection soon.	HHB
	19.		Routine duties.	HHB
	20.		The Medical Inspection rooms of the whole Division are now equipped with apparatus for rendering the earliest possible treatment of Venereal disease, i.e., Pot Permang washes and E.T.cream.	HHB
	21.		Routine duties.	HHB
	22.		The 2/1st Field Ambulance are starting the erection of huts for their hospital.	HHB

D. D. & L., London, E.C.
(A8504) Wt W1771/M2031 750,000 5/17 Sch. 52 Forms/C2118/14

Instructions regarding War Diaries and Intelligence Summaries are contained in F. S. Regs., Part II. and the Staff Manual respectively. Title pages will be prepared in manuscript.

WAR DIARY
or
INTELLIGENCE SUMMARY.

(*Erase heading not required.*)

Army Form C. 2118.

Place	Date	Hour	Summary of Events and Information	Remarks and references to Appendices
	23.		Daily sick admissions to Field Ambulances have been approximately 16-20 in number. HCMB	
	24.		Routine duties. HCMB	
	25.		Only 6 cases admitted to Field Ambulances to-day, presumably there will be more in a day or two. HMB	
	26.		Routine duties. HCMB	
	27.		Yesterday and to-day only 9 cases admitted each day to Field Ambulances. HCMB	
	28.		Routine duties. HCMB	
	29.		Routine duties. HCMB	
	30.		The A.D.M.S., went round the Artillery area and found conditions satisfactory. HMB	
	31.		Routine duties. HMB	

C. Hawkins

Colonel A.M.S.,
A.D.M.S., 61 Division.

December 31st 1918.

D. D. & L., London, E.C.
(A8204) Wt W1771/M2031 750,000 5/17 Sch. 52 Forms/C2118/14

SECRET A.D.M.S., No: 913.

MEDICAL ARRANGEMENTS - 61 DIVISION

1. The 2/1st (South Midland Field Ambulance will move on the 7th December under orders of G.O.C., 183rd Infantry Brigade, to BUIGNY L'ABBE.

2. The 2/2nd (South Midland Field Ambulance (less one Section) will move from MESNIL DOMQUEUR on the 8th instant, under orders of G.O.C. 182nd Infantry Brigade.

3. The O.C. 2/2nd (South Midland) Field Ambulance will leave one Section at MESNIL DOMQUEUR until further orders, to look after patients.

4. Collection of sick :-
(a) The 2/1st (South Midland) Field Ambulance will, on and after the 7th instant, collect sick from the 183rd Infantry Brigade Group and Divisional troops in the ST RIQUIER area.

(b) The 2/2nd (South Midland) Field Ambulance will collect sick from the 182nd Infantry Brigade Group, 184th Infantry Brigade Group, Divisional Artillery (including 315 Bde. Army Field Artillery) and the BERNAVILLE and BEAUMETZ areas.

(c) On arrival of the 2/3rd (South Midland) Field Ambulance, the 2/2nd (South Midland) Field Ambulance will collect sick from the 182nd Infantry Brigade Group and Divisional Artillery (including 315 Bde. Army Field Artillery); and the 2/3rd (South Midland)Field Ambulance will collect from the 184th Infantry Brigade Group, 1/5 D.C.L.I., (P)., and 61 Bn. M.G.C.,

(d) The O.C. 2/2nd (South Midland) Field Amb., will attend sick daily at 9.30 a.m. at the Third Army Infantry School (AUXI-LE-CHATEAU) on and after the 8th instant.

(e) The O.C. 2/2nd (South Midland) Field Amb., will render medical attention to the 61 Division Reception Camp at BERNATRE, on and after the 8th instant.

5. On arrival in new areas the Field Ambulances will be affiliated with the Infantry Brigades as follows :-

2/2nd Field Ambulance	-	182 Infantry Brigade.
2/1st Field Ambulance	-	183 Infantry Brigade.
2/3rd Field Ambulance	-	184 Infantry Brigade.

6. The A.D.M.S., office will move to ST RIQUIER on the 8th instant at a time to be notified later.

7. Field Ambulances ACKNOWLEDGE.

C Howkins

Colonel A.M.S.
A.D.M.S., 61 Division

Dec. 6th 1918.

Distribution :-

Os.C. Field Ambs.,	
61 Division "G" & "Q" for information.	
182,183,184 Inf. Bdes.	-do-
C.R.A.,	-do-
C.R.E.,	-do-
1/5 D.C.L.I.,(P)	-do-
61 Bn. M.G.C.,	-do-
O.C. Train.	-do-
Reception Camp.	-do-
D.A.P.M.,	-do-
Senior Chaplains	-do-
D.A.D.V.S.,	-do-
Camp Commandant.	-do-
D.D.M.S., XVII Corps	-do-
15 M.A.C.,	-do-

MEDICAL

14/3689

33

Jan 1919 17

CONFIDENTIAL

WAR DIARY

OF

A.D.M.S., 61st Division.

From:- January 1st 1919.

To:- January 31st 1919.

Box 2928

VOLUME 33

Army Form C. 2118.

Instructions regarding War Diaries and Intelligence Summaries are contained in F. S. Regs., Part II. and the Staff Manual respectively. Title pages will be prepared in manuscript.

WAR DIARY
or
INTELLIGENCE SUMMARY.
(Erase heading not required.)

Place	Date	Hour	Summary of Events and Information	Remarks and references to Appendices
ST RIQUI ER	Jan 1st		Routine duties.	CW
	2nd		A.D.M.S. visited Field Ambulances. The Educational scheme is working well in the Field Ambs. and a fair number of men have availed themselves of the opportunities afforded; and many and various useful classes have been formed.	CH
	3 rd		A.D.M.S. visited 183 Infantry Brigade area. Arrangements are well in hand for the construct ion of delousing chambers attached to t he various establishments of the Divisional Baths. These are being constr-ucted in order th-at men proceeding for demobilisation can have their outer and under clothing thoroughly disinfested.	CH
	4		Routine duties.	
	5		Instructions received from the Division that a demobilisation allotment was being issued for men of certain categories t o be dispersed. A.D.M.S. visited 182 Inf.Bde. area.	CH
	6 .		12 men from Field Ambulances proceeded t o Corps Concentration Camp for dispersal. Routine dut ies.	CH
	7		A.D.M.S. visited 184 Inf.Bde.area and Field Ambulances. Billeting accommodation throughout the Divisional area has been considerably improved. There is now no overcrowding and billets are well ventilated and in good order.	CH
	8		Routine duties. There is a serious shortage in the supply of new boots for the troops. This matter has been taken up with the Division who are doing all possible. It would appear, however, that there is some difficulty in getting supplies up from the Base. It is very important that supplies should be forthcoming shortly as a number of men are unable to carry on; and the healt-h of the t-roops might be affected.	CH

D. D. & L. London, E.C. (A8004) Wt W1771/M2051 750,000 5/17 Sch. 52 Forms/C2118/14

Army Form C. 2118.

WAR DIARY
or
INTELLIGENCE SUMMARY.
(Erase heading not required.)

Instructions regarding War Diaries and Intelligence Summaries are contained in F. S. Regs., Part II. and the Staff Manual respectively. Title pages will be prepared in manuscript.

Place	Date	Hour	Summary of Events and Information	Remarks and references to Appendices
	9.		A.D.M.S. visited AUXI-LE-CHATEAU and area occupied by the Divisional Artillery. The erection of disinfestation chambers is proceeding satisfactorily.	CH
	10.		21 other ranks R.A.M.C. have been demobilised since the 6th instant. This is in addition to any who may have been dispersed while on leave. Routine duties.	CH
	11.		A.D.M.S. and D.A.D.M.S. visited Field Ambulances. The general health of the Division is giving great satisfaction, and the sick percentage is getting very low.	CH
	12.		According to statistics received from Third Army the sick wastage for week ending the 11th inst., is "NIL" This is a record so far as this, and I believe other Divisions of the B.E.F., and is a gratifying result of the efforts of the Regimental Medical Officers.	CH
	13.		A.D.M.S., visited 182 Infantry Brigade area.	
	14.		Approximately 30 other ranks R.A.M.C., have now proceeded from the Field Ambulances for dispersal. After the 20th instant, however, no R.A.M.C. personnel will be demobilised except under orders of the D.G.M.S., Demobilisation so far as Administrative services are concerned will in future be carried out by the Director of the Service concerned.	CH
	15.		Routine duties.	
	16.		A.D.M.S. visited 183 Inf. Bde. There are now several delousing chambers ready and they are working well. There was some slight difficulty as regards the supply of suitable Thermometers but a few have been obtained - sufficient to carry on with.	CH
	17.		Routine duties.	
	18.		A new revised War Establishment of a Field Amb., has just been issued and a preliminary copy has been sent us by the Division. The chief change is that a Field Amb., will in future be composed of two sections only. The Bearer Division remains practically the same. The question of equipment has to be gone into.	CH

D. D. & L., London, E.C.
(A8004) Wt W1771/M2031 750,000 5/17 Sch. 52 Forms/C2118/14

Instructions regarding War Diaries and Intelligence Summaries are contained in F. S. Regs., Part II. and the Staff Manual respectively. Title pages will be prepared in manuscript.

WAR DIARY
or
INTELLIGENCE SUMMARY.
(Erase heading not required.)

Army Form C. 2118.

Place	Date	Hour	Summary of Events and Information	Remarks and references to Appendices
	19.		A.D.M.S. visited the area occupied by the Divisional Artillery. Routine duties.	CW
	20.		With regard to the equipment of a Field Amb., it is necessary that the Field Ambulance Commanders should have time to consider this question, and a Conference has therefore been arranged for the 25th inst.	CW
	21 to 23		Routine duties.	CW
	24.		Letter of congratulation received from G.O.C. 61 Division on the complete absence of sick wastage in the Division for week ending the 11th inst., He desires that his pleasure should be expressed to all Medical officers for their care of the sick which has led to such gratifying and satisfactory results. A.D.M.S. visited 182 Infantry Brigade area.	CW
	25.		A.D.M.S. HELD a Conference of Os.C. Field Ambulances with reference to revised equipment of a Field Ambulance.	CW
	26.		The question of the supply of boots is again causing anxiety and a complaint has been made by the 9th Northumberland Fusiliers. Men cannot go on parade owing to lack of boots. Every possible attention is being given to this matter. A.D.M.S. visited 183 Inf. Bde. area.	CW
	27.		Instructions received that A.D.M.S., was to inspect the 164 Prisoners of War Company at AUXI-LE-CHATEAU, and preliminary arrangements are in hand and January 29th has been fixed as a suitable date.	CW
	28.		A.D.M.S. visited AUXI-LE-CHATEAU and completed all arrangements for the inspection of the Prisoners of War Company. Routine duties.	CW

D. D. & L., London, E.C.
(A8004) Wt W1771/M2031 750,000 5/17 Sch. 52 Forms/C2118/14

Instructions regarding War Diaries and Intelligence Summaries are contained in F. S. Regs., Part II. and the Staff Manual respectively. Title pages will be prepared in manuscript.

WAR DIARY
or
INTELLIGENCE SUMMARY.
(Erase heading not required.)

Army Form C. 2118.

Place	Date	Hour	Summary of Events and Information	Remarks and references to Appendices
	29.		A.D.M.S., accompanied by the D.A.D.M.S., Lieut-Colonel H.N.Burroughes and the Divisional Intelligence Officer inspected the Prisoners of War Company and Camp. The prisoners and the conditions of the Camp generally were not very satisfac tory. A full report of the inspection was rendered to the D.D.M.S., XVII Corps.	CH
	30.		A.D.M.S., attended D.D.M.S., Conference.	CH
	31.		with reference to the question of boots. No supplies have been received from the Base. A certain number of gum boots are available for issue and will be supplied temporarily in lieu of boots ankle, until it is possible to obtain supplies of the latter. Units urgently requiring boots are invited to communicate to the Division so that an allotment of Gum boots can be made so far as they will go. Instructions have been issued to-day that the 2/4 R.Berks Regt. will leave the Division to-morrow and proceed by train to BOULOGNE base for duty. The 2/6 Bn. R.Warwick Regt. will also leave to-morrow for duty at HAVRE base. The 2/4 Oxford & Bucks Light Infantry will proceed on the 1st inst to ETAPLES base for duty. These ~~Divisions will~~ battalions will be st ruck off the strength of the Division. Routine duties.	CH

C Hinkley

Colonel A.M.S.
A.D.M.S., 61 Division.

D. D. & L., London, E.C.
(A8004) Wt W1771/M2031 750,000 5/17 Sch. 52 Forms/C2118/14

C O N F I D E N T I A L

Feb. 1919

9

MEDICAL

WO 95/3034

W A R   D I A R Y

OF

A. D. M. S., 61st DIVISION

From:- February 1st 1919.

To:- February 28th 1919.

VOLUME 3 4

Army Form C. 2118.

Instructions regarding War Diaries and Intelligence Summaries are contained in F. S. Regs., Part II. and the Staff Manual respectively. Title pages will be prepared in manuscript.

WAR DIARY
or
INTELLIGENCE SUMMARY.

(Erase heading not required.)

Place	Date	Hour	Summary of Events and Information	Remarks and references to Appendices
ST RIQUIER.	Feb. 1st.		The 2/4th Bn. Oxford & Bucks Light Infantry entrained at CONTEVILLE to-day for ETAPLES Base for duty. All arrangements were made for a motor ambulance car to be in attendance during the entrainment. No casualties were reported. Major H.E.A.Boldero. D.A.D.M.S., proceeded to ENGLAND on 14 days leave of absence, and Captain J.Manuel.M.C., 2/1st South Midland Field Ambulance reported to the A.D.M.S., for temporary duty as acting D.A.D.M.S., 25 horses from Field Ambulances were despatched to Base yesterday. This reduces the Field Ambs. to the strength now allowed by the revised War Establishment. The R.A.S.C. personnel attached to Field Ambulances rendered surplus by the revised War Establishment are to be absorbed into Divisional Trains. There are not many of such men in the Ambulances now, as a number of men have become casualties and several have been demobilised. Instructions have been received from the D.D.M.S., that an allotment of 6 places for dispersal every three days will come into force, commencing for this Division on the 5th instant. As this date falls on a Wednesday (no men being allowed to be sent to Concentration Camp on Tuesdays and Wednesdays) we shall not be able to avail ourselves of this first day's allotment. Demobilisation, so far as the Field Ambulances are concerned, has been stopped since the 20th of last month; and even now no further demobilisation can take place after a Field Amb., has been reduced to 30% of its establishment = 113 other ranks.	HEAB HEAB HEAB
	2nd.		We have to detail three medical officers for temporary duty with Labour Corps. Owing to the shortage of medical officers due to deficiencies and those on leave, it is necessary to detail Regimental Medical officers for this duty. The regiments affected will have their sick attended by the Field Ambulance nearest to them. Demobilisation will proceed until the 10th instant when particulars of strength of each Field Ambulance have to be forwarded to the Corps. Our allotment has now been altered from the 5th and 8th, to the 7th and 10th, so that 12 R.A.M.C., other ranks will be sent away. After the 10th the D.M.S., hopes to make further arrangements.	HEAB
	3rd.		The A.D. M.S. is acting D.D.M.S., XVII Corps, during the absence on leave of the D.D.M.S. Routine duties.	HEAB
	4th.		Captain J.Manuel, MC. RAMC. returned to duty with the 2/1st Field Amb, to-day, and Major AL.AYMER. RAMC. 2/2 Fd Amb., assumed duties of D.A.D.M.S . Routine duties.	HEAB

D. D. & L., London, E.C.
(A8004) Wt W1771/M2031 750,000 5/17 Sch. 52 Forms/C2118/14

Instructions regarding War Diaries and Intelligence Summaries are contained in F. S. Regs., Part II. and the Staff Manual respectively. Title pages will be prepared in manuscript.

WAR DIARY
or
INTELLIGENCE SUMMARY.
(Erase heading not required.)

Army Form C. 2118.

Place	Date	Hour	Summary of Events and Information	Remarks and references to Appendices
	5th		The 2/5 Bn.Gloucester Regiment left the Division on the 2nd instant; and to-day the 2/7 Warwicks, 1/5 D.C.L.I., and 184 Infantry Brigade Headquarters leave for duty at the ETAPLES Base. The 2/8 Worcesters will be going very shortly and this will leave the Division very depleted. The ration strength to-day is approximately 7,000 . There is a good number of Divisional motor ambul ance cars at p-resent in the workshop awaiting repair, and it is necessary in consequence to divide existing ca-rs amongst the Field Ambul-ances, having regard to the siz-e of the dail-y sick col-lecting round. No great difficulty has been experienced up to the present time. We are called on to detail three medica-l officers for duty with various L abour Groups, and these officers have proceeded to- day. This leaves the Divisio n very short of medica l officers; but with the number of units tha-t have now left, it is not anticipated that any grave difficul-ty is go-ing to be experienced. Moreover, officers on leave are gradual-ly returning, and this is rel-ievin-g the situa-tio-n. Routine duties.	####
	6th.		Orders received that the 2/8 Worcesters l-eave the Divisio-n to-morrow for temporary duty at CHERBOURG. The Medical officer of the D.C.L .I. is moving with the transp-ort of the 2/7 Warwicks, 1 /5 D.C.L.I., and 184 Bde .H.Q., in order to attend any sick on the march. The transport is all going by road. Personnel move by train; and the medical officer of 2/7 Warwicks is resp-onsibl-e for train personnel. Al-l arrangem-ents have been made for the evacuation of a-ny sick fro-m the transp-o-rt personnel. Routine duties. D.A.D.M.S. , XVII Corps called yesterday. Weather conditions are bad a-t present, and there ha-s been a downfall of snow. There is every indicatio-n, however, of an improvemen-t. A party of five R.A.M.C. men has been detailed for duty with the 70 Sanitary Section, and these men proceeded to BERNAVILLE to- day. L t.Col. C.L.LANDER.DSO. MC. called this afternoon. The 2/3rd Field Amb.a-re insom-e slight difficulty with transport as they have no cars. It has been arranged that a car fro m 2/1 Field Amb shall report to them daily for the purpose of collecting the morn ing sick.	####

D. D. & L., London, E.C.
(A8004) Wt. W1771/M2031 750,000 5/17 Sch. 52 Forms/C2118/14

Army Form C. 2118.

WAR DIARY
or
INTELLIGENCE SUMMARY.
(Erase heading not required.)

Instructions regarding War Diaries and Intelligence Summaries are contained in F. S. Regs., Part II. and the Staff Manual respectively. Title pages will be prepared in manuscript.

Place	Date	Hour	Summary of Events and Information	Remarks and references to Appendices
	7th		A.D.M.S. visited 2/1 Field Ambulance to-day. All arrangements have been made for a motor Ambulance car to be at CONTEVILLE station to-day during the entrainment of the 2/8 Worcesters, so as to deal with any cases of sick or accidents. Six R.A.M.C., men from this Division are being sent to the Corps Concentration Camp to-day for demobilisation. Captain J.K.RENNIE. MC. RAMC. has reported back from leave and has been posted to, and leaves to-day with, the 2/8 Wo-rcest-ers. Routine duties.	HEAD
	8th		Instructions were received yesterday that the 11th Suffolks and the 61 Bn. M.G.C., were leaving the Division for temporary duty at ETAPLES and ABBEVILLE respectively. Further instructions as to date of departure and times will be issued later. There is an appreciable change in the weather co nditions and a spell of hard frost has obtained for the last two or thre-e days. At least 2 motor ambulance cars have been returned from workshop to Field Ambulances. Routine duties.	HEAD
	9th		A.D.M.S. visited Corps Headquarters and spent the morning there with the D.A.D.M.S., A further allotment of demobilisation places has been given us - 6 on the 15th and 6 on the 20th. Information has been received that the 11th Bn. Suffolk Regt is entraining at LONGPRE station to-morrow the 10th instant. All arrangements have been made for a motor Ambulance and nursing orderly to be in attendance during the entrainment. The Machine Gun Battalion are moving to-morrow from BERNAVILLE to DRUCAT (N. of ABBEVILLE) and the 2/1st Field Ambulance have been instructed to collect their sick on arrival in the new area. Lieut-Colonel H.N.Burroughes. Comdg. 2/2nd Field Amb., has proceeded to-day on 14 da ys leave of absence and Major A.T.Waterhouse assumes command of t he unit. Routine duties.	HEAD
	10th		The departure of the 11th Suffolks has been postponed for one day. They will therefore entrain to-morrow commencing at 0900 hours. Instructions received that Lieut-Colonels Burroughes and Lander are required for civil employment as early as possible. Lieut-Colonel Lander desires t o go about the 18th inst. A copy of the wire has been forwarded to Acting O.C. 2/2 Field Amb., The Division comes under th e administration of the L.of.C. from the 13th inst (except the Artillery)	HEAD

D. D. & L., London, E.C.
(A8024) Wt W1771/M2031 750,000 5/17 Sch. 52 Forms/C2118/14

Army Form C. 2118.

WAR DIARY
or
INTELLIGENCE SUMMARY.
(Erase heading not required.)

Instructions regarding War Diaries and Intelligence Summaries are contained in F. S. Regs., Part II. and the Staff Manual respectively. Title pages will be prepared in manuscript.

Place	Date	Hour	Summary of Events and Information	Remarks and references to Appendices
	11th		Warning order received that the 182 Infantry Bde H.Q., and 9th North.Fus. are to move to DIEPPE. The 9th Northumberland Fusiliers are without a medical officer, and as they are only approximately 295 strong, we are endeavouring to make arrangements with the D.D.M.S. concerned for a medical officer to visitthe battalion daily on their arrival in the new area. It is quit e impossible for this Division to supply a medical officer as we are deficient of 6 on the present strength of the Division; and several are on leav e. Lieut-Colorel C.L.LANDER.DSO.MC. called with reference to his impending demobilisation. Six other ranks R.A.M.C. were despatched to Concentration Camp yesterday for dispersal. Wire received that Major A.RADFORD.MC.2/3rd Field Amb., was required as early as possib le for civil employment. The new Army forms M.N.S.(M) 16 which w ere to have been issued by the Ministry of National Service some weeks ago have not yet arrived, and as these supersede the A.Fs.Z.15 which have already been forwarded by Medical officers concerned, the officers are anxiously awaiting the new forms. Typew ritten copies of the form have therefore been made and distributed. This plan had the approval of the Corps. The spell of hard frosty weather still continues. The health of the Division generally is very good, and sick admissions are low. Lt-Col G.MACKIE.DSO.Comdg 2/1 Field Amb., returned from leave and resumed command of the unit.	HEB
	12th.		Orders received that the 2/2nd and 2/3rd Field Ambulance would move to-morrow. As the Division comes under the administration of the L. of C. from to-morrow all remaining units have to be concentrated in the 183 Inf. Bde. area. Necessary instructions for the move have been issued to all concerned. Lt.Col.G.Mackie and Major A.P.Thomson. called this morning. With regard to the move of units,there may be some slight difficulty as regards horses, owing to the fact that 25 horses have been demobilised from the Field Ambulances, and the equipment surplus owing to the revised war establishment, has not yet been disposed of. At the same time the distance to be covered in the move is only short, and there is no reason why the horses should not do the same journey the next day and so move all the equipment. Routine duties. The weather cont inues good and the spell of frost is unbroken. Appendix "A" shows the Medical arrangements which come into force after the moves of the two Field Ambulances to-morrow. D.A.D.M.S. visited the 2/2 Field Amb., this afternoon. A wire has been sent to Lt.Col.Burroughes to ascertain whether he is desirous of release from the Army. Captain Maclean RAMC.TC. formerly M.O. 11 Suffolks reported his return f rom leave this afternoon. He will proceed to No: 18 C.C.S. DOULLENS to-morrow morning in accordance with instructions from D.M.S. Third Army.	HEB

D. D. & L., London, E.C. (A8004) Wt W1771/M2031 750,000 5/17 Sch. 52 Forms/C2118/14

Army Form C. 2118.

WAR DIARY
or
INTELLIGENCE SUMMARY.
(Erase heading not required.)

Instructions regarding War Diaries and Intelligence Summaries are contained in F. S. Regs., Part II. and the Staff Manual respectively. Title pages will be prepared in manuscript.

Place	Date	Hour	Summary of Events and Information	Remarks and references to Appendices
	13.		Instructions received that 182 Infantry Brigade Headquarters, 9th Northumberland Fusiliers would not move to-day as originally arranged, but that they must hold themselves in readiness to proceed on the 14th instant. The Field Ambulances have been notified of the altered arrangement. The A.D.M.S., visited Corps Headquarters and spent the morning with the D.A.D.M.S. The Division (less Artillery) comes under the administration of the L ofC. from to-day. Field Ambulances (2/2nd and 2/3rd) are on the move to-day and are establishing their head-quarters at :- 2/2nd Field Amb., YAUCOURT BUSSUS. 2/3rd Field Amb., BUSSUS BUSSUEL. The A.D.M.S. 19th Div. has wired to say that he will look after the collection of sick from 61 Division Artillery. The general health of the Division remains good and sick admissions are low. Routine duties. Orders have now been received that the units referred to above will entrain at ST RIQUIER to-morrow the 14th inst for DIEPPE. The O.C.2/2 Field Amb., has been instructed to have a M.O. and a motor ambulance car present at the station during the entrainment and until the train has pulledout. It is impossible to detail a Medical officer to accompany the battalion owing to deficiencies. Arrangements are therefore being made with the D.M.S., L of C. to provide medical attention to the battalion on arrival at DIEPPE. In view of the fact that we have a considerable number of medical officers on detached duty in the area occupied by the Third Army, and also having in mind the fact that a number of medical officers will shortly be proceeding to ENGLAND for demobilisation; also bearing in mind the fact that the Division expects shortly to be made up to full strength; a request has been forwarded to the D.D.M.S., XVII Corps asking whether all M.Os. now temporarily detached for duty can be returned to the Division. It is important that we get these officers back if the Division is to be made up to strength. At the present time we are 6 M.Os deficient allowing for the revised War Establishment of a Field Amb., Direct orders have been received for three to be demobilised; one is on temporary duty with the Second Army and 4 are on detached duty with Laour Groups in the XVII Corps.	HHB
	14		Orders received for Captain J.R.R.RITCHIE RAMC to be demobilised. Captain M.Sommerville reported to the Division for duty to-day from ETAPLES and he is being posted to No: 47 Labour Group at PROYART in relief of Lieut R.HENSEL. MORC. Lieut Hensel will be re-posted to the 11th Bn.Suffolk Regt in relief of Captain S.R.Gleed who is proceeding to No: 51 General Hospital for duty; this is the result of his application for transfer in order that he can gain experience in the treatment of venereal disease. Lieut-Colonel C.L.Lander. DSO.MC. called this morning. A.D.M.S., visited the Field Ambulances.	HHB

D. D. & L., London, E.C. (A6004) Wt W1771/M2031 750,000 5/17 Sch. 52 Forms/C2118/14

Instructions regarding War Diaries and Intelligence Summaries are contained in F. S. Regs., Part II. and the Staff Manual respectively. Title pages will be prepared in manuscript.

WAR DIARY
or
INTELLIGENCE SUMMARY.
(Erase heading not required.)

Army Form C. 2118.

Place	Date	Hour	Summary of Events and Information	Remarks and references to Appendices
	15		The spell of frost has broken and a thaw has set in. It has been thawing rapidly for some hours, and instructions have been received to adopt Thaw precautions. Major W.V.Wood.RAMC.MC. 2/3rd Field Amb., has returned from leave to-day, having been granted two days extension. Lt-Col.Lander has now sent in his application for a vacancy to proceed by ordinary leave route to ENGLAND for demobilisation. There is no news at present of a demobilisationalotment for the R.A.M.C., of this Division. Up to the present we have only sent away 12 men this month. Application has been made to the D.M.S., L of C. At the present time the Division isdeficient of 7 medical officers. 6 others are on leave 5 are on detached duty and 2 are under orders to proceed to ENGLAND for discharge on expiration of contract. Three officers are under orders for ENGLAND for demobilisation. Routine duties.	HEM
	16		Up to the present time only 13% of personnel in Field Ambulances have been demobilised. This compares unfavourably with other branches of the service in the Division. As a result of enquiries it was ascertained that approximately 30% of other units, such as Infantry battalions had been demobilised. This question has been raised by the O.C. 2/3rd Field Ambulance, and correspondence has been passed to the D.M.S., L of C with a view to obtaining an allotment of dispersal vacancies. Since the beginning of January only 75 other ranks all told ha ve been sent away from medical units in this Division. This figure does not of course include any personnel demobilised whilst on leave. Major A.P.Thomson.MC.RAMC. 2/1st Field Amb., called. Application for leave for the A.D.M.S. approved by the Division, sailing on the 21st., subject to the approval of the D.M.S., L.o f.C. Routine duties.	HEM
	17.		Major H.E.A.Boldero. D.A.D.M.S., returned from leave to-day and Major A.L.AYMER returned to duty with the 2/2nd South Midland Field Ambulance. The general health of the Division remains very good, and the last Wastage Return received from the Third Army shows a Nil return for this Division as regards evacuation and sick wastage. The number of admissions to hospital is extremely low. The D.D.M.S., XVII Corps having returned from leave, the A.D.M.S., 61 Div. relinquished the duties of acting D.D.M.S., Routine duties. HEM	

D. D. & L., London, E.C.
(A8004) Wt W1771/M2031 750,000 5/17 Sch. 52 Forms/C2118/14

Army Form C. 2118.

Instructions regarding War Diaries and Intelligence Summaries are contained in F. S. Regs., Part II. and the Staff Manual respectively. Title pages will be prepared in manuscript.

WAR DIARY
or
INTELLIGENCE SUMMARY.

(Erase heading not required.)

Place	Date	Hour	Summary of Events and Information	Remarks and references to Appendices
	18		Routine duties. Orders have been received to-day for Captain (A/Major) A.L.AYMER. 2/2nd Field Ambulance to proceed to No: 1 Stationary Hospital for duty. Lt.Col.Lander and Major W.V.Wood called this afternoon.	
	19		A.D.M.S. and D.A.D.M.S. visited D.D.M.S. XVII Corps. Lt.Col.LANDER and Major RADFORD have proceeded to-day to ENGLAND for demobilisation. Major W.V.WOOD.MC. has assumed command of the 2/3rd South Midland Field Ambulance, and a recommendation has been submitted for the acting rank of Lieut-Colonel for him. It is understood from the A.D.M.S., ABBEVILLE that, as a result of the A.D.M.S., and D.A.D.M.S. visit to t he D.M.S., L of C., the R.A.M.C., of this Division are to have an allotment for demobilisation. All particulars have been given on the telephone to the A.D.M.S., ABBEVILLE and an allotment is expected. At the present time the Division is deficient of 12 Medical officers. Captain COATSWORTH called. Routine duties.	
	20.		A.D.M.S., and D.A.D.MS visited A.D.M.S., ABBEVILLE. Dispersal vacancies for three other ranks R.A.M.C. have been alloted to the Division to-day. Particulars of further allotments will be sent to us. Majors Thomson and Aymer called to-day. Lieut A.R.EDWARDS. MORC. has proceeded to HAVRE to-day for duty with the 2/6 Bn.R.Warwickshire Regt., in place of Lieut W A.S.MAGRATH who has proceeded to England for discharge o n expiration of contra ct. Routine duties .	
	21		A.D.M.S., proceeded to ENGLAND to-day on fourteen days leave. Lieut-Colonel G.MACKIE. DSO. Comdg 2/1st South Midland Field Ambulance is acting A.D.M.S., Routine duties.	
	22		Orders received for Captains E.F.O'CONNOR. and J.K.RENNIE.MC. RAMC. TC. to proceed to England and report personally to the War Office for instructions to attend a course of instruction in special Military Surgery. We are endeavouring to arrange medical attention for the units concerned. The Division is very short of Medical officers - there being 13 deficient. This number will be increased to 15 when the above mentioned officers depart. Six dispersal vacancies were allotted to us for to-day, and these were all given to the 2/3 Field Amb.,	
	22		D.A.D.M.S., visited 2/2 Field Amb., Three dispersal vacancies allotted to us to-day and these have been given to 2/2 Field Amb., Routine duties.	

D. D. & L., London, E.C.
(A8004) Wt. W1771/M2031 750,000 5/17 Sch. 52 Forms/C2118/14

Instructions regarding War Diaries and Intelligence Summaries are contained in F. S. Regs., Part II. and the Staff Manual respectively. Title pages will be prepared in manuscript.

WAR DIARY
or
INTELLIGENCE SUMMARY.
(Erase heading not required.)

Army Form C. 2118.

Place	Date	Hour	Summary of Events and Information	Remarks and references to Appendices
	23		D.A.D.M.S. visited 2/2 Field A mbulance this morning. T hree dispersal vacancies have been allotted to us for to-day, and these have been given to the 2/2 Field Ambulance. The D.M.S., L of C has made an allotment of three places a day to the A.D.M.S., ABBEVILLE area for the Field Ambulances of this Division. It is hoped to give us a larger allotment shortly. The sick admissions are very low, and the health of the D ivision generally is good. Routine duties. HEAB	
	24		D.A.D.M.S. visited 2/3 Field Ambulance. Notification received that Major Wood could wear the badges of rank of a Lieut-Colonel pending his gazette announcement. Three dispersal vacancies received and allotted to the 2/1 Field Amb., Routine duties. HEAB	
	25		Routine duties, HEAB	
	26.		Routine duties. 7 Demobilisation vacancies have been given to us to-day, and, in addition 4 places for P.B. Batmen. HEAB	
	27.		Lt.Col.G.Mackie called. Routine duties. HEAB	
	28.		D.A.D.M.S., visited 2/2 Field Ambulance. Routine duties. HEAB	

H.E.A. Boldero. Major for
Colonel A.M.S.
A.D.M.S., 61 Division.

D. D. & L., London, E.C.
(A8004) Wt. W1771/M2031 750,000 5/17 Sch. 52 Forms/C2118/14

A.D.M.S., No: 955/913

Medical Arrangements in connection with
61 Division Order No: 239 dated 12/2/19

1. Information. The Division (less Artillery) is transferred to L of C. area from February 13th 1919.

2. Ambulance Moves. The following moves will take place to-morrow under arrangements made by the Officers Commanding :-

2/2nd S.M.Field Amb., from AGENVILLE to YAUCOURT BUSSUS

2/3rd S.M.Field Amb., from DOMART to BUSSUS BUSSUEL.

The O.C. 2/2nd Field Amb., will arrange that suitable accommodation is left in YAUCOURT BUSSUS for a detachment of R.A.S.C.,

Information re Billeting can be arranged with Headquarters, 183 Inf. Bde.

3. Disposal of Stores. Surplus B.R.C.S., stores and Advanced Depot Medical Stores, can be taken to and stored with the 2/1st S.M. Field Amb., temporarily

4. Collection of Sick. The O.C. 2/1st Field Amb., will provide medical attention for, and collect sick from, the units remaining with the Division from and including Feby.14th.1919.

SCABIES. The 2/1st Field Amb., will take in Scabies. The O.C. 2/3rd Field Amb., will send baths etc to the O.C. 2/1st Field Amb., for that purpose.

Royal Field Artillery sick will be collected under arrangements made by A.D.M.S., 19th Division on and from the 13th instant. The M.A.C., car now with the O.C. 2/2 Field Amb., being attached to the C.R.A., 61 Division for that purpose.

Special cases. Dental cases will be sent to No: 46 C.C.S. Until further orders the present arrangement will remain for other cases.

C Hountessy

Colonel A.M.S.,
A.D.M.S., 61 Div.

61 D.H.Q.,
Feby. 12th 1919.

Copies to :-

Os.C. Field Ambulances.	
61 Div "G" and "Q" for information.	
C.R.A., 61 Div. for information.	
183 Inf. Bde.	-do-
C.R.E.,	-do-
O.C. Train.	-do-
D.D.M.S., XVII Corps	-do-
D.M.S., L of C.	-do-
A.D.M.S., 19 Div.	-do-
O.C. 15 M.A.C.,	-do-
O.C. 46 C.C.S.,	-do-
Senior Chaplains	-do-

A.D.M.S. 61st (S.M.) DIVISION

15

MEDICAL

Med 35

140/3535

CONFIDENTIAL

Mar 1919

WAR DIARIES

OF

MEDICAL UNITS 61st DIVISION

From:- March 1st 1919

To:- March 31st 1919

VOLUME No: 35.

Diaries enclosed:- A.D.M.S. 61 Div.
2/1st S.Mid.Fd.Amb.,
2/3rd S.Mid.Fd.Amb.,

H E A Boldero
Major.
for A.D.M.S. 61 Divn.

MEDICAL

CONFIDENTIAL.

WAR DIARY

OF

A. D. M. S. 61st DIVISION

From:- March 1st 1919

To:- March 31st 1919.

VOLUME NO: 35

Instructions regarding War Diaries and Intelligence Summaries are contained in F. S. Regs., Part II. and the Staff Manual respectively. Title pages will be prepared in manuscript.

WAR DIARY
or
INTELLIGENCE SUMMARY.
(Erase heading not required.)

Army Form C. 2118.

Place	Date	Hour	Summary of Events and Information	Remarks and references to Appendices
ST RIQUIER	Mar. 1st		D.A.D.M.S., visited 2/1st and 2/3rd Field Ambulances this morning. The Artillery has now definitely left the Division, and endeavours are being made for Captains Stafford and Bell to be returned to this Division. Captain E.F.O'Connor has reported back for duty from the XVII Corps, and arrangements will shortly be made for him and Captain Rennie to proceed to England and report to War Office to receive instructions as to attending a Course of Special military Surgery. The Division is still deficient of 13 Medical officers; but no particular difficulty is being experienced at present. Three other ranks reported to the Division yesterday as reinforcements and they were posted to the 2/3rd Field Amb., Demobilisation of the R.A.M.C., personnel of the Division continues steadily. To-day three men have been despatched. HEAB Routine duties.	
	2nd.		D.A.D.M.S., visited 2/1st Field Ambulance. Three men despatched for dispersal to-day. HEAB Routine duties.	
	3rd.		Lieut-Col G.Mackie called. Instructions received from the Division regarding the new Brigade areas. Routine duties. Captain W.H.H.Bell RAMC, joined the Division for duty. This officer was originally with the 306 Bde R.F.A., as Medical officer i/c. Lieut J.P.Stout MORC. M.O.i/c 307 Bde R.F.A., is also expected to rejoin the Division. The Divisional Artillery is now transferred to and administered by the XVII Corps. HEAB	
	4th.		Lieut-Colonel H.N.Burroughes called. Routine duties.	
	5th.		Lieut-Colonel G.Mackie called. Routine duties. HEAB	
	6th.		Routine duties. Lt-Col Wood called. HEAB	
	7th.		Orders received that Field Ambulances of this Division are to be reduced to Cadre strength as early as possible. Administrative Medical Officers of the Division will report to A.D.M.S., of the area to which the Division will move, for orders. The cadres of Field Ambulances will come under the administration of the A.D.M.S., area. Colonel C.H.Howkins. DSO. AMS. returned from leave to-day. HEAB	

D. D. & L., London, E.C.
(A8004) Wt W1771/M2031 750,000 5/17 Sch. 52 Forms/C2118/14

Army Form C. 2118.

WAR DIARY
or
INTELLIGENCE SUMMARY.
(Erase heading not required.)

Instructions regarding War Diaries and Intelligence Summaries are contained in F. S. Regs., Part II. and the Staff Manual respectively. Title pages will be prepared in manuscript.

Place	Date	Hour	Summary of Events and Information	Remarks and references to Appendices
	8th		A.D.M.S. and D.A.D.M.S. visited 2/1st Field Ambulance. Orders have been received that unless Lieut-Col. H.N.Burroughes is prepared to serve indefinitely, he must take his release at once. He is not so prepared, and arrangements will therefore be made for him to be sent home at an early date. Instructions also received for Capt(a/Major) W.V.Wood. Comdg 2/3rd Field Amb., to be sent home for demobilisation. This officer called to see the A.D.M.S., on this matter. The Division (less Artillery) is still 13 Medical officers deficient. HEAB Routine duties.	
	9th		Lieut-Colonel W.V.Wood called with reference to the question of his release. He does not wish to be demobilised at present, as it is his intention to remain with the cadre of his unit. Routine duties. HEAB	
	10th		Routine duties. HEAB	
	11th		A.D.M.S., and D.A.D.M.S., visited 2/1st Field Amb., Routine duties. HEAB	
	12th		Routine duties. HEAB	
	13th		A.D.M.S., and D.A.D.M.S., visited the Field Ambulances. The daily demobilisation of 3 R.A.M.C. personnelcontinues. HEAB Routine duties.	
	14th		Routine duties. HEAB	
	15th		Instructions have been received for Captain Dodd to be struck off the strength of this Division, and Lieut-Colonel H.N.Burroughes having proceeded to England yesterday for demobilisation, this makes the Division 15 Medical officers deficient excluding Artillery. Major Wood is not desirous of being demobilised at present, and elects to remain with the Army for a further period. Orders have been received to-day for the demobilisation of Colonel C.H.Howkins.DSO. AMS. ADMS. and he will proceed to England on the 17th instant. HEAB Routine duties.	

Army Form C. 2118.

Instructions regarding War Diaries and Intelligence Summaries are contained in F. S. Regs., Part II. and the Staff Manual respectively. Title pages will be prepared in manuscript.

WAR DIARY
or
INTELLIGENCE SUMMARY.

(Erase heading not required.)

Place	Date	Hour	Summary of Events and Information	Remarks and references to Appendices
	16th		An Advance party from Divisional Headquarters will proceed to Le Treport on Tuesday next the 18th instant to prepare the place and arrange accommodation. The remainder of D.H.Q., will proceed to Le Treport as soon as everything is arranged. The A.D.M.S., accompanied by the D.A.D.M.S., visited each Field Ambulance to-day. Weather conditions have been very changeable of late, but on the whole the weather is mild. HEAB Routine duties.	
	17th		A.D.M.S., proceeded to ENGLAND to-day for demobilisation. Orders received that all personnel surplus to the cadre strength of Field Ambulances are to report to A.D.M.S., ABBEVILLE to-day. They will proceed to Le Treport and thence to the Rhine for duty. Orders also received that Lieut-Colonel Wood must be demobilised forthwith and that he is not allowed to remain on in the Army. Arrangements have therefore been made for Major A.P.Thomson. 2/1st Field Amb., to be posted to the 2/3rd Field Ambulance. Routine duties. HEAB	
	18th		An advance party of 61 Divisional Headquarters proceeded to Le Treport to-day to prepare the Headquarters. It is expected that the remainder of headquarters will move there on or about Saturday next. HEAB	
	19th		Lieut-Colonel W.V.WOOD. MC. Comdg 2/3 Field Amb., proceeded to ENGLAND to-day for demobilisation. Lt-Col G.Mackie and Lt-Col A.T.Waterhouse called. D.A.D.M.S., visited 2/1st Field Amb., Routine duties. HEAB	
	20th		Lieut-Col. G.Mackie called regarding the move of the Field Ambulances and negotiations on this matter are now in process. Routine duties. HEAB	
	21st		The 2/1st and 2/3rd Field Ambulances will move to Le Treport on the 25th instant. The 2/2nd Field Ambulance will remain at its present site in order to look after the Divisional troops in the ABBEVILLE area. It will possibly be necessary to borrow some horses from the 2/2 Fd. Amb., in order to enable the other two ambulances to move, and arrangements are being made in regard to this. Lieut-Col Mackie called, also Major Waterhouse. Routine duties. HEAB	

D. D. & L., London, E.C.
(A8004) Wt W1771/M2031 750,000 5/17 Sch. 52 Forms/C2118/14

Army Form C. 2118.

Instructions regarding War Diaries and Intelligence Summaries are contained in F. S. Regs., Part II. and the Staff Manual respectively. Title pages will be prepared in manuscript.

WAR DIARY
or
INTELLIGENCE SUMMARY.
(Erase heading not required.)

Place	Date	Hour	Summary of Events and Information	Remarks and references to Appendices
	22nd		Instructions received that no personnel for leave or demobilisation or cadres are to be entrained after receipt of the instructions. This is a temporary measure rendered necessary owing to threatened strikes in England. All orders with regard to the move of the Ambulances have been issued to-day, vide Appendix "A" The men of this Division on temporary duty with the No: 18 C.C.S., are being sent back to us under orders of the D.D.M.S. XVII Corps. HGAB	
	23rd		D.A.D.M.S., visited 2/2nd South Midland Field Ambulance. Routine duties. To-date, the Division is deficient of 18 Medical officers. Routine duties. HGAB	
LE TREPORT	24th		61 D.H.Q., and advance parties of 2/1st and 2/3rd Field Ambulances moved to LE TREPORT to-day. Routine duties. HGAB	
	25th		2/1st and 2/3rd Field Ambulances duly started their journey to LE TREPORT to-day and are staging to-night at FRESSENVILLE. D.A.D.M.S., visited units in the area and found that there is a great scarcity of medical officers in the district. Arrangements were therefore made for any sick to be sent to Divisional Headquarters until more definite arrangements were made. We have asked the D.M.S., for particulars of disposal of special cases; in the meantime the Dental Surgeon attached to the Tank Corps will see any men of this Division on any day. HGAB	
	26th		Routine duties. D.A.D.M.S., visited 2/1st Field Ambulance. 2/1st Field Ambd, and 2/3rd Field Ambulance arrived at LE TREPORT to-day. HGAB Routine duties.	
	27th		D.A.D.M.S., visited 2/1st and 2/3rd Fd.Amb., Major Thomson, Comdg 2/3 Fd.Amb. has received a warrant from H.Q., L of C., to proceed to ENGLAND on one month's special leave of absence. The new Mobilisation Store Table has been received by the Field Ambulances, and we have wired the S.M.O., DIEPPE asking whether we can hand in all our surplus medical equipment. The Ambulances are practically down to cadre strength as far as personnel is concerned; and we are now making endeavours to get rid of surplus horses, ordnance and medical stores. Routine duties. HGAB	

D. D. & L., London, E.C.
(A8004) Wt W1771/M2031 750,000 5/17 Sch. 52 Forms/C2118/14

Instructions regarding War Diaries and Intelligence Summaries are contained in F. S. Regs., Part II. and the Staff Manual respectively. Title pages will be prepared in manuscript.

WAR DIARY
or
INTELLIGENCE SUMMARY.
(Erase heading not required.)

Army Form C. 2118.

Place	Date	Hour	Summary of Events and Information	Remarks and references to Appendices
	28		Routine duties. HEAB	
	29th		Routine duties. HEAB	
	30th		Orders received for Major Boldero to proceed to England forthwith and report to War Office for transfer to Home Establishment. Routine duties. The Division, less Artillery units, is now 21 Medical officers deficient. HEAB	
	31st		Routine duties. Major A.P.Thomson Comdg 2/3 Fd.Amb. proceeded on a month's special leave. HEAB	

HEABoldero
Major.
for A.D.M.S., 61 Divn.

D. D. & L., London, E.C.
(A8004) Wt W1771/M2031 750,000 5/17 Sch. 52 Forms/C2118/14

COPY NO: ______

61st DIVISION R.A.M.C. ORDER No: 103

Ref. Map ABBEVILLE 1/100,000 22-3-19

1. The Cadres of the 2/1st and 2/3rd South Midland Field Ambulances will move to LE TREPORT commencing March 25th. Horse transport will stage night 25th/26th instant at FRESSENVILLE. Os.C. concerned will arrange that one officer is in charge of the two Ambulances horse transport; and that two days rations and forage are taken.

2. The Cadre of the 2/2nd South Midland Field Ambulance will stand fast and, on move of Divisional Headquarters on March 25th, will come under the orders of G.O.C. 183 Inf. Bde.,

3. Small advance parties of 2/1st and 2/3rd South Midland Field Ambs. will proceed and report to Captain Mortimer at LE TREPORT, under arrangements made by O.C. 2/1st Field Amb.,

4. Detail of lorry or lorries available to assist in the move will be notified later.

5. On arrival at LE TREPORT sick that cannot be retained in Field Ambulances will be evacuated by car to hospitals at ABBEVILLE.

6. A.D.M.S., office will close at ST RIQUIER at 10.00 hours, and re-open on arrival at LE TREPORT on March 24th.

H E A Boldero
Major.
for A.D.M.S., 61 Div.

Issued at 10.30 hours.

Distribution :-

1-3.	2/1,2/2,2/3 Field Ambs.	
4.	183 Inf. Bde. for information.	
5.	Area Comdt.ST RIQUIER Area for information.	
6.	A.D.M.S., ABBEVILLE for information.	
7.	A.D.M.S., DIEPPE	-do-
8.	D.M.S., L of C.,	-do-
9.	61 Division "G"	-do-
10.	61 Division "Q"	-do-
11.	Captain Mortimor	-do-
12-13.	War Diary.	o
14.	File.	

www.ingramcontent.com/pod-product-compliance
Lightning Source LLC
Chambersburg PA
CBHW080814010526
44111CB00015B/2556
* 9 7 8 1 4 7 4 5 3 2 7 8 5 *